FROMMER'S

COMPREHENSIVE TRAVEL GUIDE

PUERTO VALLARTA, MANZANILLO & GUADALAJARA '94-'95

by Marita Adair

PRENTICE HALL TRAVEL

NEW YORK • LONDON • TORONTO • SYDNEY • TOKYO • SINGAPORE

FROMMER BOOKS
Published by Prentice Hall General Reference
15 Columbus Circle
New York, NY 10023

Copyright © 1992, 1994 by Simon & Schuster, Inc.

All rights reserved, including the right of reproduction in whole or in part in any form.

PRENTICE HALL is a registered trademark and colophon is a trademark of Prentice-Hall, Inc.

ISBN 0-671-86662-1
ISSN 1060-3727

Design by Robert Bull Design
Maps by Geografix Inc.

Frommer's Editorial Staff
Editorial Director: Marilyn Wood
Senior Editor/Editorial Manager: Alice Fellows
Senior Editors: Sara Hinsey Raveret, Lisa Renaud
Editors: Charlotte Allstrom, Thomas F. Hirsch, Peter Katucki, Theodore Stavrou
Assistant Editors: Margaret Bowen, Chris Hollander, Alice Thompson, Ian Wilker
Editorial Assistant: Gretchen Henderson
Managing Editor: Leanne Coupe

Special Sales
Bulk purchases (10+ copies) of Frommer's Travel Guides are available to corporations at special discounts. The Special Sales Department can produce custom editions to be used as premiums and/or for sales promotion to suit individual needs. Existing editions can be produced with custom cover imprints such as a corporate logo. For more information write to Special Sales, Prentice Hall Travel, Paramount Communications Building, 15 Columbus Circle, New York, NY 10023.

Manufactured in the United States of America

CONTENTS

FOREWORD viii

by Arthur Frommer

1 INTRODUCING MEXICO'S MID-PACIFIC REGION 1

1. Geography, Ecology, History & Politics 3
2. Mexico's Famous People 11
3. Art, Architecture & Literature 16
4. Religion, Myth & Folklore 19
5. Cultural & Social Life 20
6. Performing Arts 21
7. Sports & Recreation 22
8. Food & Drink 22
9. Recommended Books, Films & Recordings 24

SPECIAL FEATURES
- What's Special About Mexico's Pacific Coast 2
- Dateline 6

2 PLANNING A TRIP TO MEXICO'S MID-PACIFIC REGION 28

1. Information, Entry Requirements & Money 28
2. When to Go—Climate, Holidays & Events 35
3. Health & Insurance 39
4. What to Pack 42
5. Tips for the Disabled, Seniors, Singles & Families 43
6. Alternative/Adventure Travel 46
7. Shopping 46
8. Getting There 48
9. Getting Around 53

SPECIAL FEATURES
- What Things Cost in Puerto Vallarta 32
- What Things Cost in Manzanillo 33
- What Things Cost in Guadalajara 33
- Mexico Calendar of Events 36
- Fast Facts: Mexico 62

3 GETTING TO KNOW PUERTO VALLARTA 70

1. Orientation 70
2. Getting Around 72

SPECIAL FEATURES
- Did You Know . . . ? 71
- Fast Facts: Puerto Vallarta 73

4 WHERE TO STAY & DINE IN PUERTO VALLARTA 77

1. Where to Stay 77
2. Where to Dine 88

SPECIAL FEATURES
- Frommer's Smart Traveler: Hotels 79
- Frommer's Smart Traveler: Restaurants 89

5 WHAT TO SEE & DO IN PUERTO VALLARTA 96

1. Organized Tours 96
2. Sports & Recreation 97
3. Shopping 99
4. Evening Entertainment 101
5. Easy Excursions 103

SPECIAL FEATURES
- Suggested Itineraries 96
- Frommer's Favorite Puerto Vallarta Experiences 99

6 GETTING TO KNOW MANZANILLO 110

1. Orientation 110
2. Getting Around 115

SPECIAL FEATURES
- Did You Know . . . ? 111
- Fast Facts: Manzanillo 115

7 WHERE TO STAY & DINE IN MANZANILLO 116

1. Where to Stay 116
2. Where to Dine 121

8 WHAT TO SEE & DO IN MANZANILLO 128

1. Organized Tours 129
2. Sports & Recreation 129
3. Other Activities 130
4. Easy Excursions 131

SPECIAL FEATURES
- Suggested Itineraries 128
- Frommer's Favorite Manzanillo Experiences 129

9 GETTING TO KNOW GUADALAJARA 147

1. Orientation 147
2. Getting Around 152

SPECIAL FEATURES
- Did You Know . . . ? 152
- Fast Facts: Guadalajara 154

10 WHERE TO STAY & DINE IN GUADALAJARA 157

1. Where to Stay 157
2. Where to Dine 165

SPECIAL FEATURES
- Frommer's Smart Traveler: Hotels 158
- Frommer's Smart Traveler: Restaurants 166

11 WHAT TO SEE & DO IN GUADALAJARA   170

1. The Major Attractions   171
2. More Attractions   174
3. Organized Tours   176
4. Special Events   177
5. Spectator Sports   178
6. Shopping   178
7. Evening Entertainment   179

SPECIAL FEATURES
- Suggested Itineraries   170
- Walking Tour—Downtown Guadalajara   171
- Frommer's Favorite Guadalajara Experiences   175

12 EASY EXCURSIONS FROM GUADALAJARA   182

1. Tlaquepaque & Tonala   182
2. The Lake Chapala Region   188
3. Mazamitla   204
4. Tapalpa   209
5. San Juan de los Lagos & Lagos de Moreno   2‌1‌2

APPENDIX   220

A. Vocabulary   220
B. Menu Savvy   222
C. Conversion Tables   229

INDEX   231

LIST OF MAPS

MEXICO 4-5

Mexico's Mid-Pacific Coast   31

PUERTO VALLARTA

Puerto Vallarta Area   74-75
Downtown Puerto Vallarta   91

MANZANILLO

Manzanillo Area   112-113
Downtown Manzanillo   123
Barra de Navidad Bay Area   133

GUADALAJARA

Guadalajara & Environs   151
Greater Guadalajara   153
Downtown Guadalajara   163
Walking Tour—Downtown Guadalajara   173
Lake Chapala   191
Chapala Village   193
Ajijic   199

FOREWORD

by Arthur Frommer

Lying in a courtyard hammock with a paperback book, I used to spend my afternoons in Puerto Vallarta at a cheap, 12-room hotel just short steps from the village that was soon to gain worldwide fame. I'd read about Emiliano Zapata or Pancho Villa until the bells of the city's crown-shaped church tower began to signal the coming of dusk. It was time for the mariachis, and a meal of tortillas, and all the evening commerce and conversation that flowed back and forth among small groups in a town square overlooking the sea. Even before the coming of Elizabeth Taylor and Richard Burton, Puerto Vallarta was a lively place, though it had (at that time) only a single international hotel worthy of the name: the Posada Vallarta (now the immensely expanded Hotel Krystal Vallarta).

Amazingly, despite its expansion into a sprawling metropolis of multiple chain hotels, discos, galleries, and shopping arcades, Puerto Vallarta has remained to this day a distinctively Mexican city. On a trip there just several weeks before writing this preface, I strolled the streets of the original village of Puerto Vallarta, and was charmed—in fact, set aglow—by the fact that it remains Mexican and authentic. Nowadays you stay in Puerto Vallarta's modern high-rise hotels, but they are located down the coast, or far along the immense Bay of Banderas, or beyond the hills. Always, wherever you stay and however plush the hotel, there is the option to "go downtown" to that poor and lively fishing village where two movie megastars carried on the affair of the century, and thereby made "Puerto Vallarta" into a household name.

In the heart of the Mexican Riviera, of which Manzanillo is also a proud part, the colors are bright and primary. The weather is hot, the white-sand beaches go on for miles along warm Pacific waters. The beachside chairs are shaded by thatched, umbrella-like *palapas,* the waters are active with boats of every kind, the music is timelessly Mexican, the hawkers sell sombreros and serapes, visitors sip margaritas and try out their halting Spanish with a bemused hotel staff, the nighttime sybaritic and intense. And when the beachside life begins to pall (which is unlikely—it grows on you, and you'll hate for the stay to end), you have the option of traveling to the grand and stately nearby city of Guadalajara, which adds still another degree of age and culture to the seaside resorts. Despite the continuing modernization of Mexico's second largest city, great portions of its downtown area remain authentically Colonial; some structures date back to the late 16th century. Although your main goal may be a seaside vacation on the Pacific Coast, I'd urge you to consider stopping in Guadalajara on the way to, or from, the beaches. Its art, architecture, folklore, and history are fully as impressive, complex, and valuable as most any in the world—but are available here at half the price!

Certainly, the author of our guide to *Puerto Vallarta, Manzanillo & Guadalajara '94–'95* shares those views about combining a trip to the beaches with Mexico's second largest city. Marita ("Marty") Adair is a specialist in Mexico who has devoted her entire professional career to writing about that nation. Fluent in Spanish and a former staff member of the Organization of American States, she has been traveling there continually for nearly 30 years, and has written about every aspect of Mexican life, culture, and commerce for publications ranging from the *Chicago Tribune* and the *Los Angeles Times* to *Honeymoon Magazine*.

For this 1994-1995 edition, Marty has again crisscrossed the cities covered here for many weeks on end, rechecked each recommendation, dropped a number, but added more: about 40 new restaurants, 20 new hotels. The result is a book more than 20% longer than its predecessor. This revised edition also includes an important new sidetrip from Guadalajara to the religious pilgrimage site of San Juan de los Lagos, two hours north of the big city by car. Five million visitors a year, including penitents from countries all over the world, make that trip; yet Marty's discussion of it is the only one I've seen in any guidebook literature. This is also true of Marty's newly added description of the tranquil and inexpensive small village of Bucerias. Behind rock walls, 11 miles north of Puerto Vallarta, it is gaining in popularity among venturesome travelers.

And finally, Marty's guidebook keeps abreast of the single most important development hereabouts—the imminent completion of a number of ultra-elegant but moderately priced resorts at Barra de Navidad, the neighboring Isla Navidad, El Tamarindo, Costa Careyes, and Las Alamandas, all north of Manzanillo, that are bound to change the face of tourism in this area.

Frommer Guides are constantly updated, and issued in dated editions, to bring you information—the most current available—almost as a newspaper would do. And with skilled insiders like Marty Adair always on the scene, we're often able to "spot" these developments early, and bring them to your attention before anyone else does. Book them before they're discovered by others!

INVITATION TO THE READERS

In researching this book, I have come across many wonderful establishments, the best of which I've included here. I am sure that many of you will also come across appealing hotels, inns, restaurants, guest houses, shops, and attractions. Please don't keep them to yourself. Share your experiences, especially if you want to comment on places that have been included in this edition that have changed for the worse. You can address your letters to:

Marita Adair
Puerto Vallarta, Manzanillo, and Guadalajara '94–'95
Prentice Hall Travel
15 Columbus Circle
New York, NY 10023

A DISCLAIMER & SAFETY ADVISORY

Readers are advised that prices fluctuate in the course of time and that travel information changes under the impact of the varied and volatile factors that affect the travel industry. Neither the author nor the publisher can be held responsible for the experiences of readers while traveling. Readers are invited to write to the publisher with ideas, comments, and suggestions for future editions.

Whenever you're traveling in an unfamiliar city or country, stay alert. Be aware of your immediate surroundings. Wear a moneybelt and keep a close eye on your possessions. Be particularly careful with cameras, purses, and wallets, all favorite targets of thieves and pickpockets.

A WORD ABOUT PRICES

In this book, I've listed only dollar prices, which are a more reliable guide than peso prices. In this age of inflation, prices may change by the time you reach Mexico. Mexico's inflation has been running nearly 15% a year.

Mexico has a Value Added Tax of 10% (*Impuesto de Valor Agregado*, or "IVA," pronounced "ee-bah") on almost everything, including hotel rooms, restaurant meals, bus tickets, and souvenirs. This tax will not necessarily be included in the quoted price of hotels and restaurants. In addition, prices charged by hotels and restaurants have been deregulated. Mexico's new pricing freedom may cause some price variations from those quoted in this book; always ask to see a printed price sheet and ask if the tax is included. All prices given in this book already include the tax.

Important note: In 1993 Mexico introduced the New Peso, which knocks three zeros off the old currency. Old peso notes will be accepted for the time being. To acclimate users to the new currency, New Peso prices appear on price labels preceded by "NP," and next to old peso prices still bearing the zeros. In Mexico, the dollar sign is used to denote pesos, and a Mexican sign reading NP$5 means 5 New Pesos, not 5 dollars. In this book, however, the dollar sign is used only to indicate U.S. dollars. At press time, one U.S. dollar was worth around 3 New Pesos.

CHAPTER 1

INTRODUCING MEXICO'S MID-PACIFIC REGION

- **WHAT'S SPECIAL ABOUT MEXICO'S PACIFIC COAST**
1. **GEOGRAPHY, ECOLOGY, HISTORY & POLITICS**
- **DATELINE**
2. **MEXICO'S FAMOUS PEOPLE**
3. **ART, ARCHITECTURE & LITERATURE**
4. **RELIGION, MYTH & FOLKLORE**
5. **CULTURAL & SOCIAL LIFE**
6. **PERFORMING ARTS**
7. **SPORTS & RECREATION**
8. **FOOD & DRINK**
9. **RECOMMENDED BOOKS, FILMS & RECORDINGS**

Everyone north of the Río Grande has at least some idea (usually an old-fashioned one) about what Mexico is like, but only those who go there can know the real Mexico, for the country is undergoing fast-paced and far-reaching change, as are most countries touched by modern technology. Being so close to the United States and Canada, Mexico is so forcefully affected by what goes on in its neighboring countries to the north that the Old Mexico of cowboy songs and movies has long ago been replaced by a land full of familiar signs of 20th-century life. But this does not mean that a trip to Mexico will reveal people, sights, and sounds just like home, for Mexico is very much its own country, the result of a particular blending of the land itself and of ancient Indian, colonial, European, and modern industrial influences. These elements are the basis of a unique culture and tradition.

This book encompasses a triangle of cities—two resorts, Puerto Vallarta and Manzanillo, and inland through the mountains, sophisticated Guadalajara. These cities are found in two neighboring states, Jalisco (Hah-*leez*-coh), Mexico's sixth-largest state, and Colima (Coh-*lee*-mah), the second-largest state, both on Mexico's Pacific Coast. San Blas, suggested as a side trip from Puerto Vallarta, is in the state of Nayarit.

Puerto Vallarta, Jalisco, a leading Pacific Coast resort city, has a picturesque cobblestoned town center flanked by high- and low-rise resort hotels leading in and out of town. Manzanillo, Colima, 175 miles south of Puerto Vallarta, is built around a major port and a string of beaches and bays. Between them lie some of the Pacific Coast's most beautiful mountains and undeveloped coastal landscape, with beautiful beaches at Tenacatita, Careyes, and Tecuan, as well as isolated beaches all along the coast. Thick mountain vegetation and plantations of banana, mango, lime, and coconut hide remote vacation spots.

Inland 260 miles east of Puerto Vallarta and 167 miles northeast of Manzanillo is

WHAT'S SPECIAL ABOUT MEXICO'S PACIFIC COAST

Birding
- San Blas's famous mangrove trips and its 300 bird species.
- Colima's rich bird life, especially around Laguna Cuyutlán, Manzanillo's lagoon, and near the volcanoes east of Colima City.

Beaches
- Some of the country's best beaches, stretching from San Blas to Manzanillo, many of them unspoiled.

Fishing
- The abundance of marlin and sailfish.

Food & Drink
- Ceviche, birria, red pozole of Jalisco, and Colima's white version, Jalisco-style menudo, caldo michi, and tortas ahogadas from the Lake Chapala region, and frijoles boda (married beans), a Colima specialty. The town of Tequila, the heart of the tequila-producing region near Guadalajara.

Museums
- Colima's Museum of Western Cultures, with its pre-Hispanic artifacts including clay dancing dogs.
- Colima's Museum of Popular Culture Pomar, showing regional clothing from throughout Mexico.

Nightlife
- Puerto Vallarta's diverse nightlife.

Shopping
- Guadalajara, for huaraches and silver; Tonalá and Tlaquepaque, for fine decorative objects, equipale furniture, blown glass, and pottery; Colima, for pre-Hispanic reproductions; and Puerto Vallarta, for contemporary art.

Weird Phenomena
- A magnetic field near Comala that causes vehicles to move without motors turned on.

Guadalajara, Jalisco, capital of the state, and Mexico's second-largest city. The delightful metropolis provides an alternate to resort vacationing with its colonial-era center, museums, and nearby artisan villages of Tlaquepaque and Tonalá. And 34 miles south of Guadalajara is Lake Chapala, with its springlike climate and lakeside and mountain resort villages of Mazamitla and Tapalpa, all showing another completely different and very relaxed face of Jalisco. Surrounding Jalisco and Colima are other culturally interesting states, Nayarit, Zacatecas, Aguascalientes, Guanajauto, and Michoacán, all with influences on Jalisco and Colima where their borders touch.

Thirty years ago reaching Puerto Vallarta meant a two-day bus trip from Guadalajara, a journey over an unpaved mountain road from Manzanillo, or a flight to Puerto Vallarta's new airport from Tepic or Guadalajara—all cities more developed and well known than Puerto Vallarta. What a difference three decades makes! Within the last five years Puerto Vallarta has doubled the number of luxury hotel rooms, making it rival Acapulco for accommodations; there are plans to expand even more. Developers who have long eyed the coastline between Puerto Vallarta and Manzanillo (an area dubbed the Costa Alegre, or "happy coast") broke ground in a big way in early 1993. In addition to the established resorts of El Tecuan and Las Alamandas, work has begun on the grand Isla Navidad resort development adjacent to the village of Barra de Navidad; a 27-hole golf course and hotel should be finished there when you travel. Also new is the secluded and sophisticated Hotel Bel-Air El Tamarindo.

The former Hotel Costa Careyes has been transformed under new ownership and management into the secluded Hotel Bel-Air Costa Careyes. Both the Hotel Bel-Air Costa Careyes and the new Grand Bay Hotel in the Isla Navidad project plan to open state-of-the-art health spas in 1994.

Manzanillo, long a haven for condo owners from north of the border, is experiencing a small boom in hotel and restaurant construction. It's still a more tranquil alternative to beachside vacationing, as are the rustic coastal villages of San Blas, north of Puerto Vallarta, and the above-mentioned Barra de Navidad, north of Manzanillo.

Distances are easily manageable by car with most drives between points being from 45 minutes to 6 hours. Roads throughout both states are generally good except for Highway 15 west from Guadalajara through Tequila to Puerto Vallarta.

1. GEOGRAPHY, ECOLOGY, HISTORY & POLITICS

GEOGRAPHY & ECOLOGY

Mexico stretches 2,000 miles from sea to sea. Four times the size of Texas, it's bordered on the north by the United States and to the southeast by Belize, Guatemala, and the Caribbean, to the east by the Gulf of Mexico, and west by the Sea of Cortez and Pacific Ocean. Mexico lacks an extensive river system, but the longest is the Río Balsas which empties near Lázaro Cárdenas on the Pacific. The Río Grande/Río Bravo separates Texas from Mexico and the Río Usumacinta separates Mexico from Guatemala. The highest volcanic peak is the Pico de Orizaba at 18,201 feet and the largest lake is Chapala, near Guadalajara, at 666 square miles.

Colima and Jalisco occupy a region of 103,229 square miles with 265 miles of some of the country's most beautiful mountain coastline, fringed by beautiful beaches and rocky outcroppings. The snowcapped Volcano de Nevada at 14,302 feet lies completely in Jalisco although it is better seen from Colima City. The still-active Fire Volcano at 12,870 feet looms only 35 miles from Colima's city limits. It sent out a stream of lava as late as 1991 after years of nothing but willowy plumes of smoke. In Jalisco the mountains reach to the sea, but for the most part, the mountainous part of Colima is set back a bit from the coast.

Among the wildlife of the untouched coastline of both Colima and Jalisco are jaguars, alligators, and ocelots. Of 70 species of mammals, the most numerous are bats, including the vampire bat. Hundreds of bird species have been counted between Cuixmala and Teopa, near Careyes.

At least four of Mexico's nine species of marine turtles nest on the beaches of Colima and Jalisco. Just before nesting time, fishermen report seeing the turtles mating offshore. Most turtles will return to the same beach to lay eggs year after year, and as often as three times in a season. They only nest on dark beaches; lights of any kind repel them. It takes an hour or more for the turtle to dig the nest in the sand with her back flippers. Of the more than 100 eggs in each nest (*nido*) only 5% of those that hatch will live to return. Programs to save the turtles involve taking the eggs from the original nest to a fenced-off, protected area (*maya*) and placing them in a nest of identical depth and size. The hatchlings, which appear about 45 days later, wait until all their nestmates are ready before they scurry by the hundreds to the ocean. Crabs, birds, and other ocean denizens as well as humans endanger the turtles' precarious

existence. A recent Mexican law carrying serious penalties for destroying turtles or their eggs has had some effect; the belief persists, however, that turtle eggs are an aphrodisiac, and turtles are still killed for their shells and meat. The Biological Station at Chamela, near Careyes, has ongoing studies of the region and produces numerous publications describing their work.

DATELINE

- **1500–300 B.C.** Preclassic period: Olmec culture spreads over Gulf coast, southern Mexico, Central America, and lower Mexican Pacific coast. La Venta Olmec cultural zenith in 600.
- **500 B.C.** Zapotecs lay out great mountaintop plaza of Monte Alban.
- **100 B.C.** Olmec culture disintegrates.
- **A.D. 100** Building begins on Sun and Moon pyramids at Teotihuacán which eventually becomes largest city in the world. Palenque dynasty emerges in Yucatán.
- **300–900** Classic period: Xochicalco established in 300. Maya civilization develops in Yucatán and Chiapas.
- **650–800** El Tajín reaches cultural zenith on coast of Veracruz.
- **650** Teotihuacán

(continues)

HISTORY OF MEXICO

The earliest "Mexicans" were Stone Age men and women, descendants of the race that had crossed the Bering Strait and reached North America before 10,000 B.C. These were Homo sapiens who hunted mastodons and bison, and gathered other food as they could. Later (Archaic period, 5200–1500 B.C.), signs of agriculture and domestication appeared: Baskets were woven; corn, beans, squash, and tomatoes were grown; turkeys and dogs were kept for food. By 2400 B.C. the art of pot making had been discovered (use of pottery was a significant advance). "Artists" made clay figurines for use as votive offerings or household gods. Actually, "goddesses" is a better term, for all of the figurines found so far have been female, and supposedly symbolize Mother Earth or fertility.

THE PRECLASSIC PERIOD It was in the Preclassic period (1500 B.C.–A.D. 300) that the area known by archeologists as Mesoamerica (from the northern Mexico Valley to Costa Rica) began to show signs of a farming culture. Farming was either by the "slash-and-burn" method—cutting grass and trees, then setting fire to the area to clear it for planting—or by construction of terraces and irrigation ducts, this latter method being the one used principally in the highlands around what is now Mexico City, where the first large towns developed. At some time during this period, religion became an institution as certain men took the role of shaman, or guardian of magical and religious secrets. They were the predecessors of the folk healers and native priests still found in modern Mexico.

The most highly developed culture of this Preclassic period was that of the Olmecs, flourishing from 1500 to 100 B.C. They lived in what are today the states of Veracruz and Tabasco, where they used river rafts to transport the colossal multiton blocks of basalt, used to carve roundish heads. These sculptures still present problems to archeologists: What do they signify? The heads seem infantile in their roundness, but all have the peculiar "jaguar mouth" with a high-arched upper lip, the identifying mark of the Olmecs. The Olmecs were the first in Mexico to use a calendar and to develop writing, both of which were later perfected by the Maya.

The link between the Olmecs and the Maya has not been clearly established, but Izapa (400 B.C.–A.D. 400), a ceremonial site in the Chiapan cacao-growing region near the Pacific coast, appears to be one of several transitional sites between the two cultures. When it was discovered, the monuments and stelae were in place, not having undergone destruction as have so many sites.

THE CLASSIC PERIOD Most artistic and cultural achievement came during the Classic period (A.D. 300–900), when life centered in cities. Class distinctions arose as the military and religious aristocracy took control; a class of merchants and artisans grew, with the independent farmer falling under a landlord's control. The cultural centers of the Classic period were Yucatán and Guatemala (also home of the Maya), the Mexican Highlands at Teotihuacán, the Zapotec cities of Monte Alban and Mitla (near Oaxaca), and the cities of El Tajín and Zempoala on the Gulf coast.

THE POSTCLASSIC PERIOD In the Postclassic period (A.D. 900–1500), warlike cultures developed impressive societies of their own, although they never surpassed the Classic peoples. All paintings and hieroglyphs of this period show war, migration, and disruption. Somehow the glue of society became unstuck; people wandered from their homes, and the religious hierarchy lost influence. During these years Colima and Jalisco were inhabited by Otomis, Toltecs, and Tarascans and later by nomadic Chichimecas, who left abundant pottery and underground tombs, but few buildings. Finally, in the 1300s, the warlike Aztecs settled in the Mexico Valley on Lake Texcoco (site of Mexico City), with the island city of Tenochtitlán as their capital. Legend has it that as the wandering Aztecs were passing the lake they saw a sign predicted by their prophets: an eagle perched on a cactus plant with a snake in its mouth. They built their city there and it eventually became a huge (pop. 300,000) and impressive capital. The Aztec empire more or less loosely united territories of great size. The high lords of the capital became fabulously rich in gold, stores of food, cotton, and perfumes; skilled artisans were prosperous; events of state were elaborately ceremonial. Victorious Aztecs returning from battle sacrificed thousands of captives on the altars atop the pyramids, cutting their chests open with stone knives and ripping out their still living hearts to offer to the gods.

QUETZALCOATL The legend of Quetzalcoatl, a holy man who appeared during the time of troubles at the end of the Classic period, is one of the most important tales in Mexican history and folklore, and contributed to the overthrow of the Aztec empire by the Spaniards. Quetzalcoatl means "feathered serpent." Learned beyond his years, he became the high priest and leader of the Toltecs at Tula, and put an end to human sacrifice. His influence completely

DATELINE

burns and is deserted by A.D. 700. Cacaxtla begins to flourish.
- **750** Zapotecs conquer Valley of Oaxaca. Casas Grandes culture begins on northern desert.
- **800** Bonampak battle/victory mural painted.
- **900–1154** Chichimecas descend on the territories of today's Jalisco and Colima. Cacaxtla begins decline.
- **900–1500** Postclassic period: Toltec culture emerges at Tula and spreads to Chichén Itzá by 978.
- **1156 or 1168** After a fire, the Toltecs abandon Tula.
- **1230** El Tajín abandoned by this year.
- **1290** Zapotecs decline and Mixtecs emerge at Monte Alban and Mitla becomes refuge of Zapotecs by this year.
- **1325–45** Aztec capital Tenochtitlán founded. Aztecs dominate Mexico until 1521 when they are defeated by Spaniards.
- **1519–21** Conquest of Mexi-

(continues)

DATELINE

- **co:** Cortés and troops arrive near present-day Veracruz and conquest of Mexico is complete when Cortés defeats Aztecs at Tlaltelolco near Tenochtitlán in 1521.
- **1521–24** Hernán Cortés organizes Spanish empire in Mexico and begins building Mexico City on top of ruins of Tenochtitlán.
- **1523** City of Colima founded.
- **1524** First Franciscan friars arrive from Spain.
- **1531** Tepic founded. Nuño de Guzmán begins the conquest of western Mexico, terrorizing and killing inhabitants of Jalisco, Colima, Michoacán, and Nayarit.
- **1524–35** Cortés removed from leadership. Spanish king sends officials, judges, and finally an audiencia to govern.
- **1535** Cortés visits Manzanillo for the first time.
- **1535–1821** Viceregal period: Mexico governed by viceroys appointed by king of Spain; landed aristocracy emerges.

(continues)

changed the Toltecs from a group of warriors to peaceful and productive farmers, artisans, and craftspeople. But his success upset the old priests who wanted human sacrifice, and they called upon their ancient god of darkness, Texcatlipoca, to degrade Quetzalcoatl in the eyes of the people. One night the priests conspired to dress Quetzalcoatl in ridiculous garb, get him drunk, and tempt him to break his vow of chastity. The next morning shame of this night of debauchery drove him out of his own land and into the wilderness, where he lived for 20 years. He emerged in Coatzacoalcos, in the Isthmus of Tehuantepec, bade his few followers farewell, and sailed away, having promised to return in a future age. But artistic influences noted at Chichén Itzá in the Yucatán suggest that in fact he landed there and began his "ministry" again with much success among the Maya, who called him Kukulkán. He died there, but the legend of his return in a future age remained.

SPANISH CONQUISTADORES When Hernán Cortés and his men landed in 1519 the Aztec empire was ruled by Moctezuma (often misspelled Montezuma) in great splendor. The emperor was uncertain of his course; if the strangers were Quetzalcoatl and his followers returning at last, no resistance must be offered; on the other hand, if they were not, they might be a threat to his empire. Moctezuma tried to bribe them with gold to go away, but this only whetted their appetites. Despite the fact that Moctezuma and his ministers received the conquistadores with full pomp and glory when they reached Mexico City, Cortés eventually took Moctezuma captive.

Though the Spaniards were no match for the hundreds of thousands of Aztecs, they skillfully kept things under their control until a revolt threatened Cortés's entire enterprise. He retreated to the countryside, made alliances with non-Aztec tribes, and finally marched on the empire when it was governed by the last Aztec emperor, Cuauhtémoc. Though Cuauhtémoc defended his people valiantly for almost three months, he was finally captured, tortured, and ultimately executed.

The Spanish conquest had started out as an adventure, unauthorized by the Spanish Crown or its governor in Cuba. Soon Christianity was being spread through "New Spain." Guatemala and Honduras were explored and conquered, and by 1540 the territory of New Spain included Spanish possessions from Vancouver to Panama. During that time the cruel Spaniard Nuño de Guzmán was president of the governing audiencia. Before he could be deposed, he led an army of conquest to western Mexico, killing, terrorizing, and exploiting native inhabitants of the present states of Michoacán, Jalisco, Colima, and Nayarit. In the two centuries that followed, Franciscan and Augustinian friars converted great numbers of Indians to Christianity, and the Spanish lords built up huge feudal estates on which the native farmers were little more than serfs. The silver and gold that Cortés had sought made Spain the richest country in Europe.

INDEPENDENCE Mexico finally gained its independence from Spain in 1821 after a decade of upheaval. The independence movement began in 1810 when a priest, Father Miguel Hidalgo, gave the cry for independence from his pulpit in the town of Dolores, Guanajuato. The revolt soon became a revolution, and Hidalgo, Ignacio Allende, and another priest, José María Morelos, gathered an "army" of citizens and threatened Mexico City. Ultimately Hidalgo was executed, but he is honored as "the Father of Mexican Independence." Morelos kept the revolt alive until 1815, when he was executed.

When independence finally came, Agustín de Iturbide was ready to take over. Iturbide founded a short-lived "empire" with himself as emperor in 1822. The next year it fell and was followed by the proclamation of a republic with Gen. Guadalupe Victoria as first president. A succession of presidents and military dictators followed Guadalupe Victoria until one of the most bizarre and extraordinary episodes in modern times: the French intervention. In the 1860s, Mexican factions offered the Habsburg Archduke Maximilian the crown of Mexico, and with the support of the ambitious French emperor, Napoléon III, the young Austrian actually came to Mexico and "ruled" for three years (1864-67), while the country was in a state of civil war. This European interference in New World affairs was unwelcomed by the United States, and the French emperor finally withdrew his troops, leaving misguided Maximilian to be captured and executed by firing squad in Querétaro. His adversary and successor was Benito Juárez, a Zapotec lawyer and one of the most heroic figures in Mexican history. After victory over Maximilian, Juárez did his best to unify and strengthen his country before dying of a heart attack in 1872. His effect on Mexico's future was profound, however, and his plans and visions bore fruit for decades. From 1877 to 1911, a period now called the Porfiriato, the prime role in Mexico was played by Porfirio Díaz, a Juárez general. Recognized as a modernizer, he was a terror to his enemies and to challengers of his absolute power. He was forced to abdicate in 1911 by Francisco Madero and public opinion.

After the fall of the Porfirist dictatorship several factions split the country, including those led by "Pancho Villa" (whose real name was Doroteo Arango), Alvaro Obregón, Venustiano Carranza, Francisco Madero, Lázaro Cárdenas, and Emiliano Zapata. The decade that followed is referred to as the Mexican Revolution. Drastic reforms occurred in this period, and the surge of vitality and progress from this

DATELINE

- **1537** Mexico's first printing press is installed in Mexico City.
- **1538** Nuño de Guzmán imprisoned for his reign of destruction across western Mexico.
- **1542** Guadalajara founded for the final time.
- **1562** Friar Diego de Landa destroys 5,000 Mayan religious stone figures and burns 27 hieroglyphic-painted manuscripts at Maní, Yucatán.
- **1571** The Inquisition is established in Mexico.
- **1703** Population of Guadalajara is 6,000.
- **1742-48** Construction on the Seminario Conciliar de San José is finished; today it's the Regional Museum of Guadalajara.
- **1767** Jesuits expelled from New Spain.
- **1792** Guadalajara's first printing press starts operation.
- **1803** Guadalajara's population is almost 40,000.
- **1804** In Guadalajara, construction begins on Hospicio

(continues)

DATELINE

Cabañas designed by Manuel Tolsá.

- **1810** Independence War begins. Father Miguel Hidalgo starts movement for Mexico's independence from Spain and leads a large group of insurgents to Guadalajara.
- **1818** Earthquake destroys the towers of Guadalajara's cathedral.
- **1821** Independence from Spain achieved.
- **1822** First Empire: Agustín de Iturbide, independence leader, orchestrates his ascendancy to throne as emperor of Mexico. Guadalajara's population is 70,000.
- **1823** Jalisco becomes a free state.
- **1833** Cholera epidemic kills thousands in Guadalajara.
- **1838** After 34 years of construction the Hospicio Cabañas is finally finished in Guadalajara.
- **1824** Iturbide is expelled, returns, and is executed by firing squad.
- **1824** Priciliano Sanchez is elected first governor of Jalisco. Federal Re-

(continues)

exciting if turbulent time has inspired Mexicans to the present. Succeeding presidents have invoked the spirit of the revolution, which is still studied and discussed.

THE 20TH CENTURY After the turmoil of the revolution, Mexico sought stability in the form of the Partido Revolucionario Institucional (el PRI), the country's dominant political party. With the aim of "institutionalizing the revolution," el PRI (*ell-pree*) literally engulfed Mexican society, leaving little room for vigorous, independent opposition. For over half a century the monolithic party has had control of the government, labor unions, trade organizations, and other centers of power in Mexican society.

The most outstanding Mexican president of the century was Gen. Lázaro Cárdenas (1934–40). An effective leader, Cárdenas broke up vast tracts of agricultural land and distributed parcels to small cooperative farms called *ejidos,* reorganized the labor unions along democratic lines, and provided funding for village schools. His most famous action was the expropriation of Mexico's oil industry from U.S. and European interests, which became Petroleros Mexicanos (Pemex), the government petroleum monopoly.

The PRI has selected Mexico's president (and, in fact, virtually everyone else on the government payroll) from its own ranks since Cárdenas, the national election being only a confirmation of the choice. Among these men have been Avila Camacho, who continued many of Cárdenas's policies; Miguel Alemán, who expanded national industrial and infrastructural development; Adolfo López Mateos, who expanded the highway system and increased hydroelectric power sources; and Gustavo Díaz Ordaz, who provided credit and technical help to the agricultural sector.

In 1970 Luis Echeverría came to power, followed in 1976 by José López Portillo. During their presidencies there emerged a studied coolness in relations with the United States and an activist role in international affairs. This period also saw an increase in charges of large-scale corruption in the upper echelons of Mexican society. The corruption, though endemic to the system, was encouraged by the river of money from the rise in oil prices. When oil income skyrocketed, Mexican borrowing and spending did likewise. The reduction of oil prices in the 1980s left Mexico with an enormous foreign bank debt and serious infrastructure deficiencies.

MEXICO TODAY Without king oil, Mexico must rebuild agriculture and industry, cut expenditures, tame corruption, and keep creditors at bay. President Miguel de la Madrid Hurtado, who assumed the presidency in 1982, struggled with these problems, and made important progress. The present president, Carlos Salinas de Gortari, has managed to slow inflation from 200% annually to between

10% to 15%. But the economy, and society, are still under tremendous economic pressure, and charges of government corruption still abound although less so than in the past.

Mexico's current economic difficulties have led to a newly vigorous and open political life with opposition parties gaining strength. The traditionally victorious PRI party won the hotly contested presidential election in 1988, but its candidate, Carlos Salinas de Gortari, only managed to claim a historically low 50.36% of the vote amid claims of fraud by his chief rival, Cuauhtémoc Cárdenas of the newly formed National Democratic Front (FDN). Ironically, Cárdenas is the son of Mexico's beloved president who founded the PRI. However, opposition parties managed to win a few Senate seats for the first time since the PRI came to power, and recent local elections produced strong opposition candidates. Whether Sr. Salinas de Gortari's promised reforms for greater democracy will be lasting is debatable, but Mexico remains the most stable country in Latin America.

In 1994 a new president of Mexico will be elected.

MEXICAN FACTS & FIGURES The Republic of Mexico is headed today by an elected president and has a bicameral legislature. It is divided into 31 states, plus the Federal District (Mexico City). Economically, Mexico is not by any means a poor country. Only about a sixth of the economy is in agriculture. Mining is still fairly important. Mining for iron ore around Manzanillo is one of the city's major forms of income. Gold and silver and many other important minerals are still mined in the rest of Mexico, but the big industry today is oil. Mexico is also well industrialized, manufacturing textiles, food products, and everything from tape cassettes to automobiles.

In short, Mexico is well into the 20th century, with all the benefits and problems of contemporary life, and although vast sums are spent on education and public welfare, a high birthrate, high unemployment, and unequal distribution of wealth show that much remains to be done.

2. MEXICO'S FAMOUS PEOPLE

Raul Anguiano Valdez (b. 1915) Born in Guadalajara, at 21 Anguiano had his first exhibition at the Palacio de Bellas Artes in Mexico City. One of his most famous paintings, *The Thorn*, depicts a young Indian removing a thorn from her foot with a knife. It hangs in the National Museum of Art in Mexico City. His teaching career took him to the Escuela Nacional de Pintura y

DATELINE

public period begins: Guadalupe Victoria is elected first president of Mexico.
- **1828** Slavery abolished.
- **1835** Texas declares independence from Mexico.
- **1836** Santa Anna defeats Texans at Battle of the Alamo, at San Antonio, Texas, but is later defeated and captured at the Battle of San Jacinto outside Houston, Texas.
- **1838** France invades Mexico at Veracruz.
- **1845** U.S. annexes Texas.
- **1846–48** War with U.S.; for a payment of $15 million Mexico relinquishes half of its national territory to the U.S. in treaty of Guadalupe Hidalgo.
- **1855** Santos Degollado is named governor of Guadalajara. Reform years begin. Country wages three-year war on itself, pitting cities against villages and rich against poor. Benito Juárez becomes president, in fact and in exile.
- **1862** England,

(continues)

DATELINE

Spain, and France send troops to demand debt payment and all except France withdraw.

- **1864–67** Second Empire: French Emperor Napoléon III sends the Hapsburg Ferdinand Maximilian Joseph, 32, and his wife, Marie Charlotte Amélie Léopoldine, 24, to be emperor and empress of Mexico.
- **1866** Guadalajara is seized by troops loyal to Juárez.
- **1867** Juárez orders execution of Maximilian at Querétaro and resumes presidency in Mexico City until his death in 1872.
- **1872–84** Post-Reform period: Only four presidents hold office but country is nearly bankrupt.
- **1876–1911** Porfiriato: With one four-year exception, Porfirio Díaz is president/dictator of Mexico for 35 years, leading country in tremendous modernization at the expense of human rights.
- **1880** Mule-drawn trolleys serve as public

(continues)

Escultura in Mexico City in 1935 when he was only 20, where he remained until 1967. Simultaneously he became a professor at the Universidad Nacional Autónima de Mexico in Mexico City in 1959, and guest professor at Trinity University in San Antonio, Texas, in 1966. One-man shows organized for him took him to Guadalajara, the Carnegie Cultural Arts Center in Oxnard, California, and the San Diego Museum of Man.

Luis Barragán (1902–89) One of Mexico's most influential architects, he was from a wealthy Guadalajara family but spent his youth in the forested mountains of Jalisco, near Mazamitla. Though a skilled landscape architect he was known primarily as an architect/designer of homes and for his use of bold Mexican colors and incorporation of hacienda styles into modern buildings. Unschooled in either architecture or landscape gardening he nevertheless succeeded in becoming prominent in both and his techniques and designs influence Mexican architecture today. He won the coveted Pritzker Award for architecture in 1980.

Hernán Cortés (1485–1547) Brash, bold, greedy, and a brilliant military leader, 34-year-old Hernán Cortés conquered Mexico in the name of Spain without the knowledge of that country's king. He sank his ships to prevent desertion and with only 550 men and 16 horses, he conquered a nation of 30,000 and a territory larger than his native country. He became governor and captain general of New Spain immediately after the conquest and later he was given the title of Marqués of the Valley of Oaxaca and substantial landholdings. He began silver mining in Taxco and introduced sugarcane cultivation around Cuernavaca. But by 1528 he was removed from governorship and the king sent other Spaniards to take charge. Cortés died in Spain while seeking proper recognition and a more significant title from the Spanish court, which shunned him. Mexicans regard him as the destroyer of a nation and no monuments honor him. He is buried in a vault in the Church of the Hospital of Jésus Nazareño, Mexico City.

Porfirio Díaz (1830–1915) Born in Oaxaca and schooled in law, at age 32 he distinguished himself at the famous Puebla battle and within 14 years became president of Mexico. He remained as dictator for the next 34 years, with one 4-year interruption. His contributions were enormous: He moved the country from turmoil and bankruptcy into peace and stability through improvements in communication, railroads, agriculture, manufacturing, mining, port enlargement, oil exploration, and foreign investment. He built lavish public buildings, and sent promising art students to Europe on full scholarship. His love for all things French was legendary. He achieved these successes by disregarding the law and at the expense of the poor, Indians, and intellectuals who opposed his methods, all of which brought about his downfall in 1911 and the Mexican Revolution which lasted until 1917. He died in exile in Paris and is buried in the Père Lachaise Cemetery there.

Miguel Hidalgo y Costilla (1753–1811) In 1792, the man later to be known as the Father of Mexican Independence, was the parish priest in Colima. By 1810, however, he was a small-town priest in the town of Dolores, Guanajuato. At the time he was better known for his anticelibacy beliefs, and disbelief in papal supremacy. As priest he taught parishioners to grow mulberry trees for silkworms (for making silk) and grapes (for winemaking, prohibited by the crown), and to make ceramics; the latter two still thrive in the region. He was among several in his area who secretly conspired to free Mexico from Spanish domination. On the morning of September 16, 1810, a messenger from Josefa Ortiz de Dominguez brought Hidalgo word that the conspiracy was uncovered. He quickly decided to publicly call for independence (known today as the *grito* or "cry") from his parish church after which he galloped from village to village spreading the news, and gathering troops. His small home, today a museum, is on Morelos Street, corner of Hidalgo in Dolores Hidalgo, Guanajuato, and he is buried in the Independence Monument, Mexico City.

Agustín de Iturbide (1783–1824) In an elaborate ceremony that took months to plan, he was crowned emperor of Mexico and created an elaborate imperial monarchy with titles and right of succession by his children. But he reigned only briefly from 1822 to 1824, when General Santa Anna led a successful rebellion to dethrone him. He returned surreptitiously from exile but was captured and shot by a firing squad in Padilla, Tamaulipas. For years regarded as a usurper and self-interested politician, in a rare move public sentiment recognized his role in gaining Mexico's independence from Spain and his remains were interred more fittingly in the Mexico City Cathedral.

María Izquierdo (1906–55) Born in San Juan de los Lagos, Jalisco, Izquierdo's career was a brief but important one. Contemporary with Frida Kahlo (Diego Rivera's wife), her work, like Kahlo's, had a skilled but primitive edge to it. Her first art lessons began at age 6 and by 21 she spent a year in school at the Academia de San Carlos in Mexico City. The following year her first one-woman show appeared at the Galería de Arte Moderno and she began work with Rufino Tamayo, another of Mexico's renowned artists. In 1930 a one-woman show was mounted for her at the New York Art Center and in 1933 in Paris at the Galerie René Highe. Her subjects were those of everyday Mexican life. Intellectuals from around the world honored her talent and beauty with poetry and praise during her lifetime. Much of her work is in private

DATELINE

transportation in Guadalajara.

- **1884** Electric lights go on in Guadalajara for the first time.
- **1887** Gen. Ramón Corona is elected governor of Jalisco in 1887.
- **1888** The Mexico City-to-Guadalajara railroad is inaugurated.
- **1907** Electric trolleys are installed in Guadalajara.
- **1909** Francisco Madero's political tour of Mexico includes Manzanillo and Guadalajara as he becomes a more visible anti-Díaz leader. The Guadalajara-to-Manzanillo railroad is inaugurated.
- **1911–17** Mexican Revolution: Díaz resigns and many factions jockey for power. Period of great violence, national upheaval, and tremendous loss of life. Starvation reaches epidemic proportions, dramatically affecting Guadalajara.
- **1913** President Madero assassinated.
- **1914–1916** Two U.S. invasions of Mexico.

(continues)

14 • INTRODUCING MEXICO'S MID-PACIFIC REGION

DATELINE

- **1917–40** Reconstruction: Mexican constitution signed. Reforms initiated, labor unions strengthened, and Mexico expells U.S. oil companies and nationalizes all natural resources and railroads. Presidents Obregón and Carranza assassinated as are Pancho Villa and Emiliano Zapata.
- **1926–29** The Cristero Rebellion in response to President Calles's action limiting the Catholic church; violence between church and government is particularly strong in Jalisco, Colima, and Michoacán.
- **1940–present** Mexico enters period of political stability and economic progress though with continued problems of corruption, inflation, national health, and unresolved land and agricultural issues.
- **1955** Women given full voting rights.
- **1982** Nationalization of banks.
- **1988** Mexico enters the General Agreement on

(continues)

collections, but good examples are at the Museum of Modern Art in Mexico City.

Benito Juárez (1806–72) A full-blooded Zapotec, he was orphaned at the age of 3. He became governor of Oaxaca in 1847 after which he was exiled to New Orleans by grudge-holding President Santa Anna because Juárez refused to grant him asylum in Oaxaca years before. On becoming president of Mexico first in 1858, his terms were interrupted once during the Reform Wars and again during the French intervention. Juárez cast the deciding vote favoring the execution of Maximilian. He died from a heart attack before completing his fourth term. Devoid of personal excesses, Juárez had a clear vision for Mexico, that included honest leadership, separation of church and state, imposition of civilian rule, reduction of the military, and education reform. He is buried in the San Fernando Cemetery, Mexico City.

Miguel de la Madrid Hurtado (b. 1934) President of Mexico from 1982 to 1988, he was born in Colima. He received a degree in law in 1957 from the Universidad Nacional Autónima de Mexico, and in 1965 a master's degree in public administration from Harvard University. He was an able administrator and good president, who unfortunately inherited scandalous excesses of two presidents immediately before him, a bankrupt country with 200% inflation, and a mess from his immediate predecessor, José López Portillo, who, among other ill-advised acts, nationalized the banks overnight just before turning over the government to de la Madrid. Among de la Madrid's credits he began returning to the private sector many government holdings, steered Mexico toward world competition through membership in GATT (General Agreement on Trade and Tariffs), and managed to continue Mexico's payment on its enormous debt at great sacrifice by the Mexican people and economy. His presidency set the stage for the present one in which Mexico heads even faster into world trade, lower inflation, and greater stability.

Alfonso Michel (1897–1957) Born in Colima, capital of Colima state, Michel's career took him all over the world in search of study, but it wasn't until 1942 that he began to be noticed. Using his mastery of impressionism, he directed his themes to Mexican subjects and shared a studio with Roberto Montenegro from 1935 to 1940.

Roberto Montenegro (1887–1968) Another of Mexico's child prodigies, Montenegro, born in Guadalajara, began studying painting in 1903. The following year he went to Mexico City to study at the Escuela Nacional de Arte where he began acquaintances with some of Mexico's famous artists, Diego Rivera among them. On scholarship and working, he traveled, studied, and exhibited in Europe for almost 15 years, becoming one of Mexico's most skilled artists. When he returned to Mexico, he began an intense discovery of Mexican folk art and his paintings, besides featuring peasant folk, usually include folk art from everyday life. In 1934 he was appointed director of the Museo de Artes Populares de Bellas Artes, and for five years shared a studio in Guadalajara with fellow painter, Alfonso Micheĺ.

Gerardo Murillo (Dr. Atl) (1875-1964) Possessing enormous energy as well as political and artistic passion, Gerardo Murillo (who, for a political statement, changed his name to Dr. Atl, a Náhuatl word meaning water) was a painter, writer, and not-too-successful politician who was driven by art and political causes and attracted by the outdoors, mountain climbing, and science. Born in Guadalajara, he is best known for his vast landscapes, usually including volcanoes, in which he produced an aerial feeling of the Mexican landscape. His influence on Mexican art and artists was enormous. Among his students, when he was director of the San Carlos Academy, were José Clemente Orozco and David Siquieros. One of his books, *Las Artes Populares en Mexico* (Popular Arts in Mexico), produced as a catalog for the first exhibition of Mexican folk art, upheld the common artisans of Mexico and remains a classic.

José Clemente Orozco (1883-1949) Born in what today is known as Ciudad Guzmán, Jalisco, Orozco is considered one of the "Big Three" muralists along with Diego Rivera and David Alfero Siquieros. His gloomy, angry, but powerful works project his bitter view of politics. His years of struggle included a stint painting street signs and doll faces in the United States. On one trip north across the border U.S. Customs destroyed his brothel series of paintings. Alma Reed, who owned Delphic Studios in New York, took him under her wing, promoting his career. His best-known murals appear in Guadalajara and the many of his easel works are in the Alvaro Carrillo Gil Museum in Mexico City. He is buried in the Rotonda de los Ilustres of the Dolores Cemetery in Mexico City.

Antonio López de Santa Anna (1794-1876) One of the most scorned characters in Mexican history, he was president of Mexico 11 times between 1833 and 1855. Audacious, pompous, and self-absorbed, his outrageous exploits disgust and infuriate Mexicans even today, but none more than his role in losing half the territory of Mexico to the United States. Defeated and captured at the Battle of San Jacinto outside Houston, Texas, in 1836, among other things he agreed to allow Texas to be a separate republic and to mark the boundary at the Rio Grande. When the United States voted to annex Texas, it sparked the Mexican-American War which the United States won in 1848. In the Treaty of Guadalupe Hidalgo which followed between the two nations, the United States paid Mexico $15 million for Texas, New Mexico, California, Arizona, Nevada, Utah, and part of Colorado. Eventually Santa Anna was exiled, but returned two years before he died, poor, alone, and forgotten. He is buried in the Guadalupe Cemetery behind the Basilica de Guadalupe, Mexico City.

Ignacio Luis Vallarta (1830-93) Puerto Vallarta is named after this distinguished lawyer, diplomat, and governor of Jalisco. Born in Guadalajara, he studied law at the University of Guadalajara. Upon receiving his law degree at age 25,

---

DATELINE

Trade and Tariffs (GATT).
- **1991** Mexico, Canada, and the United States begin free-trade agreement negotiations.
- **1992** Sale of *ejido* land (peasant communal property) to private citizens is allowed; Mexico and the Vatican establish diplomatic relations after an interruption of 100 years.
- **1993** Mexico deregulates hotel and restaurant prices; New Peso currency begins circulation.

he served Jalisco governor Santos Degollado as personal secretary, a post he later held for Governor Pedro Ogazón. He went into exile in the United States during the French Intervention but returned to join with Benito Juárez against the French in 1866. At age 41 he became governor of Jalisco, serving from 1871 to 1875. In 1877 he became Secretary of Foreign Affairs under President Porfirio Díaz. He ended his legal and political career in 1888 as president of the nation's Supreme Court of Justice.

3. ART, ARCHITECTURE & LITERATURE

ART & ARCHITECTURE Mexico's art and architectural legacy began more than 3,000 years ago. Until the fall of the Aztec empire after the Spanish conquest of Mexico in 1521, art, architecture, politics, and religion in Mexico were inextricably intertwined and remained so to a different extent through the colonial period.

World-famous archeological sites in Mexico—more than 15,000 of them—are individually unique even when built by the same groups of people. Each year scholars decipher more information about those who built these cities, using information they left in bas-relief carvings, sculptures, pottery, murals, and hieroglyphics.

Mexico's pyramids are truncated platforms, not true pyramids, and come in many different shapes. At Tzintzuntzán, near Lake Pátzcuaro, in Michoacán state, the buildings, called *yacatas,* are distinguished by semicircular buildings attached to rectangular ones. Many sites have circular buildings, usually called the observatory and dedicated to Ehécatl, god of the wind. Few pre-Hispanic buildings remain in either Colima or Jalisco although exquisite pottery examples are preserved in museums in both states.

Pottery played an important role and different indigenous groups are distinguished by their use of color and style in pottery. In Tonalá near Guadalajara, pottery traditions begun in pre-Hispanic times continue today and the National Museum of Ceramics in that village contains many good samples of Jalisco pottery as well as pieces from around Mexico. Ancient Jalisco pottery was both off-white and dark red and often decorated with black or red. Many of the figures show the workaday world of unknown peoples, carrying children or water jugs and at play. Good examples are on display at the small museum of anthropology in Guadalajara, across from Agua Azul Park. Both Jalisco and Colima are riddled with underground burial chambers and much of the dark red pottery was found in these multiroomed vaults. Near Colima City visitors can go to some of these underground tombs. Colima is also famous for clay pieces formed into the shapes of potbellied hairless dogs, many of them dancing. But the pottery also took the shape of vegetables, especially squash. Excellent museums in Colima display the unusual work of pre-Hispanic peoples of that area. Besides the museums mentioned above, prime samples from this area are in the Museum of Anthropology in Mexico City.

With the arrival of the Spaniards a new form of architecture came to Mexico, which, for the next 300 years is known as the Viceregal era, when Spain's appointed viceroys ruled Mexico. Many sites that were occupied by indigenous groups at the time of the conquest were razed, and in their place appeared Catholic churches, public buildings, and palaces for conquerors and the king's bureaucrats. Indian artisans, who formerly worked on pyramidal structures, were recruited to give life to these structures, often guided by drawings of European buildings the Spanish architects tried to emulate. Frequently left on their own, the indigenous artisans sometimes implanted their symbolism on the buildings. They might sculpt a plaster angel

IMPRESSIONS

The revolution gave us self-confidence and a conscience for our existence and our destiny.
—José Clemente Orozco

... Mexico is a country as richly set with architecture as an Elizabethan gown with pearls. Obviously they are not all jewels, but all have their places in the great network from which such buildings as the parish church of Taxco, San Agustín Acolman, the cathedreal of Puebla, the Palacio del Gobierno in Guadalajara, or the Casa de los Azulejos in Mexico City stand out.
—Elizabeth Wilder Weismann, Art and Time in Mexico, 1985

---

swaddled in feathers reminiscent of the god Quetzalcoatl or the face of an ancient god surrounded by corn leaves or use the pre-Hispanic calendar counts or the 13 steps to heaven or the nine levels of the underworld to determine how many flowerettes to carve around the church doorway. Good examples of native symbolism are at the church in Xochimilco near Mexico City and Santa María Tonanzintla near Puebla. Native muralists had a hand in painting a knight in tiger skin on the Augustinian monastery in Ixmiquilpan, Hidalgo.

To convert the native populations, New World Spanish priests and architects altered their normal ways of building and teaching. Often before the church was built, an open-air atrium was first constructed so that large numbers of parishioners could be accommodated for service. *Posas* (shelters) at the four corners of churchyards were another architectural technique unique to Mexico, again for the purpose of accommodating crowds during holy sacraments. Because of the language barrier between the Spanish and natives, church adornment became more graphic. Biblical tales came to life in frescoes splashed across church walls and Christian symbolism in stone supplanted that of pre-Hispanic times. Out went the eagle (sun symbol), feathered serpent (symbol of fertility, rain, earth, and sky), and jaguar (power symbol) and in came Christ on a cross, saintly statues, and Franciscan, Dominican, and Augustinian symbolism on church facades. The talents of native master stone- and wood-carvers were turned to Christian subjects. It must have been a confusing time for the indigenous peoples, which accounts for the continued intermingling of Christian and pre-Hispanic ideas as they tried to make sense of it all by mixing preexisting ideas with new ones. The convenient apparition of the Virgin Mary on former pre-Hispanic religious turf made it "legal" to return there to worship and build a "Christian" shrine. Baroque became even more baroque in Mexico and was dubbed *Churrigueresque*. Excellent Mexican baroque examples are in Guadalajara in the Chapel of Our Lady of Aranzaú, and Guadalajara's Regional Museum, as well as Santa Prisca Church in Taxco and San Cayetano de la Valencia Church near Guanajuato. The term *Plateresque* was given to facade designs resembling silver design, but more planted on a structure than a part of it. Acolman Convent near the ruins of Teotihuacán has one of the best Plateresque facades in Mexico. The Viceregal Museum in Tepozotlán, north of Mexico City, holds a wealth of artwork from Mexican churches during this period.

Running concurrently with the building of religious structures, the public buildings took shape, modeled after those in European capitals. Especially around Puebla the use of locally made colorful tile, a fusion of local art and Talavera style from Spain, decorated public walls and church domes. The hacienda architecture sprang up in the countryside, resulting in often massive, thick-walled, fortresslike structures built around a central patio. Remains of haciendas, some still operating, can be seen in almost all parts of Mexico. The San Carlos Academy of Art was founded in Mexico City in 1785, taking after the renowned academies of Europe. Though the emphasis was on a Europeanized Mexico, by the end of the 19th century, the subject matter of easel artists was becoming Mexican: Still lifes with Mexican fruit and pottery, clearly Mexican landscapes with cacti and volcanoes appeared, as did portraits, whose subjects wore Mexican regional clothing. José María Velasco (1840-1912), the father of Mexican landscape painting, emerged during this time. His work and that of others of this period are at the National Museum of Art in Mexico City.

With the late 19th-century entry of Porfirio Díaz into the presidency came another infusion of Europe. Díaz idolized Europe and during this time he lavished on the country a number of striking European-style public buildings, among them opera houses still used today. He provided European scholarships to promising young artists who later returned to Mexico to produce clearly Mexican subject paintings using techniques learned abroad. While the Mexican Revolution, following the resignation and exile of Díaz, ripped the country apart between 1911 and 1917, the result was the birth of Mexico, a claiming and appreciation of it by Mexicans. In 1923 Minister of Education José Vasconcelos was charged with educating illiterate masses. As one means of reaching many people he started the muralist movement when he invited Diego Rivera and several other budding artists to paint Mexican history on the walls of the Ministry of Education building and the National Preparatory School in Mexico City. From then on, the "Big Three" muralists, David Siquieros, Guadalajara-born José Clemente Orozco, and Rivera, were joined by others in bringing Mexico's history in art to the walls of public buildings throughout the country for all to see and interpret. The years that followed eventually brought about a return to easel art, an exploration of Mexico's culture, and a new generation of artists and architects who are free to invent and draw upon subjects and styles from around the world. Among the 20th-century greats are the Big Three muralists, as well as Rufino Tamayo, Gerardo Murillo (Dr. Atl), José Guadalupe Posada, Saturnino Herrán, Francisco Goitia, Frida Kahlo, Roberto Montenegro, José María Velasco, Pedro and Rafael Coronel, Miguel Covarrubias, Olga Costa, and José Chávez Morado. Among the important architects during this period is Luis Barragán, of Guadalajara, who incorporated design elements from haciendas, and Mexican textiles, pottery, and furniture, into sleek, marble-floored structures splashed with the vivid colors of Mexico. His ideas are used by Mexican architects all over Mexico today.

LITERATURE By the time Cortés arrived in Mexico, the cultures of Mexico were already masters of literature, recording their poems and histories by painting in fanfold books (codices) made of deer skin and bark paper or carving on stone. To record history, gifted students were taught the art of book making, drawing, painting, reading, and writing. After the conquest the Spaniards deliberately destroyed native books. However, several Catholic priests, among them Bernardo de Sahugun and Diego de Landa (who was one of the book destroyers) encouraged the Indians to record their customs and history. These records are among the best we have that document life before the conquest. During the conquest Cortés wrote his now-famous five letters to Charles V, which give us the first printed conquest literature, but it was spare by contrast to the work of Díaz de Castillo. Enraged by an inaccurate account of the conquest written by a flattering friend of Cortés, 40 years after the conquest Bernal Díaz de Castillo, one of the conquerors, wrote his lively and very readable version of the event, *True History of the Conquest of Mexico;* it's regarded as the most accurate. The first printing press appeared in Mexico in 1537 and was followed by a proliferation of printing mostly on subjects about science, nature, and getting along in Mexico. The most important literary figure during the 16th century was Sor Juana Inés de la Cruz, child prodigy and later poet-nun whose works are still treasured. The first Spanish novel written in Mexico was *The Itching Parrot* by José Joaquín Fernández de Lizardi about 19th-century Mexican life. The first daily newspaper appeared in 1805. Nineteenth-century writers produced a plethora of political fiction and nonfiction. Among the more explosive was *The Presidential Succession of 1910* by Francisco Madero (who later became president) which contributed to the downfall of Porfirio Díaz and *Regeneración,* a weekly anti-Díaz magazine published by the Flores Mignon brothers. Among 20th-century writers of note are Octavio Paz, author of *The Labyrinth of Solitude* and winner of the 1991 Nobel Prize for literature, and Carlos Fuentes, who wrote *Where the Air Is Clear.* Books in Mexico are relatively inexpensive to purchase but editions are not produced in great quantity. Newspapers and magazines proliferate, but the majority of those who read devour comic-book novels, the most visible form of literature.

4. RELIGION, MYTH & FOLKLORE

RELIGION Mexico is a predominantly Catholic country, a religion introduced by the Spaniards during the conquest of Mexico. Despite the preponderance of the Catholic faith, in many places it has pre-Hispanic overtones. One need only visit the *curandero* (folk healing) section of a Mexican market, or attend a village festivity featuring pre-Hispanic dancers to understand that supernatural beliefs often run parallel to Christian ones.

Mexico's complicated mythological heritage from pre-Hispanic literature is jammed with images derived from nature—the wind, jaguars, eagles, snakes, flowers, and more, all intertwined with elaborate mythological stories that explain the universe, climate, seasons, and geography. So strong were the ancient beliefs in their mythological dieties that Mexico's indigenous peoples built their cities according to the cardinal points, with each direction assigned a particular color (the colors might vary from group to group). The sun, moon, and stars took on godlike meaning and their religious, ceremonial, and secular calendars were arranged to show tribute to these omnipotent gods.

Most groups believed in an underworld (not a hell) usually of 9 levels and heaven of 13 levels, so the numbers 9 and 13 become mythologically significant. The solar calendar count of 365 days and the ceremonial calendar of 260 days are numerically significant. How one died determined where one wound up after death, in the underworld, heaven, or at one of the four cardinal points. Everyone had to first make the journey through the underworld.

One of the richest sources of mythological tales is the *Popol Vuh,* a Maya bible of sorts, that was recorded after the conquest. The *Chilam Balam,* another such book, existed in hieroglyphic form at the conquest and was recorded using the Spanish alphabet into Mayan words that could be understood by the Spaniards. The *Chilam Balam* differed from the *Popol Vuh* in that it is the collected histories of many Maya communities.

Each of the ancient cultures had its set of gods and goddesses and while the names might not cross cultures, their characteristics or purpose often did. Chac, the hook-nosed rain god of the Maya, was Tlaloc, the mighty-figured rain god of the Aztecs; Queztalcoatl, the plumed serpent god/man of the Toltecs, became Kukulkán of the Maya. The tales of the powers and creation of these deified personages make up Mexico's rich mythology. Sorting out the pre-Hispanic pantheon and mythological beliefs in ancient Mexico can become an all-consuming study (the Maya alone had 166 deities), so below is a list of some of the most important gods.

Chac Maya rain god
Cinteotl Huastec corn god
Coatlíque Huitzilopochtli's mother, whose name means "she of serpent skirt," goddess of death and earth
Cocijo Zapotec rain god
Ehécatl Wind god whose temple is usually round; another aspect of Quetzalcoatl
Huitzilopochtli War god and primary Aztec god, son of Coatlíque
Itzamná Maya god above all, who invented corn, cocoa, and writing and reading
Ixchel Maya goddess of water, weaving, and childbirth
Kinich Ahau Maya sun god
Kukulkán Quetzalcoatl's name in the Yucatán
Mayahuel Goddess of pulque
Ometeotl God/goddess all powerful creator of the universe, ruler of heaven, earth, and underworld.
Quetzalcoatl A mortal who took on legendary characteristics as a god (or vice versa). When he left Tula in shame after a night succumbing to temptations, he promised to return; he reappeared in the Yucatán. He is also symbolized as Venus, the morning star, and Ehécatl, the wind god.
Tezcatlipoca Aztec sun god known as "Smoking Mirror"
Tláloc Aztec rain god
Tonantzin Aztec motherhood goddess
Xochipilli Aztec god of dance, flowers, and music
Xochiquetzal Flower and love goddess

5. CULTURAL & SOCIAL LIFE

The population of Mexico is 85 million, with 15% white (most of Spanish descent), 60% mestizo (mixed Spanish and Indian), and 25% pure Indian (descendants of the Maya, Aztecs, Huastecs, Otomies, Totonacs, Huichol, and other peoples). Added to this ethnic mix are Africans brought as slaves; European merchants and soldiers of fortune; and the lingering French influence from the time of Maximilian's abortive empire in the New World.

Although Spanish is the official language, about 50 indigenous languages are still spoken, mostly in the Yucatán peninsula, Oaxaca, Chiapas, Chihuahua, Nayarit, Puebla, Sonora and Veracruz, Michoacán, and Guerrero.

Modern Mexico clings to its identity while embracing outside cultures, so Mexicans enjoy the Bolshoi Ballet as readily as a family picnic or village festival. Mexicans have a knack for knowing how to enjoy life, and families, weekends, holidays, and festivities are a priority. A weekend holiday stretched into four days is called a *puente* (bridge) and with the whole family in tow, Mexicans flee the cities to visit relatives in the country, picnic, or relax at resorts.

The Mexican workday is a long one; laborers begin around 7am and get off at dusk; office workers go in around 9am and, not counting the two- to three-hour lunch, get off at 7 or 8pm. Once a working career is started, there is little time for additional study. School is supposedly mandatory and free through the sixth grade, but many youngsters quit long before that, or never go at all.

Sociologists and others have written volumes trying to explain the Mexican's special relationship with death. It is at once mocked and mourned. Day of the Dead, November 1 and 2, is a good opportunity to see Mexico's relationship with the concept of death.

6. PERFORMING ARTS

MUSIC & DANCE One has only to walk down almost any street or attend any festival to understand that Mexico's vast musical tradition is inborn; it pre-dates the conquest. Musical instruments were made from almost anything that could be made to rattle, produce a rhythm, or a sound—conch-shell trumpets, high-sounding antler horns, rattles from seashells and rattlesnake rattlers, drums of turtle shell as well as upright leather-covered wood (*tlalpanhuéhuetl*) and horizontal hollowed logs (*teponaztli*), bells of gold and copper, wind instruments of hollow reeds or fired clay, and soundmakers from leather-topped armadillo shells and gourds. Many were elaborately carved or decorated befitting the important ceremonies they accompanied. So important was music that one of Moctezuma's palaces, the Mixcoacalli, was devoted to the care and housing of musical instruments which were guarded around the clock. In Aztec times, music, dance, and religion were tied together with literature. Music was usually intended to accompany poems which were written for religious ceremonies. Children with talent were separated and trained especially as musicians and poets, two exacting professions in which mistakes carried extreme consequences. The dead were buried with musical instruments for the journey into the afterlife.

Music and dance in Mexico today is divided into three kinds, pre- and post-Hispanic, and secular. Pre-Hispanic dancing may be seen at the Ballet Folklórico de Mexico which, among other places, performs in Guadalajara. Many pre-Hispanic dances are still performed in regional village fiestas; examples are the dances of the

---

IMPRESSIONS

Jalisco is not only a state but also a magic name. The scenes for many of Mexico's modern movies and popular novels are set in Jalisco and often have the name in the title; practically all of the ranchero songs are about Jalisco or about Guadalajara, its capital. This popularity is probably traceable to a nostalgia for the good old days of Mexico which Jalisco once represented.
　—HERBERT CERWIN, *THESE ARE THE MEXICANS*, 1947

Jalisco is rich in ancient remains. Burial places are constantly discovered, though the material unearthed falls, at least to a great extent, into the hands of shrewd dealers, who sell it to tourists and thus scatter it over the earth.
　—CARL LUMHOLTZ, *UNKNOWN MEXICO*, 1902

Huicholes and Coras of Jalisco and Nayarit. Post-Hispanic music and dance first evolved to teach the native inhabitants about Christianity. "Los Santiagos" is about St. James battling heathens, and "Los Moros" shows Moors battling Christians. Others, like "Los Jardineros," were spoofs on pretentious Spanish life. Secular dances are variations of Spanish dances, characterized by lots of foot tapping, skirt-swishing, and flirtatious gestures. No Mexican fiesta night would be complete without the "Jarabe Tapatío," the national folk dance of Mexico, created in Guadalajara.

Besides the native music and dances, there are regional, state, and national orchestras. On weekends and special occasions state bands often perform free in central plazas. Mexicans have a sophisticated enjoyment of performing arts from around the world and world-class auditoriums in which they perform. Any such performance will be a sell-out, so it's possible to find national as well as international groups touring most of the year but especially in conjunction with the Cervantino Festival which takes place in Guanajuato in October and November. Invited groups perform throughout the country before and after the festival.

7. SPORTS & RECREATION

The precise rules of the ball game played by pre-Hispanic Mexicans aren't known, but it is fairly well established that some of the players were put to death when the game was over. Stone carvings of the game left on the walls of ballcourts throughout Mesoamerica depict heavily padded players elaborately decked out. With that interesting beginning, team sports are still popular in Mexico.

Bullfighting, introduced by the Spaniards, is performed countrywide today. Jai alai, another Spanish game, is played in arenas in Mexico City and Tijuana. By the 18th century the Mexican gentleman cowboy, the charro, displayed skillful horsemanship during the "charreada" a Mexican-style rodeo. Today charro associations country-wide compete all year, usually on Sunday mornings. Although supposedly illegal, in many places cockfights are held in specially built arenas. Probably the most popular spectator team sport today is soccer; turn on the TV almost any time to catch a game. Mexico has numerous golf courses, especially in the resort areas, but also excellent ones in Mexico City and Guadalajara. It is sometimes easier to rent a horse in Mexico than a car, since riding is a pastime enjoyed by many people at beach resorts as well as in the country. Sport bicycling has grown in popularity so it isn't unusual to see young men making the grind of steep mountain passes during cycling-club marathons.

Tennis, racquetball, squash, waterskiing, surfing, and scuba diving are all sports visitors can enjoy in Mexico. There's good scuba diving on the Pacific, but the best place for that sport is Mexico's Yucatán Caribbean coast. Mountain climbing and hiking volcanoes is a rugged sport where you'll meet like-minded folks from around the world.

8. FOOD & DRINK

Mexican food served in the United States isn't really Mexican food; it's a transported variation that gets less Mexican the farther you get from the border. True Mexican food usually isn't fiery hot; hot spices are added from sauces and garnishes at the table.

FOOD & DRINK • 23

While there are certain staples like tortillas and beans that appear almost universally, Mexican food and drink varies considerably from region to region; even the beans and tortillas sidestep the usual in some areas just to keep you on your toes.

DINING CUSTOMS Who you are and what you do makes a difference in when you eat. If you are a businessperson you may grab a cup of coffee or *atole* and a piece of sweet bread just before heading for work around 8am. Around 10 or 11am it's time for a real breakfast and that's when restaurants usually fill with people eating hearty breakfasts that may look more like lunch with steak, eggs, beans, and tortillas. Between 1 and 5pm patrons again converge for lunch, the main meal of the day, that begins with soup, then rice, then the main course with beans and tortillas and maybe a meager helping of a vegetable, followed by dessert and coffee. Workers return to their jobs until 7 or 8pm. Dinner is late, usually around 9 or 10pm. Although you may see many Mexicans eating in restaurants at night, big evening meals aren't traditional; a typical meal at home would be a light one with leftovers from breakfast or lunch, perhaps soup, or tortillas and jam, or a little meat and rice.

Foreigners searching for an early breakfast will often find that nothing gets going in restaurants until around 9am; that's a hint to bring your own portable coffeepot and coffee and buy bakery goodies the night before and make breakfast yourself. Markets however are bustling by 7am and that's the best place to get an early breakfast. Though Mexico grows flavorful coffee in Chiapas, Veracruz, and Oaxaca, a jar of instant coffee is often all that's offered, especially in budget restaurants.

Some of the foreigner's greatest frustrations in Mexico have to do with getting and retaining the waiter and receiving the final bill. If the waiter arrives to take your order before you are ready, you may have trouble getting him again when you are ready. Once an order is in, ordinarily the food arrives in steady sequence. While you're eating, the waiter may seem overly anxious to serve—he's likely to be there to sweep your plate away before you've finished. Once the last plate is cleared, the waiter so thoroughly disappears that getting the check becomes a difficult matter. It's considered rude for the waiter to bring it before it's requested, so you have to ask for it (sometimes more than once, when at last you've found the waiter). To summon the waiter, wave or raise your hand, but don't motion with your index finger, a demeaning gesture that may even cause the waiter to ignore you. Or if it's the check you want, a smile and a scribbling motion into the palm of your hand can send the message across the room. In many budget restaurants, waiters don't clear the table of finished plates or soft-drink bottles because they use them to figure the tab. Always double-check the addition.

MEXICO'S REGIONAL CUISINES Mexico's regional foods are a mixture of pre-Hispanic, Spanish, and French cuisines and at their best are among the most delicious in the world. Recipes developed by nuns during colonial times to please priests and visiting dignitaries have become part of the national patrimony, but much of Mexico's cuisine is derived from pre-Hispanic times. For the visitor, finding hearty, filling meals is fairly easy on a budget, but finding truly delicious food is not as easy. However, some of the best food is found in small inexpensive restaurants where regional specialties are made to please discerning locals. Explanations of specific dishes are found in the Appendix. Although the foods mentioned below originated in a particular part of the country, they frequently cross state lines and appear on menus countrywide.

Tamales are one of Mexico's traditional foods, but regional differences make trying them a treat as you travel. In northern Mexico they are small and thin with only a tiny sliver of meat inside. Chiapas has many *tamal* types, but all are plump and usually come with a sizable hunk of meat and sauce inside. A *corunda* in Michoacán is a triangular-shaped tamal wrapped in a corn leaf rather than the traditional corn husk. In Oaxaca traditional tamales come steaming in a banana leaf. The *zacahuil* of coastal Veracruz is the size of a pig's leg (which is in the center) and pit-baked in a banana leaf. *Molote,* a tiny football-shaped tamal, is a specialty around Papantla, Veracruz.

Tortillas, another Mexican basic, are not made or used equally. In northern Mexico flour tortillas are served more often than corn tortillas. Blue-corn tortillas, once a market food, have found their way to gourmet tables throughout the country. Oaxaca state boasts a large assortment of tortillas, including a hard, thick one with holes used like a cracker, and the huge tlayuda that holds an entire meal. Tortillas are fried and used as garnish in tortilla and Tarascan soup. Filled with meat they become tacos. A tortilla stuffed, rolled, or covered in a sauce and garnished results in an enchilada. A tortilla filled with cheese and lightly fried is a quesadilla. Rolled into a narrow tube, stuffed with chicken, then deep fried, it's known as a flauta. Leftover tortillas cut in wedges and crispy fried are called totopos and used to scoop beans and guacamole salad. Yesterday's tortillas mixed with eggs, chicken, peppers, and other spices are called chilaquiles. Small fried corn tortillas are delicious with ceviche or when topped with fresh lettuce, tomatoes and sauce, onions, and chicken they become tostadas. Each region has a variation of these tortilla-based dishes.

Northern Mexico is known for charro beans, made with beer, *cabrito* (roast kid), *machacada* (shredded beef), Mennonite cheese, and, around Saltillo, pulque bread, made with the alcoholic drink made from maguey.

Around Tapalpa, Jalisco, roast lamb is the specialty. Birria, both red and white, are specialties of Colima and Jalisco.

Besides being known for tamales, Oaxaca has delicious regional cheeses and green, yellow, red, and black *mole.*

Puebla is known for the many dishes created by colonial-era nuns, among them traditional *mole poblano,* Mexican-style barbecue, lamb *mixiotes, tinga,* and the eggnoglike rompope. Rompope is a local specialty sold widely in the mountains of Jalisco.

Regional drinks are almost as varied as the food in Mexico. Tequila comes from the blue agave grown near Guadalajara. Hot *ponche* (punch) is found often at festivals and is usually made with fresh fruit and spiked with tequila or rum. Baja California and the region around Querétaro is prime grape-growing land for Mexico's wine production. The best pulque supposedly comes from Hidalgo state. Beer is produced in Guadalajara, Monterrey, the Yucatán, and Veracruz. Delicious fruit-flavored waters appear on tables countrywide made from hibiscus flowers, ground rice, and melon seeds, watermelon, and other fresh fruits. Sangría is a spicy orange juice–and–pepper-based chaser for tequila shots.

9. RECOMMENDED BOOKS, FILMS & RECORDINGS

BOOKS

There is an endless supply of books written on the history, culture, and archeology of Mexico and Central America. I have listed those that I especially enjoyed.

HISTORY A *Thumbnail History of Guadalajara* (Editorial Colomos, 1983) by

José María Muriá Rouret, can be purchased in Guadalajara in English. It provides excellent background on the city's early trials and architecture. *A History of Mexico* (American Heritage Library, 1969), by Henry Bamford Parkes, is a concise, colorfully written historical account. A remarkably readable and thorough college textbook is *The Course of Mexican History* (Oxford University Press, 1987) by Michael C. Meyer and William L. Sherman. *The Conquest of New Spain* (Shoe String Press, 1988), by Bernal Díaz, is the famous story of the Mexican conquest written by Cortés's lieutenant. *The Crown of Mexico* (Holt Rinehart & Winston, 1971) by Joan Haslip, a biography of Maximilian and Carlota, reads like a novel. *Ancient Mexico: An Overview* (University of New Mexico, 1985), by Jaime Litvak is a short, very readable history of pre-Hispanic Mexico. *The Wind That Swept Mexico* (University of Texas Press, 1971), by Anita Brenner, is a classic illustrated account of the Mexican Revolution. Charles Flandrau wrote the classic *Viva Mexico: A Traveller's Account of Life in Mexico* (Eland Books, 1985) early this century, a blunt and humorous description of Mexico. Most people can't put down Gary Jennings's *Aztec* (Avon, 1981), a superbly researched and colorfully written fictionalized account of Aztec life before and after the conquest.

CULTURE *Five Families* (Basic Books, 1959) and *Children of Sanchez* (Random House, 1979), by Oscar Lewis, are sociological studies written in the late 1950s and early 1960s about typical Mexican families. *Mexican and Central American Mythology* (Peter Bedrick Books, 1983), by Irene Nicholson, is a concise illustrated book that simplifies the subject.

A good but controversial all-around introduction to contemporary Mexico and its people is *Distant Neighbors: A Portrait of the Mexicans* (Random House, 1984), by Alan Riding. Patrick Oster's *The Mexicans: A Personal Portrait of the Mexican People* (Harper & Row, 1989) is a reporter's insightful account of ordinary Mexican people. Another book with valuable insights into the Mexican character is *The Labyrinth of Solitude* (Grove Press, 1985), by Octavio Paz.

For some fascinating background on northern and western Mexico and the Copper Canyon, read *Unknown Mexico* (Dover Press, 1987), written by Carl Lumholtz, an intrepid writer and photographer around the turn of the century.

The best single source of information on Mexican music, dance, festivals, customs, and mythology is Frances Toor's *A Treasury of Mexican Folkways* (Crown, 1967). *Life in Mexico: Letters of Fanny Calderón de la Barca* (Doubleday, 1966), edited and annotated by Howard T. Fisher and Marion Hall Fisher, is as lively and entertaining today as when it first appeared in 1843, but the editor's illustrated and annotated update makes it even more contemporary. Scottish-born Fanny was married to the Spanish ambassador assigned to Mexico.

ART, ARCHEOLOGY & ARCHITECTURE *The Mexican Codices and Their Extraordinary History* (Ediciones Lara, 1985), by María Sten, tells the story of the native peoples' "painted books." *Mexico Splendors of Thirty Centuries* (Metropolitan Museum of Art, 1990), the catalog of the 1991 traveling exhibition, is a wonderful resource on Mexico's art from 1500 B.C. through the 1950s. Another superb catalog, *Images of Mexico: The Contribution of Mexico to 20th Century Art* (Dallas Museum of Art, 1987) is a fabulously illustrated and detailed account of Mexican art gathered from collections around the world. *Art and Time in Mexico: From the Conquest to the Revolution* (Harper & Row, 1985), by Elizabeth Wilder Weismann, illustrated with 351 photographs, covers Mexican religious, public, and private architecture with excellent photos and text. *Casa Mexicana* (Stewart, Tabori & Chang, 1989), by Tim Street-Porter, takes readers through the interiors of some of

Mexico's finest homes-turned-museums or public buildings and private homes using color photographs. *Mexican Interiors* (Architectural Book Publishing Co., 1962), by Verna Cook Shipway and Warren Shipway, uses black-and-white photographs to highlight architectural details from homes all over Mexico.

FOLK ART Chloë Sayer's *Costumes of Mexico* (University of Texas Press, 1985) is a beautifully illustrated and written work. *Mexican Masks* (University of Texas Press, 1980), by Donald Cordry, remains a definitive work on Mexican masks based on the author's collection and travels. Cordry's *Mexican Indian Costumes* (University of Texas Press, 1968) is another classic on the subject. The two-volume *Lo Efímero y Eterno del Arte Popular Mexicano* (Fondo Editorial de la Plastica Mexicana, 1974), produced during the Echeverría presidency, is out of print, but it's one of the most complete works ever produced on Mexican folk art and customs. The late Carlos Espejel wrote both *Mexican Folk Ceramics* and *Mexican Folk Crafts* (Editorial Blume, 1975 and 1978), two comprehensive books that explore crafts state by state. *Folk Treasures of Mexico* (Harry N. Abrams, 1990) by Marion Oettinger, curator of folk art and Latin American art at the San Antonio Museum of Art, is the fascinating illustrated story behind the 3,000-piece Mexican folk art collection amassed by Nelson Rockefeller over a 50-year period, as well as much information about individual folk artists.

NATURE The *Peterson Field Guide to Mexican Birds* (Houghton Mifflin, 1973), by Roger Tory Peterson and Edward L. Chalif, is an excellent guide to the country's birds. *A Guide to Mexican Mammals & Reptiles* (Minutiae Mexicana, 1989), by Norman Pelham Wright and Dr. Bernardo Villa Ramírez, is a small but useful guide to some of the country's wildlife.

FILMS

Mexico's first movie theater opened in 1897 in Mexico City. Almost immediately men with movie cameras began capturing everyday life in Mexico as well as what later became news, including both sides of the Mexican Revolution. All these early films are safe in Mexican archives. As an industry, it had its Mexican start with the 1918 film *The Gray Automobile Gang* (*La Banda del Automóvil Gris*) by Enrique Rosas Priego, based on an actual cops-and-robbers event in Mexico, but the industry's heyday really began in the 1930s and lasted only until the 1950s. Themes revolved around the Mexican Revolution, handsome but luckless singing cowboys, and helpless, poor-but-beautiful maidens all against a classic Mexican backdrop, at first rural or village (*rancho*) and later city neighborhood. Classic films and directors from that era are *Alla en el Rancho Grande* and *Vamonos Con Pancho Villa*, both by Fernando de Fuentes; *Champion Without a Crown* (*Campeón sin Corona*) a true-life boxing drama, by Alejandro Galindo; *The Pearl* (*La Perla*), by Emilio Fernández based on John Steinbeck's novel; *Yanco*, by Servando Gonzalez about a poor, young boy of Xochimilco who learned to play a violin; and the sad tale of *María Candelaria* also set in Xochimilco, another Fernández film starring Dolores del Río. Comedian Cantinflas starred in many Mexican films, and became known in the United States for his role in *Around the World in Eighty Days*. If Mexico's golden age of cinema didn't last long, Mexico as subject matter and location has had a long life. The Durango mountains have become the film-backdrop capital of Mexico. The *Night of the Iguana* was filmed in Puerto Vallarta, putting that seaside village on the map. *Old Gringo* was filmed in Zacatecas and *Viva Zapata!* and *Under the Volcano* were both set in Cuernavaca. Laura Esquivel's *Like Water for Chocolate* is now both a novel (Doubleday, 1992) and a wonderfully done new movie. Lusty and intimate, it intrigues with a story that intertwines the secrets of traditional Mexican food preparation with an outrageous, magical, and yet believable account of a fictional Mexican hacienda family along the Río Grande/Río Bravo at the turn of the century.

RECORDINGS

While Mexico's homegrown cinema may have hit a snag, it's recording industry has not; Mexicans take their music very seriously—just notice tapes for sale almost everywhere, nearly ceaseless music in the streets, and bus-driver collections of tapes to entertain passengers by. For the collector there are numerous choices from contemporary rock to ballads from the revolution, ranchero, salsa, and sones, and romantic trios. You'll arrive and leave the states of Jalisco and Colima with the sound of mariachi music playing. Among the top recording artists is Mariachi Vargas. No mariachi performance is complete without *Guadalajara, Las Mañanitas*, and *Jarabe Tapatío*. For trio music, some of the best is by Los Tres Diamantes, Los Tres Reyes, and Trio Los Soberanos. If you're requesting songs of a trio, good ones to ask for are *Sin Ti, Usted, Adios Mi Chaparita, Amor de la Calle*, and *Cielito Lindo*. Traditional ranchero music to request, which can be sung by soloists or trios, are *Tu Solo Tu, No Volveré*, and *Adios Mi Chaparita*. Music from the Yucatán would include the recordings by the Trio Los Soberanos and Dueto Yucalpeten. Typical Yucatecan songs are *Las Golondrinas Yucatecas, Peregrina, Ella, El Pajaro Azul*, and *Ojos Tristes*. Heartthrob soloists from years past include Pedro Vargas, Hector Cabrera, Lucho Gatica, Pepe Jara, and Alberto Vazquez. Marimba music is popular in Veracruz, Chiapas, and the Yucatán. Peña Ríos makes excellent marimba recordings. Though marimba musicians seldom ask for requests, some typical renditions would include *Huapango de Moncayo*, and *El Bolero de Ravel*. Mariachi music is played and sold all over Mexico. One of the best recordings of recent times is the Royal Philharmonic Orchestra's rendition of classic Mexican music titled *Mexicano;* directed by Luis Cobos and out on CBS/Columbia International, it's one purchase you must make. In a more popular vein Los Broncos's *Cuentame, Cuentame* is played so often you'd think it was the national song.

CHAPTER 2

PLANNING A TRIP TO MEXICO'S MID-PACIFIC REGION

1. **INFORMATION, ENTRY REQUIREMENTS & MONEY**
- **WHAT THINGS COST IN PUERTO VALLARTA**
- **WHAT THINGS COST IN MANZANILLO**
- **WHAT THINGS COST IN GUADALAJARA**
2. **WHEN TO GO—CLIMATE, HOLIDAYS & EVENTS**
- **MEXICO CALENDAR OF EVENTS**
3. **HEALTH & INSURANCE**
4. **WHAT TO PACK**
5. **TIPS FOR THE DISABLED, SENIORS, SINGLES & FAMILIES**
6. **ALTERNATIVE/ ADVENTURE TRAVEL**
7. **SHOPPING**
8. **GETTING THERE**
9. **GETTING AROUND**
- **FAST FACTS: MEXICO**

In this chapter, the where, when, and how of your trip is discussed—the advance planning that gets your trip together and takes it on the road.

Most of the questions people ask before traveling to Mexico are discussed here. This chapter addresses such important issues as when to go, whether or not to take a tour, what pretrip health precautions should be taken, what insurance coverage to investigate, and where to obtain additional information.

1. INFORMATION, ENTRY REQUIREMENTS & MONEY

SOURCES OF INFORMATION

The state of Jalisco provides information through **Casa Jalisco, State Promotion Office,** 418 Villita, San Antonio, TX 78205 (for mail); 600 Hemisfair Park (physical location) (tel. 210/227-2887; fax 512/227-2889).

For very general informational brochures on the country and answers to most commonly asked questions, call the **Mexico Hotline,** (tel. 800/446-3924 in the U.S.). **Mexican Government Tourism Offices** throughout the world include the following:

In the **United States:**
Chicago—70 E. Lake St., Suite 1413, Chicago, IL 60601 (tel. 312/565-2786); Houston—2707 N. Loop West, Suite 450, Houston, TX 77008 (tel. 713/880-5153); Los Angeles—10100 Santa Monica Blvd., Suite 224, Los Angeles, CA 90067 (tel. 213/203-8191); Miami—128 Aragon Ave., Coral Gables, FL 33134 (tel. 305/443-

INFORMATION, ENTRY REQUIREMENTS & MONEY

9167); New York—405 Park Ave., 14th Floor, New York, NY 10022 (tel. 212/755-7261); Washington, D.C.—1911 Pennsylvania Ave. NW, Washington, DC 20006 (tel. 202/728-1750).

In **Canada:** Montréal—One Place Ville-Marie, Suite 2409, Montréal, PQ H3B 3M9 (tel. 514/871-1052); Toronto—2 Bloor St. West, Suite 1801, Toronto, ON, M4W 3E2 (tel. 416/925-0704).

In **Europe:** Frankfurt—Weisenhüttenplatz 26, 06000 Frankfurt-am-Main 1 (tel. 4969/25-3541); London—60 Trafalgar Sq., 3rd floor, London WC2 N5DS (tel. 441/839-3177); Madrid—Calle de Velázquez 126, Madrid 28006 (tel. 34/261-1827); Paris—4 rue Notre-Dame-des-Victoires, 75002 Paris (tel. 331/40-210-0734); Rome—Via Barberini 3, 00187 Roma (tel. 396/474-2986).

In **Asia:** Tokyo—2.15.1 Nagata-Cho, Chiyoda-Ku, Tokyo 100 (tel. 813/580-2961 or 580-5539).

The following newsletters may be of interest to readers who want to keep up with Mexico between visits: **Sanborn's News Bulletin,** Dept. FR, P.O. Box 310, McAllen, TX 78502. It's a free newsletter produced by Sanborn's Insurance, offering tips on driving conditions, highways, hotels, economy and business, RV information, fishing, hunting, and so forth.

Travel Mexico, Apdo. Postal 6-1007, Mexico, D.F. 06600, is published six times a year by the publishers of *Traveler's Guide to Mexico*—the book frequently found in hotel rooms in Mexico. The newsletter covers a variety of topics from news about archeology, to hotel packages, new resorts and hotels, and the economy. A subscription costs $15.

Mexico Meanderings, P.O. Box 33057, Austin, TX 78764, is a new six-to-eight page newsletter with photographs featuring off-the-beaten-track destinations in Mexico. It's aimed at readers who travel by car, bus, or train, and is published six times annually. A subscription costs $18.

For other newsletters, see also "Retiring," below.

ENTRY REQUIREMENTS

DOCUMENTS All travelers are required to present **proof of citizenship,** such as an original birth certificate with a raised seal, or valid passport, or naturalization papers at the border. This proof of citizenship may also be requested to reenter both the United States and Mexico. Note that photocopies are not acceptable.

You must carry a **Mexican Tourist Permit,** which is issued free of charge by Mexican border officials after proof of citizenship is accepted. The tourist permit is more important than a passport in Mexico, so guard it carefully. If you lose it, you may not be permitted to leave the country until you can replace it, a bureaucratic hassle that takes at least several days, maybe a week, or perhaps longer.

A tourist permit can be issued for up to 180 days (don't make the mistake of automatically equating 180 days with 6 months); although you may not plan to stay south of the border for that long, get the card for the maximum time, just in case. Sometimes the officials don't ask, they just stamp a time limit, so be sure and say "180 days," or at least twice as long as you think you'll stay—you may decide to prolong your visit, and you'll thus eliminate hassle of renewing your papers.

This is especially important for people who take cars into Mexico. Additional documentation is required for driving a personal vehicle into Mexico (See "By Car" in "Getting There," below).

Note that children under age 18 traveling without parents or with only one parent must have a notarized letter from the absent parent or parents authorizing the travel.

LOST DOCUMENTS To replace a lost passport or other necessary travel document contact your embassy or nearest consular agent listed below in "Fast Facts: Mexico." You must establish a record of your citizenship, and fill out a form requesting another Mexican Tourist Permit. If the Mexican Tourist Permit is lost as well, you can't leave the country; and without an affidavit regarding your passport and citizenship, you may have hassles at Customs when you get home. So you must get it all cleared up before trying to leave.

CUSTOMS When you enter Mexico, Customs officials are tolerant as long as you have no drugs (marijuana, cocaine, etc.) or firearms. You're allowed to bring two cartons of cigarettes, or 50 cigars, plus a kilogram (2.2 lb.) of smoking tobacco; the liquor allowance is two bottles of anything, wine or hard liquor.

U.S. citizens are allowed up to $400 in purchases outside the country every 30 days. After $400, the first $1,000 is taxed at 10%. Any number of times a year Canadian citizens are allowed $20 in purchases after 24 hours' absence from the country or $100 after 48 hours or more.

Reentering the United States, federal law allows a carton (200) of cigarettes, or 50 cigars, or 2 kilograms (total, 4.4 lb.) of smoking tobacco, or proportional amounts of these items, plus 1 liter of alcoholic beverage (wine, beer, or spirits). Also remember that you are restricted by the quotas set by the state in which you reenter the United States. Liquor restrictions are most strictly applied at the border posts, less strictly at airports far from the border.

Canadian returning-resident regulations are similar to the U.S. ones: a carton of cigarettes, 50 cigars, 2 pounds (not kilos) of smoking tobacco, 1.1 liters (40 oz.) of wine or liquor, or a case of beer (8.2 liters). All provinces except Prince Edward Island and the Northwest Territories allow you to bring in more liquor and beer—up to 2 gallons (9 liters) more—but the taxes are quite high.

MONEY

CASH/CURRENCY In January 1993 the Mexican government changed the currency now called Nuevo Peso (New Peso) by dropping three zeros. The purpose was to simplify accounting since all those zeroes were becoming too difficult to manage by computers, cash registers, banks, and anyone trying to write a check. Old peso notes will still be accepted at least until January 1994. Paper currency comes in denominations of 2, 5, 10, 20, 50, and 100 bills. Coins come in denominations of 1, 2, 5, and 10 pesos, and 20 and 50 centavos (100 centavos makes 1 New Peso). The coins are somewhat confusing because different denominations have a similar appearance. New Peso prices appear written with N or NP beside them; and for a while the old peso prices will appear as well. Currently the U.S. dollar equals around NP$3, so an item costing NP$5 would be equivalent to U.S. $1.66. There are several points ripe for confusion among U.S. and Canadian travelers to Mexico with these changes. First, New Peso prices will seem very close to those in the United States and Canada and there will inevitably be confusion with some people taking advantage of the similarity. Ask. Second, for the first time in years everyone must become accustomed to small change appearing on restaurant bills and credit cards. On restaurant bills, which you pay in cash for example, the change will be rounded up or down to the nearest five-centavo multiple. But credit card bills will show the exact amount and will have N written before the amount to denote that the bill is in New Pesos. Be sure to double check any credit card vouchers to be sure the N or NP appears on the total line.

Many establishments dealing with tourists also quote prices in dollars. To avoid confusion, they use the abbreviations "Dlls." for dollars, and "m.n." (*moneda nacional*, or national currency) for pesos, so "$1,000.00 m.n." or N$100 means 1,000 pesos or 100 New Pesos.

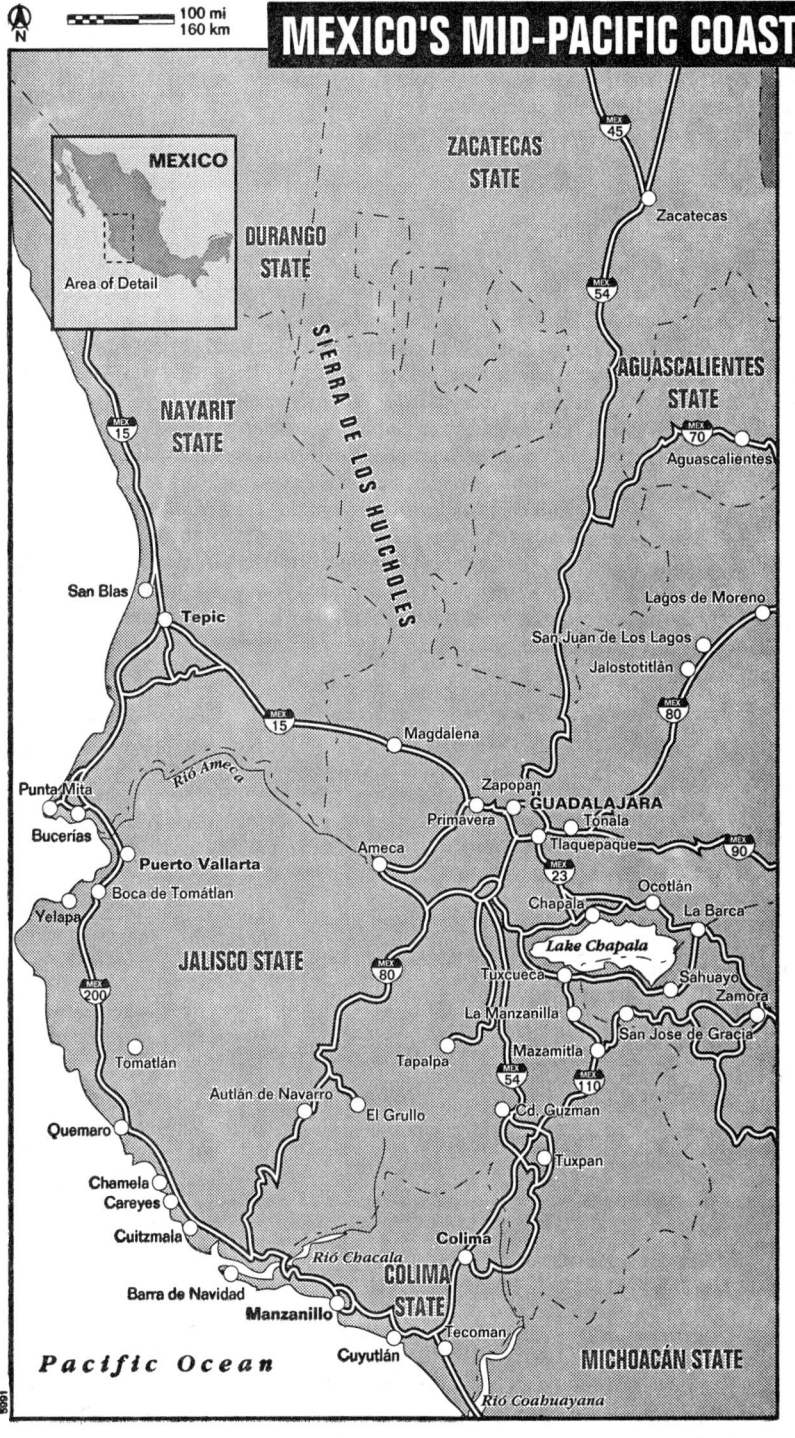

Getting change continues to be a problem in Mexico. Small denomination bills and coins are hard to come by so start collecting them early in your trip and continue as you travel. Shopkeepers everywhere seem to always be out of change and that's doubly true in a market.

Inflation in Mexico is increasing 15% to 20% per year. Every effort is made to provide the most accurate and up-to-date information in this book, but further changes are inevitable.

EXCHANGE For the fastest and least complicated service, its best to carry traveler's checks. Cash can sometimes be difficult to exchange because counterfeit dollars have been circulated recently in Mexico, and merchants and banks are wary. In some small towns, banks may refuse to accept cash. Personal checks may delay you for weeks since a bank will wait for the check to clear before giving you your money. But I always carry one blank check, just for an emergency.

Banks often give a rate of exchange below the official daily rate. Hotels usually exchange below the bank's daily rate as well. Canadian dollars seem to be most easily exchanged for pesos at branches of Banamex and Bancomer.

In Mexico, banks are open Monday through Friday from 9am to 1:30pm; a few banks in large cities offer extended afternoon hours. Although they open earlier, you'll save time at the bank or currency-exchange booths by arriving no earlier than 10am. Generally they don't receive the official rate for that day until shortly before then and they won't exchange your money until they have the daily rate.

Large airports have currency-exchange counters that sometimes stay open as long as flights are arriving or departing.

TRAVELER'S CHECKS Mexican banks pay you more for traveler's checks than for dollars in cash, but Casas de Cambio (exchange houses) pay more for cash than traveler's checks. All are examining dollars carefully. Some banks, but not all, charge a service fee, as high as 5%, to cash either dollars or traveler's checks. Sometimes banks post the service charge amount so you can see it, but they might not, so it pays to ask first and shop around for a bank without a fee.

CREDIT CARDS You'll be able to charge some hotel and restaurant bills, almost all airline tickets, and many store purchases. You can get cash advances of several hundred dollars on your card, but there may be a wait of 20 minutes to 2 hours. However, you can't charge gasoline purchases in Mexico.

VISA (Bancomer in Mexico), MasterCard (Carnet in Mexico), and less widely, American Express, are the most accepted cards. The Mexican bank named Bancomer, with branches throughout the country, has inaugurated a system of automatic teller machines linked to VISA International's network. If you are a VISA customer, you *may* be able to get peso cash from one of the Bancomer ATMs.

WHAT THINGS COST IN PUERTO VALLARTA — U.S. $

Collective van from the airport to downtown	$5.00–$7.00
Local telephone call	.10–.50
Double at the Camino Real (very expensive)	$175.00–$480.00
Double at the Quinta Real (expensive)	$140.00–$240.00
Double at the Playa Los Arcos (moderate)	$75.00–$90.00
Double at the Los Cuatro Vientos (budget)	$35.00

INFORMATION, ENTRY REQUIREMENTS & MONEY

	US$
Three-course dinner for one at Bogart's (expensive)	$50.00–$70.00
Three-course dinner for one at Chez Elena (moderate)	$25.00
Three-course lunch for one at La Casa del Almendro (moderate)	$15.00
Three-course lunch for one at Restaurant Juanita (budget)	$5.00–$10.00
Beer	$1.00–$2.00
Margarita	$2.00–$4.50
Half day of deep-sea fishing	$215.00
Half day of diving (per person)	$50.00

WHAT THINGS COST IN MANZANILLO

	U.S. $
Collective van from the airport to downtown	$4.00–$5.00
Local telephone call	.10–.50
Double at Las Hadas (very expensive)	$182.00–$420.00
Double at the Sierra Manzanillo (expensive)	$125.00–$300.00
Double at La Posada (moderate)	$52.00–$78.00
Double at the Hotel Colonial (budget)	$24.00–$26.00
Three-course dinner for one at Legazpi (expensive)	$50.00–$75.00
Three-course dinner for one at Manolo's Bistro (moderate)	$25.00–$40.00
Three-course lunch for one at La Plazuela (moderate)	$15.00–$25.00
Three-course lunch for one at Cafeterí Chantilly (budget)	$5.75
Beer	$1.00–$2.00
Margarita	$2.00–$4.50
Half day of deep-sea fishing	$200.00

WHAT THINGS COST IN GUADALAJARA

	U.S. $
Collective van from the airport to downtown	$8.00
Local telephone call	.10–.50
Double at La Quinta Real (expensive)	$198.00–$232.00

	US$
Double at the Hotel de Mendoza (moderate)	$88.00
Double at the Hotel San Francisco (budget)	$45.00
Three-course dinner for one at El Méson del Chef (expensive)	$35.00
Three-course dinner for one at Los Otates (moderate)	$18.00
Two-course dinner for one at La Chata (budget)	$8.00
Beer	$1.00–$2.00
Margarita	$2.00–$3.00
Admission to the bullfights	$1.50–$65.00
Ticket to the Degollado Theater Ballet Folklórico	$1.00–$6.00

BRIBES

Called propina (tip), mordida (bite), or worse, the custom is probably almost as old as humankind. Bribes exist in every country but in third world countries the amounts tend to be smaller and collected more often. You will meet with bribery, so you should know how to deal with it.

With the administration of President Salinas de Gortari, border officials have become more courteous, less bureaucratic, and less inclined to ask/hint for a bribe. I'm still wary, however, so just so you're prepared here are a few hints based on the past. If you don't offer a tip of a few dollars to the man who inspects your car (if you're driving), he may ask for it, as in "Give me a tip (*propina*)." Some border officials will do what they're supposed to do (stamp your passport or birth certificate and inspect your luggage) and then wave you on through. If you're charged for it, ask for a receipt. If you get no receipt, you've paid a bribe.

Officials don't ask for bribes from everybody. Travelers dressed in a formal suit and tie, with pitch-black sunglasses and a scowl on the face, are rarely asked to pay a bribe. Those who are dressed for vacation fun, seem good-natured and accommodating, are charged every time. You may not want the bother of dressing up for border crossings, but you should at least act in a formal manner, and be rather cold, dignified, and businesslike, perhaps preoccupied with "important affairs" that are on your mind. Wear those dark sunglasses. Scowl. Ignore the request. Pretend not to understand. Don't speak Spanish. But whatever you do, avoid impoliteness, and absolutely never insult a Latin American official! When an official's sense of machismo is roused, he can and will throw the book at you, and you may be in trouble. Stand your ground—politely.

SCAMS

The **shoeshine scam** is an old trick that seems to happen most often in Mexico City. Here's how it works. A tourist agrees to a shine for, say, 3,000 pesos (3 New Pesos). When the work is complete the vendor says, "that'll be 30,000" (or 30 New Pesos) and insists the shocked tourist misunderstood. A big brouhaha ensues involving bystanders who side with the shoeshine vendor. The object is to get the bewildered tourist to succumb to the howling crowd and embarrassing scene and fork over the money. A variation of the scam has the vendor saying the price quoted is per shoe. To avoid this scam, ask around about the price of a shine, and when the vendor quotes his price, write it down and show it to him *before* the shine.

Tourists are suckered daily into the **iguana scam,** especially in Puerto Vallarta and nearby Yelapa beach. Someone, often a child, strolls by carrying a huge iguana and says "wanna take my peekchur." Photo-happy tourists seize the opportunity. Just as the camera is angled properly, the holder of the iguana says (more like mumbles) "one dollar." That means a dollar per shot. Sometimes they wait until the shutter clicks to mention money.

Because hotel desk clerks are usually so helpful, I hesitate to mention the **lost-objects scam** for fear of tainting them all. But here's how it works. You "lose" your wallet after cashing money at the desk, or you leave something valuable such as a purse or camera in the lobby. You report it. The clerk has it, but instead of telling you that he does, he says he will see what he can do; meanwhile, he suggests that you offer a high reward. This one has all kinds of variations. In one story a reader wrote about, a desk clerk in Los Mochis was in cahoots with a bystander in the lobby who lifted her wallet in the elevator.

Another scam readers have written about might be called the **infraction scam.** Officials, or men presenting themselves as officials, demand money for some supposed infraction. Never get into a car with them. I avoided one with a bona-fide policeman-on-the-take when my traveling companion feigned illness and began writhing, moaning, and pretending to have the dry heaves. It was more than the policeman could handle.

Legal and necessary car searches by military personnel looking for drugs are mentioned elsewhere. But every now and then there are police-controlled yet illegal roadblocks where motorists are allowed to continue after paying.

Along these lines, if you are stopped by the police, I also suggest that you avoid handing your driver's license to a policeman. Hold it so that it can be read, but don't give it up. See also "Safety" in "Fast Facts: Mexico" later in this chapter.

My advice is intended to help you to be aware of potential hazards and how to deal with them. I log thousands of miles and many months in Mexico each year without serious incident, and I feel safer there than at home. (See also "Fast Facts: Mexico"—"Emergencies" and "Safety," below.)

2. WHEN TO GO — CLIMATE, HOLIDAYS & EVENTS

From Puerto Vallarta south to Huatulco, Mexico offers one of the world's most perfect winter climates—dry, balmy, with temperatures ranging from the 80s by day to the 60s at night. From Puerto Vallarta south you can swim year round. Temperatures range from 72° to 86°F year round along the coasts of Jalisco and Colima. In the mountain villages of Mazamitla and Tapalpa it's cold enough most of the year for gloves, heavy sweater or down jacket, wool socks, and flannel underwear.

High mountains shield Pacific beaches from *nortes* (northers—freezing blasts out of Canada via the Texas Panhandle). In summer the difference between west coast and Gulf coast temperatures is much less. Both areas become warm and rainy. Of the two regions the Gulf is far rainier, particularly in the states of Tabasco and Campeche. Jalisco and Colima, like most of Mexico, have the most rain from May through September, with the rainiest months being June through August. There is a handy temperature-conversion chart in the Appendix to this book.

HOLIDAYS

Banks, stores, and businesses are closed on national holidays. Hotels fill up quickly, and transportation is very crowded. Mexico celebrates the following national holidays:

January 1	New Year's Day
February 5	Constitution Day
March 21	Birthday of Benito Juárez
March–April (movable)	Holy Week (Good Friday through Easter Sunday)
May 1	Labor Day
May 5	Battle of Puebla, 1862 (Cinco de Mayo)
September 1	President's Message to Congress
September 16	Independence Day
October 12	Columbus Day (Mexico: Day of the Race)
November 1–2	All Saints' and All Souls' Days (Day of the Dead)
November 20	Mexican Revolution Anniversary
December 11–12	Day of the Virgin of Guadalupe (Mexico's patron saint)
December 24–25	Christmas Eve (evening), Christmas Day

MEXICO CALENDAR OF EVENTS

The following events are celebrated nationwide; special events in cities and towns in this book are mentioned in each chapter.

JANUARY

☐ **Three Kings Day** Commemorates the Three Kings' bringing of gifts to the Christ Child. On this day the Three Kings "bring" gifts to children. January 6.

FEBRUARY

☐ **Candlemas Day** On January 6, Rosca de Reyes, a round cake with a hole in the middle is baked with a tiny doll inside representing the Christ Child. Whoever gets the slice with the doll must give a party on February 2. Northwest of Guadalajara in San Juan de los Lagos, Jalisco, and Buenavista near Lagos de Moreno, Jalisco, pilgrims come from all over Mexico to honor the Virgen de San Juan de los Lagos. Also in Tecomán south of Manzanillo.

☐ **Ash Wednesday** The start of Lent and time of abstinence. It's a day of reverence nationwide, but some towns honor it with folk dancing and fairs. Movable date.

✪ **CARNAVAL** Three days before Ash Wednesday. In some towns there will be no special celebration, in others a few parades. **Where:** Especially celebrated in Tepoztlán, Morelos; Huejotzingo, Puebla; Chamula, Chiapas; Veracruz, Veracruz; Cozumel, Quintana Roo; and Mazatlán, Sinaloa. **When:** Date variable, but always the three days preceding Ash Wednesday. **How:** Transportation and hotels will be clogged, so it's best to make reservations six months in advance and arrive a couple of days ahead of the beginning of celebrations. The latter three resemble a U.S. festival-type atmosphere. In Chamula, however, the event harks back to pre-Hispanic times with ritualistic running on flaming branches. On Tuesday before Ash Wednesday, in Tepoztlán and Huejotzingo, masked and brilliantly clad dancers fill the streets.

MARCH

☐ **Benito Juárez Birthday** Celebrated with small hometown celebrations countrywide, but especially in Juaréz's birthplace, Gelatao, Oaxaca.

✪ **HOLY WEEK** *Celebrates the last week in the life of Christ from Good Friday through Easter Sunday with almost nightly somber religious processions, spoofing of Judas, and reenactments of specific biblical events, plus food and craft fairs. Businesses close and Mexicans travel far and wide during this week.*
When: *March or April.* **How:** *Reserve early with a deposit. Airlines into and out of the country will be reserved months in advance. Buses to these towns or almost anywhere in Mexico will be full, so try arriving on the Wednesday or Thursday before Good Friday. Easter Sunday is quiet.*

MAY

☐ **Labor Day** Workers' parades countrywide and everything closes. May 1.
☐ **Holy Cross Day** Día de la Santa Cruz. Workers place a cross on top of unfinished buildings and have food celebrations, bands, folk dancing, and fireworks around the work site. Celebrations are particularly colorful in Tequila, Jalisco. May 3.
☐ **Cinco de Mayo** A national holiday that celebrates the defeat of the French at the Battle of Puebla. May 5.
☐ **Feast of San Isidro** The patron saint of farmers is honored with a blessing of seeds and work animals. May 15.

JUNE

☐ **Navy Day** Celebrated by all port cities. June 1.
☐ **Corpus Christi Day** Honors the Body of Christ—the Eucharist—with religious processions, mass, and food. Celebrated nationwide. Variable date 66 days after Easter.

JULY

☐ **Saint Peter** Día de San Pedro, is celebrated wherever St. Peter is the patron saint and honors anyone named Pedro or Peter. It's especially festive at San Pedro Tlaquepaque, near Guadalajara, with numerous mariachi bands, folk dancers, and parades with floats. June 29.

JULY

☐ **Virgin of Carmen** A nationally celebrated religious festival centered at churches nationwide. July 16.
☐ **Saint James Day** Día de San Juan, is observed countrywide wherever St. James

is patron saint, and by anyone named Juan or John, or any village with Santiago in the name, often with rodeos, fireworks, and dancing. July 25.

AUGUST

- **Assumption of Virgin Mary** Venerated throughout the country with special masses and in some places processions. August 15–16.

SEPTEMBER

- **Independence Day** Celebrates Mexico's independence from Spain. A day of parades, picnics, and family reunions throughout the country. At 11pm on September 15, the president of Mexico gives the famous independence "grito" (shout) from the National Palace in Mexico City. Guadalajara has a weeklong fair and market in the central plaza. September 16 (parade day).

OCTOBER

- **Cervantino Festival** Begun in the 1970s as a cultural event bringing performing artists from all over the world to the Guanajuato, a picturesque village northeast of Mexico City, now the artists travel all over the republic after appearing in Guanajuato. Check local calendars for appearances. Mid-October through November.
- **Feast of San Francisco de Asis** Anyone named Frances or Francis or Francisco, and towns whose patron saint is San Francisco, celebrate with barbecue parties, regional dancing, and religious observances. October 4.
- **Día de la Raza** Day of the Race, or Columbus Day (the day Columbus discovered America), commemorates the fusion of two races—Spanish and Mexican. October 12.
- **Feast of San José** This festival honors Saint Joseph and anyone named Joseph (José in Spanish). Ciudad Guzmán, Jalisco, between Guadalajara and Manzanillo, celebrates with a fair, processions, and regional dancing. October 21.

NOVEMBER

- **◎ DAY OF THE DEAD** *What's commonly called Day of the Dead is actually two days. November 1, All Saints' Day, honors saints and deceased children. November 2 is All Souls' Day, honoring deceased adults. Relatives gather at cemeteries countrywide, carrying candles and food, often spending the night beside graves of loved ones. Weeks before, bakers begin producing bread formed in the shape of mummies or round loaves decorated with bread shaped like bones. Decorated sugar skulls emblazoned with glittery names are sold everywhere. Many days ahead homes and churches erect special altars laden with Day of the Dead bread, fruit, flowers, candles, and the favorite foods as well as photographs of saints and of the deceased. On the two nights children dress in costumes and masks, often carrying mock coffins through the streets and pumpkin lanterns into which they expect money will be dropped. Often there are solemn processions to the cemetery, where villagers settle in for the night.*

- **Revolution Day** Commemorates the start of the Mexican Revolution in 1910, with parades, speeches, rodeos, and patriotic events. November 20.

DECEMBER

○ **DÍA DE GUADALUPE** Throughout Mexico, the Virgin of Guadalupe, patroness of Mexico, is honored, with religious processions, street fairs, dancing, fireworks, and masses. The Virgin appeared to a small boy, Juan Diego, in December 1531, on a hill near Mexico City. He convinced the bishop that the apparition had appeared by revealing his cloak upon which the Virgin was emblazoned. It's customary for children to dress up as Juan Diego, wearing mustaches and red bandanas.

Where: The most famous and elaborate celebration takes place at the Basílica of Guadalupe, north of Mexico City, where the Virgin made her appearance. But every village in Mexico celebrates this day, often with processions of children carrying banners of the Virgin, and frequently with charreadas, bicycle races, dancing, and fireworks as well. In Jalisco this event has especially interesting celebrations in Tapalpa and El Grullo. **When:** December 12.

☐ **Christmas Posadas** Each night for 12 days before Christmas it's customary to reenact the Holy Family's search for an inn, with door-to-door candlelit processions in cities and villages nationwide.

☐ **Christmas** Mexicans extend this celebration and leave their jobs, often beginning two weeks before Christmas all the way through New Year's. Many businesses close and resorts and hotels fill up.

☐ **New Year's Eve** As in the United States, New Year's Eve is the time to gather for private parties of celebration and to explode fireworks and sound off noisemakers.

3. HEALTH & INSURANCE

HEALTH PREPARATIONS

Of course, the very best ways to avoid illness or to mitigate its effects are to make sure that you're in top health and that you don't overdo it. Travel tends to take more of your energy than a normal working day, and missed meals mean that you get less nutrition than you need. Make sure you have three good, wholesome meals a day, get more rest than you normally do, and don't push yourself if you're not feeling in top form.

TURISTA Turista is the name given to the pervasive diarrhea, often accompanied by fever, nausea, and vomiting, that attacks so many travelers to Mexico on their first trip. Doctors, who call it traveler's diarrhea, say it's not just one "bug," or factor, but a combination of different food and water, upset schedules, overtiring, and the stresses that accompany travel. Being tired and careless about food and drink is a sure ticket to turista. A good high-potency (or "therapeutic") vitamin supplement, and even extra vitamin C, is a help; yogurt is good for healthy digestion, and it's becoming more available in Mexico.

How to Prevent It The U.S. Public Health Service recommends the following measures for prevention of traveler's diarrhea:

Drink only purified water. This means tea, coffee, and other beverages made with boiled water; canned or bottled carbonated beverages, including carbonated water; beer and wine; or water that you brought to a rolling boil or otherwise purified. Avoid ice, which is often made with untreated water.

Choose food carefully. In general, avoid salads, uncooked vegetables, and unpasteurized milk or milk products (including cheese). Choose food that is freshly cooked and still hot. Peel fruit yourself. Don't eat undercooked meat, fish, or shellfish.

The Public Health Service does not recommend that you take any medicines as preventatives. All the applicable medicines, including antibiotics, bismuth subsalicylate (as in Pepto-Bismol), and difenoxine (as in Lomotil), can have nasty side effects if taken for several weeks. The best way to prevent illness is to take care with food, water, and rest, and don't overdo it.

How to Get Well   If you get sick, there are lots of medicines available in Mexico which can harm more than help. You should ask your doctor before you leave home what medicine he or she recommends for traveler's diarrhea, and follow his or her advice.

The Public Health Service guidelines are these: If there are three or more loose stools in an eight-hour period, especially with other symptoms such as nausea, vomiting, abdominal cramps, and fever, it's time to go to a doctor.

The first thing to do is go to bed and don't move until it runs its course. Traveling makes it last longer. Drink lots of liquids: tea without milk or sugar, or the Mexican *té de manzanilla* (chamomile tea), is best. Eat only *pan tostada* (dry toast). Keep to this diet for at least 24 hours, and you'll be well over the worst of it. If you fool yourself into thinking that a plate of enchiladas can't hurt, or that beer or liquor will kill the germs, you'll have a total relapse.

The Public Health Service advises that you be especially careful to replace fluids and electrolytes (potassium, sodium, etc.) during a bout of diarrhea. Do this by drinking glasses of fruit juice (high in potassium) with honey and a pinch of salt added; and also a glass of pure water with ¼ teaspoon of sodium bicarbonate (baking soda) added.

ALTITUDE SICKNESS   At high altitudes it takes about 10 days or so to acquire the extra red blood corpuscles you need to adjust to the scarcity of oxygen. At very high-altitude places, your car won't run very well, you may have trouble starting it, and you may not even sleep well at night.

This ailment results from the relative lack of oxygen and decrease in barometric pressure that come from being at high altitudes (5,000 ft./1,500m, or more). Symptoms include shortness of breath, fatigue, headache, and even nausea.

Avoid altitude sickness by taking it easy for the first few days after you arrive at high altitude. Drink extra fluids, but avoid alcoholic beverages, which not only tend to dehydrate you, but also are more potent in a low-oxygen environment. If you have heart or lung problems, talk to your doctor before going above 8,000 feet.

BUGS AND BITES   Mosquitoes and gnats are prevalent along the coast. Insect repellent (*rapellante contra insectos*) is a must, and it's not always available in Mexico. If you're sensitive to bites, pick up some antihistamine cream from a drugstore at home (Di-Delamine is available without a prescription). Rubbed on a fresh mosquito bite, the cream keeps down the swelling and reduces the itch. In Mexico, ask for "Camfo-Fenicol" (Campho-phenique), the second-best remedy.

Most readers won't ever see a scorpion, but if you're stung, it's best to go to a doctor.

MORE SERIOUS DISEASES   You don't have to worry about tropical diseases too much if your journey is for less than three months, and if you stay on the normal tourist routes (that is, you don't head out into the boondocks to camp with the locals for a week).

You can also protect yourself by taking some simple precautions. Besides being careful about what you eat and drink, do not go swimming in polluted waters. This includes any stagnant water such as ponds, and slow-moving rivers. Avoid mosquitoes because they carry malaria, dengue fever, and other serious illnesses. Cover up, avoid going out when mosquitoes are active, use repellent, sleep under mosquito netting, and stay away from places that seem to have a lot of mosquitoes. The most dangerous areas seem to be on Mexico's west coast, away from the big resorts (which are relatively safe).

To prevent malaria if you go to a malarial area, you must get a prescription for antimalarial drugs, and begin taking them before you enter the area. You must also continue to take them for a certain amount of time after you leave the malarial area. Talk to your doctor about this. It's a good idea to be inoculated against tetanus, typhoid, and diphtheria, but this isn't a guarantee against contracting the disease.

The following list of diseases should not alarm you, as their incidence is rare among tourists. But if you become ill with something more virulent than traveler's diarrhea, I want you to have this information ready at hand:

Cholera Cholera comes from water contaminated with sewage and is transmitted when the contaminated water is used for drinking, cooking, or washing food. Raw fish and raw or lightly cooked vegetables are good candidates for transmitting the disease. Outbreaks of cholera in Mexico have been isolated and contained immediately, and have not occurred in any major tourist area. Symptoms are extreme diarrhea, vomiting, abdominal pain, and rapid incapacitation. The disease is curable if treated quickly—get to a hospital immediately. Dehydration can be immediate and dangerous, so drink plenty of nonalcoholic liquids.

Dengue Fever Transmitted by mosquitoes, it comes on fast with high fever, severe headache, and joint and muscle pain. Three or four days after the onset of the disease, there's a skin rash. Highest risk is during July, August, and September. Risk for normal tourists is low.

Dysentery Caused by contaminated food or water, either amoebic or bacillary in form, it is somewhat like traveler's diarrhea, but more severe. Risk for tourists is low.

Hepatitis, Viral This virus is spread through contaminated food and water (often in rural areas), and through intimate contact with infected persons. Risk for tourists is normally low.

Malaria Spread by mosquito bites, malaria can be effectively treated if caught soon after the disease is contracted. Malaria symptoms are headache, malaise, fever, chills, sweats, anemia, and jaundice.

Rabies This virus is almost always passed by bites from infected animals or bats, rarely through broken skin or the mucous membranes (as from breathing rabid-bat-contaminated air in a cave). If you are bitten, wash the wound at once with large amounts of soap and water—this is important! Retain the animal, alive if possible, for rabies quarantine. Contact local health authorities to get rabies immunization. This is essential, as rabies is a fatal disease which can be prevented by prompt treatment.

Schistosomiasis An infestation of the larvae of parasitic worms found in freshwater snails. The larvae leave the snails in the water and can penetrate unbroken human skin. You get it by wading or swimming in fresh water where the snails are, such as in stagnant pools, streams, or cenotes. Two or three weeks after exposure, there's fever, lack of appetite, weight loss, abdominal pain, weakness, headaches, joint and muscle pain, diarrhea, nausea, and coughing. Six to eight weeks after infection, the microscopic snail eggs can be found in the stools. Once diagnosed (after a very unpleasant month or two), treatment is fast, safe, effective, and cheap. If you think you've accidentally been exposed to schistosomiasis-infected water, rub yourself vigorously with a towel, and/or spread rubbing alcohol on the exposed skin.

Typhoid Fever You can protect yourself by having a typhoid vaccination (or booster, as needed), but protection is not total; you can still get this very serious disease from contaminated food and water. Symptoms are similar to those for traveler's diarrhea, but much worse. If you get typhoid fever, you'll need close attention by a doctor, perhaps hospitalization for a short period.

Typhus Fever You should see a doctor for treatment of this disease, which is spread by lice. Risk is very low.

INSURANCE

HEALTH/ACCIDENT/LOSS It can happen anywhere in the world—you discover you've lost your wallet, your passport, your airline ticket, and your tourist permit. Whether the loss is from your negligence or by theft, you'll want to report it. Always keep a photocopy of these documents in your luggage—it makes replacing them easier. To be reimbursed for insured items once you return, you'll need to report the loss to the Mexican police and get a written report. If you don't speak Spanish, take along someone who does. The report-making involves much typewriter clacking and question answering.

If you lose official documents, you'll need to contact both Mexican and U.S. officials in Mexico before you leave the country. See "Information, Entry Requirements, and Money," above, specifically the section on "Documents."

Before leaving home ask your insurance agent what health coverage is in force while you are out of the country. Several credit-card companies include accident and trip-cancellation insurance coverage as a benefit for charging airline tickets on a charge card.

For additional coverage you may want to consider policies from the following companies:

Health Care Abroad, 107 Federal St. (P.O. Box 480), Middleburg, VA 22117 (tel. 703/687-3166, or toll free 800/237-6616), for trips lasting 10 to 90 days. Coverage includes accident and sickness, and insurance against luggage loss and trip cancellation can be added.

Access America, Inc., 6600 W. Broad St., Richmond, VA 23230 (tel. 804/285-3300, or toll free 800/628-4908), also offers medical and accident insurance as well as coverage for luggage loss and trip cancellation.

EMERGENCY EVACUATION For extreme medical emergencies there's a service from the United States that will fly people to American hospitals: Air-Evac, 24-hour air ambulance. Call collect 24 hours, 713/880-9767 in Houston, 619/278-3822 in San Diego, 305/772-0003 in Miami.

4. WHAT TO PACK

CLOTHING High-elevation cities such as Mazamitla and Tapalpa, both in the mountains of Jalisco, require warm wool clothing. For the coastal areas, however, bring lightweight cottons. The temperatures aren't high, usually less than 90°F, but the humidity often reaches 100%. In summer, generally speaking, throughout Mexico it rains almost every afternoon or evening between May and October—so take rain gear. An easily packable rain poncho is most handy, since it fits in a purse or backpack and is ready for use in an instant. Guadalajara and other nonresort cities and villages tend to be conservative in dress, so save shorts and halter tops for seaside resorts. For dining out in a nice restaurant in conservative Guadalajara, a jacket and tie for men and nice dress or suit for women is appropriate. In Puerto Vallarta nice restaurants are more casual even when they are expensive. A cool dress for women and slacks and shirt for men will do fine.

GADGETS First-class hotels generally provide washcloths, but if you're staying in moderately priced or budget hotels, bring your own, or better yet a sponge (which dries quickly)—you'll rarely find washcloths in a budget-category hotel room. A bathtub plug (one of those big round ones for all sizes) is a help since fitted plugs are frequently missing, or don't work even in expensive hotels. Blow-up (inflatable) hangers and a stretch clothesline are handy. I never leave home without a luggage cart, which saves much effort and money, and is especially useful in small towns where there are no porters at bus stations. Buy a sturdy one with at least four-inch wheels that can take the beating of cobblestone streets, stairs, and curbs. A heat-immersion coil, plastic cup, and spoon are handy for preparing coffee, tea, and instant soup. For power failures, a small flashlight is a help. A combo pocketknife (for peeling fruit) with screwdriver (for fixing cameras and eyeglasses), bottle opener, and corkscrew is a must.

5. TIPS FOR THE DISABLED, SENIORS, SINGLES & FAMILIES

FOR THE DISABLED

Travelers whose disability involves the legs, those who are unable to walk, or who are in wheelchairs or on crutches discover quickly that Mexico is one giant obstacle course. Beginning at the airport on arrival you may encounter steep stairs before finding a well-hidden elevator or escalator—if one exists. Airlines will often arrange wheelchair assistance for passengers to the baggage area. Porters are generally available to help with luggage at airports and large bus stations and once you've cleared baggage claim. Escalators (and there aren't many in the country) are often not operating. The Guadalajara airport has an up escalator to the restaurant, but no down escalator or elevator. Few handicapped-equipped rest rooms exist, or when one is available, access to it may be via a narrow passage that won't accommodate a wheelchair or someone on crutches. Many five-star and Gran Turismo hotels (the most expensive) now have rooms with handicapped bathrooms and handicap access to the hotel. For those traveling on a budget, stick with one-story hotels, or those with elevators. Even so, there will probably still be step obstacles somewhere. Stairs without handrails abound in Mexico. Intracity bus drivers generally don't bother with the courtesy step upon boarding or disembarking. On city buses the distance between the street and the bus can require considerable force to board. Generally speaking, no matter where you are, someone will lend a hand, although you may have to ask for it.

FOR SENIORS

HAZARDS Handrails are often missing. Unmarked or unguarded holes in sidewalks countrywide present problems for all visitors.

RETIRING Mexico is a popular country for retirees, although income doesn't go nearly as far as it once did. Successful transplants do several things before venturing south permanently: Stay for several weeks in any place under consideration; rent before buying; and check on the availability and quality of health care, banking, transportation, and rental costs. How much it costs to live depends on your life-style and where you choose to live. Car upkeep and insurance, clothing and health costs are important variables to consider.

The Mexican government requires foreign residents to prove a specific amount of income before permanent residence is granted, but you can visit for six months on a tourist visa and renew it every six months without committing to a "legal" status. Mexican health care is surprisingly inexpensive. You can save money by living on the local economy: Buy food at the local market, not imported items from specialty stores; use local transportation and save the car for long-distance trips. Among the most popular places for retirement in Mexico or long-term stays are Guadalajara, Lake Chapala, Ajijic, and Puerto Vallarta, all in the state of Jalisco, and Manzanillo, Colima, where U.S. condo owners abound. The following newsletters are written to inform the prospective retiree about Mexico:

AIM, Apdo. Postal 31-70, Guadalajara, Jal. 45050, Mexico, is a well-written, plain talking, and very informative newsletter on retirement in Mexico. Recent issues reported on retirement background and considerations for Lake Chapala, Aguascalientes, Alamos, Zacatecas, west coast beaches, Acapulco, and San Miguel de Allende. It costs $16 to the United States and $19 to Canada. Back issues are three for $5.

Retiring in Mexico, Apdo. Postal 5-409, Guadalajara, Jal. (tel. 36/21-2348 or 47-9924), comes in three editions—a large January edition and smaller spring and fall supplements, all for $12. Each newsletter is packed with useful information about retiring in Guadalajara. It's written by Fran and Judy Furton who also sell other packets of information as well as host an open house in their home every Tuesday for $12.

Sanborn Tours, 1007 Main Street, Bastrop, TX 78602 (tel. toll free 800/531-5440), offers a "Retire in Mexico" Guadalajara orientation tour.

FOR SINGLE TRAVELERS

Mexico may be the land for romantic honeymoons, but it's also a great place to travel on your own without really being or feeling alone. Although combined single and double rates is a slow-growing trend in Mexico, most of the moderately priced and budget hotels mentioned in this book offer singles at cheaper rates. There's so much to see and do that being bored needn't be a problem. Mexicans are very friendly and it's easy to meet other foreigners and take up with them for a day or two or a meal along the way if you desire. Certain cities like Acapulco, Manzanillo, and Huatulco have such a preponderance of twosomes that single travelers there may feel as though an appendage is missing. On the other hand, singles can feel quite comfortable in Puerto Vallarta, Barra de Navidad, and San Blas. In those places you'll find a good combination of beachlife, nightlife, and tranquility, whichever is your pleasure. Guadalajara, too, is easy on the single traveler. If you don't like the idea of traveling alone, you might try **Travel Companion Exchange,** P.O. Box 833, Amityville, NY 11701 (tel. 516/454-0880; fax 516/454-0170), which brings prospective travelers together. Members complete a profile, then place an anonymous listing of their travel interests in the newsletter. Prospective traveling companions then make contact through the exchange. Membership costs $36 to $66 for six months.

FOR WOMEN As a frequent female traveler to Mexico, most of it alone, I can tell you firsthand that I feel safer traveling in Mexico than in the United States. And no, I'm not afraid. That answers the first two questions most people ask me. Mexicans are a very warm and welcoming people and I'm not afraid to be friendly wherever I go. But I use the same common-sense precautions I use traveling anywhere else in the world: I'm alert to what's going on around me.

Mexicans in general, and men in particular, are nosy about single travelers, especially women. They want to know with whom you're traveling, whether you're married or have a boyfriend, and how many children you have. My advice to anyone exchanging these details with taxi drivers or other people whose paths you'll never cross again or with whom you don't want to become friendly, is to make up a set of answers regardless of the truth: I'm married, traveling with friends, and I have three children. Being divorced may send out a wrong message about availability or imagined degree of loneliness. Drunks are a particular nuisance to the lone female traveler; even when they can hardly walk they still muster up a "staggering" amount of machismo to speak, stumble along with you, or become a pest. Don't try to be polite, just leave or duck into a public place.

Generally women alone will feel comfortable going to a hotel lobby bar, but are asking for trouble or a hassle going into a pulquería or cantina. In restaurants, as a general rule, single women are offered the worst table and service. You'll have to be vocal about your preference and insist on service. Service may improve (but don't count on it) if you dine at off-peak hours. Tip well if you plan to return. Don't tip at all if service is bad.

And finally, remember, Mexican men learn charm early. The chase is as important as the conquest (maybe more so). Despite whatever charms *you* may possess, think twice before taking personally or seriously all the adoring, admiring words you'll hear.

FOR MEN I'm not sure why, perhaps because it's a challenge or because non-Spanish-speaking, foreign men appear innocent or weak, but they seem to be special targets for scams and pickpockets. So if you fit this description, whether traveling alone or in a pair, exercise special vigilance.

FOR FAMILIES

Mexico has a high birthrate, so small children make up a large part of the population. Mexicans travel extensively with their families, so your child will feel very welcome. Hotels will often arrange for a babysitter. Hotels in the mid- to upper range have small playgrounds for children and hire caretakers on weekends to oversee them and the children's pool so the parents can relax. Few budget hotels offer these amenities.

Before leaving for Mexico, you should check with your doctor and get advice on medicines to combat diarrhea and other ailments. Bring a supply, just to be sure. Disposable diapers are made and sold in Mexico (one popular brand is Kleen Bebé). The price is about the same as at home, but the quality is lower. Also, Gerber's baby foods are sold in many stores. Dry cereals, powdered formulas, baby bottles, and purified water are all easily available in midsize to large cities.

Cribs, however, may present a problem. Except for the largest and most luxurious hotels, few Mexican hotels provide cribs.

Many of the hotels we mention, even in noncoastal regions, have swimming pools, which can be dessert at the end of a day traveling with a child who has had it with sightseeing.

6. ALTERNATIVE/ADVENTURE TRAVEL

EDUCATIONAL/STUDY TRAVEL

SPANISH LESSONS A dozen towns south of the border are famous for their Spanish-language programs. Mexican National Tourism offices (see "Information, Entry Requirements, and Money," above) may have information about schools. Go anytime of year—you needn't really wait for a "semester" or course year to start. It's best to begin on a Monday, however.

Don't expect the best and latest in terms of language texts and materials. Many are well out-of-date. Teachers tend to be underpaid and perhaps undertrained, but very friendly and extremely patient. Seek out Mexican students of English and exchange conversation with them. This is how the best friendships are made.

Try living with a Mexican family. Pay in advance for only a week or 10 days, and if things are going well, continue. If your "family stay" ends up being little more than a room rental, feel free to go elsewhere. Family stays are not particularly cheap, by the way, so you should get your money's worth in terms of interaction and language practice.

The National Registration Center for Studies Abroad (NRCSA), 823 North 2nd St., Milwaukee, WI 53203 (tel. 414/278-0631), has a catalog ($7) of schools in Mexico. They will register you at the school of your choice, arrange for room and board with a Mexican family, and make your airline reservations, all for no extra fee. Contact them and ask for a (free) copy of their newsletter.

Homestays Spanish-language schools frequently provide lists of families who offer rooms to students. Often the experience is just like being one of the family. **World Learning Inc., The U.S. Experiment in International Living,** Kipling Road, P.O. Box 676, Brattleboro, VT 05302-0676 (tel. 802/257-7751; fax 802/258-3248), offers a wide range of options for international experiences ranging from accredited programs to homestays and Elderhostel affiliation.

ADVENTURE/WILDERNESS TRAVEL

Besides a lack of funds, Mexico is behind in its awareness and commitment to tourists' interest in ecology-oriented adventure and wilderness travel. As a result, most of the national parks and nature reserves are understaffed and/or not staffed by knowledgeable persons. Most companies offering that kind of travel are U.S. operated and trips are specialist-led. The following companies offer a variety of off-the-beaten-path travel experiences.

Victor Emanuel Tours, P.O. Box 33008, Austin, TX 78764 (tel. toll free 800/328-8368 in the U.S.), is an established leader in birding and natural history tours.

Wings, Inc., P.O. Box 31930, Tucson, AZ 85751 (tel. 602/749-1967), has a wide assortment of trips including birding in Oaxaca, Chiapas, Colima, and Jalisco.

7. SHOPPING

The charm of Mexico is no better expressed than in arts and crafts. Hardly a tourist will leave this country without having bought at least one of these handcrafted items.

SHOPPING • 47

Mexico is famous for pottery, textiles, ceramics, baskets, and onyx and silver jewelry, to mention only a few.

This guide is designed to help the traveler know some of the crafts and the regions where they can be found. Many of these items can be found in markets and shops in both Guadalajara, Puerto Vallarta, and to a lesser extent in Manzanillo and around Lake Chapala. Jalisco's craft villages include Tonala and Tlaquepaque near Guadalajara, Ajijic and Jocotepec near Lake Chapala, and Tapalpa in the mountains south of Lake Chapala. Colima makes furniture and reproductions of pre-Hispanic pottery. I have listed the cities or villages where the item is sold (and often crafted), the first place listed being the best place to buy. The larger cities, especially Guadalajara, Puerto Vallarta, and Mexico City will have many crafts from other regions in addition to crafts from Jalisco and Colima. Tables of metric conversions and clothing sizes are in the Appendix. I would add that it is very helpful to visit a government fixed-price shop before attempting to bargain. There are two government-operated Casas de Artesanías in Guadalajara. This will give you an idea of the cost versus quality of the various crafts. Following are the various crafts, in alphabetical order.

Baskets Woven of reed or straw—Oaxaca, Copper Canyon, Toluca, Yucatán, Puebla, Mexico City.

Blankets Tapalpa, Jalisco, as well as Saltillo, Toluca, Santa Ana Chiautempan, north of Puebla, Oaxaca, and Mitla (made of soft wool with some synthetic dyes; they use a lot of bird and geometric motifs). Make sure that the blanket you pick out is in fact the one you take since often the "same" blanket in the wrapper is not the same.

Cantera Stone Guadalajara and Zacatecas.

Equipale Furniture Tlaquepaque and Tonalá in Jalisco state and also Nayarit state.

Glass Hand-blown and molded—Tlaquepaque, Jalisco, and also Monterrey and Mexico City.

Guitars Made in Paracho, 25 miles north of Uruapan in the state of Michoacán on Highway 37 not far from the Jalisco state line.

Hammocks and Mosquito Netting Mérida, Campeche, Mazatlán.

Hats Mérida (Panama), made of sisal from the maguey cactus; finest-quality weaving; easy to pack and wash. Also San Cristóbal de las Casas, Chiapas.

Huaraches Leather sandals often with rubber-tire soles—abundant in Guadalajara's Mercado Libertad and San Blas.

Huipils Handwoven, embroidered, or brocaded overblouses indigenous to almost all Mexican states but especially evident in Yucatán, Chiapas, Oaxaca, Puebla, Guerrero, and Veracruz. Most of the better huipils are in fact used ones that have been bought from the village women. Huipils can be distinguished by villages; look around before buying; you'll be amazed at the variety.

Lacquer Goods Olinala, Guerrero, northeast of Acapulco, is known for ornate lacquered chests and other lacquered decorative and furniture items. Pátzcuaro and Uruapan, in Michoacán state, are also known for gold-leafed lacquered trays.

Leather Goods Guadalajara, Monterrey, Saltillo, León, Mexico City, San Cristóbal de las Casas, and Oaxaca.

Masks Wherever there is locally observed regional dancing you'll find maskmakers. The tradition is especially strong in the states of Guerrero, Chiapas, Puebla, Oaxaca, and Michoacán.

Onyx Puebla (where onyx is carved), Querétaro, Matehuala, Mexico City.

Pottery Tlaquepaque and Tonalá and whimsical daily-life figures in Santa Cruz de las Huertas near Tonalá, all in the state of Jalisco. Reproductions of Colima pottery in Colima City. Also Oaxaca, Puebla, Michoacán, Coyotepec, Izúcar de Matamoras, Veracruz, Copper Canyon, Dolores Hidalgo, and Guanajuato.

Rebozos   Sold in most markets. Women's or men's rectangular woven cloth to be worn around the shoulders, similar to a shawl—Oaxaca, Mitla, San Cristóbal de las Casas, Mexico City, and Pátzcuaro. Rebozos are generally made of wool or a blend of wool and cotton and sometimes silk, but synthetic fibers are creeping in, so check the material carefully before buying. Also compare the weave from different cloths since the fineness of the weave is proportional to the cost.

Serapes   Heavy woolen or cotton blankets with a slit for the head, to be worn as a poncho—Tapalpa, Jalisco (three hours south of Guadalajara or the same distance north of Manzanillo), Santa Ana Chiautempan (30 miles north of Puebla near Tlaxcala), San Luis Potosí, Santa María del Río (25 miles south of San Luis Potosí), Chiconcoac (one hour's drive northeast from Mexico City, near Texcoco), Saltillo, Toluca, Mexico City.

Silver   Taxco, Mexico City, Zacatecas, and Guadalajara. Sterling silver is indicated by "925" on the silver, which certifies that there are 925 grams of pure silver per kilogram, or that the silver is 92.5% pure. In Mexico they also use a spread-eagle hallmark to indicate sterling. Look for these marks or otherwise you may be paying a high price for an inferior quality that is mostly nickel, or even silver plate called alpaca.

Stones   Chalcedony, turquoise, lapis lazuli, amethyst—Querétaro, San Miguel del Allende, Durango, Saltillo, San Luis Potosí. Opals are sold in the village of Margarita off Highway 15 west of Tequila. The cost of turquoise and silver is computed by weight, so many pesos per carat.

Sweaters   Beautifully made and designed sweaters using natural dyes are a cottage industry in Tapalpa, Jalisco.

Textiles   Oaxaca, Chiapas, Santa Ana near Puebla, Guerrero, and Nayarit are known for their excellent weaving, each culturally distinct and different. Ajijic and Jocotepec, both near Lake Chapala in Jalisco state, are weaving villages.

Tortoise Shell   It's illegal to buy in Mexico and to bring into the United States.

8. GETTING THERE

From the United States, how you choose to get to Mexico will depend on the amount of time and money you have. Air travel is generally quicker. Train travel can be less harried, and bus travel can be inexpensive, long, and variable in comfort.

BY PLANE

The airline situation is changing rapidly with many new regional carriers offering scheduled service to areas previously not served or underserved. Besides regularly scheduled service, charter service direct from U.S. cities to resorts is making Mexico much more accessible.

The main airlines operating direct or nonstop flights from the United States to points in Mexico with U.S. toll-free 800 numbers are: **Aero California** (tel. 800/237-6225), **Aeromexico** (tel. 800/237-6639), **Air France** (tel. 800/237-2747), **Alaska Airlines** (tel. 800/426-0333), **American** (tel. 800/433-7300), **Continental** (tel. 800/231-0856), **Delta** (tel. 800/221-1212), **Lacsa** (tel. 800/225-2272), **Lufthansa** (tel. 800/645-3880), **Mexicana** (tel. 800/531-7921), **Northwest** (tel. 800/225-2525), and **United** (tel. 800/241-6522). **Southwest Airlines** serves the U.S. border (tel. 800/435-9792).

The main departure points for U.S. airlines are Chicago, Dallas/Fort Worth,

Denver, Houston, Los Angeles, Miami, New Orleans, New York, Orlando, Philadelphia, Raleigh/Durham, San Antonio, San Francisco, Seattle, Toronto, Tucson, and Washington, D.C.

Regional airlines operating within Mexico, with appropriate telephone numbers, are as follows: **Aero Cancún** (see Mexicana); **Aero Caribe** (see Mexicana); **Aero Leo López,** headquartered in El Paso (tel. 915/778-1022; fax 779-3534); **Aerolitoral** (see Aeromexico); **Aeromar** (tel. toll free 800/950-0747, or see Mexicana); **Aero Monterrey** (see Mexicana); **Aero Morelos,** headquartered in Cuernavaca (tel. 73/17-5588; fax 17-2320); and **Aerovias Oaxaqueñas,** based in Oaxaca (tel. 951/6-3824).

Bargain hunters rejoice! Excursion and package plans proliferate, especially in the off-season. A good travel agent will be able to give you all the latest schedules, details, and prices for both airlines, but the changes in regional airlines is ongoing, so you may have to sleuth those for yourself. The least expensive airline prices are midweek, in the off-season (after Easter to December 15). Sample off-season, midweek, round-trip fares on Mexicana are as follows: A round-trip excursion fare from New York to Guadalajara is $561; to Puerto Vallarta, $561; and Manzanillo, $661. From Los Angeles to Guadalajara a typical fare runs from $323; to Puerto Vallarta, $279; and Manzanillo, $361. From Denver, a round-trip fare to Guadalajara is $298; to Puerto Vallarta, $298; and to Manzanillo, $477. But never pay these prices without first pricing packages that include air and hotel.

CHARTERS Charter service is growing and usually is sold as a package combination of air and hotel. **Tour companies** operating charters include Club America Vacations, Asti Tours, Apple Vacations, Friendly Holidays, Gogo Tours, and Mexico Tourism Consultants (MTC).

BY TRAIN

For getting to the border by train, call Amtrak (tel. toll free 800/872-7245 in the U.S.) for fares, information, and reservations.

BY BUS

Greyhound-Trailways, or its affiliates, offers service from the United States to the border, where passengers disembark, cross the border, and buy a ticket for travel into the interior of Mexico. At many border crossings there are scheduled buses from the U.S. bus station to the Mexican bus station.

BY CAR

Driving is certainly not the cheapest way to get to Mexico, but it is the best way to see the country. Unleaded gas (Magna Sin) costs around $1.60 a gallon, and regular gas (Nova) only slightly less. Insurance costs are high (see below). Parking is a problem in the cities. Unless you have a full carload of passengers, travel by bus or train will be cheaper, and with public transport you don't have to undertake the tedious amount of driving needed to see a country this big.

If you want to drive to the Mexican border, but not into Mexico, chambers of commerce or convention and visitors' bureaus near the border can supply names of secured parking lots. You can leave your car there while you see the country by rail, bus, or plane.

CAR DOCUMENTS To drive a car into Mexico you'll need a Temporary Car Importation Permit, granted upon satisfaction of a long and strictly required list of documents. The permit can be obtained through Mexican border officials at the time you cross the border, *or,* before you travel, through American Automobile Association (AAA) border state offices in Texas, New Mexico, Arizona, and California. AAA *may* charge a fee for this service, but it will be well worth if it improves the uncertain prospects, before traveling all the way to the border, of getting your documents and car past the scrutiny of Mexican border officials. (Even if you do obtain your permit through AAA, all your credentials will still be reviewed by these officials and are still subject to questions of validity.)

Temporary Car Importation Permit regulations have changed dramatically several times since early 1992, and you'll be wise to double-check all the requirements (see below) before setting out for a driving tour to Mexico. Call your nearest Mexican consulate, Mexican Government Tourist Office, AAA, or Sanborn's for the latest regulations. And call again en route to the border; yes, folks, in the past compliance has been required with rules that changed overnight. At this time here is what is required:

- A *valid driver's license.*
- *The car's current registration or original title.* Note that if the registration is in more than one name, and not all the named people are traveling with you, a notarized letter from the absent person(s) authorizing the use of the vehicle for the trip will be required. *Important Note:* The car registration and credit card (see below) must be in the same name.
- A *notarized letter from the lien holder,* if your registration shows a lien, giving you permission to take the vehicle into Mexico.
- *Special Mexican auto insurance*—auto insurance from your home country is invalid in Mexico. Sanborn's and AAA are just two of many insurance suppliers with offices at the border, or you can get the insurance from them in advance (see "Mexican Auto Insurance," below).
- A *valid international major credit card* (Discover is not accepted). Using only your credit card (no cash or checks) you are required to pay a $10 car-importation fee. As noted above, the credit card used must be in the same name as the registration for the car.

    Those without credit cards will forgo the $10 importation fee and instead will be required to post a cash bond based on the value of the car (which is determined by a private bonding company). Sanborn's now writes these bonds using consistent criteria. I recommend using their bonding service since otherwise cost of the bond can vary wildly from 20% to 100% of the value of the car and from one border crossing to another. If you post a bond you must also leave your *original car title* and your *social security card* with the bond, both of which are returned to you when you return with your car. This, of course, necessitates coming and going through the same border entry.
- A *signed declaration* promising to return to your country of origin with the vehicle.

You must carry your Temporary Car Importation Permit, tourist permit, and proof of insurance in the car at all times. Remember too that only under certain circumstances will the driver of the car be allowed to leave the country without the car. If it's undrivable, you can leave it at a mechanic's shop *if* you get a letter to that effect from the mechanic and present it to the Secretaría de Hacienda y Credito Publico for further documentation, which you then present upon leaving the country.

Then you must return personally to retrieve the car. If the driver of the car must leave the country without the car due to an emergency, the car must be put under Customs seal at the airport and the driver's Tourist Permit must be stamped to that effect. There may be storage fees. If it's wrecked or stolen, your insurance adjuster will provide the necessary paperwork, which you must present to Hacienda officials.

As if this pile of paper weren't enough, it's a good idea to make two copies of all your documents, including your driver's license, before you leave home. Doing so may save you some time and money at the border (if you decide to obtain your permit there); border officials will otherwise make copies of everything and charge you for them.

The car permit papers will be issued for 6 months and the Tourist Permit is usually issued for 180 days—but they might stamp it for half that, so check. It's a good idea to greatly overestimate the time you'll spend in Mexico when applying for your permit, so that if something unforeseen happens and you have to (or want to) stay longer, you'll have avoided the long hassle of getting your papers renewed. But whatever you do, don't overstay either permit. Doing so invites heavy fines and/or confiscation of your vehicle, which will not be returned. *Note:* Six months does not necessarily work out to 180 days—be sure that you return before whichever expiration date comes first.

Other documentation is required for permission to enter the country (see "Entry Requirements," above).

MEXICAN AUTO INSURANCE You must purchase Mexican insurance, as U.S. or Canadian insurance is not valid in Mexico, and any party involved in an accident who has no insurance (or ready proof of it) is automatically sent to jail and the car is impounded until all claims are settled. This is true even if you just drive across the border to spend the day; and it may be true even if you are injured. Those with insurance are assumed to be good for claims and are released.

The agency where you purchase your Mexican insurance will show you a full table of current rates and will recommend the coverage it thinks adequate. The policies are written along lines similar to those north of the border with this exception: the contents of your vehicle aren't covered. It's no longer necessary to overestimate the amount of time you plan to be in Mexico because it's now possible to get your policy term lengthened by fax from the insurer. However, if you are staying longer than 48 days it's more economical to buy a nonrefundable annual policy. For example, a car with a value of $10,000 costs $133.45 to insure for 2 weeks, or $72.25 for 1 week. An annual policy for a car valued between $10,000 and $15,000 would be $372. Be sure the policy you buy will pay for repairs in either the United States or Mexico and that it will pay out in dollars, not pesos.

One of the best insurance companies for south of the border travel is **Sanborn's Mexico Insurance,** with offices at all of the border crossings in the United States. I never drive across the border without Sanborn's insurance. It costs the same as the competition, and you get a travelog that's like a mile-by-mile guide along your proposed route. Information occasionally gets a bit dated, but for the most part it's like having a knowledgeable friend in the car telling you how to get in and out of town, where to buy gas (and which stations to avoid), highway conditions, and scams. It's especially helpful in remote places. Most of Sanborn's border offices are open Monday through Friday, and a few are staffed on Saturday and Sunday. You can purchase your auto liability and collision coverage by phone in advance and have it waiting at a 24-hour location if you are crossing when their office is closed. The insurance includes a type of evacuation assistance in case of emergency, and more emergency evacuation insurance is available for a small daily fee. For information contact Sanborn's Mexico Insurance, P.O. Box 310, Dept. FR, 2009 South 10th,

McAllen, TX 78505-0310 (tel. 210/686-0711; fax 210/686-0732). AAA auto club also sells insurance.

PREPARING YOUR CAR Know the condition of your car before you cross the border. Parts made in Mexico may be inferior, but service generally is quite good and relatively inexpensive. Your cooling system should be in good condition, with the proper mixture of coolant and water. Don't risk disaster with an old radiator hose, and carry a spare fan belt. In summer for long drives, an air conditioner is not a luxury, but a necessity. You might want a spare belt for this, too, just in case. Mexican gasoline is not up to high standards, even the best of it, so it's good to be sure your car is in tune to handle it.

Remember that Mexico is a big country, and that you may put several thousand miles on your tires before you return home—can your tires last a few thousand miles on Mexican roads? Take simple tools along if you're handy with them, also a flashlight or spotlight, a cloth to wipe the windshield, toilet paper, and a tire gauge. Mexican filling stations generally have air to fill tires, but no gauge to check the pressure. If you don't carry your own gauge you'll have to find a tire repair shop to get your tires checked, then return to the gas station for air. When driving I always bring along a combination gauge/air compressor sold at U.S. automotive stores. It plugs into the car cigarette lighter, making it a simple procedure to check the tires every morning and pump them up at the same time.

Not that many Mexican cars comply, but Mexican law requires that every car have **seat belts** and a **fire extinguisher**. Be prepared.

CROSSING THE BORDER After you cross the border into Mexico from the United States, you'll stop to get your tourist/car permit (now all in one), and a tourist decal will be affixed to the front window. After that you'll come to a Mexican Customs post somewhere between 12 and 16 miles down the road. In the past every motorist had to stop and present travel documents. Now there is a new system that stops some motorists (chosen at random) for inspection. If the light is green go on through. If it's red, stop for inspection. In the Baja peninsula the procedures may differ slightly—first you get your tourist permit, then there may be no stop for the car permit. Theoretically, you should not be charged for your tourist permit, auto permit, and inspection, but the uniformed officer may try to extract a bribe from you (see "Bribes," above).

A last word: When you cross back into the United States after an extended trip in Mexico, the American Customs officials may inspect every nook and cranny of your car, your bags, even your person. They're looking for drugs, which includes illegal diet pills.

BY SHIP

Numerous cruise lines serve Mexico. Taking one, especially if it's your first time to Mexico, is one way to canvas beach resorts for a return trip. But keep in mind that a brief port call barely skims the surface. Possible trips include: from California down to the Baja peninsula (including specialized whale-watching trips), and to ports of call down the Pacific coast including Ixtapa/Zihuatanejo, Puerto Vallarta, Manzanillo, and Acapulco. Among the many cruise lines with Pacific coast itineraries is **Princess Cruises,** 10100 Santa Monica Blvd., Los Angeles, CA 90067 (tel. toll free 800/344-2626 in the U.S.). Several cruise-tour specialists arrange substantial discounts on unsold cabins at the last minute. One such company is **The Cruise Line, Inc.,** 4770 Biscayne Blvd., Penthouse 1-3, Miami, FL 33137 (tel. 305/576-0036, or toll free 800/777-0707 or 800/327-3021). **AAA** members receive cruise discounts on many different lines.

PACKAGE TOURS

Package tours offer some of the best values to the coastal resorts especially during high season from December until after Easter. Off-season packages can be real bargains. But to know for sure if the package is a cost saver you must price the package yourself by calling the airline for round-trip flight costs, and the hotel for rates. Add in the cost of transfers to and from the airport (which packages usually include) and see if it's a deal. Packages are usually per person, and single travelers pay extra. In the high season a package may be the only way of getting there because wholesalers have blocked airline seats. The airline may be completely booked when you call, but a travel agent can get you there through a package purchase. The cheapest package rates will be those in hotels in the lower range, always without as many amenities or as beautiful rooms as more costly hotels. But you can go to the public areas and beaches of any other hotel and spend the day without being a guest there. Use this book to read up on the hotels and make your selection. Travel agents, airlines, and hotels have information on specific packages.

9. GETTING AROUND

BY PLANE

U.S. and international airlines can fly to and from Mexico letting off and picking up passengers. But to fly from point to point within the country you'll rely on Mexican airlines. Mexico has two privately owned, large national carriers, **Mexicana** and **Aeromexico**, which fly from the United States to Mexico as well as within the country, and several up-and-coming regional carriers. Mexicana is Latin America's largest air carrier, dating back to 1921, and has the most extensive service within the country. Several of the new regional carriers are operated by, or can be booked through, Mexicana (**Aero Caribe, Aero Cozumel, Aeromar,** and **Aeromonterrey**) and Aeromexico (**Aerolitoral**). The regional carriers are expensive, but they go to places that were once difficult to reach. Look for this trend to continue. In each of the sections in this book, I've mentioned the regional carriers and the major ones with all pertinent telephone numbers.

Because major airlines can book some regional carriers, read your ticket carefully to see if a connecting flight is on one of these smaller carriers since they may leave from a different airport or check-in at a different counter.

AIRPORT TAXES Mexico charges an airport tax on all departures. Passengers leaving the country on an **international departure** pay $12 in cash—dollars or the peso equivalent—to get out of the country. Each **domestic departure** you make within Mexico costs around $9 unless you are on a connecting flight and already paid at the start of the flight—you shouldn't be charged again if you have to change planes for a connecting flight.

RECONFIRMING FLIGHTS Although airlines in Mexico say it is not necessary to reconfirm a flight, I always do. On several occasions I have arrived to check-in with a valid ticket only to discover my reservation had been canceled. Now I leave nothing to chance. Also be aware that airlines routinely overbook. To avoid getting bumped, check-in for an international flight the required 1½ hours in advance of travel. That will put you near the head of the line.

BY TRAIN

The Mexican Government would like to privatize the railroads and has systematically downgraded passenger service from the high it reached a few years ago. You can't count on diner or club cars or Pullman (sleeping) cars even on overnight journeys. Always board with food and water, no matter what is promised.

However, if you find a first-class train heading your way, try it. Train travel is safer and sometimes more comfortable than bus travel, though it's slower, costs more, and schedules are likely to be less convenient.

SERVICE CLASSES

Traveling **Segunda** (second class) is usually hot, overcrowded, dingy, and unpleasant. **Primera** (first class) can be the same unless you make sure to ask for **Primera Especial** (first class, reserved seat), if possible a day or so in advance. The top-of-the-line accommodations on trains, cheaper than flying but more expensive than the bus, are **Pullman** compartments (*alcoba* for two with two beds or *camarin* for one with one bed) for overnight travel. These convert to private sitting rooms during the day. Cramming extra people in either size compartment is very uncomfortable, and not recommended. Some first-class trains have a Pullman *and* diner; others have only a diner (or no diner or Pullman), but most will have reclining chairs. In all cases baggage is carried on and stored over your seat.

Service and cleanliness may vary dramatically. Cars will be clean at the start of a journey, but little may be done en route to maintain them. Trash may accumulate, toilet paper—if there was any to begin with—may vanish, the water cooler may run dry or lack paper cups, and the temperature may vary between freezing and sweltering. Conductors range from solicitous to totally indifferent.

There are two major train hubs—Mexico City and Guadalajara. If you plan to get on and off before your final destination, you must tell the agent your exact on-off schedule at the time of your ticket purchase, and there's usually a surcharge for the stops. Trains are often filled, especially on holidays or with tour groups. Here is a summary of the major rail connections.

Mexico City Hub

Regiomontaño: Runs between Nuevo Laredo at the Texas border through Monterrey and Saltillo to Mexico City.

El Constitucionalista: From Mexico City north and west to Querétaro, Irapuato, and Guanajuato.

El Tapatío: Mexico City to Guadalajara overnight.

El Oaxaqueño: Overnight between Mexico City and Oaxaca.

El Jarocho: Mexico City overnight to Veracruz passing Fortín de las Flores, Orizaba, and Córdoba en route.

El Purepecha: Suspended but may be reinstituted—overnight between Mexico City and Morelia, Pátzcuaro, and Uruapan.

División del Norte: Northward between Mexico City through Irapuato, León, Lagos de Moreno, Aguascalientes, Zacatecas, and Juárez.

Guadalajara Hub

El Tren del Pacífico: From Guadalajara along the Pacific coast to a dozen cities including Tepic, Mazatlán, Culiacán, Obregón, Hermosillo, Nogales, Puerto Peñasco, and Mexicali at the California border.

El Sinaloense: From Guadalajara to Tepic, Mazatlán, Culiacán, and Los Mochis.

Other Trains

El Nuevo Chihuahua-Pacífico: Begins at both Los Mochis and Chihuahua City and passes through Mexico's beautiful Copper Canyon.

TICKETS

For advance purchase of tickets, contact **Mexico by Train** (not to be confused with Mexico by Rail), 3015 South Martin, Laredo, TX 78043 (tel. toll free 800/321-1699). Given 10 days notice they will pre-purchase your train tickets and mail them to you. For holiday travel, make plans at least 45 days ahead of when you'd like to travel. If you leave from Nuevo Laredo, a company representative will meet you at the La Posada Hotel, check for your proper citizenship identification, secure Mexican Tourist Permits, transfer you across the border, through customs and aboard a first-class bus to Monterrey to connect with the southbound Regiomontaño train which leaves from Monterrey going to Mexico City (see "Mexico City Hub" above and specific chapters for train accessibility). For their services, they charge a percentage above the cost of the train ticket. The additional cost of this service may be worth it when you consider the tightness of your travel schedule, the hassle of going to the train station yourself, and the uncertainty of being able to reserve a seat at the last minute.

To contact the railroad directly for fares and schedule information in Mexico City, phone 5/547-6593, 547-1097, or 547-1084. If you purchase your ticket at the train station, do it as soon as your plans are firm. Although they seldom reply to mail, for the latest train itinerary or other questions, you can try writing well in advance to Commercial Passenger Department, National Railways of Mexico, Buenavista Grand Central Station, Mexico, D.F. 06358, or call 5/547-8972. For the Pacific Railroad Company write Tolsa 336, Guadalajara, Jal. Both companies have special personnel and divisions to handle group train travel. With enough lead time, they'll even put on extra cars.

TRAVEL TIME ON TRAINS

From Mexicali, the fast train takes 30 hours to Guadalajara, 45 to Mexico City. Pacific coast trains are notorious for running as much as 24 hours behind time. In general though, they take off on time.

BY BUS

Except for the Baja and Yucatán peninsulas, where bus service is not well developed, buses are frequent, readily accessible, and can get you to almost anywhere you want to go. More than a dozen Mexican companies operate large air-conditioned Greyhound-type buses between most cities. My *unofficial* method of calculating the cost of bus travel is by the hour of travel. I estimate that it now costs around $1.75 per hour of travel for first class with a reserved seat. That is, if a trip is three hours long, the cost of the ticket will be $5.25. Deluxe buses cover routes all over Mexico now and cost roughly $3 per hour of travel. These deluxe buses, known by a variety of names—*plus, de lujo, executivo,* etc.—have fewer seats than regular buses, show video movies en route, are air-conditioned, and have few stops; many have no stops until the final destination. They are well worth the extra bucks. Second-class buses have many stops and cost only slightly less than first-class or deluxe buses.

Modern buses have replaced most of the legendary "village buses" that growled and wheezed when they were overloaded, which was often. Today it's best to buy your reserved-seat ticket, often via a computerized system, a day in advance on many long-distance routes. Schedules are fairly dependable, so be at the terminal on time for departure.

Many Mexican cities, including Guadalajara, now have new central bus stations that are much like sophisticated airport terminals rather than the bewildering array of tiny private company offices scattered all over town—such as Puerto Vallarta. I've included information on bus routes along my suggested itineraries. Keep in mind that routes, times, and prices may change, and as there is no central directory of schedules for the whole country, current information must be obtained from local bus stations or travel offices.

For long trips, carry some food, water, toilet paper, and a sweater (in case the air conditioning is too strong).

See the Appendix for a list of helpful bus terms in Spanish.

BY CAR

Mexico is developing a good network of four-lane toll roads which offer convenience, and speed since they also cut the time of travel. But the cost for using them is among the highest in the world. Because of the high rates, they are relatively little used and as this edition was being prepared talks were under way to reduce the tolls, which may occur by the time you travel. Generally speaking, the toll roads will cut your travel time between destinations. In the region covered in this book there are new toll roads between Guadalajara and Manzanillo and a short one between Chapalilla and Compostela which bypasses Tepic (and cuts the travel time from 8 to 6 hours) on the road between Puerto Vallarta and Guadalajara. The old roads, are generally in good condition and are free, but overall they take longer to use since they usually pass through more mountains and carry an abundance of truck traffic. However, now that the toll roads are built, signage to the free roads is confusing and inconsistent from toll road to toll road, or is nonexistent, so it's easy to find yourself at the toll booth when you meant to take the free road.

The toll road from Guadalajara through Colima City to Manzanillo is a dream—if an expensive one. Tolls cost around $20 for the whole distance. As you cross bridges, signboards compare heights of bridges along the route to pyramids in Mexico. The Piala Bridge, for example, is 292 feet high compared to the 207 feet for the Pyramid of the Sun. The Beltrán Bridge is 459 feet high compared to the Latin American Tower in Mexico City at 590 feet. It makes for an interesting bit of trivia as you travel, and some of the deep gorges from the highway are incredibly beautiful. The two-lane, free road that covers the same route is in good shape but takes longer to drive and goes through more mountainous curves.

It may be improved by the time you travel, but when I drove it to research this book, the road between Puerto Vallarta and Tequila was so potholed as to slow traffic to a crawl, and practically negates the time gained by the new toll road if you're traveling between Guadalajara and Puerto Vallarta.

Although Mexico's new toll roads are state-of-the art, most Mexican roads are not up to northern standards of smoothness, hardness, width of curve, grade of hill, or safety marking. Cardinal rule: Never drive at night if you can avoid it. The roads aren't good enough; the trucks, carts, pedestrians, and bicycles usually have no lights; you can hit potholes, animals, rocks, dead ends, or bridges out with no warning. Enough said.

You will also have to get used to the locals' spirited driving styles, which tend to depend more on flair and good reflexes than on system and prudence. Be prepared for new procedures, as when a truck driver flips on his left-turn signal when there's not a crossroad for miles. He's probably telling you that the road's clear ahead for you to pass—after all, he's in a better position to see than you are. It's difficult to judge, however, if he really means that he intends to pull over on the left-hand shoulder.

You may have to follow trucks without mufflers and pollution-control devices for miles. Under these conditions drop back and be patient, take a side road, or stop for a break when you feel tense or tired.

Take extra care not to endanger pedestrians. People in the countryside are not good at judging the speed of an approaching car, and often panic in the middle of the road even though they could easily have reached the shoulder.

Be prepared to pay tolls on some of Mexico's expressways and bridges. Tolls are among the highest in the world. The word for "toll" in Spanish is *cuota*.

CAR RENTALS With some trepidation I wander into the subject of car-rental rules, which change often in Mexico. Guadalajara and most other large Mexican cities have several rental offices representing the various big firms and some smaller ones. You'll find rental desks at the airports, at all major hotels, and at many travel agencies. The large firms like Avis, Hertz, National, and Budget have rental offices on main streets as well.

Cars are easy to rent if you have a credit card (American Express, VISA, MasterCard, etc.), are 25 or over, and have a valid driver's license and passport with you. Without a credit card you must leave a cash deposit, usually a big one. Rent-here/leave-there arrangements are usually simple to make, but are very costly.

Costs Don't underestimate the cost of renting a car. The best prices are obtained by reserving your car at least a week in advance from your home country. But shop for the best rate before settling on one since the cost of renting can be enormously different from company to company. The least expensive car to rent is the VW Beetle with standard shift and without air conditioning. Single-day charges are much higher than the per-day rate on a car rented for a week (and arranged in advance). Besides varying from company to company, they can vary greatly from city to city and during certain times of year. I recommend taking the mileage-included option rather than mileage added because the latter can run up the cost of using a car considerably.

If you select to take mileage included, your completed estimate should look something like this for a VW Beetle rented from Avis in Guadalajara:

Basic daily charge	$49.00
Collision/Damage and personal accident insurance	$15.00
Subtotal	$64.00
IVA tax 10%	$ 6.40
Grand Daily Total	$109.40

If you purchase Budget's collision/damage insurance the deductible is $250 if the car is reparable; $400 if unreparable.

A car rented for seven days in Guadalajara, through Avis, which from the United States only rents with unlimited mileage, would be:

Basic weekly rental	$179.00
Insurance	$105 ($15.00 daily)
Subtotal	$284.00
IVA tax 10%	$ 28.40
Total	$312.40 ($44.63 a day)

The Avis deductible is five days of the basic car rental, which in this case would be 5 × $44.63 = $223.15, if you buy their insurance.

Rental Confirmation Make your reservation directly with the car-rental company using their toll-free number. Write down your confirmation number and request that a copy of the confirmation be mailed to you (rent at least a week in advance so the confirmation has time to reach you). Present that confirmation slip when you appear to collect your car. If you're dealing with a U.S. company, the confirmation must be honored, even if they have to upgrade you to another class of car—don't allow them to send you to another agency. The rental confirmation also has the agreed-on price, which prevents you from being charged more in the event that prices have changed in the interim. Insist on the rate printed on the confirmation.

Deductibles *Be careful:* Deductibles vary greatly; some are as high as $2,500, which comes out of your pocket immediately in case of car damage. So don't fail to get information about deductibles.

Insurance Many credit-card companies offer their cardholders free rental-car insurance. *Don't use it in Mexico,* for several reasons. Even though rental-car insurance is supposedly optional in Mexico, there may be major consequences if you don't have it. First, if you buy insurance, and you have an accident, you pay only the deductible, which limits your expense. Second, if you don't have insurance and you have an accident, or the car is vandalized or stolen, you'll have to pay for everything before you can leave the rental-car office. This includes full value of the car if it is irreparably damaged—a determination made only by the rental-car company. While your credit card will eventually pay your costs, you will have to lay out the money in the meantime. Third, if an accident occurs, everyone may wind up in jail until guilt is determined. If you are the guilty party, you may not be released from jail until all restitution is paid to the rental-car owners and to injured persons—made doubly difficult if you have no rental-car insurance. Insurance is offered in two parts: **Collision and damage insurance** covers your car and others if the accident is your fault, and **personal accident insurance** covers you and anyone in your car. I always take both.

Damage Always inspect your car carefully before signing the rental agreement and leaving the lot, using this checklist:

- Hubcaps
- Windshield (for nicks and cracks)
- Body (for dents, nicks, rust, etc.)
- Fenders (for dents, etc.)
- Muffler (is it smashed?)
- Trim (loose, damaged, or missing?)
- Head- and taillights
- Fire extinguisher required by law—it should be under the driver's seat

- Spare tire and tools (in the trunk)
- Seatbelts (required by law)
- Gas cap
- Outside mirror
- Floor mats

Note every damaged or missing area, no matter how minute, on your rental agreement or you may be charged for all missing or damaged parts, including missing car tags, should the police confiscate your tags for a parking infraction (very costly). I can't stress enough how important it is to check your car carefully. Car companies have attempted to rent me cars with bald tires and tires with bulges; a car with a registration that would expire before I returned the car; as well as cars with missing trim, floor mats, fire extinguisher, etc.

Fine Print Read the fine print on the back of your rental agreement. Note that insurance is invalid if you have an accident while driving on an unpaved road—and you may find it necessary to travel on many unpaved roads in Mexico.

Trouble Number Before starting out with a rental car, be sure you know their trouble number. The large firms have toll-free numbers, which may not be well staffed on weekends.

Problems, Perils, and Deals At present, I find that Avis offers the best prices and that's the company I use; generally I am a satisfied customer, though I sometimes have to dig in my heels and insist on proper service. I have had even more difficult problems with other agencies. No matter what company you deal with, stay alert. In the past several years I have encountered certain kinds of situations that could occur with any company: An attempt to push me off to a no-name company rather than upgrade me to a more expensive car when a VW Beetle wasn't available; poorly staffed offices with no extra cars, parts, or mechanics in case of a breakdown; a demand that I sign a credit-card voucher for 75% of the value of the car in case of an accident even though I had purchased insurance (I refused and still rented the car). Since potential problems are varied, I'd rather deal with a company based in the United States, so that at least I have recourse when these obstacles arise.

Signing the Rental Agreement Once you've agreed on everything, the rental clerk will tally the bill before you leave and you will sign an open credit-card voucher that will be filled in when you return the car. Read the agreement and double-check all the addition. The time to catch mistakes is before you leave, not when you return.

Picking Up/Returning the Car When you rent the car, you agree to pick it up at a certain time and return it at a certain time. If you're late in picking it up or cancel the reservation, there are usually penalties—ask what they are when you make the reservation. If you return the car more than an hour late, an expensive hourly rate kicks in. Also, you must return the car with the same amount of gas in the tank as when you drove out. If you don't, the charge added to your bill for the difference is much more than for gas bought at a public station.

GASOLINE There's one government-owned brand of gas and one gasoline station name throughout the country—Pemex (Petroleras Mexicanas). Each station has a franchise owner who buys everything from Pemex. There are two types of gas in Mexico—Nova, an 82-octane leaded gas, and Magna Sin, 87-octane unleaded gas. Magna Sin is sold from bright green pumps and costs around $1.60 a gallon. Nova, sold from blue pumps, costs about the same. In Mexico, fuel and oil are sold by the liter, which is slightly more than a quart (40 liters equals about 10½ gallons). Nova is readily available. Magna Sin is now available in most areas of Mexico, along major highways and in the larger cities. Even in areas where it should be available, you may have to hunt around. The usual station may be out of Magna Sin for a couple of days—weekends especially. Or you may be told that none is available in the area, just to get your business. Plan ahead: Fill up every chance you get; keep your tank topped off. Pemex publishes a helpful Atlas de Carreteras (road atlas), which includes a list of filling stations with Magna Sin gas, although there are some inaccuracies in the list. No credit cards are accepted for gas purchases.

Here's what to do when you have to fuel up: Drive up to the pump, close enough so that you will be able to watch the pump run as your tank is being filled. Check that the pump is turned back to zero, go to your fuel filler cap and unlock it yourself, and watch the pump and the attendant as the gas goes in. Though many service station attendants are honest, most are not. It's good to ask for a specific peso amount rather than saying "full." This is because the attendants tend to overfill, splashing gas on the car and anything within range.

As there are always lines at the gas pumps, attendants often finish fueling one vehicle, turn the pump back quickly (or don't turn it back at all), and start on another vehicle. You've got to be looking at the pump when the fueling is finished, because it may show the amount you owe for only a few seconds. This "quick draw" from car to car is another good reason to ask for a certain peso amount of gas. If you've asked for 20,000 pesos' worth, the attendant can't charge you 22,000 for it.

Once the fueling is complete, let the attendant check the oil, or radiator, or put air in the tires. Do only one thing at a time, be with him as he does it, and don't let him rush you. Get into these habits, or it'll cost you.

If you get oil, make sure that the can that is tipped into your engine is a full one. If in doubt, have the attendant check the dipstick again after the oil has supposedly been put in. Check your change, and again, don't let them rush you. Check that your locking gas cap is back in place.

DRIVING RULES If you park illegally, or commit some other infraction, and you are not around to discuss it, police are authorized to remove your license plates (*placas*). You must then trundle over to the police station and pay a fine to get them back. Mexican car-rental agencies have begun to weld the license tag to the tag frame; you may want to devise a method of your own to make the tags difficult to remove. Theoretically, this will make the policeman move on to another set of tags easier to confiscate. On the other hand, he could get his hackles up and decide to have your car towed. To weld or not to weld is up to you.

Be attentive to road signs. A drawing of a row of little bumps means that there are speed bumps (*topes*) across the road to warn you to reduce your speed while driving through towns or villages. Slow down when coming to a village whether you see the sign or not—sometimes they install the bumps but not the sign!

Kilometer stones on main highways register the distance from local population centers. There is always a shortage of directional signs, so check quite frequently that you are on the right road. Other common road signs include:

Camino en Reparación Road Repairs
Conserva Su Derecha Keep Right
Cuidado con el Ganado, el Tren Watch Out for Cattle, Trains
Curva Peligrosa Dangerous Curve
Derrumbes Earthquake Zone

Deslave Caved-in Roadbed
Despacio Slow
Desviación Detour
Disminuya Su Velocidad Slow Down
Entronque Highway Junction
Escuela School (zone)
Grava Suelta Loose Gravel
Hombres Trabajando Men Working
No Hay Paso Road Closed
Peligro Danger
Puente Angosto Narrow Bridge
Raya Continua Continuous (Solid) White Line
Tramo en Reparación Road under Construction
Un Solo Carril a 100 m. One-lane Road 100 Meters Ahead
Zona Escolar School Zone

BREAKDOWNS Your best guide to repair shops is the yellow pages. For specific makes and shops that repair them, look under *Automoviles y Camiones: Talleres de Reparación y Servicio;* auto-parts stores are listed under *Refacciones y Accessorios para Automoviles.* On the road often the sign of a mechanic simply says *Taller Mecánico.*

I've found that the Ford and Volkswagen dealerships in Mexico give prompt, courteous attention to my car problems, and prices for repairs are, in general, much lower than in the United States or Canada. I suspect that other big-name dealerships— General Motors, Chrysler, etc.—give similar, very satisfactory service. Often they will take your car right away and make repairs in just a few hours, sometimes minutes.

If your car breaks down on the road, help might already be on the way. Green, radio-equipped repair trucks manned by uniformed, English-speaking officers patrol the major highways during daylight hours to aid motorists in trouble. The "Green Angels" will perform minor repairs and adjustments free, but you pay for parts and materials.

MINOR ACCIDENTS Most motorists think it best to drive away from minor accidents if possible. Without fluent Spanish, you are at a distinct disadvantage when it comes to describing your version of what happened. Sometimes the other person's version is exaggerated, and you may end up in jail or spending days straightening out things that were not even your fault. In fact, fault often has nothing to do with it. See "Mexican Auto Insurance," above.

PARKING When you park your car on the street, lock up and leave nothing within view inside (day or night). I use guarded parking lots especially at night, to avoid vandalism and break-ins. This way you also avoid parking violations. When pay lots are not available, dozens of small boys will surround you as you stop, wanting to "watch your car for you." Pick the leader of the group, let him know you want him to guard it, and give him a peso or two when you leave. Kids may be very curious about the car and may look in, crawl underneath, or even climb on top, but they rarely do any damage.

CAMPING It's easy and relatively cheap to camp south of the border if you have a recreational vehicle or trailer. It's more difficult if you only have a tent. Some agencies selling Mexican car insurance in the United States (including Sanborn's) will give you a free list of campsites if you ask. The AAA also has a list of sites. *RV Park & Campground Directory* (previously published by Rand McNally, now published by Prentice Hall, New York) covers Mexico.

62 • PLANNING A TRIP TO THE REGION

Campgrounds here tend to be slightly below U.S. standards (with many attractive exceptions to this rule, though). Remember that campgrounds fill up just like hotels during the winter rush-to-the-sun and at holiday times. Get there early. It is not wise to camp on a beach or any other remote, unofficial place.

OTHER OPTIONS

BY RV Touring Mexico by recreational vehicle is a popular way of seeing the country. Many hotels have hookups. RV parks, while not as plentiful as in the United States, are available throughout the country.

BY FERRY Ferries connect Baja California at La Paz and Santa Rosalía with the mainland at Topolobampo and Mazatlán.

HITCHHIKING You see Mexicans hitching rides at crossroads after getting off a bus, for example, but as a general rule hitchhiking isn't done. It's especially not wise for foreigners since they may be suspected of carrying large amounts of cash.

FAST MEXICO

In this section I have tried to anticipate some of the questions that you may find yourself asking. You will probably think of many other listings yourself; if so, I would appreciate hearing about them. Such listings will be included in future versions of this book.

Abbreviations Dept.—apartments; Apdo.—post office box; Av.—Avenida; Calz.—calzada or boulevard. C on faucets stands for caliente (hot), and F stands for fría (cold). In elevators, PB (planta baja) means "ground floor."

American Express Wherever there is an office, I've mentioned it.

Business Hours In general Mexican businesses in larger cities are open between 9am and 7pm. Smaller towns may close between 2 and 4pm. Most are closed on Sunday. Bank hours are 9 or 9:30am to 1pm Monday to Friday. A few banks in large cities have extended hours.

Camera/Film Both are more expensive in Mexico than in the United States; take full advantage of your 12-roll film allowance by bringing 36 exposures per roll, and bring extra batteries. AA batteries are generally available, but AAA and small disk batteries for cameras and watches are rarely found. A few places in resort areas advertise color-film developing, but it might be cheaper to wait until you get home.

If you're a serious photographer, bring an assortment of films at various speeds as you will be photographing against glaring sand, on city streets, and at sun-baked open markets. Proper filters are a help.

Important note about camera use: Tourists wishing to use a video or still camera at any archeological site in Mexico and at many museums operated by the Instituto Nacional de Historia y Antropología must pay $8.50 per video or still camera at each site or museum visited (in some museums camera use is not permitted). When you pay the fee, your camera will be tagged and you are permitted to use the equipment. Watchmen are often posted to see that no untagged camera is used.

Cigarettes Cigarettes are much cheaper in Mexico, even U.S. brands, if you buy them at a grocery or drugstore and not a hotel tobacco shop.

Climate See "When to Go," above.

Crime See "Safety" and "Legal Aid," below, and "Scams" and "Bribes," above.

FAST FACTS: MEXICO • 63

Currency See "Information, Entry Requirements, and Money," above.

Customs Mexican Customs procedures have been streamlined. At most crossings, entering tourists are requested to punch a button. If the resulting light is green you go through without inspection. If it's red your luggage or car may be inspected thoroughly or briefly.

Doctors/Dentists Every embassy and consulate is prepared to recommend local doctors and dentists with good training and modern equipment; some of the doctors and dentists even speak English. See the list of embassies and consulates under "Embassies/Consulates," below, and remember that at the larger ones a duty officer is on call at all times. Hotels with a high clientele of foreigners are often prepared to recommend English-speaking doctors. Almost all first-class hotels in Mexico have a doctor on call.

Documents Required See "Information, Entry Requirements, and Money," above.

Driving Rules See "Getting Around," above.

Drug Laws Briefly, don't use or possess illegal drugs in Mexico. Mexicans have no tolerance of drug users and jail is the solution with very little hope of getting out until the sentence (usually a long one) is completed or heavy fines or bribes are paid. *Important Note:* It isn't uncommon to be befriended by a fellow user, only to be turned in by that "friend," who then collects a bounty for turning you in. It's no win. Bring prescription drugs in their original containers. If possible pack a copy of the original prescription with the generic name of the drug. I don't need to go into detail about the penalties for illegal drug possession upon return to the United States. Customs officials are also on the lookout for diet drugs sold in Mexico, possession of which could also land you in jail in the United States where they are illegal. If you buy antibiotics over the counter (which you can do in Mexico), say, for a sinus infection and still have some left, you probably won't be hassled by U.S. Customs.

Drugstores Drugstores (farmacias) will sell you just about anything you want, with prescription or without. Most are open Monday through Saturday from 8am to 8pm.

If you need to buy medicines after normal hours, you'll have to search for the *farmacia de turno*—pharmacies take turns staying open during the off-hours. Find any drugstore, and in its window may be a card showing the schedule of which farmacia will be open at what time.

Electricity Current in Mexico is 110 volts, 60 cycles, as in the United States and Canada, with the same flat-prong plugs and sockets. Some light bulbs have bayonet bases.

Embassies/Consulates They provide valuable lists of doctors, and lawyers, as well as regulations concerning marriages in Mexico. Contrary to popular belief, your embassy cannot get you out of a Mexican jail, provide postal or banking services, or fly you home when you run out of money. Consular officers can provide you with advice on most matters and problems, however. Most countries have a representative embassy in Mexico City and many have consular offices or representatives in the provinces.

Australia: The Australian Embassy in Mexico City is at Jaime Balmes 11, Plaza Polanco Torre B (tel. 5/395-9988); open Monday through Friday from 8am to 1pm.

Canada: The Canadian Embassy in Mexico City is at Schiller 529, in Polanco (tel. 5/254-3288); open Monday through Friday from 9am to 1pm and 2 to 5pm; at other times the name of a duty officer is posted on the embassy door. In Acapulco, the Canadian consulate is in the Hotel Club del Sol, Costera Miguel Alemán, at the corner of Reyes Catolicos (tel. 748/5-6621); open 8am to 3pm.

France: The French Embassy and the French Consulate-General is at Havre 15, between Reforma and Hamburgo, in the Zona Rosa (tel. 5/533-1360); open Monday through Friday from 8:30am to 1:00pm.

Germany: The Embajada de la República Federal de Alemania is at Lord Byron 737 (tel. 5/545-6655); open Monday through Friday from 9am to noon.

Netherlands: The Embajada Real de los Países Bajos is at Monte Urales 635 at Reforma, Col. Lomas (tel. 5/540-7788). Hours are Monday through Friday, 9am to 2pm.

New Zealand: The New Zealand Embassy is on the eighth floor of the building at Homero 229 (tel. 5/250-5914 or 250-5777); open Monday through Thursday from 9am to 2pm and from 3 to 5pm, Friday from 9am to 2pm.

United Kingdom: The British Embassy in Mexico City is at Lerma 71, at Río Sena (tel. 5/207-2089 or 207-2186). Hours are 8:30am to 2pm Monday through Friday. There are **honorary consuls** in the following cities: Acapulco, Hotel Las Brisas, Carretera Escenica (tel. 748/4-6605 or 4-1580); Ciudad Juárez, Calle Fresno 185 (tel. 161/7-5791); Guadalajara, Paulino Navarro 1165 (tel. 36/11-1678); Mérida, Calle 58 no. 450 (tel. 99/28-6152); Monterrey, Privada de Tamazunchale 104 (tel. 83/45-0692); Tampico (tel. 12/12-9784); and Veracruz, Emparan 20 OPB (tel. 29/31-0955).

United States: The American Embassy in Mexico City is right next to the Hotel Maria Isabel Sheraton at Paseo de la Reforma 305, corner of Río Danubio (tel. 5/211-0042).

There are **U.S. consulates** in Ciudad Juárez (tel. 1/613-4048), Guadalajara (tel. 3/625-2998 or 625-2700), Hermosillo (tel. 6/217-2382), Matamoros (tel. 89/12-5251), Mérida (tel. 99/25-5011), Monterrey (tel. 83/45-2120), Nuevo Laredo (tel. 871/4-0696), and Tijuana (tel. 66/81-7400).

In addition, **consular agents** reside in Acapulco (tel. 74/85-6600); Cancún (tel. 988/4-2411), open from 10am to 2pm and 4 to 7pm; Durango (tel. 181/1-2217), open weekdays from 8am to 3pm; Mulege (tel. 685/3-0111); Oaxaca (tel. 951/4-3054); Puerto Vallarta (tel. 322/2-0069); San Luis Potosí (tel. 481/7-2510), open weekdays from 9am to 1pm and 4 to 7pm; San Miguel de Allende (tel. 465/2-2357), open Monday and Wednesday from 9am to 2pm and 4 to 7pm, Tuesday and Thursday from 4 to 7pm, and by appointment on Friday, Saturday, and Sunday; Tampico (tel. 12/13-2217); and Veracruz (tel. 29/31-5821).

Emergencies The 24-hour Tourist Help Line in Mexico City is 5/250-0151, 5/525-9380, or 525-9384. See also "Legal Aid," below.

Etiquette As a general rule, Mexicans are very polite. Foreigners who ask questions politely, and say please and thank you, will be rewarded. Mexicans are also very formal; an invitation to a private home no matter how humble is an honor. And although many strangers will immediately begin using the familiar form of the verb "tu" for you, if you want to be correct, the formal "usted" is still preferred until a friendship is established. How long it takes to establish a friendship varies. I know neighbors in Mexico who are still on formal terms after 10 years. When in doubt use the formal and wait for the Mexican to change to the familiar. Mexicans are normally uncomfortable with our "Dutch treat" custom of dining and will usually insist on paying. It can be touchy, and you don't want to be insulting. But you might offer to get the drinks or insist on paying the tip. If you're invited to a home it's polite to bring a gift, perhaps a bottle of good wine or flowers.

Guides Most guides in Mexico are men. Many speak English (and occasionally other languages) and are formally trained in history and culture to qualify for a federally approved tourism license. Hiring a guide for a day at the ruins, or to squire you around Mexico City may be a worthwhile luxury *if* you establish boundaries in the beginning. Be specific about what you want to do, and how long you want the service. The guide will quote a price. Discussion may reduce the initial quote. If your guide is using his own car, is licensed (something he can prove with a credential), and speaks English, the price will be higher and is generally worth it. If you are together at lunch, it's customary to buy the guide's meal. When bus tours from the United States diminished a few years ago, many licensed English-speaking guides became taxi drivers, so it isn't unusual to find incredibly knowledgeable taxi drivers who are experienced guides. In Mexico City these licensed guides/taxi drivers often have a permanent spot outside the better hotels and are available for private duty. If the service has been out of the ordinary, a tip is in order—perhaps 10% of the daily rate. On tours, the recommended tip is $1.50 to $2 per day per person.

Hitchhiking Generally speaking hitchhiking is not a good idea in Mexico. Take a bus; they are cheap and go everywhere.

Holidays See "When to Go," above.

Information See "Information, Entry Requirements, and Money," above, and specific city for local information offices.

Language The official language is Spanish, but there are at least 50 Native American languages spoken and more than four times that many dialects. English is most widely spoken in resort cities and in better hotels. It's best to learn some basic Spanish phrases.

Laundry See information in various cities.

Legal Aid Proseco (Procuraduría Federal de Consumidor), Calle Doctor Navarro 210, 4th Piso, Col. de los Doctores, Mexico D.F. 06720 (tel. 525/761-4546; fax 525/761-3885), is a contact for tourists with legal problems. **International Legal Defense Counsel,** 111 South 15th St., Packard Building, 24th floor, Philadelphia, PA 19102 (tel. 215/977-9982), is a law firm specializing in legal difficulties of Americans abroad. See also "Embassies/Consulates" and "Emergencies," above.

Liquor Laws See "Entry Requirements," above.

Mail Mail service south of the border tends to be slow (sometimes glacial in its movements) and erratic. If you're on a two-week vacation, it's not a bad idea to buy and mail your postcards in the arrivals lounge at the airport to give them maximum time to get home before you do.

For the most reliable and convenient mail service, have your letters sent to you c/o the American Express offices in major cities, which will receive and forward mail for you *if* you are one of their clients (a travel-club card or an American Express traveler's check is proof). They charge a fee if you wish them to forward your mail.

If you don't use American Express, have your mail sent to you care of *Lista de Correos,* followed by the city, state, and country. In Mexican post offices there may actually be a "lista" posted near the Lista de Correos window bearing the names of all those for whom mail has been received. If there's no list, ask, and show them your passport so they can riffle through and look for your letters. If the city has more than one office, you'll have to go to the central post office—not a branch—to get your mail. By the way, in many post offices they return your mail to sender if it has been there for more than 10 days. Make sure people don't send you letters too early. See the Appendix for a list of postal terms.

If you don't want to rely on the post office, you might want to consider the services of DHL, Federal Express, or UPS, all of which have service between the United States and most major Mexican cities or Mexican cities with a high number of foreign residents.

Maps AAA maps to Mexico are quite good and available free to members at any AAA office in the United States. Guia Roji also has good maps.

Newspapers and Magazines The English-language newspaper *The*

News, published in Mexico City, carries world news and commentaries, and a calendar of the day's events including concerts, art shows, and plays.

Newspaper kiosks in larger Mexican cities will carry a selection of English-language magazines.

Passports See "Information, Entry Requirements, and Money" in this chapter.

Pets Taking a pet into Mexico entails a lot of red tape. Consult the Mexican Government Tourist Office nearest you.

Police Police in general in Mexico are to be suspected rather than trusted; however, you'll find many who are quite helpful with directions, even going so far as to lead you where you want to go.

Prices As this book went to press the Mexican government allowed hotels and restaurants the right to set their own prices. Previously each entity was graded by the government and given an official price structure by which to operate. Now these businesses can charge what the traffic will bear. It is unlikely that this change will alter the prices quoted in this book, since many hotels (at least) were already charging below their officially designated prices, because patrons would not pay more. When in doubt at a hotel, ask to see their rate sheet, which is required to be posted within view. If the hotel seems overpriced, leave and check with another hotel—this sends the message that the hotel is charging too much. Often desk clerks will quote a lower price if business is slack or if you suggest a slight reduction. In the past, quoted prices included the 10% IVA tax. Now a quoted price does not have to include tax, so be sure to ask before ordering a meal or taking a room. The deregulation of prices also affects taxis, tours, and car rentals.

Radio/TV Many hotels now have antennae capable of bringing in U.S. TV channels. Large cities will have English-language stations and music.

Rest Rooms The best bet in Mexico is to use rest rooms in restaurants and hotel public areas. Always carry your own toilet paper and hand soap, neither of which is in great supply in Mexican rest rooms. Public facilities, usually near the central market, vary in cleanliness and usually have an attendant who charges a few pesos for toilet use and a few squares of toilet paper. Pemex gas stations have improved the maintenance of their rest rooms along major highways. No matter where you are, even if the toilet flushes with paper, there'll be a waste basket for paper disposal. Many people come from homes without plumbing and are not accustomed to toilets that take paper, and throw paper on the floor rather than put it in the toilet—thus you'll see the basket no matter what quality of place you are in. On the other hand the water pressure in many establishments is so low that paper won't go down. There's often a sign saying "do" or "don't" flush paper.

Safety Whenever you're traveling in an unfamiliar city or country, stay alert. Be aware of your immediate surroundings. Wear a moneybelt and don't sling your camera or purse over your shoulder. This will minimize the possibility of your becoming a victim of crime.

Crime is more of a problem in Mexico than it used to be. Although you will feel physically safer in most Mexican cities than in comparable big cities at home, you must take some basic, sensible precautions.

First, remember that you're a tourist, and an obvious target for crime. Beware of pickpockets on crowded buses, the Metro, and in markets. Guard your possessions very carefully at all times; don't let packs or bags out of sight even for a second (the big first-class bus lines will store your bag in the luggage compartment under the bus, and that's generally all right, but keep your things with you on the less responsible village and some second-class buses on country routes).

Next, if you have a car, park it in an enclosed or guarded lot at night. Vans are a special mark. Don't depend on "major downtown streets" to protect your car—park it in a private lot with a guard, or at least a fence.

Women must be careful in cities when walking alone, night or day. Busy streets are no problem, but empty streets (even if empty just for afternoon siesta) are lonely places.

Important Warning: Agreeing to carry a package back to the United States for an acquaintance or a stranger could land you in jail for years and cost a lot of money to get you out. Never do it no matter how friendly, honest, or sincere the request. Perpetrators of this illegal activity prey on innocent-looking single travelers and especially senior citizens.

Allowing anyone into your room whom you don't know could invite an instant robbery. This includes someone announcing him or herself (by phone or at your hotel room door) as room service bringing a "free" meal or drinks as compliments of the house—or anything you didn't order. When you open the door expectantly, robbers burst in. Always use caution before opening your door to anyone. When in doubt call hotel security or the reception desk.

Seasons/Booking Those planning to be in resorts like Puerto Vallarta, Manzanillo, San Blas, and Barra de Navidad on major holidays (Mexican as well as international) should make hotel reservations. Christmas, New Year's, and Easter week are the worst for crowding. If you discover it's a holiday when you're en route to the resort, plan to arrive early in the day.

Several readers have written to me about difficulties they encountered in making reservations by mail, and even by toll-free reservation numbers. Some report no answer or no record of their request (or deposit check) when they've arrived. Or they are quoted a higher price than one they might have paid by just arriving without a reservation. I've experienced the same frustrations. Here's a suggestion: Only make reservations during high season if you are going to a beach area. Off-season just arrive and find out what's available by calling when you arrive.

Sightseeing As a general rule museums and archeological sites in Mexico are free on Sunday and they are free at all times to those age 13 and below, or over age 60.

Taxes There's a 10% tax on goods and services in Mexico and it may or may not be included in the posted price.

Telephone/Telex/Fax *Important Note:* Area codes were gradually being changed as this book went to press. Usually the change affects area code and first digit, or area code only. But some cities are adding exchanges and changing numbers. If you have difficulty calling long distance, ask the operator for assistance.

In 1990 Telefonos de Mexico reduced long-distance rates by 40%, and at the same time raised local rates. *Long-distance calls are still exorbitantly expensive,* especially out of the country, and now so are local calls.

Public pay phones for local use come in two types: In one, the slot at the top holds the N10- or 100-peso coin in a gentle grip until your party answers, then it drops; if there's no answer or a busy signal you can pluck your coin from the slot. With the other type, you insert a coin which disappears into the bowels of the machine, and drops into the cashbox when your call goes through, or into the return slot if it doesn't (after you hang up). This type of phone is often jammed, and your coin won't drop, so that when your party answers you will hear them but they won't hear you. Try from another pay phone.

For **long-distance calls** there are several ways to go: The most expensive is through a hotel switchboard, which may add a service charge to your already expensive bill. The least expensive way is to use Ladatel phones found increasingly in bus stations, airports, and downtown public areas of major cities and touristic zones.

(See how to use the Ladatel below.) Next in cost, and often faster and more convenient, is the *caseta de larga distancia* (long-distance telephone office), found all over Mexico. Most bus stations and airports now have specially staffed rooms exclusively for making long-distance calls and sending faxes. Often they are efficient and inexpensive, providing the client with a computer printout of the time and charges. Long-distance operators are notoriously hard to reach, so no matter what method is used, the process can be time-consuming.

To call the United States or Canada collect, dial 09, and tell the *operadora* that you want *una llamada por cobrar* (a collect call), *teléfono a teléfono* (station-to-station), or *persona a persona* (person-to-person). Collect calls are the least expensive of all, but sometimes caseta offices won't make them, so you'll have to pay on the spot.

To make a long-distance call from Mexico to another country, from a caseta or Ladatel phone first dial 95 for the United States and Canada, or 98 for anywhere else in the world. Then dial the area code and number you are calling. If you need the international (English-speaking) operator after all, dial 09.

To call long distance (abbreviated "lada") within Mexico, dial 91, the area code, then the number. Mexican area codes (*claves*) are listed in the front of the telephone directories, and in the hotel listings for each area in this book. For Mexico City, it's 5; for Acapulco, 74. (See also beginning paragraph regarding gradual changes in area codes.)

You can save considerably by calling in off-peak periods. The cheapest times to call are daily after 11pm and before 8am, and all day Saturday and Sunday. The most expensive times are Monday through Friday from 8am to 5pm.

Ladatel call stations are at major transportation termini and other public places of importance. These special pay telephones allow you to dial direct long-distance calls to anywhere in Mexico or the world, at reasonable prices. You can use N10- or 100-peso coins or a Ladatel card purchased at many drugstores and restaurants throughout the country.

To use a Ladatel phone, first, have a Ladatel card or a good supply of N10- or 100-peso coins. Next, find out the approximate rate per minute for your call by picking up the handset and punching in the long-distance code (91 for Mexico, 95 for the United States and Canada, 98 for the rest of the world), plus the area or country and city codes for the destination of your call. The charge per minute in pesos will appear on the LCD display. For instance, if you press 95-212, you'll get the charge-per-minute for a call to Manhattan. Once you know the charge per minute, count your coins or tokens, make sure you have as many as you'll need, then dial your number and insert coins. The display will keep you informed of when more coins are needed. Instructions on Ladatel phones are in Spanish, English, and French. Be patient, though; reaching an international telephone operator may take a long time.

Mexico's area codes and numbers are sometimes shorter than North American ones.

To place a call to Mexico from your home country: dial the international service (011), then Mexico's country code (52), then the Mexican area code (for Mexico City it's 5), then the local number. Thus to call the Secretaría de Turismo's information number in Mexico City, you'd dial 011-52-5-250-0123.

Keep in mind that calls to Mexico are quite expensive, even if dialed direct from your home phone. As a rule of thumb, it's usually much cheaper to call Europe or the Middle East than it is to call Mexico.

The telegraph office may be in a different place from the post office in many cities. Telex works out to be much cheaper than long-distance calls, but you must know the telex number you want to call. Many businesses, particularly in the travel industry (travel agents and hotels), have telex numbers.

The effects of reducing long-distance rates while hiking local rates means that hotels have begun to charge for local calls made from hotel-room phones. Until now these calls were free. So far, most of the inexpensive hotels listed in this book do not have the equipment to track calls made from individual rooms and, therefore, telephone-use charges are not added to the room bill. But hotels with more sophisticated telephone systems are charging 35¢ to 50¢ per call. To avoid checkout shock, ask at check-in if local calls are extra.

Time Central standard time prevails throughout most of Mexico. The west-coast states of Sonora, Sinaloa, and parts of Nayarit are on mountain standard time. The state of Baja California Norte is on Pacific standard time, but Baja California Sur is on mountain time.

Note: Beginning in the spring of 1994 Mexico will adopt daylight saving time to save on energy costs.

Tipping Throw out the iron-clad 15% rule right away in budget restaurants south of the border, no matter what other travel literature may say. Do as the locals do: for meals costing under $3, leave the loose change; for meals costing from $4 to $5, leave 6% to 10%, depending on service. Above $5, you're into the 10% to 15% bracket. However, in above-average restaurants and exclusive places, the 15% rule holds. But don't tip on top of the 15% tax. Some of the more crass high-priced restaurants will actually add a 15% "tip" to your bill.

Bellhops and porters will expect about 25¢ to 50¢ per bag. You needn't tip taxi drivers unless they've rendered some special service—carrying bags or trunks.

Tourist Offices See "Information, Entry Requirements, and Money," above, and also specific city chapters.

Villas/Condos Renting a private villa or condominium home for a vacation is a popular vacation alternative. The difference between the two, of course, is that villas are usually freestanding and condos may be part of a large or small complex. Often the villas are true private homes in exclusive neighborhoods and rented out seasonally by their owners. Condominiums, on the other hand, may seem more like a hotel, although the secluded ones feel more exclusive. Either accommodation ordinarily comes with private kitchen and dining area, maid service, and pool. Often a full-time cook, maid, or gardener/chauffeur are on duty. I've seen prices as low as $80 a night to a high of $500. Prices are seasonal with the best deals between May and October. Of course, depending on the number of bedrooms, you can get a group together and share the cost. Four companies specializing in this type of vacation rental are: **Creative Leisure,** 951 Transport Way, Petaluma, CA 94954-1484 (tel. 707/778-1800, toll free 800/426-6367); and **Mexico Condo Reservations,** 5801 Soledad Mountain Rd., La Jolla, CA 92037 (tel. 619/275-4500; toll free 800/262-4500 in the U.S., 800/654-5543 in Canada fax 619/456-1350). All have brochures with photographs of potential properties.

Water Most hotels have decanters or bottles of purified water in the rooms and the better hotels have either purified water from regular taps or special taps marked "Agua Purificada." In the resort areas, hoteliers are beginning to charge for in-room bottled water. Virtually any hotel, restaurant, or bar will bring you purified water if you specifically request it, but you'll usually be charged for it.

CHAPTER 3

GETTING TO KNOW PUERTO VALLARTA

1. ORIENTATION
• DID YOU KNOW...?
2. GETTING AROUND
• FAST FACTS: PUERTO VALLARTA

Puerto Vallarta (pop. 250,000) is gorgeous, with its tropical mountains right beside the sea, its coves and beaches, and its Mexican town of white buildings with red-tiled roofs. Puerto Vallarta's development—mostly on the outskirts of the original town—has lent prosperity without destroying charm.

Once an agricultural village on the Bay of Banderas, far from roads, airports, electricity, and tourism, Puerto Vallarta ceased to be a secret with the making of *Night of the Iguana*. Elizabeth Taylor bought a house in the village, and the growth of a booming resort started with a good highway and a jetport.

1. ORIENTATION

ARRIVING

BY PLANE **Aeromexico** flies from Los Angeles and San Diego as well as Guadalajara, La Paz, León, Mexico City, and Tijuana. **Alaska Airlines** flies from Los Angeles, Seattle, and San Francisco. **American Airlines** has direct flights from Dallas/Fort Worth. **Continental** flies nonstop from Houston. **Delta** flies nonstop from Los Angeles. **Mexicana** has direct or nonstop flights from Chicago, San Antonio, Denver, Los Angeles, and San Francisco, plus Guadalajara, Mazatlán, Los Cabos, and Mexico City. The regional airline **Aero Vallarta** flies to and from Manzanillo November through Easter. **AeroLitoral** flies from San Antonio, McAllen, Harlengen, and Monterrey. Check with a travel agent regarding seasonal charter service.

The airport is close to the north end of town on the main highway, only about six miles from downtown, where most of the budget hotels are located. Upon arriving, take the airport Transportes Terrestres' minivan (*colectivo*) for around $5 for downtown or $7 for the hotel strip, or you can walk a block to the highway and catch a city bus for about 40¢.

BY BUS Getting to Puerto Vallarta from Mexico City, Guadalajara, or points north and south along the coast is not difficult, as it is served by a whole slew of bus lines: Tres Estrellas de Oro (first class), Estrella Blanca (first class), Transportes del

PUERTO VALLARTA: ORIENTATION • 71

? DID YOU KNOW ...?

- To be legally married in Mexico a civil ceremony is required; church ceremonies are optional.
- No monuments honor Hernan Cortés in Mexico.
- The poinsettia is named after Joel Poinsett, first U.S. Minister to Mexico in 1823.
- Elizabeth Taylor wasn't a member of the cast in *Night of the Iguana*, which was filmed in Puerto Vallarta and starred Ava Gardner and Richard Burton.
- Pirates once roamed the waters off the port of San Blas.

Pacífico (first and second class), and Transportes Norte de Sonora (first and second class), and Autotransportes del Cihuatlán (second class).

When you arrive by bus, you'll be south of the river on Madero, Insurgentes, or Constitución streets and close to many of our hotel selections. The locations of the bus "stations" (most are small offices or waiting rooms) of the various lines are as follows: **Autotransportes del Cihuatlán,** Constitución and Madero; **Tres Estrellas de Oro,** Carranza 322; **Transportes Norte de Sonora,** Madero 343, near Insurgentes; **Transportes del Pacífico,** Insurgentes 282; **Estrella Blanca,** Insurgentes 180.

BY CAR From Mazatlán to the north (6 hr.) or Manzanillo to the south (3.5 hr.), the only choice is the coastal highway. From Guadalajara (8 hr.), take Highway 15 towards Tepic, but take the new toll road through Compostela which bypasses Tepic, then Highway 200 south to Puerto Vallarta.

DEPARTING

BY PLANE Airline offices: **Aeromexico,** airport (tel. 4-2777 or 1-1204); **Alaska Airlines,** airport (tel. 1-1350 or 1-1352, toll free 95-800/426-0333 in Mexico); **American Airlines,** airport (tel. 1-1927 or 1-1799); **Continental,** airport (tel. 1-1025 or 1-1096); **Delta,** airport (tel. 1-1919 or 1-1032; toll free 91-800/9-0221 in Mexico); **Mexicana,** Villas, (tel. 2-5000 or 1-1266); **AeroLitoral** (tel. 4-2777).

BY BUS Until the new bus terminal near the airport is completed, riders must make do with finding the "station" (most are small offices or waiting rooms) of their choice south of the river along Madero, Insurgentes, and Constitución streets.

The second-class **Autotransportes del Cihuatlán,** at the corner of Constitución and Madero (tel. 2-3436), has hourly buses to Manzanillo from 5am to 6pm (a 6-hr. trip), and service almost as frequent to Melaque (a 4.5-hr. trip). It also has two buses a day to Guadalajara between 8am and 8pm. Buy your ticket an hour before departure or even a day ahead. Primera class buses leave for Manzanillo at 4:30pm and 11:30pm. This is the best line for Manzanillo and Melaque.

The first-class **Tres Estrellas de Oro,** Carranza 322 (tel. 2-6666), offers 12 buses and four-plus buses daily for the 12-hour trip to Guadalajara, for which you can buy a reserved-seat ticket the day before. It also has **de paso** buses to Culiacán, Mazatlán, and Manzanillo.

Transportes Norte de Sonora, Insurgentes 282 (tel. 2-1015), has first- and second-class service to Tepic, Guadalajara, and Mexico City. The remainder are second-class buses.

Transportes del Pacífico, Insurgentes 282 (tel. 2-1015), has both first- and second-class service to Guadalajara and Mexico City and second-class to Tepic. Its Tepic buses depart every half hour from 5am to 9pm (a 3.5-hr. trip). **Estrella Blanca** (first class), Insurgentes 180 (tel. 2-0613), goes to Tepic (at 10am and 5pm), Irapuato, Mexico City (three buses daily), and Guadalajara (four buses daily). If you are going north, say to Mazatlán, you'll need to change buses in Tepic.

CITY LAYOUT

From the center of old town nearly everything in the central village is within walking distance. The seaside promenade, or *Malecón*, follows the rim of the bay from north to south, and the town stretches back into the hills a half dozen blocks. North of the airport is Nuevo Vallarta. Coming in from the airport, north of town, you'll pass the town pier, the Marina Vallarta development, and many luxury hotels; downtown the malecón is lined with shops and restaurants.

Avenida de las Palmas (formerly called Carretera Aeropuerto or airport highway) is the multilane thoroughfare leading from town to the northern hotel zone and airport. It's been completely repaved and landscaped, transforming the area from unsightly to chic.

NEIGHBORHOODS IN BRIEF

Listed below are the areas of Puerto Vallarta, beginning in the north and moving to the south.

Bucerias A village of cobblestone streets, villas behind walls, and small hotels, is located on the far side of Banderas Bay 11 miles beyond the Puerto Vallarta Airport. **Punta de Mita,** at the northern end of the bay, has always been a daytime beach hangout with palapa-style restaurants. A new resort is now under construction there.

Nuevo Vallarta Nuevo Vallarta, a planned resort community, is just north of Puerto Vallarta, the airport, and Marina Vallarta, across the Ameca River in the state of Nayarit. Besides a few small hotels, condominiums, the Jack Tar Resort Village, and a yacht marina, the new Radisson Paraiso Hotel is open. On either side of it several more as-yet unnamed highrise hotels are nearing completion. There is no public transportation to the area and taxis to and from Puerto Vallarta are expensive; most hotels in Nuevo Vallarta are all-inclusive.

Marina Vallarta Marina Vallarta, a resort-city-within-a-city, is at the northern edge of the hotel zone not far from the airport. It boasts a half dozen luxury hotels and condominium projects, a huge marina with 400 yacht slips, a golf course, restaurants and bars, an office park, and a shopping plaza.

Hotel Zone North of old town to the airport many luxury hotels, such as the Krystal, Sheraton, and Fiesta Americana, line a strip of beach.

North of the Río Cuale/old town The area north of the Río Cuale is the oldest part of town—the original Puerto Vallarta. The waterfront is lined with shops and restaurants and the town plaza and church are here.

Río Cuale The Cuale river divides north town from south town. In the middle of the river is an island now built up with numerous restaurants and shops.

South of the Río Cuale The area south of the river used to be only beach, but in the last decade it has become as built up as the old town. Today the best budget lodgings are here, as well as the bus "stations."

Mismaloya Beach About six miles south of town lies Mismaloya Beach (where *Night of the Iguana* was filmed), the Jolla de Mismaloya Resort & Spa, and, just beyond, Boca de Tomatlán, which marks the farthest development to the south. Between it and downtown are more five-star hotels on the beach and mountainside.

2. GETTING AROUND

BY BUS City buses run from the airport through the expensive hotel zone along 31 de Mayo (the waterfront street), across the Río Cuale and inland on Vallarta, looping

IMPRESSIONS

The west coast beach towns Puerto Vallarta and San Blas, once completely isolated, are now booming. Every tourist tells the next one that these places are the real Mexico, off the beaten track, tranquil, and despite a certain squalidity, also delightful. And tourists are already beginning to go there by the hundreds. Within four or five years we will probably have half a dozen rivals for Acapulco, which, with the present great influx of North Americans, has practically ceased to be a Mexican town.
—John A. Crow, Mexico Today, 1957

At the present moment the only way to reach Puerto Vallarta is by plane. . . . Although a road is sketched upon maps, only some ungainly open-air, high-wheeled buses make the trip. It takes them about 2 days [from Guadalajara] to make the 200 mile trip."
—James Norman, Terry's Guide to Mexico, 1965

---

back through the downtown hotel and restaurant districts, on Insurgentes and several other downtown streets. These will serve just about all of your transportation needs; they run frequently and are cheap—about 50¢ a ride. Buses run generally from 6am to 11pm. The No. 02 minivan (*colectivo*) bus goes south every 10 to 15 minutes to Mismaloya Beach from Plaza Lázaro Cárdenas, a few blocks south of the river at Cárdenas and Suárez. Check with the driver to make sure this is your bus—another No. 02 goes farther to Boca de Tomatlán (a fishing village) and may not stop at Mismaloya. To get to the northern hotel strip from old Puerto Vallarta, take the "Pitillal" or "Aeropuerto" bus.

BY BOAT The town pier (*muelle*), where you'll catch pleasure boats to Yelapa and for fishing excursions, is north of town near the airport and a convenient, inexpensive bus ride from town. Just take any bus marked "Pitillal" and tell the driver to let you off at the muelle. Do not confuse the town pier with the new pier south of the river at Playa Olas Altas.

BY TAXI They cost $5 for most trips downtown from the hotel strip, $15 to or from Mismaloya Beach to the south. But with such good bus service there's little reason to use them.

FAST FACTS

American Express The office is located in the Villa Vallarta shopping center on the main highway to the airport (Av. las Palmas, km 2.5), north of downtown (tel. 4-6876 or 4-6877, toll free 91-800/0-0555).

Area Code The area code is 322.

Climate Hot and humid; rain most afternoons June through August.

Consulates The U.S. Consular Agency is at Miramar and Libertad on the second floor of Parián del Puente 12A, just north of the river bridge near the market (tel. 322/2-0069, 24 hours a day for emergencies). Open Monday through Friday from 9am to 1pm.

Holidays See "Special Events" in Chapter 5; also see "When to Go" in Chapter 2.

Information The State Tourism Office, Juárez and Independencia (tel. 322/2-0242, 2-0244, or 3-0744; fax 322/2-0243), is in a corner of the white Presidencia Municipal building near the main square. This is also the office of the

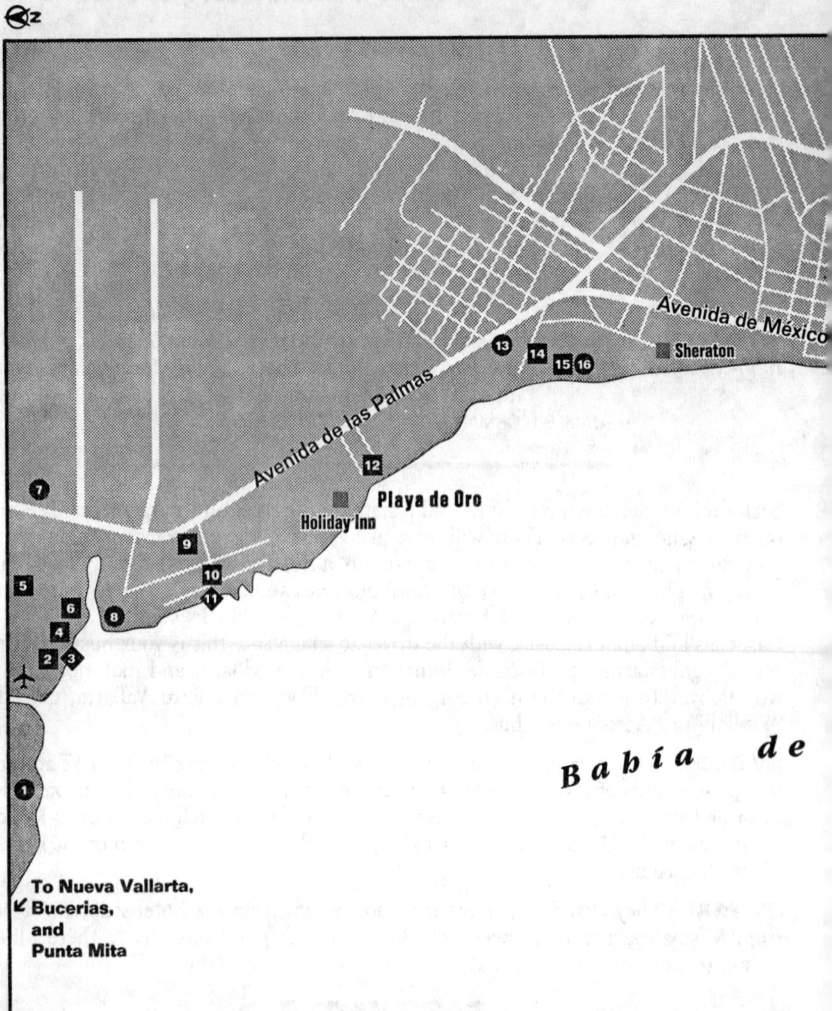

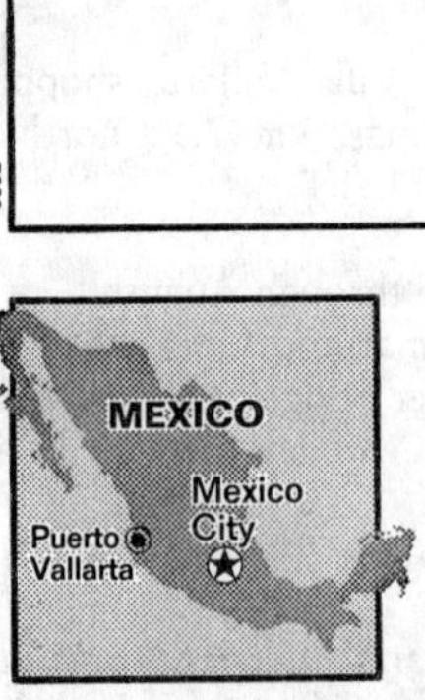

Avenida de México
Sheraton
Avenida de las Palmas
Playa de Oro
Holiday Inn
Bahía de
To Nueva Vallarta, Bucerias, and Punta Mita
5992

MEXICO
Mexico City
Puerto Vallarta

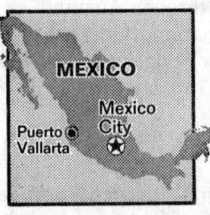

ACCOMMODATIONS:

Belaire Resort Puerto Vallarta 5
Camino Real 20
Continental Plaza Vallarta Tennis & Beach Resort 15
Fiesta Americana Puerto Vallarta 12
Hacienda Buenaventura 9
Hotel Buenaventura 17
Hyatt Coral Grand 21
La Jolla de Mismaloya 22
Krystal Vallarta 10
Marriott Casamagna 2
Melia Puerto Vallarta 6
Plaza Las Glorias Puerto Vallarta 14
Velas Vallarta Grand Suite Resort 4

PUERTO VALLARTA AREA

DINING:
Bogart's ⑪
Chico's Paradise ㉓
Mikado ③
El Set ⑲

ATTRACTIONS:
Bullring ⑦
Cruise Pier ⑧
John Newcomb Tennis Center ⑯
Nuevo Vallarta ①
Villa Vallarta Center ⑬
Zócalo ⑱

"tourist police" who hear tourist complaints. Open Monday through Friday from 9am to 9pm, Saturday from 9am to 1pm.

Important note: Beware of "tourist information" booths along the street—they are usually time-share hawkers offering "free" or cheap Jeep rentals, cruises, breakfasts, etc., as bait. If you are suckered in, you may or may not get what is offered and the experience will cost at *least* half a day of your vacation.

Laundry Lavandería Nelly on Guerrero near Matamoros will wash and dry a load of clothes for about $4. Open Monday through Friday from 9am to 1:30pm and 4 to 8pm, Saturday from 9am to 1:30pm.

Telephone See "Fast Facts: Mexico" in Chapter 2.

CHAPTER 4

WHERE TO STAY & DINE IN PUERTO VALLARTA

1. **WHERE TO STAY**
- **FROMMER'S SMART TRAVELER: HOTELS**
2. **WHERE TO DINE**
- **FROMMER'S SMART TRAVELER: RESTAURANTS**

The hotel and restaurant listings in this chapter begin in Nuevo Vallarta eight miles north of the airport and Puerto Vallarta's developed area and end past downtown at Mismaloya, the farthest development south.

1. WHERE TO STAY

NUEVO VALLARTA

Not part of Puerto Vallarta proper (it's in the state of Nayarit), Nuevo Vallarta is nevertheless an extension of the resort. For years a slightly isolated area with a few small hotels and the all-inclusive Jack Tar Resort Village, Nueva Vallarta now features a nearly completed string of new highrise hotels (including the all-inclusive Hotel Sierra Radisson); the all-inclusive Radisson Paraiso Nuevo Vallarta is already open. Public buses go only as far as the highway entrance to the development, where taxis wait for transportation the mile or more farther into the resort. Taxis charge $8 one-way to or from Nuevo Vallarta to old Puerto Vallarta. Because of transportation difficulties and the distance from Puerto Vallarta, the trend here seems to be towards all-inclusive hotels (meals and activities are included in one price). For now at least (until public transportation improves) Nuevo Vallarta might be best for those who've been to Puerto Vallarta several times and don't mind staying in one place. First-time visitors may prefer staying somewhere with easier access to town.

RADISSON PARAISO NUEVO VALLARTA, Paseo de los Cocoteros 18, Fracc. Náutico, Nuevo Vallarta, Nay. 63732. Tel. 322/7-0400, toll free 800/333-3333 in the U.S. Fax 322/7-0082. 293 rms. TV TEL

$ Rates (including all meals and tips): $150 single; $180 double; children extra. Ask about substantial summer discounts. **Parking:** Free.

Grand and spacious, this hotel is all an upscale, self-contained resort is supposed to be—spread out enough to be quiet, yet offering a complete and relaxing vacation all in one spot. The beautifully furnished, nice size rooms all have gray marble floors, ocean views, remote-control TV, and card-activated door locks. The public areas are brightened here and there by Mexican-style yellow and hot pink decoration. Sixty-five rooms on the fifth floor are reserved for nonsmokers and there are two rooms equipped for the disabled. Some rooms have balconies and hairdryers.

Dining/Entertainment: There are two restaurants, a beachside snack bar, and nightly disco and entertainment in the lobby bar plus theme nights and free drinks including soft drinks, domestic wines, beers, and cocktails. A full schedule of activities and equipment include a daily fitness walk, aerobics, tennis and snorkeling classes, bike tours, windsurfing, kayaks, pedal boats, and table games. Specialty restaurant dining and motorized water vehicles are extra as is golf at nearby courses.

Services: Travel agency, boutique, gift shop.

Facilities: Pool, two tennis courts lit for night play, beach, horses, table games, kayaks, pedal boats, bicycles, snorkeling equipment, tennis rackets.

MARINA VALLARTA

The Marina Vallarta is the northern extension of the "Hotel Zone" and is located just before the airport. The hotels below are built around the new 400-slip marina and 18-hole golf course designed by Joe Finger. All except the Quinta Real are on the beach.

BELAIRE RESORT PUERTO VALLARTA, Pelicanos 311, Marina Vallarta, Puerto Vallarta, Jal. 48300. Tel. 322/1-0800, toll free 800/648-4097 in the U.S. and Canada, 91-800/3-2832 in Mexico. Fax 322/1-0801. 67 suites and villas. A/C TV TEL

$ **Rates:** High season $140–$160 junior suite single or double; $160–$240 master suite single or double; $180–$250 grande classe; $280–$400 villa; $1,380 presidential suite.

This stylish inn is located in the heart of the Marina Vallarta development squarely between the first and 18th holes of the golf course. Few Mexican hotels can claim such masterful use of elegant Mexican furniture—many of the gorgeous pieces are replicas of furniture found in the Museo Alfenique in Puebla—a kind of Mexican Chippendale. The suites combine those designs with sculpted faces prepared especially for the hotel by the renowned Mexican sculptor Sergio Bustamante. Spacious junior suites all have balconies (some have two). Master suites all have balconies with bubbling whirlpools overlooking the golf course. Grande-classe suites have a balcony, whirlpool bath for two, and living-room area. The two-story villas have small bar areas, living rooms, dining rooms, and from one to three bedrooms and private pools.

Dining/Entertainment: The multilevel Gourmet Restaurant overlooks the golf course and pool through a wide expanse of windows and is open from 7am to 11pm. Live harp or piano music accompanies all meals. Another restaurant/bar by the pool serves snacks during the day. The lobby bar features live nightly entertainment.

Services: Laundry, room service, car rental, travel agency. Grande classe guests receive champagne and fresh juice on arrival, have separate check-in and access to the hotel's fax and secretarial services.

Facilities: Large gorgeous pool facing the golf course; 2 tennis courts, 46 private pools. A fully staffed private beach club will open in 1994 with a restaurant and water sports.

MARRIOTT CASAMAGNA, Marina Vallarta, Puerto Vallarta, Jal. Tel. 322/1-0004, toll free 800/228-9290 in the U.S. 433 rms and suites (all with bath). A/C TV TEL MINIBAR

$ Rates: High season $190 single or double sunset view; $156 single or double ocean view; $330–$480 suite.

You're first impressed with the splendid openness of this grand hotel which debuted in 1990; the enormous lobby soars and baronial hallways lead to the rooms and beach; from the lobby to the beach you cross a small artificial pond. The sound of fountains is ever present throughout the hotel. Rooms are accented in pale sienna and pale ocher and all have ocean views and balconies, hairdryers, ironing boards and irons, and in-room safety-deposit boxes. Rooms with king-size beds have a couch; those with two double beds have an easy chair and game table.

Dining/Entertainment: Mikado, the Japanese restaurant, is open for dinner; La Estancia, is open for all three meals; and Las Casitas, a poolside restaurant, is open for breakfast and lunch.

Services: Laundry, room service, travel agency, car rental, beauty salon, barber shop, gift shop, summer children's program (ages 5 to 12) at extra cost, 14 security cameras.

Facilities: Huge oceanside pool, coed gym, five tennis courts (three lighted for night play), volleyball court.

MELIA PUERTO VALLARTA, Marina Vallarta, Puerto Vallarta, Jal. 48300. Tel. 322/1-0200, toll free 800/336-3542 in the U.S. 392 rms. A/C TV TEL MINIBAR

$ Rates: High season $145 single or double.

The grand and spacious Melia Puerto Vallarta boasts a dove-shaped swimming pool that's the largest in the city, a vast stretch of beach, and a football field-size entrance courtyard illuminated by 49 tower skylights. The nine-story hotel was designed by the architect of the Barcelona Olympics facilities, and it's so high-tech that it looks more like an industrial complex than a resort hotel. However, the lushly landscaped

---

 FROMMER'S SMART TRAVELER: HOTELS

1. Purchasing a package which includes either hotel alone or airfare usually saves considerable money.
2. Never pay the public rate without first investigating package deals from your home country before arrival in Puerto Vallarta.
3. Consider travel time to and from Puerto Vallarta before purchasing a two- or three-day package (you could spend half your time traveling).
4. Most of the bargain hotels are in town, south of the Río Cuale.
5. More expensive hotels are in the Hotel Zone, Marina Vallarta, and south to Mismaloya.
6. Travel during May, August, and September through November—the slowest months of the off-season (post-Easter to mid-December). Always ask about discounted rates or special packages in those months.
7. Prices go up anywhere from 25% to 50% from mid-December through Easter week, when all the best rooms are generally booked.
8. It's best to have reservations in high season, but if you don't, arrive early in the day and start your search. If you are told that the rooms are full, ask if you can leave your name and return at checkout time to see if anyone has vacated.

grounds, with clusters of flower beds and wide brick walkways, soften the ultra-modern feeling. Guest rooms have a luxurious feel to them, and feature diagonal views of the marina or bay, private terraces, and bedside lighting control, as well as marble floors, wood and wicker furnishings, and brass accents. Each comes with remote-control TV, shower and tub combination, and hairdryers. Forty rooms are reserved as nonsmoking and five are handicap-equipped.

Dining/Entertainment: The hotel's formal restaurant, Los Vitrales, specializes in haute cuisine and grilled seafood. It's open from 6 to 11pm. The Quetzal Café, a coffee shop, is open from 7am to midnight. The beachfront restaurant, El Patio, serves sandwiches and drinks during pool hours. A daily list of activities is posted in the lobby and includes water aerobics, aquatic polo, basketball and volleyball, backgammon and bingo, and supervised activities for children. One of the two lounges has nightly entertainment.

Services: Laundry, room service, in-room safety-deposit boxes, travel agency, car rentals, shopping arcade.

Facilities: One large pool, two tennis courts, table tennis.

VELAS VALLARTA GRAND SUITE RESORT, Marina Vallarta, Puerto Vallarta, Jal. 48300. **Tel.** 322/1-0091, toll free 800/659-8477 in the U.S. and Canada. Fax 322/1-0751 or 1-0755. 361 suites. A/C TV TEL

$ Rates: High season $173 single; $310 double. **Parking:** Free.

This large, sprawling all-suite hotel is set on 10 beachfront acres built in a U shape with three two-story wings of one- and two-bedroom suites and a central area with a lobby, restaurants, bar, and shops. A colonnaded arcade separates the lobby from the lushly landscaped pool area which meanders with waterfalls and has plenty of lounging areas. Though all the spacious units are privately owned, approximately half are used for hotel purposes (the upper three floors). All have ocean views, marble floors, large living rooms, and full kitchens with coffee makers, microwaves, and blenders—the works. The large bedrooms open onto terraces running the width of the suite. Two-bedroom suites have two bathrooms, a dining table for eight, a set of doors leading to the terrace, and a small empty room ideal for a child's bedroom. All are decorated with rattan furniture in light tones and pastel fabrics.

Dining/Entertainment: The restaurant Andrea is open from 7am to 10:30pm and serves international cuisine featuring Italian cuisine. The palapa-covered Beach Club by the pool serves sandwiches and crêpes from 7am to 11pm, and La Ribera by the beach is open from 9am to 5pm. During high season there are special children's activities.

Services: Laundry, room service, travel agency, babysitting, concierge, beauty shop, car rental.

IMPRESSIONS

There are a number of apartments for rent in town [Puerto Vallarta]. They range in price from $125 to $150 per month, including maid, utilities, etc.
—JAMES NORMAN, *TERRY'S GUIDE TO MEXICO*, 1965

It becomes a virtue, almost a necessity, to do some loafing. The art of leisure is therefore one of Mexico's most stubbornly defended practises [sic] and one of her subtle appeals; a lesson in civilization which we of the hectic north need very badly to learn.
—ANITA BRENNER, *YOUR MEXICAN HOLIDAY*, 1932.

Facilities: Three interconnected swimming pools and children's pool, four tennis courts (three lighted) with tennis pro on duty, video game room, indoor and outdoor parking.

HOTEL ZONE

The main street from town and fronting the hotel zone has recently been renamed Paseo de las Palmas but locals may still refer to it as Avenida de las Garzas, or the airport road—a handy piece of information to keep in mind when reading or hearing addresses.

CONTINENTAL PLAZA VALLARTA TENNIS & BEACH RESORT, Av. de las Palmas (km 2.5 airport highway), Puerto Vallarta, Jal. 48300. Tel. 322/40123, toll free 800/882-6684 in the U.S. and Canada. Fax 322/4-5236. 438 rms and suites. A/C TV TEL MINIBAR

$ Rates: High season $162 single or double. **Parking:** Free.

An airy atrium lobby surrounded by two-story stucco arches is the centerpiece of the Mediterranean village style of this five-story beachfront hotel. Its pastel wings frame a huge courtyard with a large free-form pool facing the beach. The medium-size rooms are decorated with florals and attractive cane and wood furniture. There are marble-trimmed baths and counters (with shower and tub), purified tap water, and private balconies. Rooms have ocean, pool, or garden views. It's conveniently located within the Plaza Vallarta shopping area, with shops and restaurants a short stroll away.

Dining/Entertainment: The elegant La Parilla, open from 6:30 to 11:30pm, features French cuisine and live piano music. Condesa del Mar, the coffee shop, features Mexican and international favorites and is open from 6:30am to 11:30pm. Los Cantaros serves steaks, chicken, and fish prepared to guest specifications and is open from 6:30 to 11pm. Los Peces, the oceanside restaurant, serves seafood either on the terrace or at the swimup bar from noon to 5pm. In the evening the lobby bar has live music for dancing.

Services: Laundry, room service, business center, beauty shop, travel agency, shopping arcade, tennis shop, concierge, babysitting.

Facilities: John Newcombe Tennis Club with four lighted indoor courts and four outdoor clay courts (see Chapter 5 "What to See and Do" below), large pool, sauna, massage by appointment, tennis pro on duty.

FIESTA AMERICANA PUERTO VALLARTA, Av. de las Palmas s/n, Puerto Vallarta, Jal. 48300. Tel. 322/2-2010, toll free 800/223-2332 in the U.S. 363 rms and suites. A/C TV TEL MINIBAR

$ Rates: High season $195–$216 single or double superior or deluxe room. **Parking:** Free.

The Fiesta Americana's enormous thatched palapa lobby is a landmark along hotel row and is equally impressive once you enter the spacious lobby. With lots of plants, splashing fountains, breezes, and sitting areas, the lobby sets a casual South Seas tone. The nine-story building embraces a large plaza with pool facing the beach. Marble-trimmed rooms in neutral tones with pastel accents come with pretty, carved headboards and comfortable furniture. All have private balconies with sea views.

Dining/Entertainment: Chula Vista is open from breakfast through dinner, La Pergola is open from 7am to 11pm; and El Morocco is open for fine dining from 7pm to midnight. There's live music nightly in the lobby bar. Friday López is the popular disco, open from 10:30pm to 3am.

Services: Laundry, room service, travel agency, beauty shop, in-room hairdryers.

82 • WHERE TO STAY & DINE IN PUERTO VALLARTA

Facilities: Pool, six tennis courts, tennis privileges at the Fiesta Americana Plaza Vallarta, health club with sauna and massages.

KRYSTAL VALLARTA, Av. de las Palmas s/n, Puerto Vallarta, Jal. 48300. Tel. 322/2-1041, toll free 800/231-9860 in the U.S. and Canada. Fax 322/4-0150 or 4-222. 359 rms, suites, and villas. A/C TV TEL MINIBAR

$ Rates: High season $180 deluxe room and villa single or double; $210 junior suite single or double; $325–$460 master suite.

Built to resemble a Mexican village with cobblestone streets, this completely self-contained resort oasis is spread out over 37 plant- and fountain-filled acres with a prime beachfront location. Interwoven in this setting are the accommodations in one- and two-story buildings. Although the resort is large, there is still a sense of seclusion, with many shaded interior walkways linking the various pool areas and restaurants. In fact, with seven restaurants and numerous bars, you can dine and drink without ever leaving the place, should that be your choice. All the guest rooms were completely refurnished and renewed in 1991. The four varieties of accommodations include 38 three-bedroom villas with private pools, 22 suites with spacious living rooms, 48 junior suites, and 251 deluxe rooms. Trios of villas share a private pool; large suites come with refrigerators. All come with tile floors, area rugs, tasteful loomed bedspreads, balconies or patios, and in-room security boxes. Electric carts take guests to and from their rooms, for, depending on where your room is, it can be a long walk within the grounds. The hotel is not far from the main pier and airport.

Dining/Entertainment: Seven restaurants are open daily including: Bogart's, one of the finest restaurants in Puerto Vallarta, open from 6pm to midnight; Kamakura, an excellent Japanese restaurant, open from 5pm to midnight; Tango, featuring specialties from Argentina, open from 6pm to midnight; El Palmara, open for buffet breakfast from 8 to 11am; Rarotonga, seafood restaurant by the pool, open from 1 to 5pm; and La Noria coffee shop, open from 7am to midnight. Among the six bars, the lobby bar has live music nightly. For evening entertainment there's Christine's disco, open from 10:30pm to 3am; Le Café in the lobby for special coffees, tea, and pastries, Fiesta Brava, is held Thursday in winter, and guests are seated for a Mexican dinner at tables overlooking a bullring where the show is held.

Services: Laundry, room service, travel agency, shops, babysitting with 12 hours' advance notice, wedding arrangements with advance notice, car rental.

Facilities: Olympic-size pool, 2 free-form pools, 38 private pools, 2 tennis courts, racquetball court.

PLAZA LAS GLORIAS PUERTO VALLARTA, Av. de las Palmas s/n, Puerto Vallarta, Jal. 48300. Tel. 322/4-4444, toll free 800/342-2644 in the U.S. Fax 322/2-2465. 389 rms, suites, and villas. A/C TV TEL MINIBAR

$ Rates: High season $102 single or double. **Parking:** Free.

Designed in a contemporary style with white stucco, terra-cotta tile, and handcrafted Mexican touches, this four-story hotel is arranged around a palm-shaded pool area facing the sea. A huge palapa bar/restaurant is next to the pool and individual shade palapas line its beach. The standard rooms are small to medium size, with cool marble floors, ivory walls, blond rattan furniture, and usually balconies. The 140 villas include kitchenettes. It's adjacent to the Plaza Vallarta shopping center, which has 100 shops.

Dining/Entertainment: Las Pergolas offers international cuisine from 7:30 to 11:30am and 6 to 11pm; La Terraza, the poolside restaurant, serves snacks from 1 to 5pm. Of the three bars, the pool often features live music from 7 to 11pm.

Services: Laundry, room service, travel agency, car rental, shops, concierge, babysitting.

Facilities: Two pools, sauna, massage by appointment, tennis privileges at the nearby Continental Plaza Vallarta.

NORTH OF THE RÍO CUALE

This is the real center of town, where the market, principal plazas, church, and town hall all lie. Budget lodgings are scarce here, although most of the hotels are moderately priced.

MODERATE

HACIENDA BUENAVENTURA, Paseo de la Palma, Apdo. Postal 95-B, Puerto Vallarta, Jal. 48310. Tel. 322/4-6667. Fax 322/4-6400. 155 rms (all with bath). A/C TEL

$ Rates: High season $45–$57 single; $57–$69 double. Low season $29–$37 single; $36–$44 double. (In low season ask about a free fourth night).

You can stay right on the hotel strip and skip the high prices at this congenial hotel, which offers a real Mexican colonial atmosphere, inside and out. Hacienda-style rooms have soft colors on stucco walls, alcove-type windows, and are built around tropical gardens that include a functioning aqueduct. The far end of the gigantic pool encircles a large palapa-roofed swim-up bar and the other end fronts the restaurant La Cascada. Although the Hacienda has no beachfront of its own, guests are provided passes for use of the facilities next door at the luxury Krystal Vallarta.

HOTEL BUENAVENTURA, Av. Mexico 1301, Puerto Vallarta, Jal. 48350. Tel. 322/2-3737, toll free 800/223-6764 in the U.S. 210 rms. A/C TEL

$ Rates: High season $70 single; $93 double. Low season $45 single; $52 double.

★ The giant wood roof of the hotel lobby and restaurant set the tone for the breezy, jungle-lush interior filled with *equipales* leather furniture. Somewhat off the beaten tourist track, the Buenaventura holds its place in the market with appealing prices, comfort, and its beautiful beachfront. The attractive rooms have beam-and-brick ceilings and tiled floors, and some have balconies. There's also a swimming pool next to the beach. Only fourth-floor rooms have color TV with U.S. channels and these rooms cost $6 extra. It's on the beach about six blocks north of the malecón between Nicaragua and San Salvador.

BUDGET

LOS CUATRO VIENTOS, Matamoros 520, Puerto Vallarta, Jal. 48350. Tel. 322/2-0161. 13 rms. FAN

$ Rates (including continental breakfast): $35 single or double; low-season discounts.

A quiet secluded cozy inn set on a hillside overlooking Banderas Bay, Los Cuatro Vientos's rooms are built around a small central patio and swimming pool. Access is up a flight of stairs to the second-floor patio, pool, and the Chez Elena restaurant (see "Where to Dine" below), which is open in the evenings. Each of the cheerful and spotless rooms has a small tiled bathroom, brick ceiling, red tile floor, glass louvered windows facing outdoors, and its own unique color scheme. All are decorated with simple Mexican furnishings and accented with local crafts. There's a rooftop deck for sunning and a pool on the patio level. Continental breakfast is served on the terrace for guests only from 8 to 10:30am. The friendly owner, Gloria Whiting, is from Los Angeles and is usually around to attend guests personally. It's located on a hill above the central part of town at the corner of Matamoros and Corona.

HOTEL ENCINO, Juárez 122, Puerto Vallarta, Jal. 48380. **Tel. 322/2-0280** or 2-0406. Fax 322/2-2573. 75 rms. A/C TEL
$ Rates: High season $32 single; $48 double. Low season $30 single; $36 double; $52–$64 suite for up to five people.

$ The hotel's spotless rooms are cheerfully decorated with turquoise-blue furniture and other bright touches, white walls, and tiled floors. Most have their own private balconies with sliding glass doors and views of the ocean, river, or mountains and town. Rooms also come with radios. Especially nice are the rooftop swimming pool and the restaurant/bar, Vista Cuale, which enjoy lovely vistas of mountains and sea. The four-story hotel, however, has no elevator. To find it head south on Juárez to the place where Vallarta crosses the river; it's next to the bridge.

SOUTH OF THE RÍO CUALE

MODERATE

CASA CORAZON, 326 Amapas (Apdo. Postal 66), Puerto Vallarta, Jal. 48380. **Tel. 322/2-1371** at the restaurant. 12 rms (all with bath). FAN
$ Rates (including breakfast): High season $45–$70 single or double; low season inquire about lower rates. *Note:* No children under 12.

Perched on a hill beside the beach Playa del Sol, this four-story villa has been converted by its American owners into a delightful bed-and-breakfast inn. It prides itself on its friendly, casual atmosphere, where guests get together over the complete breakfast served on the expansive terrace. The front gate opens onto the beach, where the inn has a bar and restaurant.

To get there, walk 10 blocks south of the river on Vallarta, turn right onto Pilita for an uphill walk of three blocks, then left for ½ block on Amapas. For reservations write to P.O. Box 937, Las Cruces, NM 88004 (tel. *505/523-4666* or *522-4684*).

HOTEL FONTANA DEL MAR, Dieguez 171, Puerto Vallarta, Jal. 48380. **Tel. 322/2-0583** or 2-0712, toll free 800/458-6888 in the U.S. 27 rms, 15 suites (all with bath). A/C TV TEL
$ Rates: High season $46 single; $55 double. Low season $30 single; $35 double.

One of the best budget hotels in the area is on a quiet side street in downtown Vallarta, only two blocks from the beach, Playa del Sol. The inviting decor includes curly white iron and royal blue. The clean, comfortable rooms overlook the plant-filled courtyard with more frilly iron trim. Rooms have showers or bathtubs, and the suites come with balconies or kitchenettes. Guests can use the small rooftop swimming pool or the pool and beach-club facilities at the Hotel Playa Los Arcos a block away.

HOTEL MOLINO DE AGUA, Vallarta 130 (Apdo. Postal 54), Puerto Vallarta, Jal. 48380. **Tel. 322/2-1907** or 2-1957, toll free 800/423-5512 in California, 800/826-9408 elsewhere in the U.S. Fax 322/2-6056. 20 rms, 16 suites, 29 cabins. A/C
$ Rates: High season $60–$95; low season $40–$80. **Parking:** Free.

This complex of luxury cabins and small buildings, reached by winding walkways, is

PUERTO VALLARTA: WHERE TO STAY • 85

nestled into lush tropical gardens beside the river and sea. Although on a main street and centrally located, with all its big trees and open space it's a completely tranquil oasis. Some units are individual bungalows with private patios and there's a small three-story building near the beach. Amenities include a Jacuzzi beside the pool and an excellent restaurant/bar, the Aquarena, and its off-shoot, The Lion's Court, in the garden. Parking is protected. It's ½ block south of the river on Vallarta.

PLAYA LOS ARCOS, Olas Altas 390, Puerto Vallarta, Jal. 48380. Tel. 322/2-1583, toll free 800/648-2403 in the U.S. Fax 322/2-0583. 135 rms, 10 suites. A/C TEL

$ Rates: Dec 18–Easter $65–$80 single; $75–$90 double; $109–$125 suite. Ask about further discounts in June and Sept–Oct.

Conveniently located downtown, this popular four-story hotel is shaped like a U facing the beach, with a swimming pool in the courtyard. Rooms with private balconies overlook the pool, while the 10 suites have ocean views and kitchenettes. The standard rooms are small but pleasantly decorated with pink floral spreads and carved wooden furniture painted pale pink—two double beds, a dresser, a table, and two chairs. On the premises there are tennis courts, a restaurant, coffee shop, and beachside bar with occasional live entertainment. It's seven blocks south of the river.

To find it, walk five blocks south of the river on Vallarta, then right on Badillo two blocks, then left on Olas Atlas.

BUDGET

HOTEL MARSOL, Rodriguez 103 (Apdo. Postal 4), Puerto Vallarta, Jal. 48380. Tel. 332/2-1365 or 2-0865. 138 rms, 22 apartments. A/C (22 apartments) FAN

$ Rates: $38 single; $48 double; $66 apartment for one or two.

Right on Playa del Sol beach, this large, airy hotel has nothing but a row of coconut palms and a retaining wall between its veranda and the beach, while oceanside restaurants are a mere 50 yards away. The apartments have balconies facing the sea and screened windows. The other rooms face the mountains and town. There's also a pool.

To get there walk seven blocks south of the river on Vallarta, then right on Rodriguez to the beach.

HOTEL POSADA DE ROGER, Badillo 237, Puerto Vallarta, Jal. 48380. Tel. 322/2-0836 or 2-0639. 52 rms. A/C (24 rms) FAN TEL

$ Rates: $25 single; $30 double.

This former pension is now a hotel with simple but homey, comfortable, and spotless rooms at a good price. Guests enjoy the small, second-floor swimming pool and choose from several levels of terraces with tropical plants and bougainvillea. The hotel has retained its friendly ambience, and guests still gather in the attractive courtyard for conversation and entertainment. The hotel's restaurant/bar, El Tucán, is downstairs.

To get here walk five blocks south of the river on Vallarta, then right on Badillo ½ block.

POSADA RIO CUALE, Serdan 242 (Apdo. Postal 146), Puerto Vallarta, Jal. 48380. Tel. 322/2-0450 or 2-0914. 21 rms. A/C

$ Rates: High season $48 single; $55 double. Low season $25 single; $30 double. This delightful two-story hotel occupies one of the town's busiest intersections. Its large rooms have arched brick windows and wooden shutters; the quietest are away from Calle Vallarta. At night the swimming pool becomes a lighted fountain, and the courtyard around it is part of the popular Restaurant Gourmet, which has mariachi music on Friday, Saturday, and Sunday nights from 8 to 10:30pm. Park in front on the street.

Walk one block south of the river at Serdan and Vallarta.

SOUTH TO MISMALOYA

EXPENSIVE

CAMINO REAL, Hwy. 200 south to Mismaloya, km 3.2. Tel. 322/2-0002, toll free 800/228-3000 through Westin Hotels in the U.S. and Canada. 337 rms and suites (all with bath). A/C TV TEL MINIBAR

$ Rates: $175–$216 single or double main building; $240–$290 single or double Royal Beach Club; $480 Fiesta Suite.

Not so long ago the Camino Real was the most remote hotel or establishment of any kind, 2½ miles south of town. Though it has neighbors now, on down the highway, it's still set apart with a lush mountain backdrop and retains that exclusivity that made it popular from the beginning. The hotel is actually two buildings: the 250-room main hotel curving gently with the shape of the Playa Las Estacas (beach), and the new 11-story, 87-room Royal Beach Club, also on the beach. Rooms in the main building are large, some with sliding doors facing the bay, and others with balconies. Royal Beach Club rooms from the sixth floor up have balconies with whirlpool spas. The top floor is divided among six two-bedroom Fiesta Suites with whirlpool spas on the balcony, and each has a private swimming pool. All rooms are accented with the vibrant colors of Mexico and come with hairdryers, remote-control TV (with U.S. channels), and in-room safe-deposit boxes. Royal Beach Club rooms have robes besides other amenities mentioned below.

Dining/Entertainment: Restaurants, all open daily include: La Perla, open from 7pm to midnight, features nouvelle-French cuisine; Azulejos, on a patio terrace by the beach, is open from 7am to midnight; La Brisa, on the north end of the beach, open from 11am to 6pm, serves seafood specialties; and the Snack Shack near the pool serves drinks and sandwiches from 11am to 6pm. The lobby bar, with a view of the bay, opens from 5pm to 1am with live bands each evening and dancing on weekends.

Services: Laundry; room service; travel agency; car rental; children's program December, June, July, and August.

Facilities: Two swimming pools; two lighted tennis courts; health club with weights, sauna, steam room, and weekday aerobic classes; boutiques, and convenience store. Royal Beach Club guests enjoy separate check-in and concierge, daily complimentary continental breakfast, and evening cocktails and hors d'oeuvres.

HYATT CORAL GRAND, Hwy. 200, km 8.5 (Apdo. Postal 448), Puerto Vallarta, Jal. 48300. Tel. 322/3-0707 or 2-5191, toll free 800/233-1234. 120 suites. A/C TV TEL MINIBAR

$ Rates: $145–$190 superior single or double; $155–$200 deluxe; $175–$245 club; $385–$495 master suite; $635–$880 presidential suite.

On a beautiful beach five miles south of town, this 10-story white hotel has window boxes spilling over with vines and bougainvillea. The open-air lobby is accessed from a bridge that connects it to the street four stories above the beach. There's a serene, intimate ambience here, with spacious suites done in white with pastel accents, tasteful art, comfortable furniture, and queen or double beds. Each suite has a living room with a couch that makes into a bed, and small balconies provide a view of the ocean. Deluxe suites have whirlpool baths, king-size beds, and robes. Master suites have two bedrooms and a whirlpool. The presidential suite has gorgeous hardwood floors, an indoor tile swimming pool with adjacent whirlpool, a waterfall, a steam room, fireplace, dining area, and huge bar. There are two handicap-equipped rooms on the first floor and wheelchair access to the pool.

Dining/Entertainment: El Coral, the gourmet restaurant open 6pm to midnight, serves international cuisine by candlelight. The Colibri restaurant, open 7am to 6pm, specializes in seafood. The swim-up Oyster Bar faces the ocean and is open for lunch only. La Cascada, the poolside bar, is open daylight hours and the lobby bar opens at 5:30pm, with live entertainment in the evenings.

Services: Laundry, room service, travel agency, concierge, babysitting.

Facilities: One large pool, children's pool, one tennis court lighted at night, table tennis and pool tables, plus other board games, children's game room, water sports, gym with massage service and steam baths.

LA JOLLA DE MISMALOYA, Hwy. 200 south to Mismaloya, km 10.5 (Apdo. Postal 158B), Puerto Vallarta, Jal. Tel. 322/3-0660, toll free 800/322-2343 in California, 800/322-2344 elsewhere in the U.S. 304 suites. A/C TV TEL

$ Rates: $175–$235 one- or two-bedroom suite. Prices are higher Christmas and Easter week.

This hotel's three nine-story buildings are arranged around beautiful Mismaloya Beach, where *Night of the Iguana* was filmed. One building is set into a cliff overlooking the cove, while the two buildings on the beach are connected by a U-shaped arcade that frames a large courtyard of interlaced pools, palapas, patios, and lush gardens facing the sea. Shops, restaurants, and lounges are intermingled in this courtyard and arcade area. White stucco and large arches create the feeling of a spacious modern hacienda. Each of the guest quarters is a spacious suite many of which are equipped with kitchenettes with a counter that doubles as a bar with high stools. The majority have one bedroom with bath, but many have two baths and some have two bedrooms and two baths. All have ocean views and balconies and are decorated in a luxurious contemporary style in whites and pastels with marble counters and floors. On a hill above the cove you can still see the ruins of the movie set. The hotel is 6½ miles south of town. Two floors are reserved for nonsmokers and there are two handicap-equipped rooms.

Dining/Entertainment: The Patio Restaurant, in the courtyard with a view of the beach, is open from 8am to 11pm. The Beach Club is open for lunch near the pool and features sandwiches and drinks. La Jolla, open from 8am to 11pm, features Mexican food from its perch on the cliff overlooking the cove. Terrace of the Stars lounge has marvelous views of the cove and is open from noon to 1am. The Cantina Shack, a refreshment bar near the pool, is open from 10am to 6pm. On Tuesday night the hotel holds a Beach Party with open bar, buffet, and live music from 7 to 10pm for $30; on Saturday night, from 7 to 10pm, it hosts a Mexican Fiesta with open bar, buffet, mariachis, folkloric dancing, and fireworks for $30.

Services: Laundry, room service, travel agency, concierge, purified tap water, beauty shop, car rental, shopping arcade, babysitting by reservation.

Facilities: Five pools (one for children), three tennis courts (with resident pro), four outdoor whirlpools, gym with steambath, and massages and facials are available,

2. WHERE TO DINE

Although eating out in Puerto Vallarta has become more expensive, some bargains and good values remain.

MARINA VALLARTA

MIKADO RESTAURANT, Marriott CasaMagna Hotel, Marina Vallarta.
Tel. 1-0004 Ext. 6248.
Cuisine: JAPANESE.
$ Prices: Sushi appetizers $3–$30; main courses $20–$35.
Open: Daily 6–11pm.

Puerto Vallarta's newest Japanese eatery is truly elegant. Though it offers the same type of grilled-at-the-table food as others of its kind, that's where the resemblance ends. The setting is royal Japanese, featuring high ceilings, elegant chandeliers, porcelain vases, and marble everywhere. Ferns and a generous use of wood and a collection of silk kimonos grace the walls. Food and service are superb. The menu features grilled seafood, with shrimp and lobster specialties, plus an extensive sushi menu. Each selection is presented as a beautiful artistic arrangement complemented by fresh ginger and mustard.

HOTEL ZONE

BOGART'S, Krystal Vallarta Hotel, Av. de las Garzas s/n. Tel. 4-0202.
Cuisine: CONTINENTAL/ECLECTIC.
$ Prices: Full meal $50–$70.
Open: Daily 6pm–midnight.

Pointed Moorish arches, murmuring fountains, a silky tent ceiling, and high-backed peacock chairs create the mysterious mood of Casablanca in this softly lighted, sumptuous restaurant. A pianist plays in the background while waiters out of *Arabian Nights* serve such delicacies as Persian Crêpes (sour cream, cheese, and caviar), escargots, sorbet between courses, and flambéed Shrimp Krystal. For a big splurge or a special occasion, a dinner in this fantasy place is unforgettable. It's north of town near the main pier; take the "Muelle" bus. Bogart's is on the front of the hotel property, facing the main boulevard.

NORTH OF THE RÍO CUALE

EXPENSIVE

CAFÉ DES ARTISTES, Guadalupe Sánchez 740. Tel. 2-3228.
Cuisine: INTERNATIONAL.
$ Prices: Main courses $16–$35.
Open: Daily 7–11pm.

FROMMER'S SMART TRAVELER: RESTAURANTS

1. South of the river is the best area for finding inexpensive-to-moderate restaurants. One cluster centers around the street Olas Altas, quite close to the beach; another edges Vallarta. But the hottest new food street is Badillo, fast becoming the south side's unofficial "restaurant row."
2. North of the river, a nice snack as you stroll along the malecón is an *elote* (corn-on-the-cob) served on a stick either roasted or broiled, sold at little stands in the evening. Try it with mayonnaise and cheese, or with lemon, salt, and chile, the way the Mexicans like it.
3. You can pick up inexpensive fruit, vegetables, and picnic fixings at the municipal market beside the Río Cuale where Libertad and Rodriguez meet. You can also eat upstairs at one of the many little *loncherías*—just choose what is freshly cooked and hot.
4. Restaurants fronting the malecón and those on the beach will be more expensive and not necessarily better in quality than others in less prime locations.
5. Fine dining in Puerto Vallarta, however, can be just as exquisite but much less expensive than the equivalent in the United States.

The Café des Artistes, located at the corner of Vicario three blocks from the malecón, is slightly off the beaten path—it's easy to miss this charming indoor/outdoor eatery. Opened in 1990, it's a sophisticated little place with lots of light, a black and white decor, and an interesting menu. Among the appetizers you'll find crêpes, quiche, and chilled cream of watercress soup. The seafood menu is extensive and includes sautéed shrimp with cheese and ravioli in a champagne basil sauce. There's an interesting spring chicken flambé, stuffed with prunes and dates. It's worth a trip just to read the menu. The unusual combinations are enough to make you order something even if you're not hungry.

CHEF ROGER, A. Rodriguez 267, Tel. 2-5900.
  Cuisine: NOUVELLE MEXICAN.
$ Prices: Appetizers $5–$15; main courses $10–$20.
  Open: Mon–Sat 6:30–11pm.

This sophisticated little dinner-only restaurant has developed quite a following since it opened in 1989, a success that owes something to owner Roger Dreir's prior reputation as a caterer in the city. A European-trained chef, he's combined elements of the cuisines of Europe, the American Southwest, and Mexico and created a highly personal style of cooking. Guests enjoy their meals on the patio or in one of the adjoining half open-air dining rooms. There are five or six daily specials using whatever is fresh; these might include steaks and lobster and such interesting combinations as pasta with crêpes huitlacoche. The restaurant is catercorner from the craft market between Matamoros and Hidalgo.

CHEZ ELENA, Matamoros 520. Tel. 2-0161.
  Cuisine: CONTINENTAL.
$ Prices: Appetizers $4.50–$10; main courses $7.50–$21.50.
  Open: 6–11pm.

Perched on a hillside with a magnificent view of the ocean, this exclusive little restaurant is on the first-floor patio of the cozy inn Los Cuatro Vientos (See "Where to Stay" above). Furnished in equipales chairs and tables covered in pink cloths and flickering candles, it's casually elegant and worthy of a special night out, yet prices are moderate. A soloist entertains softly most evenings and service is attentive and refined without being stuffy. Regular menu items include a Mexican plate; an Indonesian beef, pork, and shrimp brochet with peanut sauce; catch of the day; chicken in orange or curry sauce; and a vegetarian platter. Specialty flaming coffee mulatto is one of the desserts plus delicious cheesecake and pecan pie. It's located on a hill above the central part of town at the corner of Matamoros and Corona.

MODERATE

LA CASA DEL ALMENDRO, Galeana 180. Tel. 2-4670.
- **Cuisine:** MEXICAN/INTERNATIONAL.
- **$ Prices:** Appetizers $2–$5; main courses $8–$30.
- **Open:** Noon–11pm.

Built around the beautiful interior patio of a 19th-century home shaded by a huge almond tree in the middle, this charming restaurant is said to be the oldest house in Puerto Vallarta; it retains the atmosphere of a Mexican home and family members provide excellent service. Meals are served upstairs or down. The lunch menu offers mostly Mexican specialties. At night candlelight flickers on checkered tablecloths. There's a downstairs bar as well. It's known for its seafood and to honor its name, the restaurant serves almond-stuffed lobster and almond-cream pie. However, there are steaks to choose from and Italian entrées as well. You'll find the restaurant just off the malecón 1½ blocks inland on Galeana.

BUDGET

HELADOS BING, Juárez 280. Tel. 2-1627.
- **Cuisine:** ICE CREAM.
- **$ Prices:** Single cone 90¢; special sundae $3.
- **Open:** Daily 8:30am–10:30pm.

The most popular ice-cream shop in town has a long list of flavors to choose from. It also has branches at Cárdenas and Constitución south of the river; at the airport; and at Villa Vallarta, the shopping center near the big hotels north of town. Just look for its pink-and-white decor. It's on Juárez near Guerrero, about two blocks in from the malecón and half a block from the main plaza.

PIETRO PASTAS & PIZZAS, Zaragoza 245 at Hidalgo. Tel. 2-3233.
- **Cuisine:** ITALIAN.
- **$ Prices:** Appetizers $3.50–$7; main courses $8–$12; 12-inch pizzas $7.50–$10.
- **Open:** Daily noon–midnight.

Italian music and swags of braided garlic on the wall above a big brick oven set the mood for menu offerings: ravioli, cannelloni, lasagne, calzone, and, of course, pizza. And the pasta is homemade. It's across the street and just south of the cathedral.

RESTAURANT JUANITA, Av. Mexico 1067. Tel. 2-1458.
- **Cuisine:** MEXICAN.
- **$ Prices:** Appetizers $2–$3.50; main courses $3–$10; comida corrida $3–$4; pozole $2; giant shrimp $10.
- **Open:** Daily 8am–10:30pm; comida corrida noon–5pm.

Decorated with bright piñatas, paintings, and plaid tablecloths, this simple and cheerful restaurant is open to the sidewalk. Try the pozole (a hearty stew with meat

DOWNTOWN PUERTO VALLARTA

ACCOMMODATIONS:
Casa Corazon 32
Los Cuatro Vientos 7
Hotel Encino 15
Hotel Fontana del Mar 24
Hotel Marsol 30
Hotel Molina de Agua 18
Hotel Posada de Roger 25
Playa Los Arcos 23
Posada Rio Cuale 20

ATTRACTIONS:
Burton-Taylor bridge 13
Gringo Gulch (neighborhood) 12
Museo del Río Cuale 16
Plaza Cardenas 21
Zócalo/Main Square 9

DINING:
Archie's Wok 31
Café Adobe 29
Café des Artistes 4
Carlos O'Brians 3
La Casa del Almendro 6
Chef Roger 14
Chez Elena 8
El Dorado 33
Fonda La China Poblana 22
Franzi Cafe 17
Helados Bing 11
El Palomar de los Gonzalez 34
The Pancake House 28
Pietro Pastas & Pizzas 10
Pizza Joe 26
Puerto Nuevo 27
Restaurant/Bar Aquarena 19
Restaurant/Bar Zapata 2
Restaurant Juanita 1
Tuti Frutti 5

and hominy) or splurge on the giant shrimp with garlic. To find Juanita's, from the river, walk north on the malecón several blocks; it's on Mexico near Venezuela.

TUTI FRUTTI, Morelos and Corona. Tel. 2-1068.
   Cuisine: HEALTH/VEGETARIAN/AMERICAN.
$ Prices: Appetizers $1.50; main courses $1.50–$5; cinnamon coffee 50¢; fresh juices or licuados made with fresh fruit and milk or purified water $1.50; sandwiches $1.50–$2; three quesadillas and beans $3; hamburger and fries $4.
   Open: Mon–Sat 8am–10pm.

This is a good spot for a quick snack near the malecón. The menu includes grilled or cold sandwiches with all the trimmings. You can eat at the counter or take your meal out. You'll find it one block inland from the malecón.

SOUTH OF THE RÍO CUALE
MODERATE

ARCHIE'S WOK, Rodriguez 130. Tel. 2-0411.
   Cuisine: ORIENTAL/ECLECTIC.
$ Prices: Appetizers $3.50–$6.50; main courses $9–$14.
   Open: Daily 1–10pm.

After training as a chef in California, Archie Alpenia brought his family to Puerto Vallarta and ended up as chef to the late John Huston, director of *Night of the Iguana*. Today Archie's Wok stirs up delightfully eclectic Asian fare: Filipino eggrolls, Thai coconut fish, chicken Singapore, and spicy red curry, to name but a few dishes. Desserts surprise with homemade fudge brownies, lime pie, and carrot cake. To find it, walk 7 blocks south of the river on Vallarta, then left on Rodriguez 2½ blocks.

CAFÉ ADOBE, Badillo 300. Tel. 2-6720.
   Cuisine: INTERNATIONAL.
$ Prices: Appetizers $4–$7; main courses $7–$12.
   Open: Wed–Mon 6–11pm. **Closed:** Aug and Sept.

The Café Adobe is casually chic with a trendy southwestern flair. Waiters wearing jeans and checkered shirts serve the imaginative food—"Adobe-style" fettuccine with shrimp and pesto, red snapper with a mango hollandaise sauce, and chicken in cheese sauce with chipotle chiles—to name just a few specialties. Café Adobe is located at the corner of Badillo and Constitución opposite the Casa de Hotcakes.

EL DORADO, Pulpito s/n. Tel. 2-1511.
   Cuisine: MEXICAN.
$ Prices: Breakfast $2.50–$11; appetizers $3–$12; main courses $7–$16; green salad or sandwiches $4.50–$10.
   Open: Daily 8am–9pm.

This open-air, palapa-roofed restaurant on the beach is a local favorite, especially for a hearty breakfast by the sea. Try the Huevos Motulenos—Yucatecan-style eggs on tortillas with black beans, cheese, and a tangy salsa. In the late afternoon watch the surfers and parasailors while sipping a cool drink. Seafood is another specialty, and iced tea is always available. To find it, walk nine blocks south of the river on Vallarta, then right on Pulpito to its end at the beach.

FONDA LA CHINA POBLANA, Insurgentes 222. Tel. 2-4049.
   Cuisine: MEXICAN.
$ Prices: Breakfast $2–$3; appetizers $4–$9; main courses $7–$13; tacos $4.75.
   Open: Daily 24 hours.

In the heart of the bustling bus station area, this orderly café with checked tablecloths and brick arches is a real find—and it's open 'round the clock. You can watch food sizzling on the grill while downing tacos, steak, black-bean soup, or shrimp or oysters prepared five ways. The restaurant is on Insurgentes between Madero and Cárdenas.

EL PALOMAR DE LOS GONZALEZ, Aguacate 425. Tel. 2-0795 or 2-2795.
   Cuisine: INTERNATIONAL.
$ Prices: Appetizers $5–$15; main courses $8–$30.
   Open: Sept–June daily 6–11pm; July–Aug Mon–Sat 6–11pm.
On top of a steep hill overlooking Puerto Vallarta, this rooftop restaurant is a delight. The terrace catches the breezes and some evenings it's cool enough for a light wrap; the restaurant provides shawls for the ladies. Owned by Juan Ramon Gonzalez (who opened the restaurant on the top floor of his parents' home), it's become a fine-dining tradition that's popular with locals as well as tourists. His mother and wife take charge of the menu, which is a mix of Spanish and Mexican dishes. The special of the day might be a feast of a seafood platter with smoked octopus, crab, red snapper, scallops, lobster tail, and jumbo shrimp. The shrimp are enormous here, so count on getting your money's worth with any shrimp dish. The restaurant is a bit hard to find. Look for the large sign advertising Felipe's restaurant on a hill above the highway that leads out of town just at the edge of town proper. El Palomar is on a steep street to the right of that sign. Take a taxi or be prepared to ask lots of directions since streets are dark and not well marked, and there's no sign for the restaurant until you reach the front door.

PIZZA JOE, Badillo 269. Tel. 2-2477.
   Cuisine: ITALIAN.
$ Prices: Main courses $6–$11; pizza $7–$19.
   Open: Mon–Sat 9am–11pm.
Behind a high brick wall lies a garden patio with twinkle lights in the trees, soft music, and red-checked tablecloths, where you can *mangi* under the stars on some of the best Italian *cucina* in town. Besides pizza there's a good range of pastas, as well as vegetarian and meat lasagne. Brunch includes omelets, crêpes and pizza. The simply decadent homemade cheesecake comes in several flavors: lemon-lime, orange, Kahlúa, and chocolate-almond. The young American-Canadian couple who own it, Joe and Clara, make everyone feel welcome. It's on Badillo, left, ½ block from Vallarta.

PUERTO NUEVO, Badillo 284. No phone.
   Cuisine: MEXICAN/SEAFOOD.
$ Prices: Appetizers $4–$8; main courses $7.50–$17.
   Open: Daily 12:30–11pm.
Owner and chef Roberto Castellon presents seafood with inventive flair: Try the crab enchiladas, shrimp "filet mignon," or smoked marlin—or the unusual manta ray tacos. Dine inside or in the roofed, open-air sidewalk area hung with plants for a jungle effect. You'll find it 5 blocks south of the river off Vallarta, ½ block left on Badillo.

RESTAURANT/BAR AQUARENA, Hotel Molino de Agua, Vallarta 130. Tel. 2-1907 or 2-1957.
   Cuisine: MEXICAN/SEAFOOD.
$ Prices: Breakfast $4–$6.50; main courses $4–$11 at lunch, $10–$18 at dinner; breakfast $3–$6.
   Open: Daily 7:30am–11pm; breakfast to 11:30am; happy hour 6–9pm.

Have a relaxing meal in the beautiful dining room decorated with bamboo, or on the shady terrace looking out on the pool and tropical gardens. While the pianist plays every night from 6 to 9:30pm (during high season), savor well-executed margaritas followed by the grilled seafood platter—a large tray of succulent lobster, shrimp, fish, and tender squid—the latter in a velvety, exquisitely spiced *adobo* sauce. For lunch the tortilla soup is a filling and budget-wise winner. Afterward, take a stroll around the romantic gardens. It's immediately south of the river on Vallarta.

BUDGET

THE PANCAKE HOUSE (CASA DE HOTCAKES), Badillo 289.
   Cuisine: AMERICAN/MEXICAN BREAKFAST.
   $ Prices: Breakfast $4.50–$8.
   Open: High season daily 8am–2pm; low season Tues–Sun 8am–2pm.

For a hearty, American-style breakfast or brunch, stop at "the only pancake house on the west coast of Mexico." In a restaurant that's invitingly airy with lots of tile and white stucco, owner/travel writer Memo Barroso hosts the village's most popular breakfast eatery, which is definitely not limited to pancakes. Mouth-watering pancakes and waffles are imaginatively mixed with fruit, chocolate, nuts, and even peanut butter. You can also pig out on eggs Benedict, cheese blintzes, breakfast burritos, or omelets. It's at the corner of Badillo and Constitución.

SPECIALTY DINING

JUNGLE RESTAURANTS

One of the unique attractions of Puerto Vallarta is its "jungle restaurants," located to the south, toward Mismaloya. Each one offers open-air dining in a magnificent tropical setting, by the sea or beside a mountain river. Determine the distance from town by the kilometer in the address. For minivan transportation see "Getting Around" in Chapter 3.

CHICO'S PARADISE, Hwy. 200, km 20. Tel. 2-0747.
   Cuisine: MEXICAN/SEAFOOD.
   $ Prices: Appetizers $7–$14; main courses $9–$19; grilled seafood platter for two $65.
   Open: Daily 11am–6pm.

Lunch at this lively tropical place, perched on the edge of a clear, boulder-framed river gorge under a big thatched roof, can easily be a day's outing. Arrive early (noon) to get a good table, then enjoy the river view and the serenading trios. Among the tasty dishes are barbecued ribs, fish *sarandeado* (grilled in a special way), seafood *cazuelas* (casseroles), black-bean soup, and the seafood platter for two. After dining, hike down to the river to swim and sunbathe, or explore the crafts and souvenir shops on the premises. Don't forget to bring your swimsuit, tennis shoes, and beach towels!

Chico's is about 13 miles south of town on the main highway. *Note:* Round-trip cab fare is about $30 (get a group of four to share). Or take the no. 02 minivan (50¢) to Boca de Tomatlán, a fishing village, then get a taxi from there—a relatively short distance. (See "Getting Around" in Chapter 3.)

CHINO'S PARAISO, Hwy. 200, km 6.5. Tel. 3-0102.
   Cuisine: GRILLED SEAFOOD/STEAK.
   $ Prices: Main courses $12–$30.
   Open: Daily noon–5pm.

Tucked into some rock formations, this jungle restaurant offers five open-air terraces overlooking a green river flanked by giant boulders under grand palapas. Guests often take a dip in the swimming holes and waterfalls before or after eating. The setting is usually shady and cool, and quite festive when the marimbas play, which is usually 1 to 3pm. To get there take a cab or minivan as far as the entrance to La Jolla de Mismaloya Resort, then hike or hire a taxi about a mile on the dirt road on the landward side of the highway, you'll see the road and Chino's sign opposite La Jolla Resort.

EL EDÉN, off Hwy. 200, km 6.5. No phone.
   Cuisine: GRILLED SEAFOOD/STEAK/CHICKEN.
   $ Prices: Main courses $15–$30.
   Open: Daily 11am–6pm.

With just enough jungle cleared in this luxuriant spot beside a clear river to set up movie cameras, a crew shot scenes here for *The Predator*, starring Arnold Schwarzenegger. Then the current owner turned the set into a restaurant. Guests can dine while watching other guests dropping into the inviting green river Tarzan-style from a rope swing. Corn tortillas made on the spot usually come with the dinners. It's three miles off the highway on the mountain side farther on the same road to Chino's (see above). There's a small fee to stay without eating. It has no phone, so check first with a travel agent or at the tourist office to confirm it is open.

EL SET, Conchas Chinas, Hwy. 200, km 2.5. Tel. 2-1056 or 2-0302.
   Cuisine: GRILLED SEAFOOD, MEAT/INTERNATIONAL.
   $ Prices: Appetizers $3.50–$7.75; main courses $10.50–$20.
   Open: Daily 8am–11pm.

This charming, stylishly informal restaurant has been a favorite of visitors for years. Terraces lush with palms, shady manzanillo trees and bougainvillea on a cliff above the sea and sturdy leather tables and chairs create a relaxed tropical mood. Spectacular sunsets and Conchas Chinas Casserole are the specialties of this place. Live music accompanies dinners of grilled steaks and seafood, spareribs, soups, and salads. It's between the Conchas Chinas Hotel and Linda Mar Resort; there's an obscure sign.

PICNIC SUPPLIES

The **Supermercado Gutierrez Ruiz,** Serdan and Constitución, has an especially large bakery and cold cut and cheese selection as does **Gigante** on the northern hotel strip fronting Av. de las Palmas.

CHAPTER 5

WHAT TO SEE & DO IN PUERTO VALLARTA

- **SUGGESTED ITINERARIES**
1. **ORGANIZED TOURS**
2. **SPORTS & RECREATION**
- **FROMMER'S FAVORITE PUERTO VALLARTA EXPERIENCES**
3. **SHOPPING**
4. **EVENING ENTERTAINMENT**
5. **EASY EXCURSIONS**

Puerto Vallarta's beaches are its main attraction. The tourism offices and travel agencies can provide information on what to see and do. Puerto Vallarta is above all a place to relax and enjoy yourself.

SUGGESTED ITINERARIES

IF YOU HAVE 2 DAYS On your first day, relax, amble along the beach, and have a peaceful dinner. Sleep late on your second day, then stroll around the central village. Have lunch at one of the beachside restaurants, and later select a good sunset spot from one of the restaurants mentioned in Chapter 4 and stay on for dinner.

IF YOU HAVE 3 DAYS Spend your first two days taking it easy on Puerto Vallarta's beaches. On your third day, take one of the boats to Yelapa or Las Animas and spend the day or afternoon on the beach, taking lunch and refreshments at one of the palapa-topped restaurants there. In the evening find an outdoor restaurant, and enjoy one of the festive Mexican entertainment nights that usually include folkloric dancing, dinner, and refreshments.

IF YOU HAVE 5 DAYS With an extended stay in Puerto Vallarta to play with, you might want to break up your sun and sand sessions with a visit to one of the jungle restaurants with a pool, a scuba-diving excursion to one of the interesting spots not far off shore, or, if you're there on a Saturday, the house and garden tour detailed below. In the evenings make sure you avail yourself of the sunset cruises and Puerto Vallarta's growing nightlife, whether in throbbing dance clubs, the lobby bars of hotels, or the many lively restaurants that double as nightspots.

1. ORGANIZED TOURS

The State Tourism Office (see "Fast Facts: Puerto Vallarta" in Chapter 3) and travel agencies can provide information on what to see and do, and travel agencies can arrange tours, car rentals, and other activities. I highly recommend the agencies Viajes Toucan Tours (tel. 2-4600 or 2-4646) and Enrique Tovar (tel. 2-1877; fax 2-6585).

TOURS City tours, jungle tours, and horseback-riding tours at several different ranches in the country can be arranged through travel agencies. They cost from $15 to $35 per person.

A **house and garden tour** of four private homes in town is offered every Saturday at 11am by the International Friendship Club for a donation of $15 per person. The tour bus departs from the main plaza by the State Tourism Office (which has information about this event). Proceeds are donated to local charities.

BOAT TRIPS Puerto Vallarta offers a number of different boat trips, including sunset cruises and excursions to Yelapa (a tiny town on a lovely cove), Las Animas Beach, La Manzanilla Beach, and Quimixto Falls. Some make a stop at the Los Arcos rock formations for snorkeling, some include lunch, and most provide music and an open bar on board. Prices are around $50 for an all-day outing. Viajes Toucan Tours (tel. 2-4600 or 2-4646) and other travel agencies have tickets and information. Operadura Buenaventura (tel. 3-0309 or 3-0875) offers relaxing sunset dinner cruises on the *Tuna I* through the mangrove lagoons and canals north of Puerto Vallarta for around $45. *Note:* The town pier/marina used by most pleasure boats is north of downtown near the airport. Do not confuse it with the new pier at Playa Olas Altas south of the river.

2. SPORTS & RECREATION

THE BEACHES Puerto Vallarta's beaches start well north of town, out by the airport, with **Playa de Oro,** and extend all around the broad Bay of Banderas. The most popular are **Playa Olas Altas,** also known as Playa Muertos or Playa del Sol, just off Calle Olas Altas, south of the Río Cuale; and **Playa Mismaloya,** in a beautiful sheltered cove about six miles south of town along Highway 200. It was at Mismaloya that *Night of the Iguana* was filmed. You can still see and hike up to the stone buildings that were constructed for the movie, on the point framing the south side of the cove. The Jolla de Mismaloya Resort is on this beach, as well as several rustic seafood restaurants; this and all beaches in Mexico are public.

To get to Mismaloya, take the no. 02 minivan from Plaza Lázaro Cárdenas (see "Getting Around" in Chapter 3). Along this route to Mismaloya are many other fine beaches, including **Punta Negra,** with soft white sand, an enjoyable view, and a little palapa restaurant. You can ask the driver to let you off at any point and explore the area for yourself.

Around the rocky point **south of Playa Olas Altas** are quite a number of small, sheltered coves that get very little use and are much nicer than the Coney Island atmosphere of the main beach.

Waterskiing, parasailing, and other water sports are available at many beaches along the Bay of Banderas.

BULLFIGHTS Bullfights are held from November through April on Wednesday afternoons at the bullring La Paloma, across the highway from the town pier. Tickets can be arranged through a travel agency or through Foto Taurina (tel. 2-1158).

DIVING & SNORKELING While Puerto Vallarta is not the diving mecca that Cozumel is, there's enough here to make it worthwhile. Three diving areas are of interest: Las Mariettas Islands, where there are caves; Quimixto, where there's good visibility and lots of fish; and Los Arcos (a rock formation), which is shallow with good color changes. Local travel agencies can make arrangements and the cost is around $50 per person. Expert divers and beginners can arrange scuba diving at

98 • WHAT TO SEE & DO IN PUERTO VALLARTA

Chico's Dive Shop, Díaz Ordaz 770-5 (tel. 2-5439). Snorkeling trips through Chico's start at $24.

FISHING For **deep-sea fishing,** September through November is best for sailfish; marlin, dorado, and roosterfish are found all year. Cost is around $215 for ½ day and $500 for a full day depending on how far out you go, and the boat and provisions chosen. Trips can be arranged through travel agencies or through the Cooperativa de Pescadores (fishing cooperative) on the Malecón next door to the Rosita Hotel and across from McDonald's. Or you can try your luck by negotiating directly at the town pier or the Las Peinas marina farther north, where many dive and charter boats are docked.

Freshwater fishing is available at the Cajon de Peña Reservoir, 70 miles south of Puerto Vallarta, a 7,000-acre artificial lake stocked with bass; the fishing is good all year. Since the lake also irrigates local crops, depending on the season, you'll see rice, sorghum, corn, and tropical fruit orchards. Ask local travel agents for details.

GOLF Puerto Vallarta has two golf courses: an 18-hole private course at Marina Vallarta for members only; and the 18-hole Los Flamingos Club de Golf five minutes north of Nuevo Vallarta (tel. 8-0280). Los Flamingos is open from 9am to 5pm daily and has a restaurant and full pro shop. The greens fee is $25, plus $14 if you rent clubs, and $22 for a motorized cart or $4 for a pull cart. Golf packages are available through several hotels including the Villas Quinta Real and Marriott CasaMagna, both in Marina Vallarta, and Hotel Garza Blanca south of Puerto Vallarta.

TENNIS Besides the hotels mentioned in "Where to Stay" in Chapter 4 that have tennis courts, there's also the **John Newcombe Tennis Center** with four outdoor (clay) and four indoor courts. It's next to the Continental behind the Las Glorias Shopping Center. Nonguests of the hotel pay $12 an hour for court use; guests pay $10. A tennis pro is on duty for lessons at an extra charge. It's open daily from 7am to 9pm. For reservations call 4-0123, extension 500.

WHALE WATCHING Whales are often seen offshore during February and March from Punta Mita, north of Puerto Vallarta.

A STROLL THROUGH TOWN Puerto Vallarta's tightly knit cobblestone streets are a delight to explore (with good walking shoes!), full of tiny shops, rows of windows edged with curling wrought iron, and vistas of red-tiled roofs and sea. Start with a walk up and down the malecón, the seafront boulevard. Among the sights not to miss is the **municipal building** on the main square (next to the State Tourism Office), which has a large mural by Manuel Lepe inside in its stairwell.

Nearby, up Independencia, sits the **cathedral** topped with its curious crown; on its steps women sell colorful herbs and spices to cure common ailments. Here Richard Burton and Elizabeth Taylor were married the first time—she in a Mexican wedding dress, he in a Mexican charro outfit. Of course afterward they had fireworks! Three

---

IMPRESSIONS

A remote charming fishing village [Puerto Vallarta] on Bahia de Banderas, one of the west coast's most beautiful bays. The town, climbing up the slopes of mountains that surround the bay is Mexico's nearest equivalent to a quiet Mediterranean village, even to the tourists who are beginning to discover it.
—JAMES NORMAN, TERRY'S GUIDE TO MEXICO, 1965.

blocks south of the church, head uphill on **Libertad,** lined with small shops and pretty upper windows; it brings you to the **public market** on the river.

After exploring the market, cross the bridge to the **island in the river;** sometimes a painter is at work on its banks. Walk down the center of the island towards the sea, and you come to the tiny **Museo del Cuale,** which exhibits pre-Columbian ceramics and local artists; it's open daily from 9am to 2pm and 3pm to 8pm. Then retrace your steps to the market and Libertad, and climb up steep **Miramar to Zaragoza:** at the top is a magnificent view over rooftops to the sea. Up Zaragoza to the right two blocks is the famous pink-arched bridge that once connected Richard Burton's and Elizabeth Taylor's houses. This area is known as **Gringo Gulch,** where many Americans have houses.

SPECIAL EVENTS The week leading up to **December 12**—the "birthday" of Mexico's patron saint, the **Virgin of Guadalupe**—this is an important day all over Mexico, and is celebrated with processions of "Las Peregrinas" (religious pilgrims) and much merrymaking.

3. SHOPPING

Excellent quality merchandise is brought to Puerto Vallarta from all over Mexico and sold in hundreds of little shops all over town. The prices here are higher than in the

FROMMER'S FAVORITE PUERTO VALLARTA EXPERIENCES

A Lazy Day on the Beach Spend a day or more relaxing on any of Puerto Vallarta's fine wide beaches dozing, reading a book, and watching the waves.

Sunset Watching Search out just the right place to see the sunset—an important part of a Puerto Vallarta vacation. One of the best ways to end the day is aboard a sunset dinner cruise. My favorite goes north of Puerto Vallarta among the mangroves and canals.

Yelapa Beach Let the boat you came on leave without you, pick one of the palapa restaurants as a base for refreshments, and spend the day on the beach. Use your ticket for the last boat back.

Deep-Sea Fishing A half day or day far out at sea can be a thrilling and relaxing experience, especially if the fishing is good to great. Bring back your catch and have one of the restaurants prepare it for dinner.

Jungle Restaurants Spend an afternoon at one of the jungle restaurants swimming, relaxing, and eating.

House and Garden Tour Join the Saturday tour to see what's behind the walls of Puerto Vallarta's elite homes.

places of origin, so if you're planning to visit other parts of Mexico, you might want to wait and make your purchases at the sources. In Tonalá and Tlaquepaque near Guadalajara, six hours away by bus, prices are considerably lower.

Puerto Vallarta's **municipal market** is just north of the Río Cuale where Libertad and Rodriguez meet. The mercado sells clothes, jewelry, serapes, shawls, leather accessories and suitcases, papier-mâché parrots, stuffed frogs and armadillos, and of course T-shirts. Be sure to do some comparative shopping before buying. It's open daily from 8am to 8pm.

Calle Libertad next to the market is the place to buy *huaraches*—comfortable, practical sandals made of leather strips and rubber-tire soles. Buy a pair that fits very tightly—they stretch out quickly and can become too floppy.

CRAFTS & FOLK ART

ARTE MAGICO HUICHOL, Corona 164. Tel. 2-4210.

This may be the best gallery of Huichol art in all of Mexico. It carries very fine large and small yarn paintings by recognized Huichol artists, as well as intricately beaded masks, bowls, and ceremonial objects. It's closed from 2 to 3pm during low season. Open: Mon–Sat 10am–9pm.

GALLERY INDIGENA, Juárez 168. Tel. 2-4210.

More Mexican folk art, silver, and handmade wares await down the street from Olinala Gallery. The store specializes in masks, plus Olinalá lacquer chests. It's between A. Rodriguez and Libertad. Open: Mon–Sat 10am–2pm and 5–8pm.

NACHO'S, Libertad 160A. Tel. 2-3007.

Beautifully made silver jewelry from Taxco and lacquerware from Olinala are sold here. When buying sterling, always look for the .925 stamp on the back. Open: Mon–Sat 10am–2pm and 5–9pm.

OLINALA GALLERY, Cárdenas 274. Tel. 2-4995.

The fine indigenous Mexican crafts and folk art here include an impressive collection of authentic masks and Huichol beaded art. Priced from $45 to $2,000 for museum-quality pieces, most of the masks have been worn in ceremonies rather than created for tourists. Reference books and other literature are available in English, and the knowledgeable staff will gladly answer questions. Open: Mon–Sat 10am–2pm and 5–9pm.

QUERUBINES, Juárez 501-A. Tel. 2-2988.

"Cherubs" offers Guatemalan and Mexican wares, including embroidered and handwoven clothing, Oaxaca wood carvings, wool rugs, jewelry, straw bags, Guatemala fabric, and Panama hats. Open: Mon–Sat 9am–9pm, Sun 10am–6pm.

LA REJA, Juárez 501. Tel. 2-2272.

A great selection of Mexican ceramics and some lovely Guatemalan fabrics are among the crafts here. Open: Mon–Sat 9am–2pm and 4–8pm.

CONTEMPORARY ART

The galleries below carry contemporary Mexican and/or foreign artists.

BROOKS DE GOOYER, Morelos 589. Tel. 2-1982.

Among the works featured here is that of Marta Gilberta, a local artist whose reputation as an artist is growing. Open: Mon–Sat 10am–2pm and 4–8pm.

SERGIO BUSTAMANTE GALLERY, Juárez 275. Tel. 2-1129.

Fantastic creatures emerging from eggs and other colorful, surreal images in three-dimensional ceramics are Bustamante's trademark. Open: Mon–Sat 9am–9pm.

GALERÍA UNO, Morelos 561. Tel. 2-0908.
Open: Mon–Sat 10am–9pm.

4. EVENING ENTERTAINMENT

Wander down the malecón after dark and you'll hear music pouring out from half a dozen inviting restaurant/bars with their windows open to the sea. The beach doesn't go to sleep at night, either. Bands play under the palapas and there's dancing on the beach. Restaurants with live music can also provide a pleasant evening.

RESTAURANT/BARS

ANDALE, Olas Altas 425. Tel. 2-1054.
South of the river, Andale can be one of the wildest watering holes in town for youthful vacationers. Drinks are reasonably priced and sometimes the Tequila Slammers are on the house. Its restaurant upstairs is a bit quieter, with tables overlooking the street. Open: Daily 10am–4am.
Admission: Free. **Prices:** Margaritas $3; beer $1.50.

CARLOS O'BRIAN'S, Paseo Díaz Ordaz 786 (the malecón) at Pipila. Tel. 2-1444.
The young-at-heart form a long line out front in the evening as they wait to get inside and join the party. Late at night the scene resembles a rowdy college party. Revelers have been known to dance on the tables and chairs. Open: Daily 11am–2am; happy hour 6–8pm.
Admission: Free. **Prices:** Drinks $2.50–$6.

FRANZI CAFE, Río Cuale. No phone.
At this pleasant spot under shady trees on the island in the middle of the river, talented groups play live jazz in the evening. Dinner is expensive, but you can always stop by for drinks or to trade paperback books. Open: Daily 8am–midnight; live jazz nightly 8–11pm.
Admission: Free. **Prices:** Drinks $2.50–$5.50; fancy coffee $6; Sun brunch $12.

MOGAMBO, Paseo Díaz Ordaz 644 (the malecón). Tel. 2-3476.
Live jazz lures in passersby to sit beneath the crocodiles and other stuffed creatures on the walls of this African-theme bar and restaurant. Open: Daily 8am–2am; live jazz nightly 9pm–2am.
Admission: Usually free. **Prices:** Drinks $2.50 and up; fancy coffee $5.50.

RESTAURANT/BAR ZAPATA, Paseo Díaz Ordaz 522 (the malecón). Tel. 2-4748.
Photographs and memorabilia from the Mexican Revolution surround you as you listen to live South American music. You can sit at the bar on one of the revolving horse-saddle stools. Open: Daily noon–1:30am; live music 7pm–midnight.
Admission: Free. **Prices:** National drinks $3.

DISCOS

The discos are loud and expensive, but a lot of fun. Admission is $3.50 to $16, and you'll generally pay $3 for a margarita, $2 for a beer, more for a whiskey and mix. Keep an eye out for free disco passes frequently available in hotels, restaurants, and other tourist spots. Most discos are open from 10pm to 4am.

The malecón now has competition for the after-dark crowd. The new area is the south side of old Puerto Vallarta and contains parts of Vallarta, Cárdenas, Carranza, and Badillo. Some of the newer places heavily frequented by tourists are **XC,** between Cárdenas and Carranza, for live salsa and other music; **El Torito,** Vallarta 290, a sports bar with a giant TV; and **Banana Max,** Vallarta and Cárdenas, for food, drinks, and fun.

CACTUS, Dieguez and Vallarta 399. Tel. 2-6037 or 2-6077.

A current favorite, this large disco offers pounding music, sculpted cavelike walls sprouting trees and cactus, and several tiers of seating that frames the large, high-tech dance floor on three sides. Open: Nightly 10pm–5am.

Admission: $12. **Prices:** $2–$5.

CHRISTINE, Krystal Vallarta Hotel, Av. de las Palmas, north of downtown off airport road. Tel. 2-1459.

With its Victorian "streetlamps" and ceiling spangled with tiny lights, the interior resembles a cross between an octagonal jewel box and a turn-of-the-century gazebo in a park—until the opening light show. Then the stage fogs up, lights swing down and start flashing, and suddenly you're enveloped in booming classical music like you've *never* heard it before. After the show, video screens and disco sounds take over. Open: Nightly 10pm–4am; opening light show at 11pm.

Admission: $16. **Prices:** Drinks $2–$7. *Note:* No shorts for men, tennis shoes, or thongs.

FRIDAY LÓPEZ, Hotel Fiesta Americana Puerto Vallarta, north of downtown off Av. de las Palmas. Tel. 4-2010.

Live bands and the upstairs-downstairs Spanish colonial–style setting keep everyone hopping in this festive night spot. Classic rock-and-roll "gold" is the music of choice. Open: Nightly 10pm–3am.

Admission: $8; women free on Wed. **Prices:** Drinks $2.50–$6.

SUNDANCE, Cárdenas 329. Tel. 2-2296.

Columns, arches, and comfortable furniture surround the black-lighted dance floor in the middle of the large room. This nightspot is popular with well-heeled locals but draws its share of tourists, too. Open: Nightly 10pm–4am.

Admission: Free Sun–Thurs, $8 Fri–Sat. **Prices:** Drinks $3.50–$7.

MEXICAN FIESTAS & HOTEL EVENTS

LA IGUANA, Cárdenas 311 between Constitución and Insurgentes. Tel. 2-0105.

☆ For a real extravaganza, go to La Iguana for an evening of entertainment that includes an open bar and an all-you-can-eat buffet. The owner-chef-showman-host, Gustavo Fong Salazar, was born in Mexico to a Chinese father and Mexican mother, went to school in Hong Kong, managed the American Club there, and served in the American armed services in China during World War II. Returning to Mexico several decades ago, after seeing great shows in many parts of the world, he originated the concept of Mexican folk shows for tourists, which have since become popular all over the country. The show is as eclectic as its owner's experience, with

Mexican folkloric dancing, mariachis, rope-twirling, piñatas, fireworks, and an orchestra for dancing. Open: Thurs and Sun 7–10:30pm.
Admission: $30.

KRYSTAL VALLARTA HOTEL, Av. de las Palmas, north of downtown off the airport road. Tel. 2-1459.

Mexican fiestas are held just about every night at major hotels around town and generally include a Mexican buffet, open bar, and live music and entertainment. One of the best is hosted by the Krystal Vallarta on Tuesday and Saturday at 7pm. The hotel also puts on a comic **"Charreada"**—a Mexican rodeo—with lots of audience participation (it also includes dinner and drinks) during high season on Thursday at 7pm. The State Tourism Office and local travel agencies can provide information on these and other hotel events; agencies can arrange tickets.
Admission: $38.

5. EASY EXCURSIONS

PLAYA YELAPA

A cove as inviting as a tropical fantasy is a two-hour trip by boat down the coast. Go to the town marina and catch the 9am boat, the *Serape*, to Yelapa for $17 round-trip, returning around 4pm. The fare includes two drinks on board but you need to bring your own lunch or buy it in Yelapa. Several other boats and cruises go to Yelapa and include lunch and open bar for $30 to $35. Travel agencies can provide tickets and information.

At Yelapa you can lie in the sun, swim, eat fresh grilled crayfish or seafood at a restaurant right on the beach (try Vagabundo's), have your picture taken with an iguana (for $1 a shot!), and let local "guides" take you on a tour of the town or up the river to see the waterfall.

BUCERÍAS

Only 11 miles north from the airport, Bucerías, Nayarit, (pronounced boo-sah-*ree*-ahs, pop. 8,000), is a small coastal fishing village on Banderas Bay (but across the state line in the state of Nayarit) that's beginning to catch on as an inexpensive alternative to Puerto Vallarta. Turn left when you see all the cook stands and, before you reach town center, you'll see cobblestone streets leading from the highway to the beach and hints of the villas and town houses behind high walls. Bucerías has already been discovered by second-home owners and about 1,000 transplanted Americans as a peaceful getaway, and casual tourists are beginning to discover its relaxed pace as well. To get here from Puerto Vallarta, take a minivan or city bus to the airport, then catch a minivan marked Bucerías (it runs from 6am to midnight, and costs $1.15 one way). The last stop is the town square, also the pick-up point for the return to PV.

WHAT TO SEE & DO

Come for a day trip from Puerto Vallarta just to enjoy the uncrowded beach and good seafood offered at the restaurants on the beach. Or you may be inclined to stay a few days to relax inexpensively and explore more of Bucerías; perhaps you'll find a hotel or restaurant worthy of another visit. Sunday is street-market day but it doesn't get going until around noon—in keeping with Bucerías's well-earned reputation for a casual pace.

WHERE TO STAY

Several small hotels, beachfront bungalows, and condominiums rent rooms here. Those mentioned below will get you started while you scout others to suit your particular idea of peace, quiet, and relaxation. **Los Pericos Travel in Bucerías** (tel. 322/8-0060 or 8-0061) will book accommodations. Call ahead or ask in Bucerías for directions to their office, which is open Monday through Friday from 9am to 5pm.

COSTA FLAMINGOS HOTEL, Lázaro Cárdenas 150, Bucerías, Nay. 63732. Tel. 322/8-0226. Fax 322/8-0333. 115 rms. A/C TV

$ **Rates:** $40 single or double.

You'll see a large sign pointing left from the main highway to this new beachfront hotel before you reach Bucerías proper. The architecture is that of a pastel mediterranean village and the three stories of rooms all have ocean views and balconies. Furnishings are modern, with tile floors and small bathrooms. It had just opened when I checked and prices were at promotional lows; they may increase by the time you travel. For the moment no other establishment shares the beach, so it's a fairly tranquil spot.

Dining/Entertainment: One restaurant is open daily from 8am to 10pm and serves all three meals.

Services: Guests can use the phone at the reception desk.

Facilities: Beach and large pool.

POSADA OLAS ALTAS, Calle Heroes de Nacozari s/n, Bucerías, Nay. 63732. Tel. 322/8-0407. 22 rms. FAN

$ **Rates:** $11.50–$15.50 one bed; $15.50–$20 two beds; $25 king-size bed.

Parking: Free, on the street.

Fronting the highway and just down (left) from the cook shops, this is an ideal and inexpensive place to make your base while getting to know the area. Rooms are cheery and clean, with scored concrete floors, bathrooms with doors and walls but no ceiling separating it from the rest of the room, hanging racks for clothes, and blue iron doors and window frames. Most rooms have a single and double bed or two doubles, and one room on the roof has both a king-size bed and a double bed. There's no hot water unless you ask for it and the room price is the same with or without it. A fine inexpensive restaurant in the lobby is open daily from 7am to 7pm.

WHERE TO DINE

Besides the line of seafood restaurants near the town square and lining the beach, there are inexpensive outdoor kitchens on the street fronting the highway serving delicious grilled chicken marinated in orange juice.

ADRIANO'S, Av. Pacifico 2. Tel. 8-0088.

Cuisine: SEAFOOD.

$ **Prices:** Breakfast $2.50–$5.75; seafood $9.25–$17; beer $1.35.

Open: Daily 8am–11pm.

Just off Bucerías's main square and on the beach, Adriano's is an inviting place to eat while spending the day on the beach. Piñatas decorate the ceiling in the large dining room and the outdoor terrace faces the beach. The extensive menu includes french toast and shrimp omelets at breakfast, and seafood and nachos at other meals. The *plato campechano* is a seafood platter.

MARK'S, Lázaro Cárdenas 56. No phone.
  Cuisine: PIZZA/SANDWICHES/SUNDAY BRUNCH.
  $ Prices: Pizza $8–$13.50; meatball sandwich $5.75; Sunday brunch $6.
  Open: Mon–Sat 5–11pm; Sunday brunch 10am–1pm.
The most popular American hangout is also a relaxed place to catch the breezes and the latest U.S. news and sporting events on the wide-screen TV. Mike McMahon from Michigan opened the restaurant in 1990, and specializes in whole-wheat pizzas seasoned with fresh herbs grown in his garden. Sunday brunch includes omelets, waffles, bacon, fresh juice, diced potatoes, and toast. When you see the ice factory on the inland side of the highway into town, turn toward the beach and the restaurant is straight ahead, one block before the beach.

PIE IN THE SKY BAKERY, Carretera 200. Tel. 8-0306.
  Cuisine: PASTRIES.
  $ Prices: $1.50–$6.
  Open: Mon–Sat 9am–5pm.
Whatever you do, don't miss the experience of sampling the goodies from this wonderful bakery. It's worth the effort to find it. Owners Don and Teri Murray turn out *Besos* (kisses)—an out-of-this-world cross between a brownie and a muffin (great fresh or frozen)—three fabulous flavors of cheesecake (scaled for a crowd or for one), three sizes of rich carrot cake with rum-soaked raisins, and exotic pecan pie. Eat some, take some for a do-it-yourself breakfast or dessert, and buy some for your friends—they'll love you forever. While you're there you can also buy a copy of *Cooking in Puerto Vallarta* by Bea Bender for $15. Bender's 320-page book blends recipes with stories of local food tradition providing colorful insight into the village that you won't find anywhere else. To find the bakery, go on Highway 200 towards Tepic to the edge of Bucerías and start looking for the small PIE IN THE SKY sign on your right. Turn left when you see it, then immediately left again; it's down about a block on the right.

SAN BLAS

San Blas, Nayarit (pop. 10,000), is a rather ugly Pacific-coast fishing village. Surveying the dirt streets and rag-tag central square when you arrive may well make you wonder "Is this it?" The uninviting wide beaches, with hard-packed thick-grained sand, sport few palm trees. At night, especially during the rainy season, the whole town is infested with no-see-ums that will send you scrambling for the insect repellent. Were it not for its reputation as a birders' mecca and surfers' delight, the town might well languish as an undesirable outpost. Still, most of the year it attracts an assortment of tourists, some looking for an inexpensive retreat on this ever more expensive coast, and others who come just to see the birds or to surf. Hotels are few, but often full, especially on major Mexican holidays.

Only 150 miles from Puerto Vallarta, it's an easy trip in 3½ hours, now that the new non-toll highway bypasses Tepic. This new two-lane paved highway had just opened when I traveled it and didn't have a number, but the turn-off to it begins at Las Varas off Highway 200 (there's a sign for Las Varas) and goes through the villages of Santa Cruz and Aticama before connecting with the two-lane highway into San Blas. Ask directions. Buses from Puerto Vallarta were still taking the long way (five hours) through Tepic and were not yet traveling the new route when I checked; it's likely they will by the time you travel. If they aren't going direct, then take a **Pacifico bus** to Las Varas, and change there to a San Blas–bound bus; there may be a wait so try to get to Las Varas before noon. October is the wettest month of the rainy season (which runs from May through October) brings the worst of the no-see-ums. Bring plenty of insect repellent. Summer is hot and steamy.

As you enter the village, you'll be on **Avenida Juárez,** the principal street, which leads to the main plaza on the right. At its far end sits the old church, with a new one next to it. Across the street from the church is the bus station, and on the other side of the churches is the market. After passing the square, the first one-way street to the left is **Batallón,** an important street that passes a bakery, a medical clinic, several hotels, and Los Cocos Trailer Park, and ends up at **Borrego Beach,** with its many outdoor fish restaurants. Nearly everything is within walking distance, and there are public buses that go to the farther beaches (Matanchen and Los Cocos) on their way to the next village to the south, Santa Cruz.

The **tourist office,** next door to McDonald's Restaurant on Avenida Juárez, is open Monday through Friday from 9am to 3pm.

WHAT TO SEE & DO

After you've walked around the town and taken the river cruise, there is not a lot to do besides relax, swim, read, walk the beach, and eat fish—unless you're a serious birdwatcher or surfer. During the winter months, however, you can also look for **whales** off the coast of San Blas.

PORT OF SAN BLAS Like Acapulco, San Blas was once a very important port for New Spain's trade with the Philippines. Pirates would attempt to intercept the rich Spanish galleons headed for San Blas, and so the town was fortified. Ruins of the fortifications complete with cannons, the old church, and houses all overgrown with jungle are still visible atop the hill, **La Contadura.** The fortress settlement was destroyed during the struggle for independence in 1811, and has been in ruins ever since. From San Blas Father Junípero Serra also set out to establish missions in California during the 18th century.

The view from La Contadura is definitely worth the trouble of getting there: The entire surrounding area stretches out before you, a panorama of coconut plantations, coastline, town, and lighthouse at Playa Del Rey. To reach the ruins from San Blas, head east on Avenida Juárez about ½ mile, as if going out of town. Just before the bridge, take the stone path that winds up the hill to your right.

BEACHES & WATER SPORTS One of the closest beaches is **Borrego Beach,** south from the town plaza on Batallón until it ends. This is a gray sand beach edged with palapa restaurants selling fish. For a more secluded place to swim, pay a fisherman to take you across El Pozo Estuary at the southwest edge of town to the "island," actually **El Rey Beach.** Walk to the other side of the island and you might have it all to yourself. Or try the beach on the other side of the lighthouse on this island. Bring your own shade, for there are no trees. The fisherman "ferry" charges about $1 one-way and operates from 6am to 6pm. Canoes and small boats can also be rented at the harbor on the west side of town, following Avenida Juárez.

About three miles south of San Blas is **Matanchen Bay.** If driving, head out Avenida Juárez towards Tepic, cross the bridge, and turn right at the sign to **Matanchen.** A bus also stops there on its way south to the village of Santa Cruz, departing from the bus station on the main square at 9am, 11am, 1pm, 3pm, and 5pm; check on the return stops at Matanchen Bay, which are generally an hour later. There's a little settlement here where you can have a snack or a meal, or rent a boat and guide for the jungle river cruise.

A half mile past the settlement is a dirt road to **Las Islitas Beach,** a magnificent swath of sand stretching for miles, with a few beach-shack eateries. This is the famous surfing beach of the mile-long waves, and real and would-be surfing champions come from Mexico and the United States to test their mettle here, especially during September and October, when storms create the biggest waves. If you don't have a surfboard, you can usually rent one from one of the local surfers. The bodysurfing at Islitas and Matanchen is good, too. A taxi to Islitas will cost about $6 from downtown San Blas.

Farther south from Matanchen is beautiful **Playa Los Cocos,** lined with coconut palms. It's also on the bus route to Santa Cruz, but double-check on stops and schedules before boarding in San Blas.

JUNGLE CRUISE TO TOVARA SPRINGS Almost the moment you hit San Blas, you'll be approached by a "guide" who offers "a **boat ride** into the jungle." This can be exciting, but expensive as well, depending on how many people share the cost: about $40 for a boatload of one to four persons for the three- to four-hour trip from the bridge at the edge of town on Juárez. It's less (about $30) for the shorter, two-hour trip from the Embarcadero near Matanchen Bay, out of town. Either way it's worth it if you take the early morning cruise—through shady mangrove mazes and tunnels, past tropical birds and cane fields, to the beautiful natural springs, La Tovara, where you can swim. There's a restaurant here, too, but stick to soft drinks or beer. This is one of the unique tropical experiences in Mexico, and to make the most of it, find a guide who will leave at 6:30 or 7am: The first boat on the river encounters the most birds, and the Tovara River is like glass then, unruffled by breezes. Around 9am the boatloads of tour groups start arriving, and the serenity evaporates like the morning mist.

Note: The guide may also offer to take you to **"The Plantation"**—pineapple and banana plantations on a hill outside of town. The additional cost of this trip, for most people, is not worth it.

BIRDWATCHING As many as 300 species of birds have been sighted here, one of the highest counts in the Western Hemisphere. **Birders and hikers** should pick up a copy of the booklet, *Where to Find Birds in San Blas, Nayarit,* by Rosalind Novick and Lon Sing Wu, on sale at Hotel Las Brisas Resort. With maps and directions it details all the best birding spots and walks—including hikes to some lovely waterfalls where nonbirdwatchers can swim, too. Probably the best bilingual guide to birds and the area is **Manuel Lomelli,** who can be reached through Las Brisas Motel (tel. 321/5-0307 or 5-0558). A day's tour will cost around $100, which can be divided among the participants. Birding is best from mid-October to April.

WHERE TO STAY

For additional lodging choices, especially for a long stay, check the ads posted at McDonald's restaurant.

Moderate

HOTEL LAS BRISAS RESORT, Calle Paredes Sur s/n, San Blas, Nay. 63740. Tel. 321/5-0480 or 5-0307. Fax 321/5-0308 or 5-0112. 42 units, 5 minisuites. A/C TV FAN

$ Rates (including breakfast): $58 single; $81 double; $104 suite. **Parking:** Free.

A block inland from the waterfront and nestled among pretty gardens of palms, hibiscus, and other tropical plants are the cottagelike fourplexes and other buildings (one with three stories) of this oasis of a resort. The tranquil ambience, two pools (one for toddlers), and one of the best restaurant/bars in town all add to the appeal of the nicest place to stay in San Blas. Rooms are modern, bright, airy, and immaculate with well-screened windows and fans as well as air conditioning. Several rooms have a kitchen and come with king-size beds, otherwise most have two double beds and a few have an extra single bed. Each room has an in-room safety box. Another bonus is the manager, María Josefina Vazquez, one of the most knowledgeable and helpful people I've met on the Pacific coast!

To get here walk south from the square on Batallón about six blocks, then right on Campeche across from the Marino Inn, then left on the next street, Paredes Sur.

Budget

HOTEL LOS BUCANEROS, Av. Juárez 74 Pte., San Blas, Nay. 63740. Tel. 321/5-0101. 33 rms. FAN
$ Rates: $20 single; $25 double.

A six-foot-long stuffed crocodile smiles with open jaws at visitors who venture into the lobby. The neat and freshly painted rooms are built around a courtyard, and guests enjoy the swimming pool and patio. The hotel is on the main street, one block west of the town plaza.

MOTEL POSADA DEL REY, Calle Campeche 10, San Blas, Nay. 63740. Tel. 321/5-0123. 12 rms. FAN
$ Rates: $23 single; $27 double.

Rooms at the Posada del Rey circle a tiny courtyard taken up entirely by a little swimming pool. An open-air bar on the third floor provides a lovely view of the ocean and palms. The motel is one block in from the waterfront at El Pozo Estuary, five blocks south of the town plaza. To find it turn right at the Marina Inn and the hotel is straight ahead two blocks on the right.

Camping

For camping, try the **Los Cocos Trailer Park** on Avenida Batallón and Calle José Azueta (tel. 321/5-0055), near the beach. It has 100 spaces and charges $6 single, $8 double per day for a basic hookup in its grassy park with palm trees. It also has a Laundromat and a bar.

WHERE TO DINE

For an inexpensive meal, try fresh grilled fish from one of the little shacks on the beach. A fairly large fish (filet or whole) with hot tortillas and fresh coconut milk to drink will cost about $5. The prices are the same at all of these places. From town, take Avenida Batallón south from the plaza, follow your nose when you smell the fish grilling.

Moderate

LA ISLA, Mercado and Paredes s/n. Tel. 5-0407.
   Cuisine: SEAFOOD/BEEF.
$ Prices: Appetizers $4; main courses $6.25–$13.50.
   Open: Tues–Sun 2–10pm.

★ Some swear the best seafood in San Blas is served here. A nautical decor of hanging shark jawbones, fishnets, and shells set the mood for the excellent shrimp, oysters, lobster, and fish. Or try the filet mignon with mushrooms. The restaurant is near the post office about two blocks south of the plaza.

RESTAURANT EL DELFIN, Hotel Las Brisas Resort, Calle Paredes Sur s/n. Tel. 5-0112.

Cuisine: INTERNATIONAL.
$ Prices: Appetizers $5.75–$11; main courses $7–$17.50.
Open: Daily 8am–9:30pm.

★ This hotel restaurant serves the best food in San Blas in a beautiful air-conditioned dining room with marble floors and a pink and green decor. Soft light, soft music, and comfortable captain's chairs add to the serene ambience. The chef masterfully plays from a wide repertoire of sauces: Try the steak with mustard sauce (ask for it if it's not on the menu), the chicken Orange, or the exquisite shrimp or chicken with a creamy *chipotle* pepper sauce. The spaghetti choices include seafood marinara and spaghetti alfredo with seafood. Homemade soups and desserts deserve encores, too.

Budget

MCDONALD'S, Juárez 36 Pte.
Cuisine: MEXICAN.
$ Prices: Breakfast $2.50–$4; appetizers $2–$5; main courses $5–$10.
Open: Nov–June, daily 7am–10pm; July–Oct, Wed–Mon 7am–10pm.

This isn't what you're thinking—in fact this family-run restaurant, founded by Glenn McDonald of Iowa, has been operating in San Blas for 35 years. Specialties of the house include a seafood platter of fish, oysters, and shrimp; and a shish kebab of seafood and beef tenderloin. You'll find it one block west of the town square.

EN ROUTE TO MANZANILLO

Several coastal resorts between Puerto Vallarta and Manzanillo are within reasonable driving distance from Puerto Vallarta. See "Easy Excursions" from Manzanillo in Chapter 8 for Las Alamandas, an exclusive small resort Hotel Bel-Air El Tamarindo, Hotel Bel-Air Costa Careyes, and Club Med Playa Blanca, all four of which are from 2½ to 3 hours from Puerto Vallarta.

CHAPTER 6
GETTING TO KNOW MANZANILLO

1. ORIENTATION
* DID YOU KNOW . . . ?
2. GETTING AROUND
* FAST FACTS: MANZANILLO

Outsiders think of Manzanillo, Colima, as a resort community, but this city of 90,000 is today Mexico's foremost Pacific port. The port and fishing industries and iron-ore mining all generate more income than the tourist business. Manzanillo remains one of the Pacific coast's hidden retreats; it's without abundant airline service, and is over 150 miles from both Puerto Vallarta and Guadalajara. Tourists don't come in droves, as they do to those cities, and the overall cost of a holiday here is slightly less than at Puerto Vallarta.

Manzanillo first began to attract foreigners seeking relief from north-of-the-border winters in the 1970s; condominiums were built on hillsides and on the beaches, setting a pattern for tourism that still holds true today—lots of little private enclaves strung out for more than 20 miles from town center toward the airport and occupying some of the most prime bay property. Hotels are few, relative to private dwellings and to other Mexican resort cities, and are just as scattered as the condominiums.

Manzanillo still isn't much to look at; its town center faces the port and railroad tracks, and outlying roadways are veiled in a swirl of dust. Recently the city has begun a long-overdue program to beautify itself, widening and resurfacing its streets and planting palms and flowers in the center medians. But whatever deficiencies can be found in the appearance of the town and its main boulevards have always been made up for by the beauty of the bays, the excellent climate, a few good beaches, and a relaxing pace. Manzanillo has a delightful laid-back ambience, some very good restaurants, and it's the ideal point from which to launch further explorations north to the coastal villages of Barra de Navidad and Melaque; inland to Colima, the capital; and to the chilly mountain villages of Jalisco state.

1. ORIENTATION

ARRIVING

BY AIR Aeromexico and Mexicana offer flights between Manzanillo and Mexico City, Guadalajara, and Los Angeles. There are connecting flights several times a week for Chicago, Dallas/Fort Worth, Monterrey, Reno, Sacramento, San Diego, San Francisco, and a few other cities.

The airport is a 45-minute ride north of town center. Colectivo vans meet each flight and you buy tickets ($6.50) inside the terminal.

BY TRAIN *El Colimense*, the first-class train running between Manzanillo,

DID YOU KNOW...?

- Colima is derived from the Náhuatl word "Coliman" which has many interpretations—place of the mountain, place of the volcano, place of the god of fire, or place of our ancestors.
- Manzanillo is named after a poisonous tree found growing where the port's first pier was built.
- In 1954 Manzanillo became "Mexico's Sailfish Capital" after a record catch of more than 300 sailfish in three days.
- The name Jalisco is a corruption of a Náhuatl word, "Xaliaco," meaning "sandy place."
- Before the conquest of Mexico, Jalisco was occupied by Purépecha and Náhuatl-speaking tribes.
- The Revillagigedo Islands, south of Baja California belong to Colima.
- López de Legazpi set sail for the Philippines from Barra de Navidad in 1564 and began the trade route of the Spanish Galleons (Nao de China) which brought riches from the Orient to Mexico.
- The Volcán de Colima (Colima volcano) first erupted in 1576 and most recently in 1991.
- In 1959 a typhoon nearly destroyed Manzanillo and Cuyutlán.
- In pre-Hispanic times in Colima a small hairless dog was bred to eat and traveled along with nomadic traders as their "portable" provisions.
- Colima is the second smallest Mexican state after Tlaxcala.

Colima, and Guadalajara, has been suspended, but may be reinstituted. Otherwise there's a slow (8 hr. or longer) second-class train. The train station is opposite the waterfront near the zócalo.

BY BUS Several bus lines have frequent service to Manzanillo from Colima (1½ hours), Guadalajara (4 hours), Puerto Vallarta (6 hours) and Barra de Navidad/Melaque (1½ hours). Manzanillo's Central Camionera (bus station) is about 12 long blocks east of town. Taxis to town line up out front and cost around $5 to town center. Though not one of the new stations in Mexico, you can buy a sandwich, send a fax, or make a long distance call here. If you're just in Manzanillo to look around for the day before moving on, there's a place to store luggage (*guarda equipaje*).

BY CAR Coastal Highway 200 leads from Acapulco and Puerto Vallarta. From Guadalajara take Highway 54 through Colima. Outside of Colima you have a choice of an expensive toll road, which is faster but less scenic, into Manzanillo.

DEPARTING

BY PLANE Transportes Terrestres (tel. 3-2470), the colectivo airport service, picks up passengers at hotels. Call a day ahead for reservations. One-way, the cost is $6.50. The downtown Manzanillo office of **Aeromexico,** between Quintero and Galindo, is in the Centro Comercial "Carrillo Puerto" (tel. 333/2-1267 or 2-1711). Another Aeromexico office (tel. 3-0910 or 3-0911) is in the Plaza Santiago next to Banco Internacional. **Mexicana** is at Avenida Mexico 380 (tel. 333/2-1972 or 2-1009; airport 3-2323). The airport is 45 minutes northwest of town at Playa de Oro. A colectivo van will cost $6.50 from the airport to downtown Manzanillo.

BY BUS Manzanillo's **Central Camionera** (bus station) is about 12 long blocks east of town. Follow Hidalgo east and the camionera will be on the right. **Autotransportes Colima** (also known as Los Altos—no phone) goes to Colima every 15 minutes. On a "Directo" the trip takes 1½ hours with two stops. An "Ordinario" takes two hours and stops many times. Both types drop off passengers within two blocks of Colima's main square rather than Colima's outlying Central Camionera. To Barra de Navidad, an hour north, the company with the most frequent service is **Auto Camiones de Pacifico** (tel. 2-0515), with deluxe service (de paso) which they call "Primera Plus" (quite confusing since there's also a line by that name)

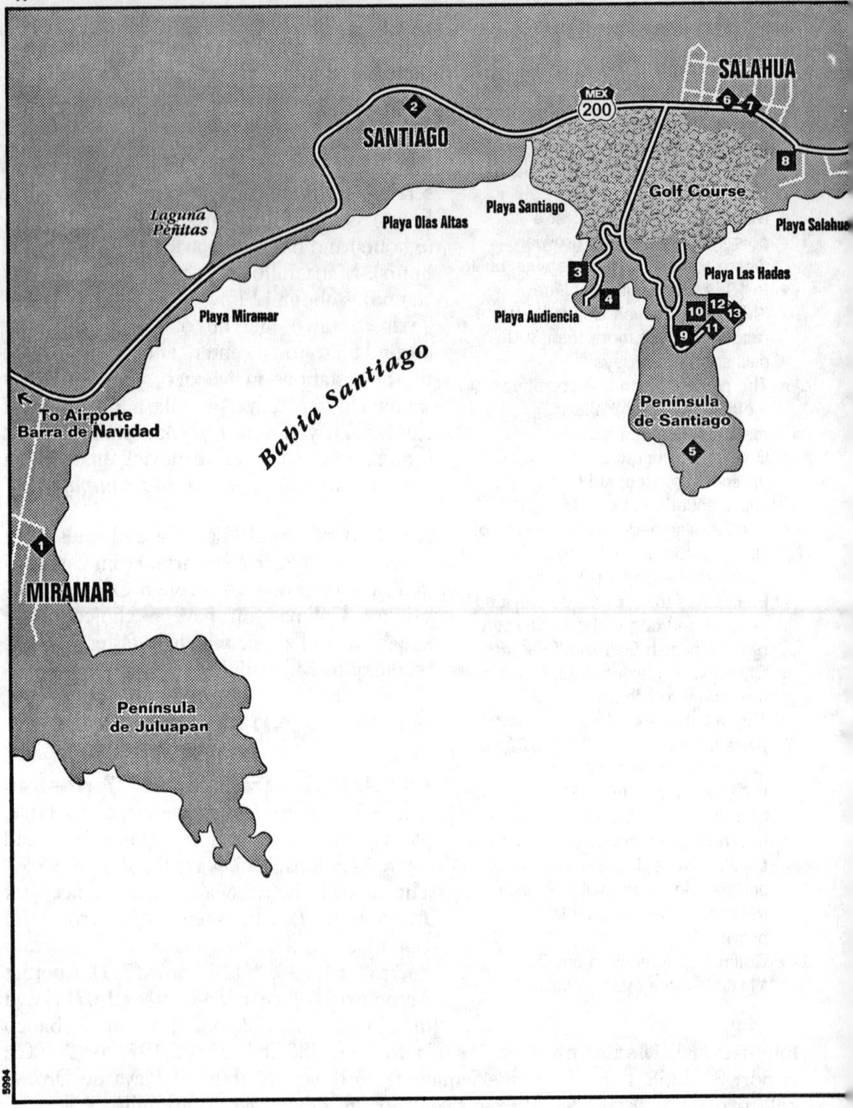

ACCOMMODATIONS:

Club Vacacional 17
Condominios Arco Iris 8
Las Hadas 12
Hotel la Posada 18
Hotel Marlyn 3
Hotel Playa de Santiago 4
Hotel Plaza las Glorias 10
Hotel Ruiseñores 19
Hotel Sierra Manzanillo 9

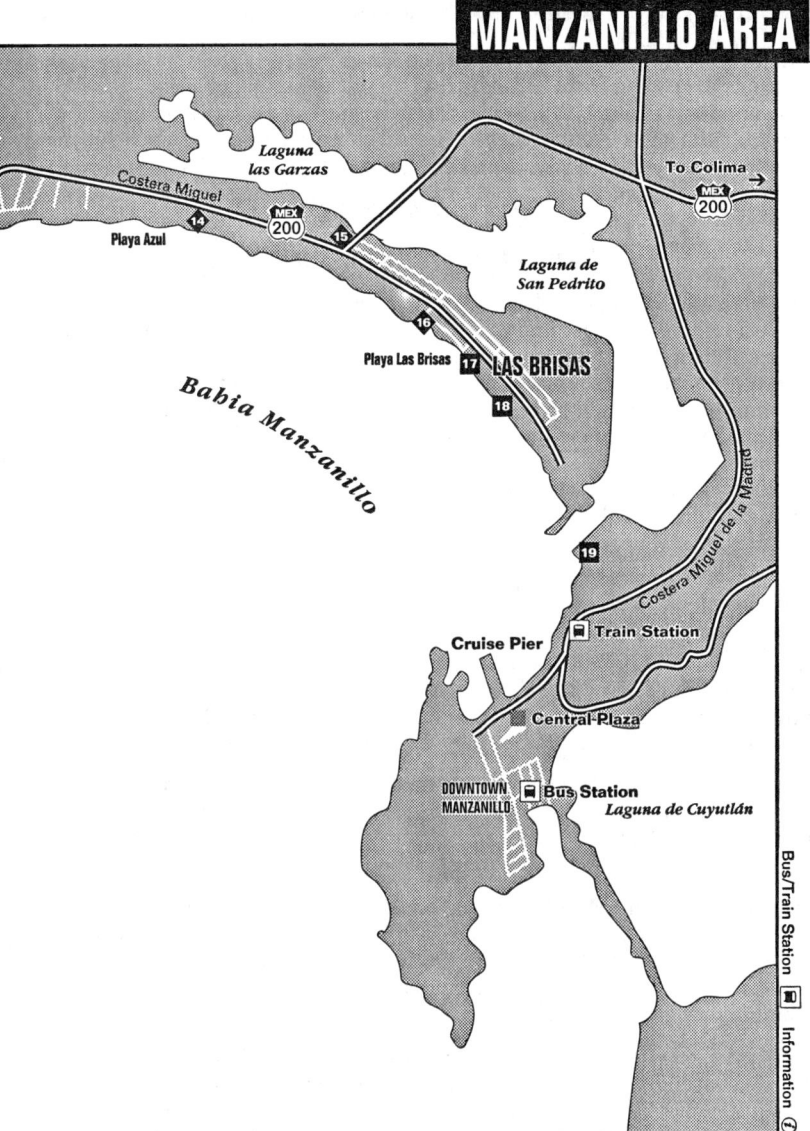

DINING:
Carlos 'n' Charlie's ⑭
Juanito's ②
Legazpi ⑭
Manolo's Bistro ⑥
Oasis ①

Ostería Bugatti ⑮
La Plazuela Restaurant ⑪
Restaurant la Audencia ⑤
El Vaquero Campestre ⑦
Willy's ⑯

six times a day and 10 second-class buses. **La Linea** (tel. 2-0123) has first-class service to Colima (1½ hours) and Guadalajara (4½ hours) 10 times daily. **Servicios Coordinados** (tel. 2-0210) has first-class buses to Guadalajara nine times a day. **Primera Plus** (tel. 2-0210) has deluxe buses with video movies and air conditioning several times daily to Guadalajara and Puerto Vallarta.

CITY LAYOUT
NEIGHBORHOODS IN BRIEF

Downtown The town, which is less attractive than you might expect, is at one end of a seven-mile-long curving beach, facing Manzanillo Bay, with four beach sections—Playa Las Brisas, Playa Azul, Playa Salahua, and Playa Las Hadas. The northern terminus of the beaches is the Santiago Peninsula. Downtown activity centers around the plaza which has a brilliant poinciana tree with red blossoms, a fountain, kiosk, and a view of the bay. Train tracks parallel the street leading into the downtown area, then cut across the street to go inland. Large ships dock at the pier nearby. Avenida Mexico, the street leading out from the plaza's central gazebo, is the town's principal commercial thoroughfare. Walking along here you will find a few shops, small eateries, and juice stands. At night swallows by the hundreds come to roost on the telephone wires around the plaza.

Las Brisas Las Brisas peninsula fronts Manzanillo Bay and is separated from downtown by a cut large enough for ships to pass. It's between downtown and the Santiago Peninsula and it's reached by the Boulevard Costera Miguel de la Madrid (named for a president of Mexico born in the state capital of Colima). Turn back left at the Las Brisas intersection. A narrow paved road leads back down the peninsula past a row of small hotels fronting the beautiful Playa Las Brisas beach.

Salahua Once you leave downtown the line of commercial buildings along the highway seems almost endless, and it's difficult to tell without a map when you've left one settlement and arrived at another. Salahua (the name means "salt water"), is one such settlement after Las Brisas and just before Santiago.

Lagoons **Laguna de Cuyutlán,** almost behind the city, stretches for miles south paralleling the coast. **Laguna de San Pedrito,** north of the city, parallels the Costera Madrid and it's behind Playa Las Brisas beach. **Playa del las Garzas,** a short distance farther north, is separated from Laguna San Pedrito by a small strip of land and is behind Playa Azul. All are good for birdwatching.

Santiago Peninsula Beyond the San Pedrito and Las Garzas lagoons is Salahua, the subdivision on the right, and the Santiago Peninsula on the left, seven miles from downtown. The high rocky mountain peninsula juts out into the bay separating Manzanillo Bay from Santiago Bay. It's the site of many beautiful homes, Las Hadas Resort and Las Hadas's La Mantarraya Golf Course, and the best hotels in the area. The beach, Playa Las Hadas, is on the south side of the peninsula facing Manzanillo Bay and Playa Audiencia is on the north side facing Santiago Bay. Santiago and town are linked by the Costera de la Madrid. This stretch of road is also called the Santiago Highway, especially the extension beyond Santiago Peninsula.

Bays **Manzanillo Bay** has the harbor, town, and beaches closest to town and it's separated by the Santiago Peninsula from the second bay, **Santiago,** which also has several beaches.

IMPRESSIONS

Manzanillo, the main Pacific port for Guadalajara, Michoacán and Mexico City is a turn-of-the-century holdover, skipped over by main highways, tourists, airlines and tourist agents.
—JAMES NORMAN, *TERRY'S GUIDE TO MEXICO*, 1965

The place [Barra de Navidad] is tropically picturesque, has magnificent stretches of golden beach and is just beginning to develop as a tourist haven.
—JAMES NORMAN, *TERRY'S GUIDE TO MEXICO*, 1965

2. GETTING AROUND

BY BUS The local buses (called camionetas) make a circuit from downtown in front of the train station out along the lagoon opposite Playa Azul, and then along the Bay of Manzanillo to the Santiago Peninsula and the Bay of Santiago to the north. The "Las Brisas" buses are the main ones; they go to the Las Brisas crossroads, then onto the Las Brisas Peninsula and back to town. "Miramar," "Santiago," and "Salahua" buses go to outlying settlements along the bays and to most restaurants mentioned in Chapter 7. Buses marked "Las Hadas" go onto the peninsula and make a circuit by the Las Hadas resort and the Sierra Manzanillo and Plaza las Glorias hotels. This is an inexpensive way to see the coast as far as Santiago and to take a tour of the Santiago Peninsula.

BY TAXI Taxis in Manzanillo supposedly have fixed rates for trips within town, as well as to points more distant, but they aren't posted; ask your hotel what a ride should cost to get a feel for what's right, then bargain. A ride from the Central Camionera to the Salahua area costs around $5; to town center, about $4.

FAST FACTS

American Express Representative is Bahías Gemelas Travel Agency, Boulevard Costera Madrid, km 10 (tel. 3-1000 or 3-1053; fax 3-0649).

Area Code The area code is 333.

Banks Banamex downtown is just off the plaza on Avenida Mexico. It's open Monday through Friday from 9:30am to 1:30pm but changes foreign currency only until 12:30pm.

Climate Manzanillo's tropical climate is hot and humid in the summer.

Holidays See "When to Go" in Chapter 2.

Information The tourism office (tel. 3-2277 or 3-2264) in Manzanillo is on the Costera Miguel de la Madrid 4960, km 8.5. It's open Monday through Friday from 9am to 3:30pm.

Telephone See "Fast Facts: Mexico" in Chapter 2.

CHAPTER 7
WHERE TO STAY & DINE IN MANZANILLO

1. WHERE TO STAY
2. WHERE TO DINE

In Manzanillo where you stay tends to be your vacation experience more so than in other Mexican resort cities that have numerous side attractions. All areas are reasonably convenient to one another by either bus or taxi. Reservations are recommended for the Christmas, New Year's, and Easter holidays.

1. WHERE TO STAY

DOWNTOWN
BUDGET

HOTEL COLONIAL, Av. Mexico 100 and Gonzales Bocanegra, Manzanillo, Col. 28200. Tel. 333/2-1080 or 2-1134. 40 rms.
$ Rates: $24 single or double with fan; $26 single or double with A/C.
An old favorite, this three-story colonial-style hotel changes little from year to year—the same beautiful blue and yellow tilework and colonial-style carved doors and windows adorn the lobby and restaurant, and the same minimal furniture, red-tiled floors, and basic comfort at ever-increasing prices characterize the rooms. Twenty-five rooms are equipped with air conditioning; the other 15 rooms have fans. In the central courtyard is a restaurant/bar. It's one block inland from the plaza at Galindo; the hotel is on the right corner.

HOTEL EMPERADOR, Balvino Davalos 69, Manzanillo, Col. 28200. Tel. 333/2-2374. 28 rms. FAN
$ Rates: $12–$14 single bed; $18 two beds.
This very basic low-budget hotel offers clean, bare rooms with hot water and a fan. Most look out onto the tiny inner courtyard, which is more like an airshaft. Walk through the restaurant to find the reception desk on the left. It's one block west (left) of the plaza almost to the corner of Carrillo Puerto.

HOTEL RUISEÑORES, Tte. Azueta s/n. Tel. 333/2-2424 or 2-0646. 72 rms. FAN
$ Rates: $20 single; $27 double.
Though it's a little off the main path, the Hotel Ruiseñores is located on the main

public beach and therefore is close to downtown and transportation. Rooms are clean, freshly painted, and comfortable though sparsely furnished. Each comes with a small closet, desk/vanity, tile floors, and worn but clean bathrooms. In the courtyard facing the beach and ocean is a pool for adults and another for children; a second-story terrace on the courtyard is the place to catch the breeze. Most rooms have ceiling fans but some have only a small table fan. To find it follow the road to the edge of downtown going toward the Costera. On the right you'll see a sign at a small traffic circle which reads OFICINAS POTUARIOS where you turn left and cross the railroad tracks. It's on the left.

LAS BRISAS

Buses run out to Las Brisas from downtown. Look for "Brisas Direc" on the signboard. It's a six-mile trundle around Manzanillo Bay, ultimately curving southward. Most hotels, bungalows, and condominiums are on the single main road.

MODERATE

CLUB VACACIONAL LAS BRISAS, Av. Lázaro Cárdenas 207, Las Brisas, Manzanillo, Col. 28200. Tel. 333/3-2075 or 3-1717. 56 bungalows. A/C (24rms) FAN (32rms) TEL

$ Rates: $29 single with fan, $42 single with A/C; $46 double with fan, $63 double with A/C. **Parking:** Free, in front.

This beachfront hostelry has plain but comfortable bungalows with kitchenettes surrounding a large pool and grassy interior lawn shaded by palms. Besides the pool there's one tennis court, and a restaurant open for all three meals. It's extremely popular with Mexican families on weekends. It's about halfway down the Las Brisas Peninsula.

HOTEL LA POSADA, Av. Lázaro Cárdenas 201, Las Brisas (Apdo. Postal 135), Manzanillo, Col. 28200. Tel. and fax 333/3-1899. 24 rms. FAN

$ Rates (including breakfast): High season $78 single or double. Low season $52 single or double.

Another longtime favorite of traveling cognoscenti, this small inn has a shocking-pink stucco facade with a large arch that leads to a broad tiled patio right on the beautiful beach. The rooms have exposed brick walls and simple but very tasteful furnishings with Mexican decorative accents. The atmosphere here is casual and informal—you can help yourself to beer and soft drinks all day long, and at the end of your stay, owner Bart Varelmann (a native of Ohio) counts the bottle caps you deposited in a bowl with your room number. All three meals are served in the dining room or out by the pool. If you want to come for a meal, breakfast, served between 8 and 11am, costs around $5; lunch and dinner (sandwiches), served between 1:30 and 8pm, cost about the same. During low season the restaurant is open only from 8am to 3pm. Or just come for a drink at sunset; the bar's open until 9pm all year. It's at the far end of Las Brisas Peninsula—the end closest to downtown. From town center take the "Las Brisas" bus.

SALAHUA

CONDOMINIOS ARCO IRIS, Costera Madrid, km 9.5 (Apdo. Postal 359), Manzanillo, Col. 28200. Tel. 333/3-0168. 21 rms. FAN

$ Rates: $70–$80 large quadruple; $47 small double.

More like a motel with kitchenettes, than what we normally regard as condominiums, it's in a shaded parklike area set back off the busy Costera; the beach is close by the back of the property. Large quarters have two bedrooms and small ones have one bedroom. All the cottages have tile floors, kitchens, dining and living-room areas (some of which are in the kitchen), patios in front, screened windows, and small bathrooms. There's a pool in the center of the grounds. This is a popular place for Mexican families on weekends and holidays, but midweek it's quite tranquil. It's beside Jalapeño's restaurant on the bay side, and the sign to it is easily missed.

SANTIAGO PENINSULA

Three miles north of Las Brisas is the wide Santiago Peninsula. At one end is the settlement of Salahua, on the highway where you enter the peninsula to reach the hotels Las Hadas, Plaza las Glorias, and Sierra Manzanillo as well as the Mantarraya Golf Course. Buses from town marked "Las Hadas" go every 20 minutes into the interior of the peninsula and by those hotels. Past the Salahua turnoff, at the end of the settlement of Santiago, an obscure road on the left is poorly marked ZONA DE PLAYAS; it leads to the hotels on the other side of the peninsula—hotels Marlyn and Playa de Santiago. To get to the latter hotels, take a bus to the main Santiago bus stop and transfer there to a taxi (available at all hours).

VERY EXPENSIVE

LAS HADAS, Santiago Peninsula, Manzanillo, Col. 28200. Tel. 333/3-0000, toll free 800/228-3000 in the U.S. and Canada. 220 rms and suites. A/C TV TEL MINIBAR

$ Rates: High season $260–$295 single or double; $355–$420 Royal Beach Club. Low season $182–$205 single or double; $305–$370 Royal Beach Club.

Anyone who has ever heard of Manzanillo has heard of Las Hadas; or say Las Hadas and a lot of people think that *is* Manzanillo. You may remember it from the movie *10* which featured Bo Derek and Las Hadas. The self-contained Eden that put Manzanillo on the map was the brainchild of the Bolivian entrepreneur Antenor Patino, featuring Moorish-style architecture that started a trend in Mexico and still has hardly an equal for lavishness. Built on the beach and up a half-moon shaped curve of the peninsula, the elegant white resort hotel is one of the most famous, popular, and exclusive in Mexico; it's among the exclusive "Leading Hotels of the World." The rooms, built around the hillside overlooking the bay, are connected by cobbled lanes lined with colorful flowers and palms. Covered, motorized carts are on call for transportation within the property. Though it's a large resort, it maintains an air of seclusion since rooms are large, spread out, and tucked here and there in short rows among the landscaped grounds. The six categories of accommodations are roughly divided among those with views of partial views and those with extra amenities. The understated, elegant, and spacious rooms have white-marble floors, sitting areas, and comfortably furnished balconies. Royal Beach Club guests have rooms on the upper tier with great bay views and some have private pools. They receive special amenities such as robes and hairdryers. Room 804 in the Royal Beach Club has a whirlpool on the patio with a fabulous view of the bay.

Entry, through a guarded gate, is to hotel guests, those who come for the daily guided tour of the resort, occupants of condominiums on an adjacent hill, patrons with restaurant reservations, or to bearers of tickets for the sunset cruise that takes off from here.

Dining/Entertainment: El Palmar, open from 5:30am to midnight is an open-air restaurant overlooking the pool. Los Delfines, open from 1 to 6pm and near the water, specializes in seafood. Elegant Legazpi Restaurant and Lounge is the formal place to dine, open from 6pm to midnight (see "Where to Dine," below). El Terral is open in winter only from 7pm to 1am and serves Mexican specialties. There are five lounges and bars with live entertainment somewhere on the property almost every evening, plus the disco, Cartouche, which opens at 10pm. Hours and restaurants may vary during low season.

Services: Laundry, room service, shopping arcade, travel agency, beauty and barber shops, child care. Royal Beach Club guests have rapid check-in, continental breakfast, cocktails, concierge, preferred restaurant reservations, and late checkout.

Facilities: Club Las Hadas includes La Mantarraya, the hotel's 18-hole golf course; two pools; beach with shade tents; 10 tennis courts (8 hard-surface, 2 clay); marina for 70 vessels; and water sports—scuba diving, snorkeling, sailing, and trimaran cruises. Royal Beach Club guests have an exclusive pool and reserved lounge chairs at the pool and beach.

EXPENSIVE

HOTEL PLAZA LAS GLORIAS, Av. de Tesoro s/n, Santiago Peninsula. Manzanillo, Jal. 28200. Tel. 3-0812 or 3-0622; toll free 800/342-2644 in the U.S., toll free 91-800/3-6566 in Guadalajara. Fax 333/3-1395. 86 rms, 17 Beach Club suites. A/C TV TEL

$ Rates: High season $105–$155 single or double; low season $90–$125 single or double. (Prices may vary more with season or holiday.)

The deep burnt-orange-colored walls of this pueblo-like hotel ramble over a hillside on Santiago Peninsula. From the restaurant on top and from most rooms is a broad vista of other red-tiled rooftops and either the palm-filled golf course or bay. It's one of Manzanillo's hidden resorts, known more to wealthy Mexicans than to Americans. Originally conceived as private condominiums, the quarters were designed for living; each accommodation is spacious, stylishly furnished, and very comfortable. Each unit has a huge living room; a small kitchen/bar open to the living room; one, two, or three large bedrooms with Saltillo-tile or brick floors; large Mexican tiled bathrooms; huge closets; and large furnished private patios with views. A few of the rooms can be partitioned off and rented by the bedroom room only. Water is purified in the tap and each room has a key-locked security box. Try to get a room on the restaurant and pool level—otherwise there'll be a lot of stairs to climb. However, there's a hillside rail elevator that goes from top to bottom, but doesn't stop in between. Beach Club suites, which are not as luxurious as those in the main hotel, are at another location on Las Brisas Beach, several miles from the main hotel. Standard Beach Club suites have two bedrooms, two bathrooms, a fully equipped kitchen, and a separate dining area open to the sunken living room (off of which there is a terrace or balcony). Penthouse suites are two stories with the living and kitchen/dining area and a bedroom and bathroom downstairs, two bedrooms and a bathroom upstairs, and balconies on both levels. The hotel is often full weekends and holidays, so make reservations early. Package rates can cut the cost of your stay.

Dining/Entertainment: La Plazuela restaurant (see "Where to Dine" below), a casual and informal restaurant shaped like a half-moon, is beside the pool and fronts the bay side to capture both the views and breezes. It's open for all three meals. Live musicians often serenade diners.

Services: Laundry, room service, elevator from bottom of property to top, babysitters arranged with advance notice.

Facilities: One pool on the restaurant level; Beach Club on Las Brisas beach, where there's a pool and small restaurant; transportation to the Beach Club from the main hotel in the morning with return transportation in the afternoon; golf privileges at La Mantarraya Golf Course; use of facilities at Las Hadas.

WHERE TO STAY & DINE IN MANZANILLO

HOTEL SIERRA MANZANILLO, Av. La Audiencia 1, Los Riscos, Manzanillo, Col. 28200. Tel. 333/3-2000; toll free 800/333-3333 in the U.S. Fax 333/3-2272. 350 rms and suites. A/C TV TEL MINIBAR
$ Rates: $125–$300 single or double; $1,500 presidential suite.

One of the most luxurious hotels in Mexico, the Sierra Manzanillo opened in 1990; its 21 floors overlook La Audiencia beach. Architecturally it mimics the white Moorish style that has become so popular in Manzanillo. Inside it's palatial in scale and awash in pale grey marble. Room decor picks up the pale grey theme with washed grey armoires that conceal the TV and minibar. Most standard rooms have two double beds or a king-size bed plus a small table, chairs, and desk. Several rooms at the end of most floors are small, with one double bed, small windows, no balcony, and no view. Most rooms, however, have balconies and either ocean or hillside views. The 10 gorgeous honeymoon suites are carpeted and have sculpted shell-shaped headboards, king-size beds, and chaise longue. Junior suites have a sitting area with couch and large bathrooms.

Dining/Entertainment: La Hidra is an informal restaurant overlooking the pool and beach and is open from 7am to 11pm. El Sol is on the pool terrace and has swim-up service from 10am to 6pm. La Palapa, next to the beach and tennis courts, serves snacks from noon to 6pm. Los Tibores, an elegant, formal restaurant on the 7th floor, serves international specialties from 6 to 11pm. Evenings from 8pm to 2am there's live music for dancing in Bar Sierra, the lobby bar, from 1pm to midnight. La Porticada, an upper terrace bar, is open from 5 to 11pm.

Services: Laundry, room service, ice machine on each floor, hairdryers, beauty salon with massage available, travel agency, 24-hour currency exchange.

Facilities: Grand pool on the beach; children's pool; four lighted tennis courts; extra cost health spa with exercise equipment, scheduled aerobics, hot tub, and separate sauna and steam rooms for men and women; access to Las Hadas golf course.

MODERATE

HOTEL MARLYN, Santiago Peninsula (Apdo. Postal 288), Manzanillo, Col. 28200. Tel. 333/3-0107. 42 rms and suites. A/C (4 suites) FAN (38 rms)
$ Rates: $30 single; $35 double; $135 bungalow for four.

White and airy, this hotel has a little swimming pool and a beachfront café. Some rooms have a sea view, but rates are much lower on the side facing inland. It's on the Audiencia Bay side of Santiago Peninsula. Taxis know the way.

HOTEL PLAYA DE SANTIAGO, Santiago Peninsula (Apdo. Postal 147), Manzanillo, Col. 28860. Tel. 333/3-0055 or 3-0270. Fax 333/3-0344. 105 rms, 24 bungalows. FAN TEL
$ Rates: $40 single or double; $35 bungalow. **Parking:** Free.

One of those 1960s-era hotels aimed at the jet set (which has migrated around the peninsula to Hotel Plaza Las Glorias and Las Hadas) the Playa de Santiago still gives you the essence of glamor at a fraction of the price. On a small beach. Rooms in the main hotel building, which is situated on a small beach, are small and clean with nearly up-to-date furnishings, tile floors, tiny closets, and balconies facing the ocean. Most have two double beds. Bungalows are in a separate building next door and are rather dreary, with dark green bedspreads, old furniture, small bathrooms, and walls that need painting. Some bungalows have kitchenettes and all have a nice-size patio—but no patio furniture. The restaurant and bar is positioned for views and there's a swimming pool and tennis court.

2. WHERE TO DINE

For picnic fixings there's a big supermarket, the Centro Comercial Conasuper on the road leading into town, ½ block from the plaza at Morelos. The huge store sells food, produce, household goods, clothes, hardware, and more. Open daily from 8am until 8pm.

DOWNTOWN

MODERATE

BENEDETTI'S PIZZA, Av. Mexico 1019. Tel. 2-5719 or 2-5869.
  Cuisine: PIZZA.
  $ Prices: $6.75 medium pizza; $9 large pizza; extra ingredients $1.25–$2.25 each depending on pizza size.
  Open: Daily 10am–6pm.
With several branches in town (some other branches are called Giovanni's Pizza), Benedetti's probably has an outlet not too far from where you are, and they deliver within a mile of each location. The variety isn't extensive, but the pizzas are quite good. This branch is downtown, one block inland from the plaza. Other branches stay open until midnight. If you're on the Costera coming from town center, the most visible one is on the right a short distance before the turnoff to La Mantarraya Golf Course and Las Hadas (tel. 3-2420 and 3-2426).

LY CHEE, Niños Heroes 397. Tel. 2-1103.
  Cuisine: CHINESE/INTERNATIONAL.
  $ Prices: Chinese $7–$15; seafood $10–$50; steaks $11.50.
  Open: Tues–Sun 2–10pm.
The most pleasurable of the waterfront restaurants faces the harbor under a huge palapa. The fare is about half Cantonese with international dishes such as steaks and seafood making up the other half. The Chinese food is filling but lacks flavor, so stick with seafood or steaks. It's on the waterfront, catercorner from the train station and plaza.

BUDGET

CAFETERÍA/NEVERIA CHANTILLY, Juárez and Madero (across from the plaza). Tel. 2-0194.
  Cuisine: MEXICAN.
  $ Prices: Breakfast $3–$4.75; main courses $3.75–$7.75; comida corrida $5.75.
  Open: Sun–Fri 7am–10pm; comida corrida 1–4pm.
Join the locals at this informal corner café facing the plaza. The large menu includes club sandwiches, hamburgers, carne asada a la Tampiqueña, enchiladas, fish, shrimp, and vegetable salads. The full comida corrida, a real value, might begin with fresh fruit cocktail, followed by soup, rice, the main course, dessert, and coffee. It's tasty and filling.

HELADOS BING, Av. Morelos and 21 de Marzo. No phone.
  Cuisine: ICE CREAM.
  $ Prices: Single cones 70¢; double cones $1.50.
  Open: Daily 8am–10pm.
Look for Bing's pink-and-white awning on the northeast corner of the plaza opposite the harbor, and trundle over for the best ice cream in Mexico. Have it by the cone, in

a cup, or piled with calories like the Bing special in a glass with fruit, hot chocolate, cream, and nuts; or a Bing roll, a 10-inch roll of cake and ice cream.

LA PERLITA RESTAURANT, Perlita Plaza. Tel. 2-2770.
    Cuisine: MEXICAN.
$ Prices: Tacos and sandwiches $2–$3; main courses $8.50–$14.
    Open: Daily 10am–6pm.

Look for the orange awnings and yellow umbrellas at this restaurant on the waterfront. Its white wrought-iron tables are set out on the shady plaza overlooking the harbor. Main courses are a bit overpriced, so save your bucks for a nicer place; stick with the sandwiches and tacos if you're hungry. La Perlita is, however, a pleasant place to rest and have a drink—the big draw here is the extensive alcoholic drink list that goes well beyond a beer. It's located one block to the right of the plaza, opposite the train station and next to the Sunset Cruise ticket office.

Botaneros

Botaneros are a tradition almost exclusive to Manzanillo. For the price of a beer or soft drink, they serve complimentary delicious snacks—ceviche, soup, shark stew, pickled pigs' feet, tacos—the list goes on. The more you drink, the more the food appears. Bring a group of four or more and platters really arrive. It's customary to order at least two drinks and to tip the waitress well. She puts a box for your empties at your table and tallies the tab from its contents when you're ready to leave. Sometimes roving musicians come in to serenade; you pay per song, so settle on the price in advance. And most botaneros have a form of betting game, which you'll have to get a local to explain. Besides those below, there's also El Menudazo on the way to Santiago. Most are open daily from noon to 8pm and all charge about the same for a beer or soft drink.

BAR SOCIAL, facing the plaza.
    Cuisine: DRINKS/SNACKS.
$ Prices: Beer or soft drink $1.75.
    Open: Mon–Sat noon–11pm.

More like a traditional Mexican cantina, with swinging doors and a room full of men, it's one of the original botaneros that's as popular with locals as it is with tourists. Women, however, will feel more comfortable in groups or with a male companion. Tables and booths are against the walls and an enormous bar takes up the center of the room. By early evening it gets noisy, crowded, and drunk inside, and tourists will probably want to exit before all that happens.

EL ULTIMO TREN, Niños Heroes. Tel. 2-3144.
    Cuisine: DRINKS/SNACKS.
$ Prices: Beer or soft drink $1.75.
    Open: Daily noon–8pm.

Among the cheeriest of the botaneros, El Último Tren (the last train), is covered by a grand high palapa with ceiling fans to stir up the breeze. There's enough of a family feel to the place to bring older children, although technically they aren't allowed. It's not far from downtown proper, on the right, several blocks past the train station. Just in case—women's rest rooms are named *máquinas* (cars) and the men's room is a *garrotero* (signalman).

SANTIAGO ROAD

The restaurants below are on the Costera Madrid between downtown and the Santiago Peninsula and includes an area known as Salahua.

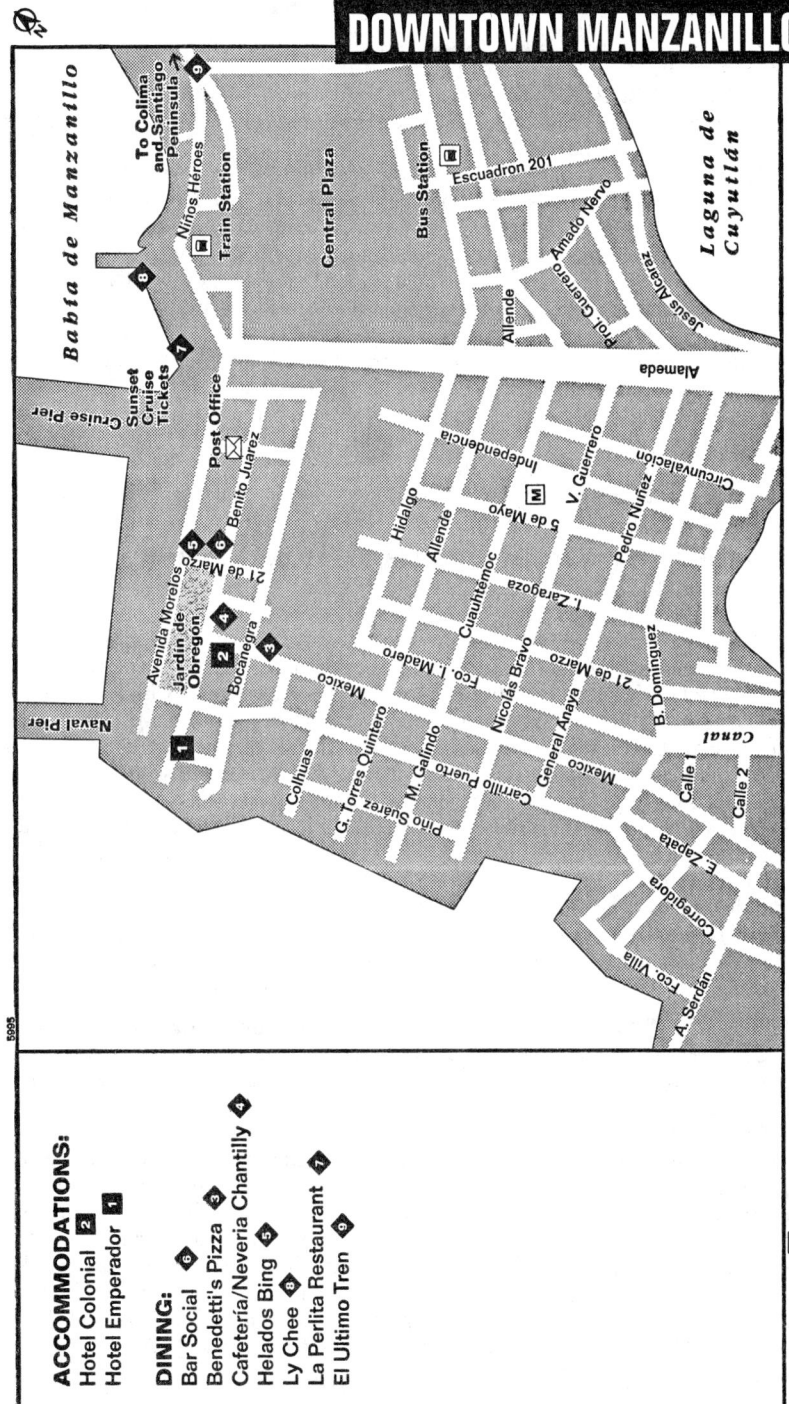

EXPENSIVE

CARLOS 'n' CHARLIES, Costera Madrid, km 6. Tel. 3-1150.
  Cuisine: GRILLED SPECIALTIES. **Reservations:** Recommended after 6pm.
  $ Prices: Main courses $11–$23.
  Open: High season daily 1pm–1am; low season daily 6pm–1am.

This franchise restaurant offers the trademark silliness and good food that has made the Anderson chain popular throughout Mexico. It starts with the facade that shows a dancing elephant, singing iguana, and shimmying mermaid, and continues inside with a decor of snorkeling fins, records, surfboards, hard hats, and cloth fish hanging from the ceiling. Of course you can't miss the enormous reclining mermaid or the giant boat/bar. Eat inside or outside with a view of the beach and bay—great for sunset; both dining areas have nice breezes. Come before 9pm for a good table. Seafood and beef are grilled outdoors; other specialties include beer-batter shrimp and "grande" margaritas. In the evening during high season there may be a required minimum order/cover if you come just to drink, but the "cover" includes three drinks. On weekends and during high season they open the new dance area and serve fast food and snacks there. To get here from town center take the "Salahua," "Miramar," or "Santiago" bus; to return to town take the "Estacion" bus.

MANOLO'S BISTRO, Costera Madrid, km 10.5. Tel. 3-2140.
  Cuisine: INTERNATIONAL/STEAK/SEAFOOD.
  $ Prices: Main courses $12–$22.
  Open: Mon–Sat 6–11pm.

Manolo's has moved next door, from under the casual thatched palapa into a smaller, more refined space with a French flair. Cloth-covered tables are set with a single fresh flower and handsome wood-backed chairs with a patina reminiscent of a European dining room. The menu continues as before and friendly owners Manuel and Juanita Lopez and family do the serving. They cater to American tastes with "safe" salad dispensed from a salad bar. Among the popular entrées is filet of fish Manolo on a bed of spinach with melted cheese Florentine style, and frogs' legs in brandy batter. They claim the onion soup is "the best this side of Paris." And most people can't leave without first being tempted by the fresh coconut or homemade pecan pie. Coming from downtown, Manolo's is on the right about three blocks before the turn to Las Hadas, its rose-colored walls almost dwarfed next to the sprawling burnt-orange walls of El Vaquero Campestre. By bus from town center take a "Miramar," "Salahua," or "Santiago" bus and return on an "Estacion" bus.

OSTERIA BUGATTI, Santiago and Las Brisas crossroads. Tel. 3-2999.
  Cuisine: INTERNATIONAL. **Reservations:** Recommended after 8pm.
  $ Prices: Appetizers $5–$9; Sonora steaks and seafood $10.75–$17; pasta $7–$8.50.
  Open: Daily 1pm–1am. **Closed:** Sept 15–27.

One of the best restaurants in town is in a dark, vaulted cellar with a brick ceiling and soft lighting. Your English-speaking waiter arrives bearing a platter laden with quality Sonora beef, plus pork and seafood. Your selection will be cooked to your specifications. Seafood selections include lobster, red snapper, and shrimp. There's a small selection of pastas too, including spaghetti alla bolognese and lasagna. Air conditioning, plus a complete international bar, help to make this a popular place. It's at the Las Brisas crossroads, several miles north of town center. Take the "Las Brisas," "Salahua," "Santiago," or "Miramar" bus from town center and get off at the Las Brisas crossroads. Take the "Estacion" bus back to town.

EL VAQUERO CAMPESTRE, km 12, Salahua. Tel. 3-0475.

Cuisine: GRILLED MEATS.
$ Prices: Main courses $11–$16; beer $2.50; wine $4.
Open: Daily 10am–11pm.

It's hard to miss the sprawling burnt-orange stucco wall and wagon wheels along the iron work and over the door of this restaurant. It's in Bistro Manolo's former spot; cloth-covered plastic tables and chairs are set under a couple of grand thatched palapas. The specialty here is Sonora beef cut just about any way you can think of on either side of the border—T-bone, mignon, ribeye, tampiqueña, etc. The arrachera is similar to the tampiqueña (a long thin cut) but the meat is softer. The churrasco is a filet for two people, charcoal-grilled then sliced and served with potatoes, beans, and tortillas. Most meats are served with grilled onions, beans, and tortillas. Most cuts are also available by the kilo for two or more people. To get here take the "Santiago," "Salahua," or "Miramar" bus.

LAS BRISAS

WILLY'S, Las Brisas crossroads. Tel. 3-1794.
Cuisine: SEAFOOD/INTERNATIONAL. **Reservations:** Recommended.
$ Prices: Appetizers $4.50; main courses $9–$21.
Open: Daily 7pm–midnight.

You're in for a treat at one of Manzanillo's most popular restaurants. It's breezy, casual, and small with perhaps 20 tables inside and 10 more on the narrow balcony over the bay. Among the outdoor grilled specialties is shrimp filet imperial wrapped in bacon, red snapper tarragon, dorado basil, and robalo with mango and ginger, homemade pâté, and coconut flan. This is food with a flair that's a winner with locals and tourists alike. Double back left at the Las Brisas crossroads and Willy's is on the right down a short side street to the ocean. To get there via public transportation from the train station, take a "Las Brisas" bus and ask the driver to let you off at Willy's, then walk half a block toward the ocean.

SANTIAGO PENINSULA

VERY EXPENSIVE

LEGAZPI, Hotel Las Hadas hotel, Santiago Peninsula. Tel. 3-0000.
Cuisine: INTERNATIONAL.
$ Prices: Appetizers $11–$18; main courses $20–$40.
Open: Daily 6pm–midnight.

For sheer elegance, gracious service, and outstanding food, don't miss the opportunity to dine here. The candlelit room announces dining tranquillity with tables, covered in pale pink and white and set with silver and flowers; a pianist plays softly in the background. Enormous bell-shaped windows on two sides show off the sparkling bay below. Meals begin with a basket of warm breads, and courses are interspersed with servings of fresh-fruit sorbet. The sophisticated menu includes prosciutto with melon marinated in port wine, crayfish bisque, broiled salmon, roast duck, lobster, or veal, and flaming desserts from crêpes to Irish coffee. It's a dining experience you won't soon forget.

EXPENSIVE

LA PLAZUELA RESTAURANT, Hotel Plaza Las Glorias, Av. de Tesoro s/n, Santiago Peninsula. Tel. 3-0440 or **3-0550.**

Cuisine: INTERNATIONAL.
$ Prices: Appetizers $4–$7.75; main courses $7.75–$17.50.
Open: Daily 8:30–11am, 1–5pm, and 7–11:30pm.

For meal on an outdoor mountainside terrace with a fabulous bay view, try this restaurant. It's breezy, casual, and cool any time of day but makes a great night out, what with the city lights twinkling around the bay and breezes brushing the mountain top. Main courses include steaks and fish prepared to your liking, and there's a fine selection of Mexican platters as well as chicken, tacos, and enchiladas. It's on the Manzanillo Bay side of Santiago Peninsula near Las Hadas. The "Las Hadas" bus from town center will drop you within walking distance.

BUDGET

RESTAURANT LA AUDIENCIA, La Audiencia beach. Tel. 3-0955.
Cuisine: INTERNATIONAL. **Bus:** Take the "Las Hadas" bus.
$ Prices: Breakfast $2.50–$4.75; hamburgers and sandwiches $2.50–$5.75; pizza $7–$19; Mexican specialties $5.75–$9; comida corrida $5.75.
Open: High season Tues–Sun 9am–10pm; low season 9am–6pm.

This pleasant little indoor/outdoor restaurant, half a block from La Audiencia beach, offers something to please just about everybody—and at reasonable prices. Besides fast food–style hamburgers and pizzas, there's fish fixed just about any way and popular Mexican specialties such as milanesa, carne asada, and enchiladas. If you stay for a meal (rather than order take-out), the owner, Magdalena Contreras Espinosa, usually treats diners to a delicious fruit drink, a specialty of the house. To get here get off the "Las Hadas" bus when it turns on Calle La Audiencia and walk down the hill towards the beach.

BEYOND SANTIAGO

EXPENSIVE

OASIS, Club Santiago. Hwy. 200 to Barra de Navidad, km 18. Tel. 3-0937.
Cuisine: SEAFOOD.
$ Prices: Soup $4–$6; main courses $18–$35.
Open: Tues–Sun 11am–2am.

Opened in 1991 by the owners of Willy's, the ambience here is entirely different. Enter through the great bamboo doors and you'll find rustic elegance while dining under this gigantic palapa overlooking the bay and open to the breezes. The menu is similar to Willy's except that it's primarily seafood with a few chicken, pork, and beef main courses. Among the specialties you'll find red snapper provençal, shrimp curry, and sea bass tarragon with apples. To find the Oasis go 10 miles from downtown and turn left at the Club Santiago sign. Turn left again at the first street and it's all the way to the end.

L' RÉCIFE RESTAURANT & BAR. Punta Juliapan, Hwy. 200 to Barra de Navidad. Tel. 3-0624.
Cuisine: STEAK/SEAFOOD. **Reservations:** Recommended.
$ Prices: Main courses lunch $7–$27, dinner $13–$35.
Open: Bar daily 10am–11:30pm; restaurant daily 1–5pm and 7–11:30pm. (Last half of Sept usually closed).

It's almost 20 miles beyond town to the turnoff to this mountaintop restaurant, but it's worth the drive. You'll see the sign pointing left on the highway. Follow that road for a couple of miles. The restaurant spreads out from a giant palapa covering around the terrace and swimming pool and overlooks a beautiful cove. It's a delightful place to come for a swim and lunch or for a romantic dinner. Among the specialties you'll find prime rib, chateaubriand, and duck. The seafood grill is excellent.

MODERATE

JUANITO'S, Costera Madrid, km 14. Tel. 3-1388 or fax 3-2019.
  Cuisine: HAMBURGERS/MEXICAN/AMERICAN.
  $ Prices: Breakfast $2–$4; hamburgers $2–$4.75; ribs $7.
  Open: Daily 8am–11pm.

The motto here is *Come Mucho, Pague Poco* (Eat a Lot and Pay a Little). I've watched this immaculate, family-run restaurant grow and prosper over the years and their recipe for success is simple: Serve the most popular mainstays of the U.S. and Mexican cuisines. John "Juanito" Corey and his wife Esperanza and children are always on duty serving hamburgers and fries, hot dogs, club sandwiches, fried chicken, barbecued chicken and ribs, tacos, tostadas, enchiladas, milkshakes, lemonade, pie, and ice cream. Now there are a few items beyond fast food, such as beef or fish filet and chicken in white sauce. The hamburgers taste just like home, although they're smaller and the portion of fries is not as large as in the States. It's 8½ miles from downtown Manzanillo on the highway going to Barra de Navidad and it's before the Club Maeva resort. To get here from town center, take the "Miramar" or "Fco. Villa" bus.

CHAPTER 8

WHAT TO SEE & DO IN MANZANILLO

- **SUGGESTED ITINERARIES**
1. **ORGANIZED TOURS**
- **FROMMER'S FAVORITE MANZANILLO EXPERIENCES**
2. **SPORTS & RECREATION**
3. **OTHER ACTIVITIES**
4. **EASY EXCURSIONS**

Activities in Manzanillo depend on where you stay. Most resort hotels here are completely self-contained, with restaurants and sports all on the premises. Manzanillo is a good jumping-off point for crossing into Jalisco state, north to Barra de Navidad and Melaque, to the individual beach resorts of Fiesta Americana Los Angeles Locos Tenecatita (yes, that's all one name), Hotel Tecuan, Hotel Bel-Air El Tamarindo, Hotel Bel-Air Costa Careyes, Club Med Playa Blanca, and Las Alamandas, a new, luxurious and ultra-exclusive inn. The curvy drive through the mountains after passing Barra de Navidad is a beautiful one. It's also easy to make excursions southeast of Manzanillo, inland to Colima, capital of Colima state, an hour away, and on to the mountain resort towns of Tapalpa and Mazamitla, both a three-hour drive from Manzanillo in Jalisco state (see Chapter 12).

SUGGESTED ITINERARIES

IF YOU HAVE 2 DAYS Take it easy on your first day—go for a dip in the ocean or a pool, and have dinner at a nearby restaurant. Sleep in on day two, then treat yourself to a room service breakfast and dine at leisure on your own patio. Spend the rest of the day by the pool or on the beach. In the evening take a sunset cruise, then have dinner at an outdoor restaurant such as L'Récife or Las Plazuelas.

IF YOU HAVE 3 DAYS Get into the slow swing of Manzanillo on your first two days as suggested above, then on the third day rise early and take a side trip to see the museums in Colima, the state capital located an hour to the southeast. Or spend the day on the beach at the coastal village of Barra de Navidad 45 minutes south.

IF YOU HAVE 5 DAYS With an extended stay in Manzanillo, you'll have time to sample the activities described above, and then perhaps you might want to explore the beautiful coast south of Manzanillo. Select from one or two of the resorts mentioned in the "Easy Excursions" section below. Or for a true change of pace, spend one or two nights at one of the chilly mountain resorts of Jalisco—Tapalpa or Mazamitla—located three hours to the southeast and covered in in Chapter 12.

1. ORGANIZED TOURS

CITY TOURS/EXCURSIONS   Because Manzanillo is so spread out, you might consider a city tour, or one to Barra de Navidad. I highly recommend the services of Luis Jorje Alvarez at the **Viajes Lujo,** Avenida Mexico 143-2, Manzanillo, Col. 28200 (tel. 333/2-2919; fax 333/2-4075). Office hours are Monday through Friday from 9am to 2pm and 4 to 7pm and Saturday from 9am to noon, but tours in or out of town can be anytime. A ½-day city tour costs around $20; a trip to Barra de Navidad costs around $45 per person. He can also arrange fishing and provide trips to the mountain resorts of Tapalpa and Mazamitla. He uses air-conditioned vans and speaks English.

SUNSET CRUISE   Many charter boats are available along the waterfront. For a sunset cruise, buy tickets from travel agents, at Las Hadas, or downtown at La Perlita Dock fronting the harbor (across from the train station). The ticket outlet at La Perlita is open daily from 10am to 2pm and 4 to 7pm; tickets cost around $19. Cruises from Las Hadas cost $23. Both cruises include two drinks. During high season it's a good idea to buy the ticket a day ahead, since hotels and travel agencies in town also book these cruises. But during low season you can take a chance and just show up at 5pm. Cruises last 1½ to 2 hours.

2. SPORTS & RECREATION

BEACHES   **La Audiencia beach,** on the way to Santiago, offers the best swimming, but **Playa Las Brisas,** shallow for a long way out, is the most popular because it is much closer to the downtown area. **Playa Miramar,** on the Bahía de Santiago, up past the Santiago Peninsula, is another of the town's most popular beaches, well worth the ride out there on the local bus from town. The major part of

---

FROMMER'S FAVORITE MANZANILLO EXPERIENCES

Lazy Days   Manzanillo's lack of good shopping and sightseeing attractions makes it easy to relax without that nagging feeling that you should be touring.

Terrace Dining   Manzanillo excels in good restaurants where you can enjoy the view and soothing breezes.

Sunset Cruise   There's nothing like winding up the day with the smell of fresh sea air and the sound of a ship skimming through the water while the sun goes down.

Deep-Sea Fishing   Fishing is superb here, and a day spent far out at sea is synonymous with a Manzanillo vacation.

the **Playa Azul** drops off a little too steeply for safe swimming, and is not recommended for waders.

BIRDING There are many lagoons along the coast. As you go from Manzanillo up past Las Brisas to Santiago, you'll pass the **Laguna de San Pedrito** and **Laguna de las Garzas** (lagoon of the herons) where herons, pelicans, and other coastal waterfowl congregate. The herons nest here in December and January. In back of town, on the road leading to Colima (the capital), is the **Laguna de Cuyutlán.** The toll road to Guadalajara crosses the lagoon and if you pull off after the bridge, you may spot many birds along the shoreline.

FISHING Manzanillo is also famous for its fishing, particularly for sailfish. Marlin and sailfish are abundant year round. Winter is best for dolphin fish, and in summer wahoo and roosterfish are in greater supply. The **international sailfish competition** is held around the November 20 holiday, and the **national sailfish competition** is sometime in February. Fishing can be arranged through travel agencies or directly at the **fishermen's cooperative** (tel. 2-1031), located downtown where the fishing boats are moored. I can recommend **Gerardo Montes** (tel. 2-0817 or 2-5085), whose boats the *Albatros I* and *Albatros II* are generally docked at the Lychee Restaurant catercorner from the train station. Fishing costs $30 an hour in a 28-foot boat and $40 an hour in a 38-foot boat, with a five-hour minimum. The cost can be shared by up to seven people in the larger boat and four in the smaller boat.

GOLF La Mantarraya Golf Club (tel. 3-0000), adjacent to Las Hadas, is open from 7am to 7pm and visitors are welcome to play. Greens fees are $50 for 18 holes or $30 for 9 holes. Carts rent for $27 to $40, clubs $24, caddies $10 to $16.

TENNIS Several of the hotels mentioned in Chapter 7 have tennis courts with a resident pro. But you can also play at La Mantarraya Golf Club next to Las Hadas. The cost is $15 an hour during the day and $24 at night (4:30–10pm). Tennis classes at the club cost $33.

3. OTHER ACTIVITIES

SHOPPING Only a few shops carry Mexican crafts and clothing and almost all are downtown on the streets near the central plaza. You can also try exploring the new malls on the road to Santiago and the arcades of the better hotels, all of which have fashionable shops.

EVENING ENTERTAINMENT Nightlife in Manzanillo consists mainly of finding a good spot for dinner and a sunset and then a good night's sleep. However, for the more active among you, **Carlos 'n' Charlies** (see "Where to Dine" in Chapter 7) is always a fun choice for both food and fun. **Cartouche Disco,** at Las Hadas resort, opens at 10pm and costs around $16 to enter. **El Bar de Felix,** between Salahua and Las Brisas by the Avis car-rental office, is open Tuesday through Sunday from 9pm to 2am and there's no cover charge. Next door, and open the same days, **VOC Disco** opens from 10pm to 4am and charges a $12 cover. The light show at 11pm splatters light beams over the waterfall and rock walls and large central dance floor. Most of these establishments have a dress code that prohibits patrons wearing *huaraches* (sandals) or shorts—but the prohibition generally applies to males more than females.

4. EASY EXCURSIONS

BARRA DE NAVIDAD & MELAQUE

Only 65 miles north of Manzanillo (a 1½-hour drive), this pair of modest beachside villages are located three miles apart on a gorgeous crescent-shaped bay with curious rock outcroppings. Both boast perfect beaches and a peaceful ambience, and have been attracting vacationers for decades. Traditionally Barra de Navidad and Melaque have appealed to those looking less for upscale, modern, and sophisticated than for quaint, quiet, and inexpensive, but the development of the Isla de Navidad resort is expected to attract a flashier set of tourists.

Highway 200 from Manzanillo north to Barra de Navidad and Melaque twists through some of the Pacific coast's most beautiful mountains, covered in oak and coconut palm and acres of banana plantations. Buses from Manzanillo run the route up the coast frequently on their way to Puerto Vallarta and Guadalajara, and most stop in the central villages of both Barra de Navidad and Melaque. A bus trip from the Navidad Bay area to Puerto Vallarta will take about five hours.

BARRA DE NAVIDAD

Barra de Navidad, which was the 17th-century harbor of the Spanish fleet (galleons set off to find China from here in 1654), has been to this point the "discovery" of a small number of budget-minded travelers who come from December through Easter and on weekends during summer. It's been a quiet getaway, with a pick of rooms and an easy pace for most of the year, but all of this is bound to change now that the long-awaited **Isla Navidad Resort** project has begun, just across the water from Barra's main pier. The final nine holes of the new resort's 27-hole golf course (designed by Robert Von Hagge) should be completed in 1993, part of a grand plan that will include hotels, homes, and condominiums. The 269-room **Grand Bay Hotel**, with a complete state-of-the-art spa, is scheduled to open there in the fall of 1994 (tel. 305/445-2493 in the U.S. for further information). And the village of Barra de Navidad itself is sprucing up to welcome the upscale clientele that the resort will bring.

Barra's hotels and main beach street, **Legazpi**, are two blocks in front of the bus station. Two blocks behind it and to the right is the lagoon side with its main street, **Morelos/Veracruz**, and more hotels and restaurants. Few streets are marked, but 10 minutes of wandering will give you the village's entire layout.

The **tourism office** for both Barra de Navidad and Melaque is in Barra at the end of Legazpi (heading out of town) in the DIF building complex (tel. 333/7-0159); it's open Monday through Friday from 9am to 5pm.

What to See & Do

Swimming and enjoying the lovely beach and bay view take up most people's time. If you want a **boat ride,** go to your right, just about ½ block south of the Restaurant Eloy on Calle Veracruz, until you come to the tiny boatmen's cooperative, with fixed prices posted on the wall. Someone will take you wherever you want to go. A round-trip to the village of **Colimilla,** just across the lagoon, popular for its many pleasant restaurants, costs $12 for up to eight people and you stay as long as you like; for a 30-minute **tour around the lagoon,** it's $19; or out on the sea, $24. **Deep-sea fishing** costs $24 per hour and up to six people can share the cost. **Waterskiing** costs $64 an hour.

132 • WHAT TO SEE & DO IN MANZANILLO

Where to Stay

During low season (May through November) it doesn't hurt to ask for a discount even on low-season rates.

HOTEL CABO BLANCO, Pueblo Nuevo (Apdo. Postal 31), Barra de Navidad, Jal. 48970. Tel. 333/7-0103. Fax 333/7-0168. 101 rms and condos/suites. A/C TEL

$ Rates: $65 single; $70 double; $100 junior suite; $150 suite; $200 master suite. This inland hotel, five minutes from the beach, is Barra's best, built more for yacht owners than beach lovers. A marina harbors most vessels or owners can dock in the canal in front of the row of condos. The main hotel section is built around large interior grounds and a pool with a swim-up bar, and edged by lawns, palms, and tropical foliage. The condo section is farther back with a separate pool. Hotel rooms have a patio or balcony facing either the pool or interior garden and each has a semicomplete kitchen with bar and sink. The condo section features one-, two-, and three-bedroom quarters, with as many stories. Each has a complete kitchen, living room, and bathrooms off each bedroom.

Dining/Entertainment: The hotel has two restaurants, one indoor and one outdoor.

Services: Laundry, room service, lobby TV with U.S. channels, travel agency, babysitting by reservation.

Facilities: Swimming pool for adults and one for children, two tennis courts, yacht marina.

HOTEL DELPHÍN, Calle Morelos 23, Barra de Navidad, Jal. 48987. Tel. 333/7-0068. Fax 333/7-4020. 25 rms, 3 apartments. FAN

$ Rates: $27 single; $35 double. **Parking:** Free, across street.

Among Barra's better-maintained hotels, this three-story hotel offers nice, well-cared-for rooms, each with red-tile floors and either double or two single beds. Outside each room are tables and chairs on the covered walkways. The courtyard with small pool and lounge chairs is shaded by an enormous tree. A breakfast buffet is served during high season on the lovely second-level breakfast terrace and costs $5 to $6 (see "Where to Dine" below). It's on the landward side of the lagoon about midway down.

HOTEL SANDS, Morelos 24, Barra de Navidad, Jal. 48987. Tel. 333/7-0018 or 7-0148. 43 rms. FAN

$ Rates: High season $34 single; $50 double. Low season $28 single; $38 double. The colonial-style Sands offers small but homey rooms, with red-tiled floors, and windows with both screens and glass. Lower rooms look onto a public walkway and wide courtyard. Upstairs rooms are brighter. In back is a beautiful pool by the lagoon. The hotel is known for its high-season "happy hour" from 2 to 6pm at the pool-terrace bar. After 6pm, the hotel is quiet again. It's catercorner from the Hotel Delphín, on the lagoon side at Jalisco.

HOTEL TROPICAL, Legazpi 96, Barra de Navidad, Jal. 48987. Tel. 333/7-0020. Fax 333/7-0149. 57 rms. FAN

$ Rates: High season $71 single; $88 double. Low season $50 single; $61 double. Located on the beach, this hotel offers nice (but very overpriced) rooms with either a view of the sea or lagoon. Rooms all have two double beds. Oceanview rooms have a narrow terrace and wall of windows, making the rooms bright and cheery. The breezy seaview terrace restaurant has a separate bar, and a tiny children's pool. It's at the far end of Legazpi facing the bay.

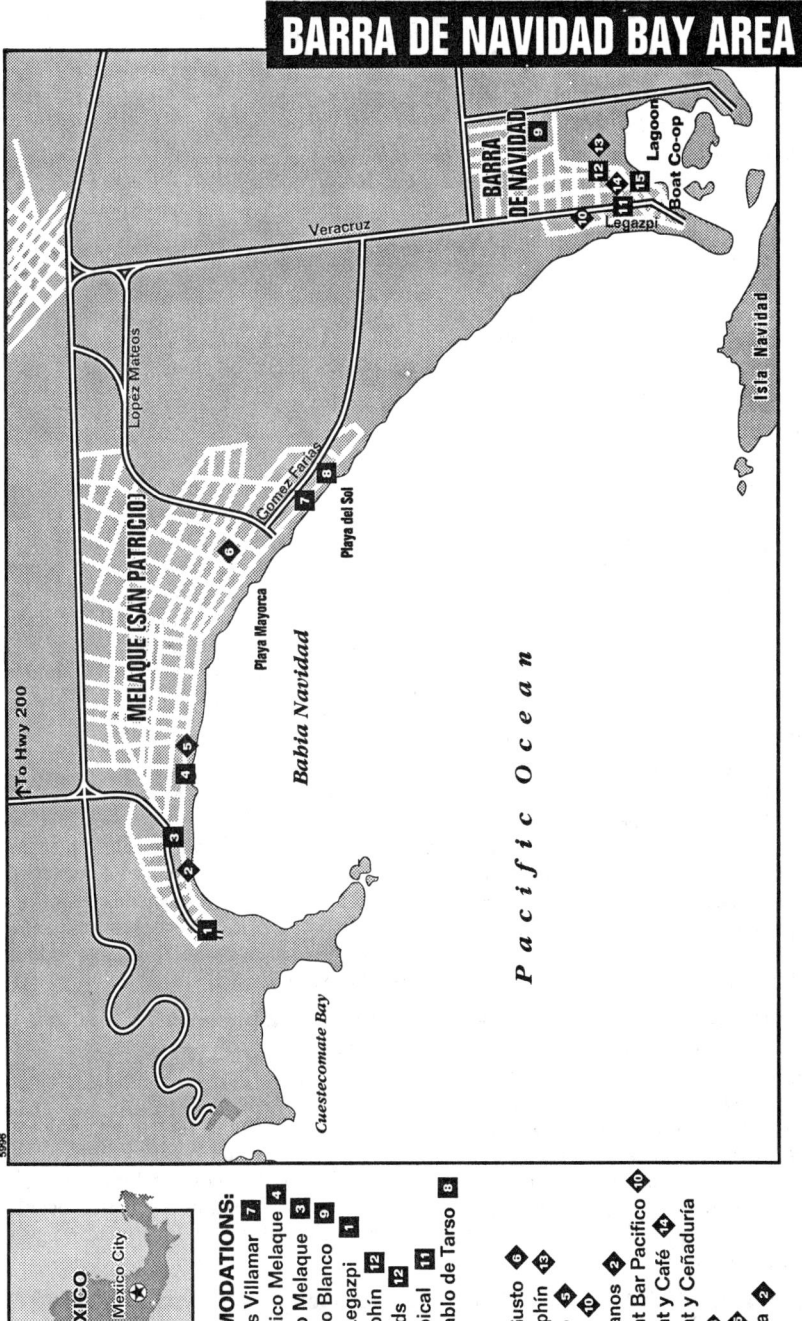

Where to Dine

HOTEL DELPHÍN, Calle Morelos 23. Tel. 7-0068.
   Cuisine: INTERNATIONAL.
$ Prices: Breakfast buffet $4.75–$5.75.
   Open: Daily 8–11am; high-season beer garden noon–5pm.

The second-story terrace of this small hotel is the most pleasant place to begin the day in Barra. The help-yourself buffet breakfast offers an assortment of fresh fruit, juices, granola, yogurt, milk, and pastries. For a few pesos more you can order eggs benedict and the delicious banana pancakes for which the restaurant is rightfully well known. The owner's son-in-law, Gerhard Hetz, winner of two world championships in swimming, was planning to offer fresh, grilled German sausage, snacks, and beer during high-season afternoons. By the way, the sausage is delicious and served on a fresh bun with mustard.

PANCHOS, Legazpi 53. Tel. 7-0176.
   Cuisine: SEAFOOD.
$ Prices: Breakfast $1.50–$4; fish $5.75–$15.50; shrimp plates $10–$16.
   Open: Daily 9am–11pm.

★ For the most popular place where locals hang out for the food and conversation, pull up a chair on the sand floor. Roving musicians drop in and bananas hang on a string. In the afternoon it's the place to chew the fat (besides the food), play a game of dominoes, and have a big lunch. You must try the spicy deviled shrimp that was invented here. The ground marlin ceviche is fabulous in a sauce of tomatoes and hot peppers. An order is plenty for two people. You'll find it towards the far end of Legazpi, next to Restaurant Bar Pacífico.

RESTAURANT BAR PACIFICO, Legazpi 206. No phone.
   Cuisine: SEAFOOD.
$ Prices: Seafood $6.25–$17.50; chicken $4.50.
   Open: Daily 8am–9pm; happy hour 4–7pm.

Facing the beach and bay, this is a popular place for a snack or whole meal. Appetizers include nachos, ceviche, and queso fundido. The seafood platter for two comes with lobster, ceviche, and fish filet. The combination Mexican plate has enchiladas, tacos, quesadillas, rice, beans, and guacamole and the combo plate has steak, shrimp, and chicken. They also serve hamburgers and good margaritas. There's a large indoor dining room and a row of tables outside on the beach.

RESTAURANT Y CAFÉ, Av. Veracruz 101-A. No phone.
   Cuisine: CREPES/VEGETARIAN/MEXICAN.
$ Prices: Breakfast $2.75; crêpes $5.75–$8.50.
   Open: Daily 8am–10pm; happy hour 11am–2pm. **Closed:** Sept.

Up a flight of stairs in a building at the corner of Veracruz and Jalisco (opposite the Restaurant y Ceñaduría Patty), you'll find this cozy restaurant open to the breezes. The crêpes are named after towns in France; the delicious *crepa Paris*, for example, is filled with chicken, potatoes, spinach, and green sauce. Mexican specialties include tortas and quesadillas. For something lighter try a seafood or fruit salad. Highly recommended.

RESTAURANT Y CEÑADURÍA PATTY, Jalisco at Veracruz. Tel. 7-1007.
   Cuisine: MEXICAN/REGIONAL.
$ Prices: Breakfast $2.75–$3.25; main courses $1.75–$4.
   Open: Daily 8am–11pm.

This cute little corner café is a pleasant place to eat; the checked tablecloths, concrete floor, and pastel walls of its interior are all open to the breeze. The menu includes the popular mainstays of pozole, tostadas, tacos, and sopa at dinner. The lunch menu is a bit more stout with beef, fish, and shrimp platters.

VELEROS, Veracruz 64. No phone.
Cuisine: SEAFOOD/BEEF.
$ Prices: Seafood $8-$12; chicken and beef $6-$10.
Open: Low season daily noon-11pm; high season daily 8am-11pm.

At this restaurant on the lagoon, it's tranquilizing to watch fishing boats float by. The ambience is clean, classy, and casual with cloth-covered tables, an ivy-covered brick wall, impeccable service, and dependably good food. Seafood specialties include shrimp brochet and fish filet, but there's also peppersteak, filet mignon, and grilled chicken. It's on the lagoon, near the boat rental and Restaurant Eloy.

MELAQUE

For a change of scenery you may want to wander over to Melaque (also known as **San Patricio**) three miles from Barra and on the same bay. You can walk to it on the beach from Barra or take one of the frequent local buses from the bus station near the main square in Barra. If you can imagine it, Melaque's pace is even more laid-back than Barra's, and though it's a larger village it seems smaller, has fewer restaurants, and less going on. The paved road ends where the town begins. A few yachts bob in the harbor and the palm-lined beach is gorgeous.

If you come by bus from Barra, you'll be dropped off at the new bus station near town center a block from the beach. Restaurants and hotels line the beach and it's impossible to get lost, but a word of orientation will help. Coming into town from the main road, you'll be on the town's main street, **Avenida López Mateos.** You'll pass the main square and come down to the waterfront, where there's a trailer park. The street going left (southeast) along the bay is **Avenida Gomez Farías;** the one going right (northwest) is **Avenida Miguel Ochoa López.**

Where to Stay

The prices mentioned below are for low season (May to October). From November to the end of Easter week, prices may go up 25% to 30% in some hotels.

All along this seaside avenue, you'll see signs for hotels as well as bungalows. In Melaque, bungalows are rooms with a kitchen and sometimes a sitting room as well.

Be aware that the sound of the pounding surf in Melaque is loud enough to disturb a good night's sleep.

BUNGALOWS VILLAMAR, Hidalgo 1, Melaque, Jal. 48980. Tel. and fax 333/7-0005. 5 bungalows. FAN
$ Rates: $16-$20 single; $20-$25 double bungalow; $25-$31 larger bungalow. Discounts for longer stays.

It's a quiet place where you can watch waves breaking and the palm trees swishing in the garden. Clean, but well used, the bungalows enjoyed a fresh coat of paint in 1990. Most have two bedrooms, living room and kitchen, bath, private patio out back, and a private sitting terrace with chairs out front by the garden. There is also an elevated terrace overlooking the beach and bay. Manager Roberto Ramirez speaks perfect

136 • WHAT TO SEE & DO IN MANZANILLO

English and is friendly and helpful. It's almost always full during winter months, so make reservations well ahead. It's on the corner, next to Posada Gaviotas.

CLUB NÁUTICO MELAQUE, Gómez Farías s/n, Melaque, Jal. 48980. Tel. 333/7-0770 or 7-0766. Fax 333/7-0239. 56 rms (all with bath). FAN
$ Rates: $60 single; $74 double.

⭐ One of Melaque's better inns, rooms are nicely furnished and immaculate. Some have private balconies. There's a swimming pool in front (street side) of the hotel. El Dorado, the hotel's huge breezy beachside palapa restaurant and bar with a total bay view is one of the nicest on the beach (see "Where to Dine" below). To find it, walk right from the front of the bus station, it's on the left facing the beach.

COCO CLUB MELAQUE, Miguel Ochoa López (Apdo. Postal 8), Melaque, Jal. 48940. Tel. 333/7-0001. Fax 333/7-03882. 236 rms and suites. A/C
$ Rates (including all meals and open bar): $60–$95 single; $90–$130 double; $90–$100 suite per person.

Recently bought by the Club Maeva chain, this is Melaque's best hotel and it's located at the far end of the beach. The all-inclusive concept features buffet-style meals, open bar all day, a selection of water sports at no extra charge, plenty of loud music, and bikini-clad staff. There are only a few pieces of water-sports equipment, so there may be a wait. Rooms are decorated in soft apricot pastels with sculpted plaster shell headboards and all have balconies facing the ocean.

Dining/Entertainment: The large restaurant doubles as the entertainment arena in the evening when the staff puts on shows.

Facilities: Pool facing the beach; use of water-sports equipment included in the price.

HOTEL DE LEGAZPI, Av. de las Palmas, Melaque, Jal. 48980. Tel. 333/7-0397; in the U.S., call 317/846-2566 Apr–Nov (ask for owner Martin Curley). 14 rms. FAN Discounts for stays of a month or more.
$ Rates: $30 single; $37 double.

💲 American owned, this two-story hotel at the north end of the bay has a nice secluded location on a beautiful portion of beach. The large rooms are simply furnished and have tile floors. It's a 10-minute walk to town and there are several palapa-style restaurants nearby. There's TV with U.S. channels in the lobby, a community kitchen, and a swimming pool in front of the hotel.

POSADA PABLO DE TARSO, Gomez Farías 49, Melaque, Jal. 48980. Tel. 333/7-0117 or 7-0268; in Guadalajara tel. and fax 3/616-4850. 27 rms (all with bath). FAN (13 rms) A/C (14 rms)
$ Rates: $35 single; $56 double. **Parking:** Free.

This two-level hotel offers exceptionally tidy rooms with fans. Twelve have kitchens and sitting rooms. There's a grassy courtyard, a seaside terrace, and large swimming pool. To find it, walk left of the bus station; it's past the Posada las Gaviotas.

Where to Dine

Besides the restaurants below, there are also many rustic palapa restaurants at the end of the beach.

EL BUEN GUSTO, López Mateos 18, at Gómez Farías. No phone.
Cuisine: MEXICAN.
$ Prices: Breakfast $1.75–$3; tamales 50¢; pozole $2; roast chicken $3; hamburgers $3; soft drinks 60¢; beer $1.25.

Open: Daily 8am–11pm.

Run by the Benjamin Macías family, this eatery, currently half a block from the square going toward the beach, keeps moving and I keep seeking it out because the food is both good and cheap. Wherever they are, the decor always features metal tables and folding wooden chairs. The food is homestyle, which is why there's always a loyal following of Mexicans around. The bowl of pozole is large, tasty, and filling. If they've moved again, ask around, or look for the Buen Gusto sign.

EL DORADO, Club Náutico Melaque, Gómez Farías s/n. Tel. 7-0770.
Cuisine: INTERNATIONAL.
$ Prices: Breakfast $2.50–$4; main courses $10–$30; seafood platter for two $30.
Open: Daily 7:30am–10pm.

The most inviting restaurant in central Melaque, El Dorado fronts the beach behind the Club Náutico Melaque which is recommended as a hotel (see "Where To Stay" above). Because it's open to the breezes on three sides, it's cool dining on both patio levels. Try the fish amadine, in an almond butter sauce which comes with rice and vegetables. The seafood tray serves two and comes with beer-batter-fried shrimp, or boiled if you prefer, octopus, plus broiled and Veracruz-style fish. To find it, walk to the right from the front of the bus station, it's on the left facing the beach.

LOS PELICANOS, north end of Melaque beach. Tel. 7-0268.
Cuisine: INTERNATIONAL.
$ Prices: Breakfast $3.25; seafood platter $8.50; Mexican plates $4–$5.
Open: High season daily 9am–10pm; low season daily 9am–7pm.

At this beachfront eatery, friendly ex-Pennsylvanian Phil Garcia and her spouse, Trine, treat everyone as though they are long-lost family and prepares meals like you might find at home. During high season you might find pork roast and mashed potatoes along with her usual seafood specialties. Plus, you can find burritos, nachos, and hamburgers anytime. Stake out a nearby spot on the beach and use the restaurant as your day-long headquarters for sipping and nipping. If you have any good used clothing or toys you can deposit them with Phil who will distribute them among needy children in the area.

VIVA MARIA, north end of Melaque beach. Tel. 7-0077.
Cuisine: SEAFOOD/INTERNATIONAL.
$ Prices: Main courses $4.75–$13.50.
Open: Nov–May daily noon–9pm. **Closed:** June–Oct.

Located at the far end of Melaque's beach and before the Hotel Legazpi, Viva Maria is named after the women who took up the fight during the revolution and who were called "Maria." The English-speaking owners do a lot to make the menu appealing to foreigners. The chicken burritos are more like an enchilada—the filling is wrapped in a flour tortilla and covered in a green sauce and sour cream and served with rice and beans. There's also pizza, crêpes, nachos, lobster, steaks, and hamburgers.

Evening Entertainment in Barra & Melaque

During high season there is always happy hour (from 2 to 6pm) at the Hotel Sands poolside/lagoonside bar in Barra.

DISCO EL GALLEON, Hotel Sands, Calle Morelos, Barra de Navidad.

Cushioned benches and cement tables encircle the round dance floor. It's all open air, but garden walls restrict air flow and there are few fans so you can really work up a sweat dancing the night away. They serve drinks only, no snacks. Open: Daily 8pm–2am.
Admission: Mon–Thurs $1.75–$2.50, Fri–Sat $3.50.

TANGA, Coco Club, Melaque. Tel. 7-0001.
Opened in 1991, it's located on a corner of the Coco Club Melaque Hotel. Open: High season Wed–Sun 10:30pm–3am; low season Fri–Sat 10:30pm–3am.
Admission: $4; free for hotel guests.

TENACATITA

After Barra de Navidad and about 40 miles from Manzanillo on Highway 200, you come to an obscure sign on the left pointing to Fiesta Americana Los Angeles Locos Tenacatita, an all-inclusive resort.

FIESTA AMERICANA LOS ANGELES LOCOS TENACATITA, Apdo. Postal 7, Melanque, Jal. Tel. 333/7-0220, toll free 800/223-2332 in the U.S. Fax 333/7-0229. 180 rms. A/C TV TEL

$ Rates (including all meals, domestic drinks, water sports, and activities): High season $150 per person; low season $100 per person.

Entrance to the hotel is via a winding cobblestone road through an Edenic coconut grove. Once past the guarded entry you see the hotel beside one of the Pacific coast's most beautiful beaches. There's a daily list of activities posted in the lobby including torpedo rides, aerobics and water exercises, windsurfing classes, water polo, jazz classes, tennis clinic, snorkeling, and waterskiing. The travel agency can arrange excursions for deep-sea fishing and to Puerto Vallarta, Manzanillo, and Colima. Rooms are nicely furnished and all have balconies and ocean views. It's very popular with vacationing Mexican families and is likely to be booked for major Mexican holidays. The big drawback here (and it may not be for some people) is that you're miles from anything, and because of the minimum-stay requirement, if you don't like it, you're stuck. The hotel is approximately 30 miles north of the Manzanillo airport on Highway 200 to Barra–Puerto Vallarta.

Dining/Entertainment: Meals are served from 7 to 11:30am, 1 to 4:30pm, and 9 to 10pm.
Services: Laundry, travel agency.
Facilities: Large oceanside pool; all water-sports equipment; tennis, jazz, windsurfing, and aerobics classes.

TECUAN

About 45 minutes from Barra de Navidad continuing north on Highway 200 and after the turnoff to Tenacatita, you'll see a white cone-shaped silo painted with a sign to El Tecuan. Turn left and drive 6½ miles on a curvy cobblestone road through a mango *ejido* (plantation). The road ends at the El Tecuan hotel.

EL TECUAN, Hwy. 200, km 33.5. Tel. 333/7-0132. Fax 333/16-6615. Reservations: Garibaldi 1676, Guadalajara, Jal. 44680 (tel. 3/616-0183; fax 3/616-6615). 40 rms, suites, and villas. A/C

$ Rates: $50 standard single, $60 standard double; $55 single junior suite, $65 double junior suite; $75–$105 villa.

Built on a hill overlooking a wide half-moon bay and beach, El Tecuan is a comfortable and moderately priced standby on this coast that's getting ever more expensive. Besides the wide bay spreading out in front of the hotel, there's a big, beautiful, natural lagoon to the left that's perfect for canoeing. The main building, made of stone and stucco, is built around the swimming pool and faces the bay. Suites and villas are connected via a boardwalk to the main section. Rooms have red-tiled floors and are comfortably furnished. Villas are two stories and have kitchens. Most rooms have ocean views. Like other hotels along this coast, what you see is the first part of a grand scheme of building that has yet to take place.

Dining/Entertainment: There's one restaurant serving all three meals from 8:30am to 10:30pm.

Facilities: Tennis court, swimming pool, basketball and volleyball courts. Bicycles, horses, and canoes for rent.

EL TAMARINDO

After Tecuan, about 21 miles north of the Manzanillo airport, you'll see a sign pointing left to El Tamarindo; turn and follow the narrow road 9½ miles through the forest to this new and very exclusive resort. It's part of a larger plan that eventually will include private residences.

HOTEL BEL-AIR EL TAMARINDO, Reservations: 311 Pelicanos Marina Vallarta, Puerto Vallarta, Jal. Tel. 3/321-0800; toll free through the Bel-Air Hotel Company 800/648-4097 in the U.S. Fax 3/321-0801. 60 villas. A/C TV TEL MINIBAR

$ Rates: $300–$500 single or double; call for spa rates.

The Hotel Bel-Air El Tamarindo's 60 villas, set on 2,000 tropical wooded acres with nine miles of ocean front, are scheduled to open in the spring of 1994. It was unfinished when I checked, but promises to be as luxurious as (if completely different from) its newly redone sister 21 miles farther up the highway—the Hotel Bel-Air Costa Careyes. The two will share amenities. Each of the 1,500- to 3,000-square-foot individual villas will have a private palapa-shaded patio and pool with ocean views. The beach is steps away.

Dining/Entertainment: There will be one beachfront restaurant featuring American and Mexican cuisines with an emphasis on fresh, local ingredients. Low-key musical entertainment will be presented nightly.

Services: Helicopter transfer service 10 minutes from the Manzanillo airport, full personalized butler service for each room, laundry and 24-hour room service, twice-daily maid service. Airport pickup can be arranged when you make your reservation. Boutiques; gift shop; gourmet shop with picnic foods, fine imported deli items, wines, and liquor.

Facilities: One free-form pool by the beach, 60 private pools, four tennis courts. The marina for 40 yachts will be added, and the 18-hole golf course is scheduled to open in 1994. Guests have the use of facilities at the Hotel Bel-Air Costa Careyes, including the equestrian center and excursions for birding, turtle nesting, fishing, and picnics.

COSTA CAREYES

The next development is Costa Careyes (which means turtle coast) with two resorts—The **Hotel Bel-Air Costa Careyes** (formerly the Hotel Costa Careyes), part of a 2,500-acre development, and **Club Med Playa Blanca.** Each resort has its own beaches, resort amenities, and a small, beautiful bay all to itself. The two bays adjoin, but are completely separated by bluffs.

The two resorts are roughly 42 miles north of Manzanillo and 100 miles south of Puerto Vallarta. It's about a 1½-hour drive north of Manzanillo on Highway 200, but only about 1 hour from the Manzanillo airport. If you haven't arranged for transportation through either hotel, taxis from the Manzanillo airport charge around $70 one-way for the trip. There are car rentals at the Manzanillo airport as well, which are convenient for exploring the coast from your hotel base. The property runs more than four miles along the highway and has eight miles of shoreline dotted with beaches, bluffs, and thick forest. After you turn left off the highway (where there's a noticeable sign to both resorts) you'll see another sign to one branch of the cobbled road going to Hotel Careyes and the other to Club Med. The area is rich in wildlife: 135 bird species have been counted in the Careyes area alone; four species of marine turtles nest on the beaches between July and December; 70 species of bats (including the vampire bat) have been sighted; and there are fox, ocelot, and alligators among the jungle animals.

HOTEL BEL-AIR COSTA CAREYES, Hwy. 200, km 47. Careyes, Jal. Tel. **3/337-0107,** toll free through the Bel-Air Hotels 800/648-4097 in the U.S.
$ Rates: $165–$275 single or double.

Purchased by Grupo Situr and Grupo Plan in 1992 and completely remodeled by the exclusive Bel-Air Hotel Company, the former Hotel Costa Careyes is a thing of the past. All of the existing rooms were gutted to make larger ones, but they retain the earthy-but-elegant Mexican tiles and decorative accents that were part of the old hotel's charm. Built in an enormous U shape with a courtyard and forest of palms leading to the beach, the Bel-Air Costa Careyes resembles a miniature Mediterranean village. It's both sophisticated and rustic, with the room facades awash in scrubbed pastels. A covered arcaded walkway, lined with trendy clothing and decorative arts shops, links the U and leads to the rooms. Guest quarters all have terraces with ocean views; a terry-cloth bathrobe is provided for each guest in the room. Twenty rooms have private pools. The emphasis here, as at the Hotel Bel-Air El Tamarindo (a sibling resort 21 miles to the south), is on a restful and relaxing holiday built on a foundation of privacy and personalized service.

The Hotel Bel-Air Costa Careyes runs a number of special-interest activities for its guests. Named after the hawksbill turtle (*careyes* in Spanish), the hotel, with a staff biologist, sponsors a "save the turtle" program. From July through December, guests can participate in a nightly **turtle watch** when the turtles come ashore at night to lay eggs. The hatchlings appear 45 days later so some guests may witness both events. Pacific Ridley, leatherback, black, and hawksbill turtles all nest on Playa Teopa, a nearby beach belonging to the hotel, and all are in danger of extinction. There's no guarantee you'll see a turtle nesting, but the hotel posts a "Turtle Probability Calendar" at the desk with dates when the possibility is best. Then guests sign up to go with a biologist for the "turtle watch" outings usually starting around 10pm and ending around 1 or 2am. Don't miss the **birdwatching** opportunities at nearby Bird Island, a natural habitat for nesting boobies between July and September. You see the birds close-up sitting on their ground nests. The dry months of November to June are good for birding on the mainland since many fly over during migration, but there are no official birding walks; you're on your own. Hour-long **boat tours** and half-day boat and coastline tours with snorkeling and lunch on a private beach are offered as well as **deep-sea fishing.** Specialists in tropical plants are on hand to show guests through the **tropical nursery** and talk about gardening with tropical plants. Guests can perfect their horse-riding skills with guided horseback excursions and riding lessons at the **equestrian center.** Polo clubs from around the world converge here for **polo** season, December through April, to play on the hotel's two polo fields. There's a polo club membership fee as well as additional charges for horse rental, tournament fee, stable fee, boarding (if you bring your own horse), groom's quarters and food, and private lessons.

Dining/Entertainment: The Restaurant (that's it's name) on a courtyard by the pool and beach, is open for dinner. The Terrace Café, also near the pool and beach, offers all three meals under a breezy pergola. Both offer contemporary Mexican and American cuisine with an emphasis on regionally produced fruits and vegetables as well as fresh seafood. The bar is by The Restaurant and pool. "Just Us Kids" is a program of activities for children and for adults there's live (but not rowdy) entertainment nightly. A movie theater provides another evening activity option, and the library provides an assortment of reading material. Guests here have access to services and amenities at Hotel Bel-Air El Tamarindo.

Services: Laundry, purified tap water, 24-hour room service, twice-daily maid service. Helicopter or taxi transportation to the resort is available at the Manzanillo airport if you make arrangements with your hotel reservation.

Facilities: One large free-form pool on the beach, 20 private pools, 2 tennis courts, equestrian center. Golf available at El Tamarindo in 1994. A marina is part of the master plan, and a full-service health and beauty spa is scheduled for completion in early 1994.

CLUB MED PLAYA BLANCA. Tel. and fax 333/7-0734; toll free 800/258-2633 in the U.S. and Canada. 558 rms. A/C

$ Rates (including all meals and most sports activities): $100 per person double; $650 per person double for a week. Higher rates during holidays and for week-long packages that include air transportation and transportation to and from the hotel; 20% extra for single occupancy.

On a beautiful bay separated by grand bluffs from the Hotel Bel-Air Costa Careyes, this sienna-colored hotel spills up, around, and down a lovely, lushly landscaped hillside to the beach. Rooms are large and bright and have two full beds. A king-size bed in a room is available upon advance request. Each Club Med has a different personality and clientele. This one has always been popular with active singles and young couples, which the extensive and innovative program of activities indicates. Children age 12 and over are welcome. Prices are usually based on double occupancy, but at certain times of year single reservations are accepted at an additional charge. Transportation from either Puerto Vallarta or Manzanilla is extra for those not booking a package that includes air transportation.

Numerous special-interest activities are included in the price. **Rock climbing,** dubbed the new sport of the 1990s, can be sampled here—you can learn to scale vertical surfaces on an artificial wall. You can also avail yourself of the **circus workshop** and learn to fly from a high trapeze, jump on a trampoline, juggle, and walk the highwire. There are free PADI or NAUI **scuba certification** classes available, but no exploration dives. Usually there are twice daily **boat excursions** which include snorkeling and a picnic at a nearby secluded beach. Other special-interest activities are offered at an additional charge, among them **intensive horseback riding**—an individualized program where you'll learn all aspects of riding. Two-and-a-half hours of daily ring instruction leads to lessons in dressage and jumping. Price includes all equipment, the same horse all week, and a videotape that charts your progress. Daily **trail rides** are open for all levels of riders. There are daily opportunities for **excursions** to nearby Bird Island (a natural habitat for nesting boobies), out into the ocean for deep-sea fishing, and to nearby Manzanillo, Barra de Navidad, Puerto Vallarta, and more. Plus there are massages available and arts and crafts workshops with a small charge for materials.

Dining/Entertainment: The main dining room, above the bar and pool, is open for breakfast, lunch, and dinner (all three meals are served buffet-style) and features Mexican and continental food. El Pelicano on the beach serves extended breakfast and lunch buffets, or for two or more, seafood dinners are served at the table. El Zapata, also on the beach, serves steaks. Bars include one by the pool, a disco bar, and a beach bar. The staff provides evening entertainment in a combination of shows and games that involve guests and there's disco dancing every night.

Services: In-room safes, irons and ironing boards available, token-operated washers and dryers, infirmary, telephone messages are posted.

Facilities: One Olympic-size pool; six tennis courts (four night lit); equipment for sailing, kayaking, snorkeling, archery, volleyball, basketball, Ping Pong, bocce ball, and billiards. Fitness center with aerobics and calisthenics classes.

LAS ALAMANDAS

In 1990, Isabel Goldsmith, granddaughter of Ateñor Patino (who developed Las Hadas), opened Las Alamandas, a super-exclusive hideaway between Manzanillo and Puerto Vallarta. It's intended as the beginning of a larger resort, but for now there are only five villas and no further construction is under way. Details on where it is and how to get there are given when guests make reservations. There's no sign on the highway. Entrance to the property is by prior request only. It's about 1½ hours by car from Manzanillo and 1 hour and 45 minutes from Puerto Vallarta.

LAS ALAMANDAS, Hwy 200, Manzanillo–Puerto Vallarta. Tel. 333/7-0259 or 7-0147. Fax 333/7-0161. Information and reservations: toll free 800/223-6510 in the U.S.; tel. 5/540-7657 or fax 5/540-7658 in Mexico City.

$ Rates: High season Casa del Sol $576–$1,008 single or double, $1,656–$2,160 entire villa for six people; Casa del Domo $576–$942 single or double, $1,320–$1,656 entire villa for four people; Casa Azul $432–$810 single or double; Casita San Miguel $432–$600 single or double; Casa Rosa $2,124–$2,388 entire villa for four people. (Prices include some meals or all meals depending on package purchased.) Minimum two-night stay required. Reduced rates in summer.

Part of a 1,500-acre estate and set on 70 acres against a low hill, this resort's small cluster of buildings almost spreads to the wide, clean beach. It's a beautifully landscaped spot, on an entirely private beach. Designed by Guadalajara architect Gabriel Nuñez, it's a mixture of Mediterranean, Mexican, and Southwestern styles, and it's been featured in *Architectural Digest, Casa Gente,* and *Conde Nast Traveler.* The furnishings, selected by Isabel Goldsmith, are a fabulous blend of Mexican handcrafted furniture, pottery, and folk art, with cushy sofas, beds, and pillows covered in bright textiles from Mexico and Guatemala, giving the rooms a relaxed, casual feel. The combined effect of architecture and furnishings is stunning, yet comfortable. You definitely feel like kicking back here—only 20 guests can be accommodated at any one time, and the threat of crowds is nonexistent. All of the guest quarters are grouped around a small cobbled plaza, lush with vegetation. All villas are spacious and have high-pitched tiled roofs, cool tiled floors, and tiled verandas with sea views. And each guest bedroom has its own bathroom. Casa del Sol, at beach level, is painted bright yellow and has three bedrooms; a large, completely equipped kitchen; living room; and common entry foyer as well as separate entrances for each bedroom plus a TV/VCR. Casa del Domo, painted hot pink, has a dome in the entry, two large bedrooms each with a private terrace, shared living room and full kitchen plus a TV/VCR. Casa Azul (blue house), set on a hill, has great views and breezes and three bedrooms which can be rented individually or all together. All bedrooms in Casa Azul have their own entrance, oversize bath and private terrace and a seating area in each bedroom. The views and breezes in Casa Azul are great. Casita San Miguel next to Casa Azul, has one bedroom with a minibar and a private terrace. Casa Rosa is a beachfront villa with a veranda, living room, fully equipped kitchen, rooftop terrace and a TV/VCR. Reservation preference is given for rental of entire villas.

Dining/Entertainment: Oasis is the festive sheltered restaurant serving all three meals and featuring fresh grilled food and Mexican specialties. There is also an honor bar.

Services: Nightly turndown service and room service. Fishing, boat rides, and diving trips are arranged on request. Transportation to and from Manzanillo ($150–$200 one way) and Puerto Vallarta ($200–$230 one way) can be arranged.

Facilities: 60-foot swimming pool; lighted tennis court; fully equipped gym with treadmill, Stairmaster, Versclimber, and Lifecycle. Large-screen TV in the bar. VCR in several villas with video library for rentals, stable of horses, hiking trails. Private 3,000-foot paved landing strip capable of accommodating a King Air turbo prop, make advance arrangements for landing.

CUYUTLÁN

Thirty miles south of Manzanillo and five miles east off Highway 200 is Cuyutlán. It's a small, tidy, budget-priced coastal village lined with modest hotels and restaurants. The attraction is the black-sand beach. A wood-slat path leads across the hot black sand to the rows of umbrella-covered chairs for rent lined up facing the ocean. Weekends and holidays the beach becomes crowded, but weekdays it's a tranquil place to be. The waves are big and strong here, so be very careful of the undertow. The Cuyutlán lagoon is behind the town a mile or more and it's a haven for many colorful birds. Ask a local to point the way.

COLIMA

Many Americans, who think Colima begins and ends with the popular port of Manzanillo, are missing a lot by overlooking the state's attractive capital, a balmy metropolis of 116,000 inhabitants only a two-hour drive 60 miles southwest of Manzanillo and 165 miles southwest of Guadalajara. Its founder in 1523, was the conquistador Gonzalo de Sandoval, youngest member of Cortés's staff.

Although one of Mexico's smallest states, Colima has an incredible range of climate and topography. The northern part contains pine forests and part of Mexico's second-highest active volcano, Volcán de Colima (12,870 ft.), which last erupted in 1991. The rest of the volcano lies in Jalisco. While the capital, Colima, lies virtually at the foot of the volcano, its 1,640-foot altitude allows it to have a climate similar to Manzanillo's. An even higher mountain, visible if you come from Guadalajara, is the 14,000-foot Nevado de Colima, which, in spite of its name, lies entirely in the state of Jalisco.

You can get there by plane on Aero California from Tijuana and Mexico City, with connections to La Paz. The first-class train between Guadalajara and Manzanillo has been suspended. There's a second-class train from Manzanillo and Guadalajara, but it could take forever. The train station is south of the town center. By bus there's frequent service from Manzanillo and Guadalajara. The new, very comfortable Primera Plus bus costs more but it's air conditioned, has video movies, vending machine refreshments, and fewer seats than regular buses. Colima's new central bus station is out of town and there's taxi service to town, or get a city bus marked "Centro." (See "Departing by Bus" in Chapter 6, "Getting to Know Manzanillo," for details on bus travel from Manzanillo to Colima.) If you come by car from Manzanillo, follow the signs out of town. After several miles you'll see the turnoff to Highway 54 and a few miles farther a choice of a toll road, or continuing on the nontoll road. They don't give you much warning and you may wind up entering the toll road whether you intended to or not.

Colima's beautiful central plaza, surrounded by the palatial colonial-era buildings, is one of the most handsome in Mexico. From the Plaza Hidalgo and Madero go east and west of it and from Reforma and Barrera go north and south.

The **State Tourist Office**, Portal Hidalgo 20 (tel. 2-4360 or 2-8360), is on the plaza. You can get maps and brochures here, or make reservations to stay at the state-owned inn in the mountains outside of Comala. Most sights are within walking distance of the central plaza.

Two notes: Unlike other Mexican cities, not all of Colima's museums are open on Sunday. Policemen in this city are abundant and overeager to hand out citations for speeding and minor infractions like going the wrong way on a street—so beware.

WHAT TO SEE & DO

MUSEO DE OCCIDENTE DE GOBIERNO DE ESTADO, [Museum of Western Cultures] at Ejército Nacional. Galvan. No phone.

Also known as the Museum of Anthropology, this is one of my favorite museums in the country. It has many pre-Hispanic pieces, including the famous clay dancing dogs of Colima. There are fine examples of clay, shell, and bone jewelry, exquisite clay human and animal figures, and diagrams of tombs showing unusual funeral customs.

Admission: Free.
Open: Daily 9am–7:30pm.

MUSEUM OF POPULAR CULTURE MARÍA TERESA POMAR, University of Colima, 27 de Septiembre and Gabino Barrera. Tel. 2-5140.

One of the city's most interesting museums contains regional costumes and musical instruments from all over Mexico, photographs showing the day-to-day use of costumes and masks, and folk art from Oaxaca, Guerrero, and elsewhere. The section devoted to Mexico's sweet bread (pan dulce) is set up like an authentic bakery with each bread labeled. At the entrance is a shop selling Mexican folk art.

Admission: 50¢.
Open: Tues–Sat 9am–2pm and 4–7pm, Sun 9am–2pm. **Directions:** From the Museo de Occidente de Gobierno go left out the front door. Walk five long and short blocks to the wide Av. Galvan at Ejército. Cross it and the museum is on your right.

MUSEO DE HISTORIA DE COLIMA, Portal Morelos 1. Tel. 2-9228.

Opened in 1988, the city's newest showcase is dedicated to state history. The beautiful colonial building is the former Hotel Casino, the birthplace of former Mexican president Miguel de la Madrid Hurtado. It's on the plaza opposite the Hotel Ceballos. The collection includes pre-Hispanic pottery, baskets, furniture, and dance masks. More than 5,000 pre-Hispanic pieces are packed away awaiting the renovation of the upper floor. Between the pottery at this museum and the Museo de Occidente, you'll begin to understand why the Aztec name for Colima meant "place where pottery is made." Colima is also known for the variety of pre-Hispanic tombs, and one of the best displays here shows drawings of many kinds of tombs. You may be asked to leave your purse or bag with the guard as you enter.

Admission: Free.
Open: Mon–Sat 10am–2pm and 4–8pm. Sun bookstore only, same hours.

SALA DE EXPOSICIONES, Portal Morelos 1. No phone.

Next to the Museo de Historia de Colima opposite the main plaza, this museum is sponsored by the University of Colima. It's a changing showcase for fine artists from all over the world.

Admission: Free.
Open: Tues–Sat 10am–2pm and 4–8pm; Sun 10am–2pm.

WHERE TO STAY

HOTEL AMERICA, Morelos 162, Colima, Col. 28000. Tel. 331/2-7488.
Fax 331/4-4425. 55 rms (all with bath). A/C TV TEL **Directions:** Walk 1½ blocks west of the plaza to Morelos; it's on the right ½ block down.
$ **Rates:** $60 single or double. **Parking:** Free.
This downtown hotel offers large and tastefully furnished rooms. It's almost always full of traveling businesspeople, so get here early in the day if you want a room. There's laundry service, a restaurant, and bar, and for men there's a gym with a sauna, hot tub, and vapor bath.

HOTEL CEBALLOS, Portal Medellin 12, Colima, Col. 28000. Tel. 331/2-4444. 60 rms (all with bath). A/C (6 rms) FAN (54 rms)
$ **Rates:** $25–$35 single or double.
On the east side of the main plaza, this hotel looks great from the outside, however, they've done a lot of squeezing to make more rooms, and the interior has lost much of its charm as well as its courtyard. The cell-like rooms are clean and freshly painted. The desk clerk will try to pressure you into taking a higher-priced room than you want. Insist that she tell you the lowest rate. Higher prices are for rooms with air conditioning, which really isn't necessary.

WHERE TO DINE

LOS NARANJOS (The Orange Trees), Gabino Barrera 43. Tel. 2-0029.
Cuisine: MEXICAN.
$ **Prices:** Main courses $5–$13; tacos $1–$5.
Open: Daily 8am–11:30pm.
The leading restaurant downtown is handsomely decorated with orange and white linens, light blue walls, and orange fruit designs hand-painted on the chairs. For the quality of decor you'd expect higher prices. I highly recommend the pollo caserola, a vegetable and meat stew of carrots, potatoes, and peas in a delicious tomato broth, all served in a clay casserole with a side order of fresh corn tortillas. It's enough for two. There are also sandwiches and beef cuts in several incarnations. To find it, from the zócalo walk down Madero (left of the cathedral) and take the first street on the left.

LAS PALMAS, Callejon del Caco. Tel. 2-4444 or 4-0388.
Cuisine: MEXICAN.
$ **Prices:** Breakfast $2.50–$5; main courses $2–$7.
Open: Mon–Sat 8am–10pm.
There's a sign on the sidewalk, directing you through a small interior mall to the back and the tranquil little restaurant. There's covered dining space as well as umbrella-shaded patio tables. The food is Mexican fast food such as tacos, quesadillas, and soup, plus hamburgers and french fries. It's behind the Hotel Ceballos (on the plaza) just off the pedestrian-only street.

COMALA

From the old Colima bus station buses go to Comala every 15 minutes. The trip takes 20 minutes and costs 35¢. By taxi it will cost $7. This picturesque little village is near a mysterious magnetic zone out on the highway. Get one of the taxi drivers on the square to run you out to this area, a few miles from town. When he gets there he'll kill the engine. Then the magnetic pull takes control and the car gathers speed uphill without engine power. The phenomenon was discovered by accident a few years ago when a motorist had car trouble, but couldn't get the vehicle to stop. If you keep going on this road you'll reach the Volcán de Colima, which disappears behind the mountain, then reappears, larger and larger with each loop around the curves—quite a twilight zone experience. There is a state-owned lodge here, where you can arrange to stay overnight in rustic cabins. Volcanic ash is everywhere.

Back in town, the village is liveliest on Sunday when roving bands of mariachis gather to serenade diners under the arcades around the central plaza. As many as five different groups sing at once. The food, drink, and atmosphere of this village make for a perfect day in Mexico. Get here before 3pm to get a good seat for all the wholesome revelry that really gets going around 3:30pm.

On the outskirts of town, an artisans' school is open Monday through Saturday. Visitors are welcome to come in and browse.

CHAPTER 9
GETTING TO KNOW GUADALAJARA

1. **ORIENTATION**
- **DID YOU KNOW...?**
2. **GETTING AROUND**
- **FAST FACTS: GUADALAJARA**

Known as the "City of Roses," Guadalajara is a great metropolis, the second largest in Mexico. It is considered by many the most Mexican of cities. Given its charter in 1542 as *muy leal y muy noble ciudad* ("most loyal and noble city") by none other than Emperor Charles V, it has held a prominent place in Mexican affairs ever since. Charles, who ran most of Europe and a lot of the world at the time, certainly knew what he was doing. Guadalajara (pop. 3,300,000), capital of the state of Jalisco, celebrated its 450th anniversary in February 1992. Sophisticated and beautiful though it is, the once very visible roses which decorated the city appear only occasionally these days.

As though to emphasize the great things that were expected of it, Guadalajara's Spanish builders gave the city not one but four beautiful plazas in its center. Today the city's leaders have given it a fifth, the enormous **Plaza Tapatía,** an ambitious stretch of urban redevelopment extending for about a mile through the urban landscape. Scattered with trees and monuments, sprinkled with fountains, the super-plaza links the city's major colonial buildings, opens new perspectives for viewing them, and joins the past with the great new buildings of the present. This ambitious project is very "Mexican" in its grand scope.

By the way, *tapatío* (or *tapatía*) is a word you'll come across often in this city. No one is certain quite where it originated, but tapatío means "Guadalajaran"—a thing, a person, even an idea. The way a charro (Mexican cowboy) gives his all, or the way a mariachi sings his heart out—that's tapatío!

Guadalajara is as sophisticated, and at least as formal as Mexico City. Dress is conservative; resort wear is out of place here.

Important Note: The tragic water main explosion that drew attention to Guadalajara in early 1992 occurred in a city suburb. The historic downtown section and all other areas of touristic interest in and around the city were unaffected by the explosion.

1. ORIENTATION

ARRIVING

BY PLANE **Aero California** reaches Guadalajara through Tijuana, Puebla, La Paz, Los Mochis, Torreon, Durango, and San Diego. **Aero Guadalajara** flies from Monterrey, San Luis Potosí, Zacatecas, and Tampico. **Aeromexico** connects Guadalajara to the United States via Houston, New Orleans, San Diego, and Los Angeles. In Mexico, Aeromexico flies from Guadalajara directly to and from Acapulco, Cancún, Culiacán, Chihuahua, and Puerto Vallarta. **Alaska Airlines** has service from San Francisco and Los Angeles. **American Airlines** connects through Dallas/Fort Worth. **Continental Airlines** connects U.S. flights through Houston. **Delta** flies from Los Angeles. **Mexicana** has three Mexican hub cities—Mexico City, Monterrey, and Cancún—offering connections to most major and many minor destinations in the country.

Guadalajara's international airport is a 25-minute ride from the city. Collectivo minivans are lined up in front of the airport. Drivers will direct you to the correct van; you pay after you board. Tickets cost $8 to the downtown area. For the return trip, the company picks up at residences only, charging around the same. So to save money, pick a residence address anywhere in the downtown area and wait there for the van. Taxis charge around $13.

BY TRAIN Guadalajara is the country's second-largest train hub. The **National Railways of Mexico** (tel. 50-0826) link Mexico City and Guadalajara. Pacific coast trains are notoriously off-schedule. *El Tapatío* runs from Mexico City to Guadalajara leaving Mexico City at 8:30pm, arriving in Guadalajara at 8:10am.

From Mexicali, on the California border, *El Tren del Pacífico* departs at 9am Pacific standard time, arriving in Guadalajara at 7pm the next day. From Nogales, Del Pacífico departs at 3:30pm and arrives in Guadalajara at 7pm a day later. *El Sinaloense* also goes along the Pacific coast from Los Mochis through Mazatlán and Tepic, but it isn't as good or convenient a train.

The train station on Calzada Independencia is within walking distance (with light luggage) of a couple of recommended hotels. Buses marked "Centro" go downtown, and those marked "Estación" go to the station from downtown. Otherwise you're at the mercy of the taxis that charge almost $5 to go the short distance anywhere between the station and the city center.

BY BUS If you arrive at the *old* bus station you'll be around 12 blocks south of the city center. The new bus station is six miles south of the city center. There, city buses pick up passengers in front of each terminal building and can become incredibly crowded. Unless you get a seat, there will be no space for even a small suitcase. Any bus marked "Centro" goes downtown.

White **minivans (combis)** holding 16 or more passengers also serve the terminal and are more comfortable and convenient. Combi 40, with "Centro" or "Nva." or "Nueva Central" on the windshield, travels along Revolucíon and begins and ends its route on Calle Ferrocarril between 16 de Septiembre and Corona, just a few blocks from the Plaza Tapatía and many of our recommended hotels. Use these if your suitcase fits on your lap. Buses and minivans often empty at the beginning of the "U" where traffic enters in front of the Flecha Amarilla terminal. There it's easier to get a seat before they get crowded.

Buy fixed-price taxi tickets from a booth inside each terminal near the exit doors. Rates vary according to destination.

BY CAR From Nogales on the Arizona border, follow Highway 15. From Barra de Navidad, or southeast on the coast, take Highway 80. From Mexico City, Highway 90 leads to Guadalajara. Coming from Manzanillo or Colima on the Pacific coast, take Mex 110, either the new toll road or the free road. The toll road shortens the trip by 1½ hours and tolls cost around $20 one-way. The free road, which winds through the mountains, is in good condition.

DEPARTING

BY PLANE International flights require check-in 90 minutes before takeoff and domestic flights, at least 60 minutes before departure. **Auto Transportaciones**

GUADALAJARA: ORIENTATION • 149

Aeropuerto (tel. 612-4278, 612-4308, or 612-9337) runs minivans between the airport and city 24 hours a day. **Aero California** (tel. 626-1901 or 626-1064; airport 689-0924). **Aero Guadalajara** (tel. 647-2770; airport 689-2689). **Aeromexico** (tel. 626-1889; airport 689-0028). **Alaska Airlines** (tel. toll free 95/800-426-0333 in Mexico). **American Airlines** (tel. 689-0304; airport 689-0480). **Continental Airlines** (tel. 689-0433 or 689-0261). **Delta** (tel. 630-3530 or 630-3226). **Mexicana** (tel. 647-2222; airport 689-0119).

BY TRAIN Going to Mexicali, on the California border, *Del Pacífico* departs Guadalajara at 8:15am, arrives in Tepic at 1:55pm, Mazatlán at 6:50pm, and Mexicali at 4:30pm, the next day. For Nogales, near the Arizona border, *Del Pacífico* departs Guadalajara at 8:15am, arrives in Mazatlán at 6:50pm, and arrives in Nogales at 11am. There are no sleeping cars. *El Tapatío,* a train with overnight sleeping compartments, leaves Guadalajara at 8:55pm and arrives in Mexico City at 8:10am. This is a popular train; reserve a place early.

BY BUS Two bus stations serve Guadalajara—the old one near downtown and the new one six miles out on the way to Tonalá. A semi-convenient place for bus information is **Servicios Coordinados,** 254 Calzada Independencia, a kind of "bus travel agency" located under the Plaza Tapatía. There travelers can make reservations, buy tickets, and receive information on the six *main* bus lines to most points in Mexico—much better than trekking out to the no-longer "central" Central Camionera (see below). Since this agency only sells tickets to major destinations on the main bus lines, you can't use their service to buy tickets to nearby villages mentioned in Chapter 12.

The Old Bus Station: For bus trips within a 60-mile radius of Guadalajara, including Lake Chapala, Ajijic, and Jocotepec, go to the old bus terminal on Niños Heroes off of Calzada Independencia Sur and look for **Transportes Guadalajara-Chapala** (tel. 619-5675), which has frequent buses and combi service beginning at 6am to Chapala and Ajijic. (For Tlaquepaque and Tonalá, see in Chapter 12).

The New Bus Station: The **Central Camionera,** about six miles and a 20-minute ride east of downtown toward Tonalá, provides bus service to or from virtually any point in Mexico. The new terminal resembles an international airport: Seven separate buildings are connected by a covered walkway in a U shape, with one-way traffic entering on the right. Each building houses several first- and second-class bus lines. And that's the only drawback—you must go to each one to find the line or service that suits you best. It's one of the nicest bus stations in Mexico, with amenities like shuttle buses, restaurants, gift shops, luggage storage (*guarda equipaje*), book and magazine shops, liquor stores, Ladatel long-distance telephones, and hotel information. There's also a large, budget hotel next door (see "Where to Stay" in Chapter 10). To get to the new Central Camionera by bus, stand under the arches opposite the cathedral downtown and take the 275 A, which discharges passengers at the bus station. Or, if all of them are full and you have light luggage, then take the 275 R which will let you off across the street.

The price difference between first and second class is small, but the difference in speed, comfort, and convenience is sometimes, but not always, great. None of the buses from here are of the school-bus variety. To get you started here are a few hints on served areas. All the lines to **Aguascalientes** or **Zacatecas** are on the left and include Camiones de los Altos (tel. 657-6158 and 657-6151), Estrella Blanca (tel. 657-6158 and 657-6151), Transportes Chihuahenses (tel. 657-7431 or 657-8199), Transportes del Norte (tel. 657-8455), and Autobuses al Aguila (tel. 657-8128). To **Tepic** or **San Blas** on the Pacific coast, try Estrella Blanca. If you want to go to **Manzanillo**, try the first-class Primera Plus (tel. 657-7310) which costs more but has only 34 seats, self-service refreshments, air conditioning, and video movies. Or try Flecha Amarilla (tel. 657-7316), Autobuses del Occidente (tel. 657-6460), or Unidos de la Costa (tel. 657-4933). Or to travel to **Barra de Navidad** and **San Melaque** (San Patricio), go to Auto Camiones del Pacífico (tel. 657-4805), or Unidos de la Costa (mentioned above). To get to **Pátzcuaro, Morelia,** or **Uruapan,** use Flecha Amarilla (tel. 657-7310), Autobuses del Occident (tel. 657-6460), or Tres Estrellas de Oro (tel. 657-6969 or 657-7225).

CITY LAYOUT

Guadalajara is not a difficult city to negotiate, but it certainly is big. While most of the main attractions are within walking distance of the historic downtown area, others, such as the nearby villages of Tonalá, Tlaquepaque, and farther away, Lake Chapala and Ajijic are accessible by bus.

Street names change at the cathedral.

NEIGHBORHOODS IN BRIEF

Historic Center The heart of the city takes in the Plaza de Armas, Plaza de los Laureles, Los Hombres Ilustres, Plaza Liberación, and the Plaza Tapatía. It's the tourist center and includes major museums, theaters, restaurants, hotels, and the largest covered market in Latin America, all linked by wide boulevards and pedestrian-only streets. It's bounded east and west by 16 de Septiembre/Alcalde and Prosperidad (across Calzada Independencia) and north and south by Hidalgo and Morelos.

Parque Agua Azul An enormous city park directly south (20 blocks) of the historic center, with a children's area and rubber-wheeled train. Nearby are the state crafts shop, performing arts theaters, and the anthropology museum.

Chapultepec A fashionable neighborhood with shops and restaurants 25 blocks west of the historic center reached by Avenida Vallarta, with Chapultepec as the main artery through the neighborhood.

Minerva Circle Almost 40 blocks west of the historic center, the Minerva Circle is at the confluence of Avenidas Vallarta, López Mateos, and Circunvalación Washington. A fashionable neighborhood, it has several good restaurants and the Hotel Fiesta Americana, all reached by the Par Vial.

Plaza del Sol The largest shopping center in the city, south of the Minerva Circle and southwest of the historic center near the intersection of López Mateos and Mariano Otero.

Zapopan Once a separate village founded in 1542, now a full-fledged suburb 20 minutes northwest of the Plaza Tapatía via Avenida Avila Camacho. It's most noted for its 18th-century basilica and the revered 16th-century image of the Virgin of Zapopan made of corn paste and honored every October 12. The city's fashionable country club is just south of Zapopan.

Tlaquepaque Seven miles southeast of the historic center, a village of mansions-turned-shops fronting pedestrian-only streets and plazas.

GUADALAJARA & ENVIRONS

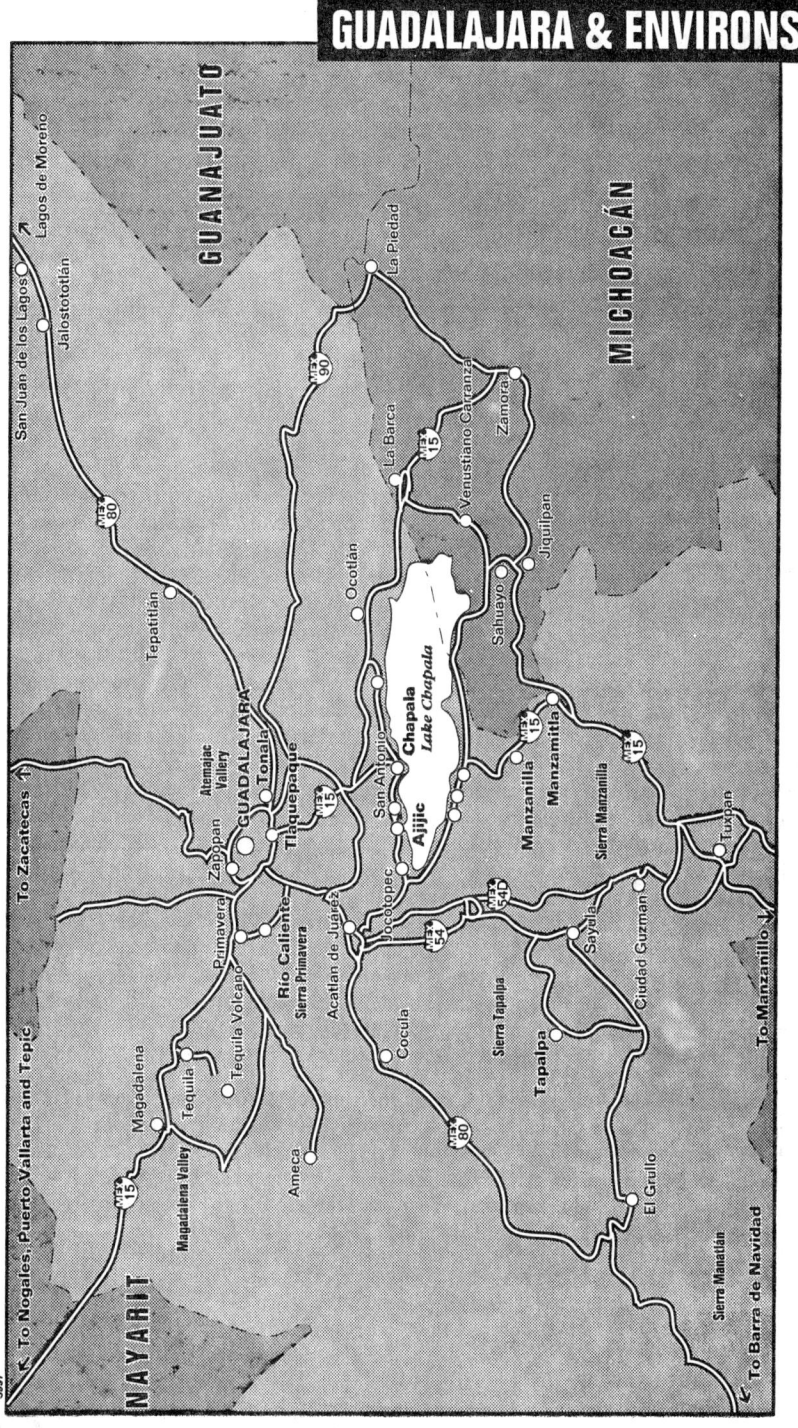

? DID YOU KNOW...?

- Guadalajara is Mexico's second largest city.
- Lake Chapala is the largest lake in Mexico.
- Jalisco is the sixth largest Mexican state.
- One of Mexico's "big three" muralists, José Clemente Orozco, was born in Guadalajara in 1883.
- The Jarabe Tapatío (Mexican Hat Dance) was developed in Guadalajara.
- The blue agave, from which tequila is made, grows around Guadalajara near the town of Tequila.
- Mariachi music developed in Cocula, a small town near Guadalajara, where there are now no mariachis.
- During the 300 years that Mexico belonged to Spain, no Spanish king ever visited the country.

Tonalá Four miles from Tlaquepaque, a village of more than 400 artists working in metal, clay, and paper, with a huge street market on Sunday and Thursday.

2. GETTING AROUND

BY BUS & TROLLEY You may find normal bus routes are detoured while the second part of the new *Tren Lijero* is under construction through 1994. The **Tren Lijero,** the new "light rail train," is the city's "metro" which goes above and below ground along its route. Route 1, which is already finished, serves few tourist needs since it runs north to south along Federalismo curving the distance of Camino de Sur/Prel Colón. Route 2, to be completed in 1994, will be of use to the tourist since it will run east to west along Vallarta/Juárez and Avenida Javier Mina, the eastern extension of Vallarta/Juárez. During my last inspection, the new electric trolleys were suspended entirely while *Tren Lijero* construction progressed, but they may be partly or wholly operational when you travel depending on the status of construction. Normally, however, the trolley routes are the same as bus routes and are quieter, newer, and more pleasant to ride; they also cost the same—40¢. Two bus routes will satisfy 90% of your intracity transportation needs. Buses bearing the sign **"Par Vial"** run a rectangular route going east along Hidalgo to the Mercado Libertad and then west along Juárez (becoming Vallarta) to the Glorieta Minerva, near the western edge of the city.

Many buses run north-south along the Calzada Independencia (not to be confused with Calle Independencia), but the **"San Juan de Dios-Estacion"** bus goes between the points you want: San Juan de Dios church, next to the Mercado Libertad, and the railroad station past Parque Agua Azul. This bus is best because most other buses on Calzada Independencia have longer routes (out to the suburbs, for instance) and thus tend to be more heavily crowded all the time.

For getting to Tlaquepaque and Tonala by bus see in Chapter 12.

BY COLECTIVO Colectivos are minivans running throughout the city day and night picking up and discharging passengers at fixed and unfixed points. They are often a faster and more convenient way to travel than the bus. There are no printed schedules, and the routes and fixed stops change frequently. However, locals know the routes by heart and can tell you where and how to use the colectivos. Prices are only slightly higher than the bus.

BY TAXI Taxis are an expensive way to get around town. A short 10- to 15-minute ride, for instance, from the Plaza de Armas to the Plaza del Sol restaurant costs an exorbitant $6 or $7, whereas a bus there costs only 40¢.

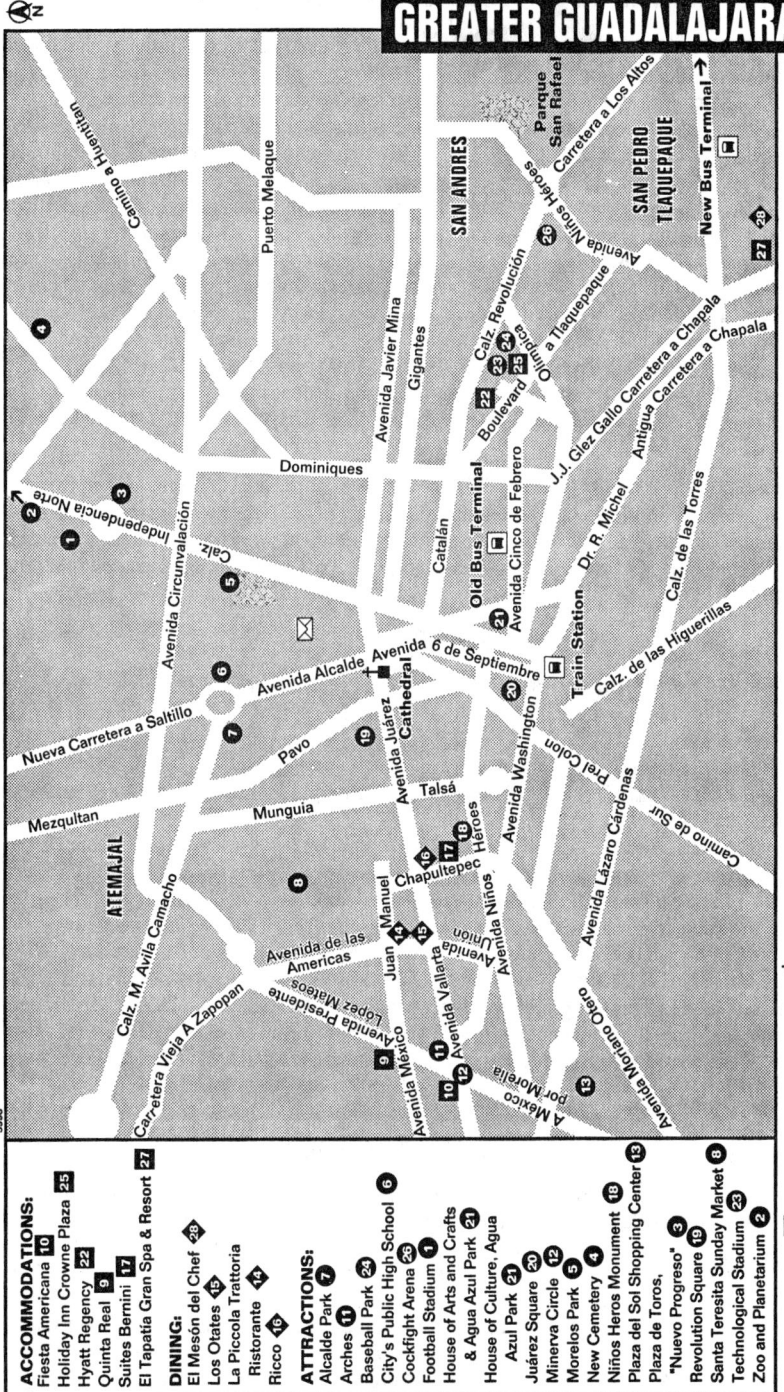

BY CAR All major car-rental agencies are represented with booths at the airport and at various locations in town. The least expensive rates are found by arranging the rental from your home country at least seven days in advance of arrival in Guadalajara. As an example, Avis rates are $49 per day, plus $15 a day insurance and 10% tax. Weekly rates are $179 plus the daily insurance and tax. Both are with unlimited mileage. This rate may be higher if you pick up the car on a weekend or major holiday. As you chauffeur yourself around keep in mind several main arteries. The **Periferico** is a loop around the city that connects to most other highways entering the city. Traffic on the Periferico is slow because it is heavily potholed, filled with trucks, and is only a two-lane road. Several important freeway-style thoroughfares crisscross the city. **Gonzalez Gallo** leads south from town center and connects to the road to Tonalá and Tlaquepaque or leads straight to Lake Chapala. **Highway 15** from Tepic intersects with both **Avenida Vallarta** and **Calzada Lázaro Cárdenas**. Vallarta then goes straight to the Plaza Tapatía area. Cárdenas crosses the whole city and intersects at the southern edge with the road to Chapala and to Tlaquepaque and Tonalá.

BY HORSE-DRAWN CARRIAGE Take one of the elegant horse-drawn carriages for a spin around town. The cost is about $15 to $20, depending on the route and length of ride—usually about 45 minutes. Drivers congregate near the Mercado Libertad and also behind the Plaza/Rotonda de Los Hombres Ilustres and other spots around town.

FAST FACTS

American Express The office is at Vallarta 2440, Plaza Los Arcos (tel. 630-0200). It's open Monday through Friday from 9am to 2pm and Saturday from 9am to noon.

Area Code The area code is 3.

Babysitters Hotels can usually recommend babysitters; ask at the reception desk.

Bookstores Gonvil is a popular chain of bookstores throughout the city. There's one across from the Plaza de Los Hombres Ilustres on Alcalde and another a few blocks south at 16 de Septiembre 118 (Alcalde becomes 16 de Septiembre south of the cathedral). Sanborn's at the corner of Juárez and 16 de Septiembre always has a tremendous selection of magazines, newspapers, and books in English.

Business Hours In Guadalajara most stores are open Monday through Friday from 10am to 7pm. Other offices such as travel agencies or other services may open at 9am. In Tlaquepaque and Tonalá, many shops close from 2 to 4pm.

Car Rentals Two to try are Auto-Rent de Guadalajara, Avenida Federalismo

---

IMPRESSIONS

The wonderful progress that Mexico has made within recent years is strikingly exemplified in the case of Guadalajara, which, less than twenty years ago, was a sleepy, backward place but little known to the outside world. The nearest railway was then some distance away, and travellers from the capital were obliged to make a large part of the journey in slow, uncomfortable stage-coaches. To-day, [sic] Guadalajara has become a busy, cosmopolitan city and an important railway center . . .
   —W. E. CARSON, MEXICO: THE WONDERLAND OF THE SOUTH, 1909

GUADALAJARA: GETTING AROUND • 155

480 at La Paz (tel. 626-6989); and Aguila, Avenida Juárez 845-A (tel. 625-9554). There are many agencies in the airport-arrivals area or ask at your hotel. See also Chapter 2, "Planning a Trip to Mexico's Mid-Pacific Region," for how to cut the cost of renting a car by reserving from your home country.

Climate Guadalajara has a mild, pleasant, and dry climate year round. Bring a sweater for evenings during November through March. From June through September it's rainy and a bit cooler. The months of March, April, and May are also hot and dry.

Consulates The world's largest American consular offices are here at Progreso 175 (tel. 625-4445, or for emergencies 626-5553). It's open Monday through Friday from 8am to 4:30pm. Death or accident is considered an emergency but Visa problems are not.

Currency Exchange Banks will change money and traveler's checks Monday through Friday from 9am to noon. Many travelers will be delighted/relieved to find handy **Pocket Tellers.** There's a 24-hour Pocket Teller that takes VISA, Cirrus, and MasterCard at the Banamex bank at the corner of Corona and Juárez. Look for the seven-story gray building catercorner from the Café Madrid.

Dentist Ask at your hotel lobby.

Doctors Guadalajara has many English-speaking doctors. Ask your hotel for a referral.

Drugstores Ask at your hotel where the closest pharmacy is. Farmacías Guadalajara, a chain with outlets throughout the city, offers late-night service; there's one near downtown on Avenida López Cotilla (tel. 614-2810) open daily from 8am to 10pm. Farmacía Varela, Pedro Moreno 620 (tel. 614-1433), is open Monday through Saturday from 9am to 11pm and Sunday from 11am to 4pm; Farmacía Corona, Hidalgo 601 (tel. 614-2201 or 613-2132), is open from 9am to 9pm and has delivery service in the downtown area.

Emergencies For police call 617-5838 (state) or 621-7194 (highways). During the day, call the tourist office (tel. 614-0606, ext. 114). For extreme medical emergencies there's a service from the United States that will fly people to American hospitals: Air-Evac, 24-hour air ambulance; call collect 24 hours, 713/880-9767 in Houston, 619/278-3822 in San Diego, 305/772-0003 in Miami.

Etiquette Like most Mexicans, Guadalajarans are reserved and formal at first, but warm up quickly with a few words of conversation. I have found Guadalajarans generally to be among the most helpful of any city I visit. On several occasions over the years while trying to find my way by car alone, I have asked a fellow motorist directions (usually a family or woman) and been given not only the directions, but told "follow me, I'll lead you there." In every case, it was plain to see they took immense pleasure in helping the tourist.

Eyeglasses Look for the optic shop right across the plaza from the tourism office.

Holidays See "Special Events" in Chapter 11. February and October are the big festival months. On Christmas and Easter, many things are closed or have different hours, and the renowned Ballet Folklórico has no performances.

Hospitals Contact the Hospital Mexico-Americano, Colomos 2110 (tel. 641-0089).

Information The state of Jalisco's tourist information office is at Morelos 102 (tel. 658-2222; fax 613-1185), in the Plaza Tapatía—at the crossroads of Paseo Degollado and Paraje del Rincón del Diablo. It's open Monday through Friday from 9am to 9pm, and Saturday from 9am to 1pm. The English-speaking staff provides good information and an excellent map.

Also check here for information on cultural happenings around town.

Laundry/Dry Cleaning There are no laundries in the historic downtown area. Hotels generally offer this service (at a high price).

Lost Property Call the American consulate, police, or your bus company or airline (for property lost in transit).

Luggage Storage/Lockers Luggage storage is available in the main bus station, the Central Camionera and at the Guadalajara airport.

Newspapers/Magazines The Hotel Fénix (on the corner of Calle Corona and Avenida López Cotillo), has English-language newspapers and magazines and maps. It's also a good place to buy Guadalajara's English newspaper, *The Colony Reporter,* which is published every Saturday, if you don't spot it on a newsstand. Sanborn's at the corner of Juárez and 16 de Septiembre has a wide selection of U.S. and Mexican newspapers and magazines.

Police See "Emergencies," above.

Post Office It's at the corner of Carranza and Calle Independencia, about four blocks northeast of the cathedral. Standing in the plaza behind the cathedral and facing the Degollado Theater, walk to the left and turn left on Carranza. Walk past the Hotel de Mendoza, cross Calle Independencia, and look for the post office on the left-hand side.

Radio/TV Many English-speaking U.S. cable TV stations are broadcast in Guadalajara.

Religious Services Check *The Colony Reporter* newspaper.

Rest Rooms Use the facilities in a restaurant, museum, or hotel lobby area. Always carry your own paper and soap.

Safety As in any large city, don't be careless with belongings. Women should avoid walking around alone late at night.

Schools Several schools offer Spanish-language study for foreigners including: the Foreign Student Study Center, University of Guadalajara, Calle Guanajuato 1047 (Apdo. Postal 12130), Guadalajara, Jal. 44100 (tel. 653-6024; fax 653-2150), most of whose courses run five weeks; the Spanish Language School, 12 de Diciembre no. 359, Col. Chapalita, Guadalajara, Jal. 45042 (tel. 621-4774), where most classes are by the semester, but shorter lengths are accepted when space is available; and the Instituto Cultural Mexicano-Norteamerican de Jalisco, Enrique Díaz de León 300, Guadalajara, Jal. 44170 (tel. 625-5838; fax 625-1671).

Taxis See "Getting Around" in this chapter.

Transit Information See "Getting Around" in this chapter.

CHAPTER 10

WHERE TO STAY & DINE IN GUADALAJARA

- **1. WHERE TO STAY**
- **FROMMER'S SMART TRAVELER: HOTELS**
- **2. WHERE TO DINE**
- **FROMMER'S SMART TRAVELER: RESTAURANTS**

Guadalajara offers all the amenities in the way of hotels and restaurants of a major city. There are hotels for every budget, and restaurants offer cuisine from around the world.

1. WHERE TO STAY

EXPENSIVE

CARLTON HOTEL, Av. Niños Heroes and 16 de Septiembre, Guadalajara, Jal. 44190. Tel. 36/14-7272, toll free 91-800/3-6200 in Mexico. Fax 3/613-5539. 222 rms and suites. AC TV TEL MINIBAR

$ Rates: $131 standard single or double; $185 master suite; $195 executive suite. Ask about weekend discounts.

Formerly the Sheraton Hotel, the Carlton is near Agua Azul Park and a short distance from the historic center. The nicely furnished rooms are unusually spacious. Standard rooms have either two double beds or one king-size bed. All have hairdryers and remote-control TV with U.S. channels. Master suites have a large living-room area, while junior suites have a small sitting area. Each of the fifth-floor executive suites includes terry robes, continental breakfast, afternoon coffee and sweets, and open bar in the early evening. The 10th floor is reserved for nonsmokers. You'll save money by purchasing a package for this hotel through a travel agent in the United States.

Dining/Entertainment: La Pergula restaurant open daily from 7am to midnight, faces the pool with indoor or outdoor dining. There are two bars. Genesis Video Disco is open from 9:30pm to 1am Thursday through Saturday.

Services: Laundry, room service, travel agency, purified tap water. For an extra charge guests may use the hotel's fax and copy machine.

Facilities: Large pool. Small, fully equipped fitness center for men.

**FIESTA AMERICANA, Aurello Aceves 225, Glorieta Minerva, Guadalaja-

ra, Jal. 44100. Tel. 3/625-3434 or 625-4848, toll free 800/223-2332 in the U.S. Fax 3/630-3725. 396 rms (all with bath). A/C TV TEL MINIBAR
$ Rates: $160 single or double; $190 Fiesta Club.

A 22-story luxury hotel on a grand scale, it caters to the exacting demands of travelers arriving for both business and pleasure. It's a bustling hotel with a 14-story lobby and popular lobby bar with ongoing live entertainment. Like the public areas of the hotel, the rooms are spacious and beautifully coordinated, all with TV with U.S. channels. The 27 exclusive Fiesta Club rooms and 3 suites on the 12th and 14th floors, come with special amenities (see below). One room is handicap-equipped.

Dining/Entertainment: The Chula Vista restaurant, open from 7am to 1am, offers an international menu, with a German buffet on Thursday evening and an Italian buffet on Friday evening. La Hacienda serves Mexican fare from 1pm to 1am, and Place de la Concorde is the international restaurant, open from 7pm to 1am. The lobby bar is open from noon to 2am. For more on the hotel's entertainment list see "Nightclub/Cabaret" in Chapter 11.

Services: Laundry, dry cleaning, room service, travel agency.

Facilities: Heated rooftop swimming pool, two lighted tennis courts, and purified tap water. Fiesta Club guests have key-only access to club floors, separate check-in and checkout, concierge, remote-control TV, continental breakfast and afternoon wine and hors d'oeuvres daily, as well as business services such as secretaries, fax, copy machine, and conference room.

HOLIDAY INN CROWNE PLAZA, López Mateos Sur 2500, Guadalajara, Jal. 45050. Tel. 3/631-5566, toll free 800/465-4329 in the U.S. Fax 3/631-9393. 300 rms and suites (all with bath). A/C TV TEL MINIBAR
$ Rates: $190 standard single or double; $220 concierge floors; $728 presidential suite. Ask about summer discounts.

With a recent complete renovation this long-established hotel rose to the standard of the Crowne Plaza, the best of the Holiday Inn chain. There are two sections, the tower section in front and the two-story garden section in back. Although the tower section is the most popular, I prefer the tranquillity of the garden section. With the exception

---

 FROMMER'S SMART TRAVELER: HOTELS

1. Hotels in the "expensive" category often reduce prices on weekends, and weekdays especially in summer, meaning savings of as much as 50% off normal rates.
2. Hotels in the budget and moderate price category will often discount the quoted price if the hotel isn't full. It never hurts to ask.
3. Because of the daily devaluation of the peso, you will pay less in the long run if you use a credit card to pay the hotel bill.
4. Many budget-quality hotels don't accept credit cards even if there's a sticker on the window that says they do.
5. Although prices may vary from those quoted here, to avoid being overcharged, if a price seems too high when compared to the price quoted in this book, ask to see their printed rates. This applies especially to budget-category hotels where clerks have been known to jack up the price and pocket the difference.

of the presidential suite, all rooms are basically furnished in the same beautifully coordinated furniture. They come with either two double beds or a king-size bed, love seat and two side chairs, balcony or terrace. The plush two-story presidential suite has a handsome bar, separate dining and living room downstairs, and enormous bedroom upstairs with a giant jet tub in the bathroom. Concierge rooms are in the garden section and include separate check-in, valet, business center, continental breakfast, and afternoon drinks.

Dining/Entertainment: La Fuente Restaurant off the lobby is open 24 hours. El Kiosco is the outdoor restaurant near the pool. Jacarandas is the gourmet restaurant open from 1pm to 1am. Da Vinci discotheque opens between 10pm and 3am nightly. La Fiesta nightclub has live music, national and international shows, and is open from 10pm to 3am.

Services: Laundry, dry cleaning, room service, travel agency, safety-deposit box in each room. Guests on the commercial program have access to the hotel's fax and copier.

Facilities: Swimming pool, two lighted tennis courts, small gym with workout equipment, sauna separate for men and women, massage by appointment, play area for children, 2 handicapped rooms, and 32 no-smoking rooms.

HYATT REGENCY, Av. López Mateos Sur y, Moctezuma, Guadalajara, Jal. 45050. Tel. 3/622-7778, toll free 800/228-9000 in the U.S. and Canada. Fax 3/622-9877. 347 rms and suites. A/C TV TEL MINIBAR
$ Rates: $154 standard single or double; $265 junior suite; $190 Regency Club.
Parking: Free.

The elegant 14-story Hyatt Regency Hotel anchors one end of the Plaza del Sol, the city's largest and most fashionable shopping center. Glass elevators whish up and down the soaring lobby, and guest rooms are as stylish as the hotel's public areas. Rooms vary in size but all are decorated in rose and green with natural wood furniture and all have a tub/shower combination. Four key-only floors are reserved for Regency Club guests who receive special amenities. No-smoking rooms are on the 12th floor.

Dining/Entertainment: Arco Iris coffee shop opens for breakfast at 7am and closes at 1:30pm. The festive La Moreña opens with a Mexican buffet breakfast from 7 to 11:30am, then reopens from 1:30pm to midnight. Aquarius snack bar is in the pool area. The lobby bar serves between 11am and 2am with live music from 8 to 11:30pm. There's live music in El Pueblito Cantina Monday through Thursday from 8pm to 3am and Friday and Saturday from 6pm to 3am.

Services: Laundry, dry cleaning, room service, beauty shop, travel agency, car rental, business center with bilingual secretarial services, and 24-hour doctor. Regency Club guests receive a daily newspaper, continental breakfast, and evening cocktails in the club's separate lounge.

Facilities: Swimming pool on the 12th floor, gym, separate sauna for men and women, ice-skating rink.

QUINTA REAL, Av. Mexico 2727, Guadalajara, Jal. 44680. Tel. 3/615-0000; toll free 800/445-4565 in the U.S. and Canada, 91-800/3-6015 in Mexico. Fax 36/30-1797. 78 suites. A/C TV TEL MINIBAR
$ Rates: $198 junior suite; $232 master suite; $253 grand-class suite.

Opened in 1986, this is the city's most intimate hotel. Its casual-but-sophisticated restaurant and bar are the place to be seen if you're climbing any social or political ladder. The hotel hosts many business meetings and is frequently full. Each of the guest rooms is different: Eight have brick cupolas, some have balconies, several have conch-shaped headboards, and four come with whirlpool bath in the bathroom. All have elegant antique decorative touches, remote-control TV with U.S. channels, tub/shower combination, and king-size beds. It's located west of the city center two blocks from the Minerva Circle on Avenida Mexico at López Mateos.

Dining/Entertainment: The elegant off-lobby restaurant with both terrace and indoor dining is open for all meals from 7am to 1am. The adjacent bar opens from 1pm to 2am.

Services: Concierge, laundry and dry cleaning, massage by reservation, video players for rent, travel agency.

Facilities: Small heated pool.

EL TAPATÍO GRAN SPA & RESORT, Blvd. Aeropuerto 4275, Guadalajara, Jal. 45500 (Apdo. Postal 2953, Guadalajara, Jal. 44100). Tel. 3/635-6050; toll free 800/472-6772 in the U.S., 914/632-0595 in New York. Fax 3/635-6664. 120 rms, 34 suites. A/C TV TEL MINIBAR

$ Rates: $145 standard single or double; $180 deluxe single or double. Ask about spa packages.

Located on a mountaintop between city center and the airport, no Guadalajara hotel exceeds this one for view or for getaway resort feeling, though the city is minutes away. Guests enter through guarded gates on a cobblestone lane that snakes up and around the mountain to the lobby and guest rooms. All of the rooms are tastefully furnished and 34 are in the deluxe category with remote-control TV. The new state-of-the-art spa was not open when I checked and no date for opening was scheduled. Besides being the hotel nearest the airport, it's also near both Tlaquepaque and Tonalá.

Dining/Entertainment: Los Laurales faces the pool and serves all three meals. Mesón del Chef (see "Where to Dine" below) is the elegant restaurant with an international menu and a panoramic view of Guadalajara below. It's open evenings only. There's a city view from the off-lobby bar, Puesta del Sol. Memories Disco is open nightly from 8pm to 3am and is free to hotel guests.

Services: Laundry, room service, and travel agency.

Facilities: General guest facilities include pool with swim-up bar near restaurants and rooms, horseback riding, racquet club with 10 clay tennis courts (4 lighted) and instructor, gymnasium, jogging track, sauna, steam and massage rooms, and pro shop. When it opens, spa guest facilities in a separate building will include outdoor hot jet-air pools and chiller pool, hydrotherapy tubs, inhalation room, Turkish and Russian baths, Finnish sauna, herbal wraps, Loofa, salt-glow and soap rubs, massage, Scotch shower, aerobics, indoor gym, and juice bar.

MODERATE

CALINDA ROMA, Av. Juárez 170, Guadalajara, Jal. 14100. Tel. 3/614-8650; toll free 800/228-5151 in the U.S., 91-800/9-000 in Mexico. Fax 3/613-0557. 172 rms. A/C TV TEL MINIBAR

$ Rates: $55–$70 single; $82 double. **Parking:** $1 daily.

Ideally situated within walking distance of all downtown sights and restaurants, this is the best hotel in the city center. For its 100th birthday in 1993, it was completely renovated and prices may go up as a result. It's a good choice considering the location, plus it's quiet and very comfortable—the rooftop garden is a great place to unwind. The hotel is at the corner of Juárez and Degollado.

Dining/Entertainment: There's an excellent restaurant in the lobby as well as a lobby bar.

Services: Laundry, room service, travel agency.
Facilities: Rooftop garden with real grass, putting green, and swimming pool.

HOTEL ARANZAZU, Av. Revolución 110, Guadalajara, Jal. 44100. Tel. 3/613-3232. Fax 3/613-6650. 500 rms. A/C TV TEL

$ Rates: $71 single; $80 double. **Parking:** $8 per day.

Located near the intersection of Corona and Degollado, this comfortable hotel has a fine location within walking distance of all major downtown sights and restaurants. Check your bed, though; some mattresses sag. To get there from the Plaza de Las Armas, walk one block east on Moreno and turn right (south) on Corona and walk six blocks.

Dining/Entertainment: There is a restaurant/bar and nightclub.
Services: Laundry and room service.
Facilities: Swimming pool.

HOTEL DE MENDOZA, Carranza 16, Guadalajara, Jal. 45120. Tel. 3/613-4646, toll free 800/221-6509 in the U.S. Fax 3/613-7310. 104 rms (all with bath). TV TEL

$ Rates: $75 single; $88 double.

This beautifully restored hotel is popular with foreigners for its quiet, colonial atmosphere and modern conveniences. It's at the corner of Hidalgo, only steps from Liberation Plaza and the Teatro Degollado. Almost all of the large rooms have wall-to-wall carpeting, and some have a tub and a shower. Rooms face either the street or an interior court with a swimming pool. Rates may be higher if you call or reserve them from the United States. Walk-in rates are cheaper—get them quoted in pesos. To get there from the Teatro Degollado, go to the left of the theater and look for Carranza, a block down on the left; turn left at the corner church, adjoining the hotel.

Dining/Entertainment: The hotel has one restaurant, La Forga, which is very good. El Campañario bar offers dance music.
Services: Laundry and room service.
Facilities: Swimming pool.

RÍO CALIENTE SPA, Primavera Forest, La Primavera, Jal. No phone. Reservations: Barbara Dane Associates, 480 California Terrace, Pasadena, CA 91105 (tel. 818/796-5577). 48 rms.

$ Rates (including all meals): Patio area $80 single; $135 double. Pool area $90 single; $160 double. Discounts Sept–Oct.

⭐ Word of mouth keeps this popular and very casual spa busy. Built along the hills of the Primavera forest and on a thermal water river, the setting, at 5,550 feet, is both rugged and serene. Temperatures average 80°F year round. Individual rooms are clustered in two areas. Those near the activity area are smaller and more simply furnished and cost less than the newer and more stylish rooms with patios near the river and pool. All have one double and one single bed, fireplace, full-length mirror, in-room safety-deposit box, desk, chest, and bedside reading lamps. Water is purified in the pools and kitchen, and jars of fresh purified water are supplied daily in each room. Extra spa programs vary throughout the year and might include special instructors for Spanish, nutrition, and electro-acupuncture face-lifts at an extra cost. A doctor comes daily. Huichol Indians sell crafts on Sunday. To save money on transportation from the Guadalajara airport, take one of the airport's colectivo vans to the Fiesta Americana Hotel, then change to a yellow cab. If you're driving, follow Avenida Vallarta west which becomes Highway 15 with signs to Nogales. Go straight for almost 10½ miles and pass the village called La Venta del

Astillero. Take the next left after La Venta and follow the rough road through the village of La Primavera for almost five miles. Keep bearing left through the forest until you see the hotel's sign on the left. There's no phone at the spa; reservations are through the United States only.

Dining/Entertainment: The help-yourself vegetarian meals are served in the cozy dining room. There's an activities room with nightly video movies or satellite TV, plus bingo and honor library.

Facilities: Two public-area outdoor thermal water pools and two private pools and sunning areas separate for men and women.

Services: Massage, with a choice of male or female massage therapist, mud wrap, anti-stress and anti-aging therapies, live-cell therapy, horseback riding, sightseeing and shopping excursions are available at extra cost. Included in the cost, besides meals, are daily guided hikes, yoga and pool exercises, use of scented steam room with natural steam from underground river.

BUDGET

HOTEL DON QUIJOTE PLAZA, Heroes 91, Guadalajara, Jal. 44100. Tel. 3/656-1299. Fax 3/614-2845. 32 rms, 1 suite. TV TEL
$ Rates: $45 single; $55 double.

This hotel, at Prisciliano Sanchez, was converted from a huge, three-story town house. It's near the Hotel Aranzazu and the Hotel Posada San Francisco. You'd expect to pay much more for the rooms which are softly luxurious with heavy drapes, fashionable pastel furnishings, and wall-to-wall carpeting. The spacious suite has a corner balcony overlooking Priciliano Sanchez and would be an elegant splurge. To reach the hotel from the Plaza de Armas, walk five blocks south on 16 de Septiembre, turn left on Sanchez and walk two blocks to the hotel.

Dining/Entertainment: There's a bar on the first-floor interior patio and a small excellent restaurant off the lobby.

HOTEL SAN FRANCISCO PLAZA, Degollado 267, Guadalajara, Jal. 44100. Tel. 3/613-8954 or 613-8971. 60 rms. A/C TV TEL
$ Rates: $35 single; $45 double. **Parking:** Free.

For a touch of class on a budget, try this highly recommended hotel facing a tiny square near Prisciliano Sanchez. They are authorized to charge much more, so you get a lot for the money. Stone arches, brick-tile floors, bronze sculptures, and potted plants decorate the four spacious central courtyards. All rooms are large and attractive. They include either a double bed, king-size bed, or two double beds. The English-speaking staff is friendly and helpful. To find the hotel from the Plaza de Armas, walk five blocks south on 16 de Septiembre, turn left on Sanchez and walk two blocks to Degollado and the hotel. There's an off-lobby restaurant open from 7am to 11pm.

POSADA REGIS, Av. Corona 171, Guadalajara, Jal. 44100. Tel. 3/613-3026 or 614-8633. 19 rms.
$ Rates: $31 single; $39 double. (Ask about discounts for stays of a week or more.)

Opposite the Hotel Fénix, the Posada Regis occupies the second floor of a restored (long ago) old mansion. The carpeted rooms are simply furnished, and arranged around a large, tranquil covered courtyard with sitting areas, a little restaurant, and potted plants. Rooms with balconies facing the street can be quite noisy. Windowless interior rooms are stuffy, so ask for a fan. The beds have plastic covers and "nonbreathing" nylon-type sheets. Bathrooms, which were added to the rooms, are not particularly private with an open ceiling and no door. I've stayed here

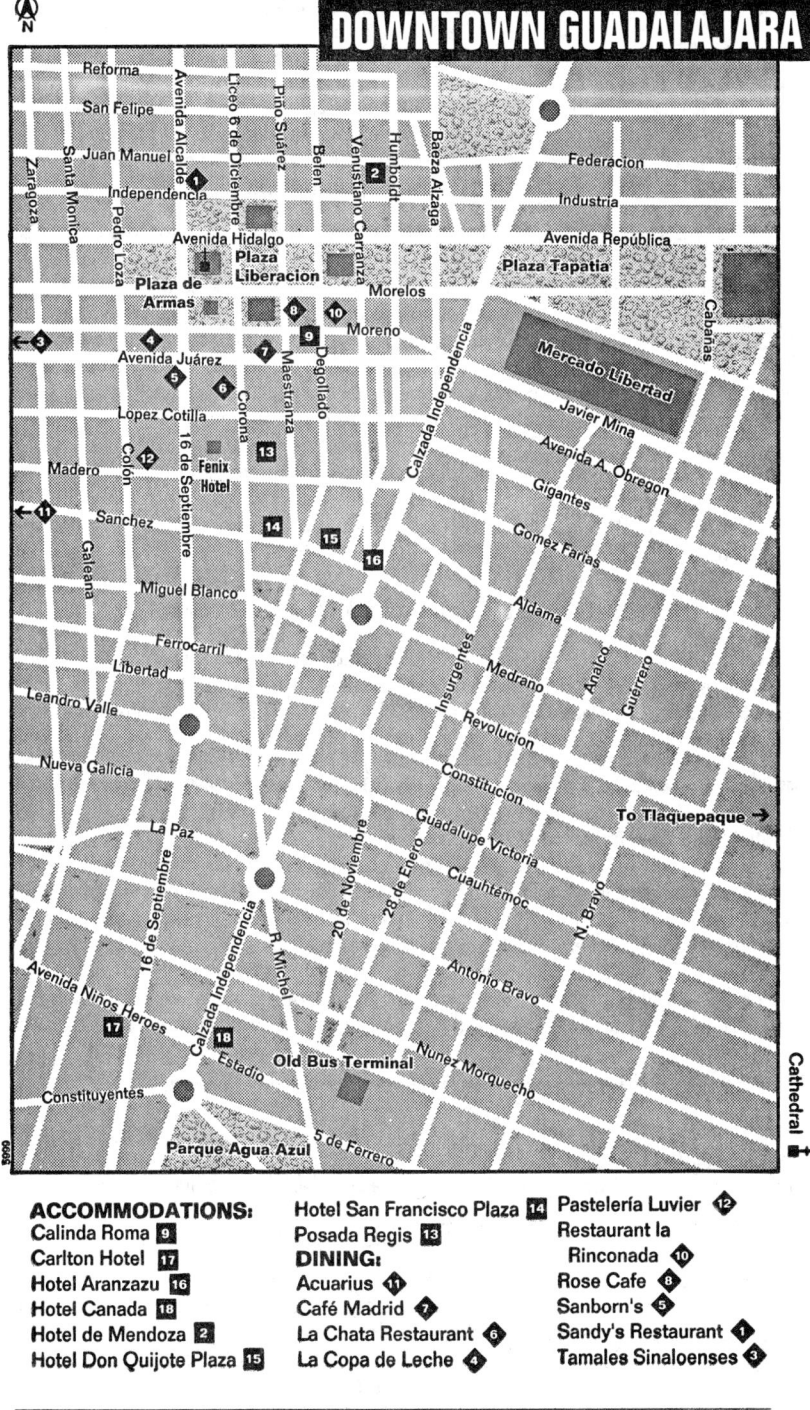

DOWNTOWN GUADALAJARA

ACCOMMODATIONS:
Calinda Roma 9
Carlton Hotel 17
Hotel Aranzazu 16
Hotel Canada 18
Hotel de Mendoza 2
Hotel Don Quijote Plaza 15
Hotel San Francisco Plaza 14
Posada Regis 13

DINING:
Acuarius 11
Café Madrid 7
La Chata Restaurant 6
La Copa de Leche 4
Pastelería Luvier 12
Restaurant la Rinconada 10
Rose Cafe 8
Sanborn's 5
Sandy's Restaurant 1
Tamales Sinaloenses 3

164 • WHERE TO STAY & DINE IN GUADALAJARA

and find it particularly serves my budget and my needs for safety and proximity to downtown. A friendly and comfortable atmosphere prevails, with personal attention from the English-speaking manager. Video movies are shown every evening. The restaurant serves a very good and inexpensive breakfast and lunch. There's personal laundry service, too. To find it walk south of Plaza de Armas on 16 de Septiembre, three blocks to López Cotillo, turn left and then the next right.

SUITES BERNINI, Av. Vallarta 1881, Guadalajara, Jal. 44140. Tel. 3/616-6736. 15 suites. TV TEL
$ Rates: $50 one-bedroom suite; $85 two-bedroom suite. **Parking:** Free.

If you don't mind being a 10- or 15-minute bus ride (on the electric "Par Vial" bus) from the center of town, by all means try the Suites Bernini, on the corner of Union. (Avenida Juárez, one of the main streets in the center of town, changes names and becomes Avenida Vallarta as it heads west.) Marble steps, guarded by stone lions, lead to the entrance of this elegant 16-story tower. Each suite has a king-size bed, kitchen, and floor-to-ceiling windows, with a magnificent view. The rooms are decorated with potted palms, plush pale-blue carpeting, and artwork—really lovely and spotlessly clean. To get there, take the "Par Vial" bus west on Avenida Juárez, two blocks south of the cathedral; it's at the corner of Union.

NEAR THE TRAIN & OLD BUS STATIONS

Now that the central bus station has been relocated to near Tlaquepaque, there's little reason to stay in this area south of the town center, unless you can't find reasonably priced lodgings elsewhere or want to be close to the old bus station or the train station. It's a 25-minute walk to downtown.

HOTEL CANADA, Estadio 77, Guadalajara, Jal. 44440. Tel. 3/619-4014. 120 rms. TEL
$ Rates: $15–$22 single; $20–$25 double.

My top pick in this area was recently remodeled, which added a bright, cheery feel to the lobby. The rooms got a face-lift as well, with fresh paint, and in most rooms new mattresses and bedspreads. You probably wouldn't want to hang around the streets at night here, but it's decent enough for an economical multiday stay in the city. Desk clerks are helpful, but speak only Spanish. The hotel is ½ block from the old bus station and should not be confused with the Gran Hotel Canada, which faces the old bus station and is more expensive. To get there from the train station, go out the front

---

IMPRESSIONS

[Guadalajara] is famous for the small feet and lovely faces of its women, the reckless poetry of its men, for its music, its piety and its tequila, and the fame is in every case warranted.
—ANITA BRENNER, *YOUR MEXICAN HOLIDAY*, 1932

The men [of Guadalajara] are also handsome and cling to their attractive charro outfits and extremely large sombreros. At one time the brims of their hats were so wide that they were declared a public nuisance. Any man caught wearing a sombrero with a brim that extended much beyond his shoulders was arrested and fined.
—BURTON HOLMES, *MEXICO*, 1939.

door and walk straight on Independencia four long blocks, turn right on Estadio; it's on the left.

NEAR THE NEW BUS STATION

HOTEL EL PARADOR, Carretera a Zapotlanejo 1500, Guadalajara, Jal. Tel. 3/659-0142. 754 rms. TV
$ Rates: $32 single or double.

This sprawling hotel is the only lodging near the new Central Camionera. Facilities include a 24-hour restaurant, two swimming pools, and saunas for men. Rooms are clean, simple, and comfortable, with two twin beds, but the tile hallways carry noise like a megaphone. You'll see the hotel's large sign as you exit the bus station.

2. WHERE TO DINE

Some travelers find it comforting to know that U.S. franchise restaurants such as Kentucky Fried Chicken and Dunkin' Donuts are beginning to proliferate in Guadalajara. But as long as you're in Guadalajara, or anywhere in the state of Jalisco for that matter, I urge you to try a local dish—**birria**. It's a hearty soup-like dish of lamb, pork, or goat meat in a tasty chicken and tomato broth, lightly thickened with masa (corn meal) and spiced with oregano, garlic, onions, cumin, chiles, allspice, and cilantro. Restaurants around El Parián in Tlaquepaque have it on the menu daily.

For those on a truly low budget, the second floor of **Mercado Libertad** will look like heaven. You can get a comida corrida here for $2 at any of what seem like hundreds of little restaurant stands. There's a vegetarian section, too, and lots of places for tacos, tamales with atole, and enchiladas. But be careful about cleanliness—some people say you should never eat here. Nonetheless, hundreds of people do eat here every day, and seem to be surviving just fine—I've even done it myself. Check it out—it's a fascinating slice of Mexican life, even if all you end up doing is looking. If you're planning to eat, the best time to go is early in the morning, while the food is the freshest.

EXPENSIVE

LA COPA DE LECHE, Juárez 414. Tel. 614-5347 or 614-1845.
   Cuisine: INTERNATIONAL.
$ Prices: Appetizers $2.70–$5.75; main courses $6.25–$13.50; seafood $11.50–$13.50; comida corrida $8.50.
   Open: Daily 7am–11pm; comida corrida served noon–5pm.
Close to the cathedral, the most famous and long-lived restaurant in Guadalajara has a sidewalk café and balcony, plus upstairs and downstairs dining rooms. An organist playing live lunch music helps drown out the relentless din on Juárez. The eclectic menu includes Mexican, American, Italian, and Greek specialties. To find the restaurant from the Plaza de Armas, walk 1 block to Juárez, turn right, and walk 1½ blocks. The restaurant is on the right.

EL MESÓN DEL CHEF, Hotel El Tapatío Spa & Resort, Aeropuerto 4275, Tel. 635-6050.
   Cuisine: INTERNATIONAL.

$ Prices: Full meal $35–$40.
Open: Mon–Sat 8pm–midnight.

For the ultimate combination of view and elegant dining this hilltop restaurant in the Hotel El Tapatío can't be beat. There's a full wall of windows overlooking the city and at night, with the city lights and flickering candlelight and handsomely clad tables, it's a fitting place for a special night out. Service is polished and the menu includes beef, chicken, and fish specialties with a combination of preparations that includes Italian, French, and Mexican. The dessert selection is small but wonderful, and there's a good wine list.

ROSE CAFE, Hotel Frances, Maestranza 35. Tel. 613-1252.
   Cuisine: INTERNATIONAL.
$ Prices: Appetizers $3–$10; main courses $6–$28 (chateaubriand for two); comida corrida $8.
   Open: Daily 7am–10:30pm.

I can't recommend the Hotel Frances because of the nightly disco noise, but the off-lobby restaurant of the hotel, with its international offerings, is a pleasant change from more traditional Mexican restaurants downtown. Nice but not elegant, the decor features soft pastel tones of rose, turquoise, and cream with art deco accents; each chair is carved with a slightly scarlet-tinted rose. Try the spaghetti primavera (natural carrot-and-spinach pasta with fresh vegetables and parmesan cheese), or the coq au vin, or something more American like the steak sandwich. From the Plaza de Armas, walk one block east on Moreno to Maestranza and turn right. The hotel and restaurant are on the left.

MODERATE

CAFÉ MADRID, Juárez 264. Tel. 614-9504.
   Cuisine: MEXICAN.
$ Prices: Breakfast $3.25–$6.25; main courses $3–$8; comida corrida $7.
   Open: Daily 8am–10:30pm; comida corrida 1–5 or 6pm.

Conveniently located, this popular café serves the best coffee in Guadalajara. The smell of coffee wafts outside the café in the morning—americano, espresso, cappuccino, and café con leche are all excellent eye-openers. Signs above the counter advertise chilaquiles and "ricos wafles" which are just that and served with warm syrup. For a light and inexpensive lunch, try the generous fruit cocktail, chilaquiles rojo or verde (red or green sauce), or a sandwich with french fries

---

FROMMER'S SMART TRAVELER: RESTAURANTS

1. Stock up on fruit or bakery goods for an inexpensive breakfast.
2. Make lunch the main meal when prices are generally less expensive.
3. Fine dining is cheaper in Guadalajara than a comparable meal in the United States, so this is the place for an all-out splurge.
4. For a meal in a bowl, try hearty soups like tlalpeño, tortilla, and pozole.
5. Drink Mexican-made liquor and wine which are inexpensive compared to any imported version.

GUADALAJARA: WHERE TO DINE • 167

or salad. The extra-hearty platillo tapatío includes fried chicken, a taco, an enchilada, and potatoes. To reach the restaurant from the Plaza de Armas, walk one block on Corona to Juárez and turn left. It's on the left.

LOS OTATES, Av. Americas 28 at Hidalgo. Tel. 615-0481.
   Cuisine: MEXICAN/REGIONAL.
$ **Prices:** Main courses $3.50-$10.50; tacos 80¢-$8.
   Open: Daily 1pm-midnight.

This nicely furnished and well-run restaurant is the place to try some of Mexico's delectable street food—without the risk. Established in 1940, it's one of the most popular places for locals to savor their own food prepared just the way they like it, and in a softly lit atmosphere with bright tablecloths and traditional pottery decorations. The menu is short—tacos, quesadillas, machaca, pig skin (*chicarron*), brains (*cesos*—considered a treat), pork, beans, al pastor meat, and beef all served with fresh tortillas or tostadas. Other main courses include enchiladas, chalupas, tamales, chiles rellenos, carne asada tampiqueño, and fresh pozole daily. The fruit water is made with purified water, so this is a good place to try that refreshing Mexican drink. There's another branch at Avenida Mexico 2455 at San Francisco Rojas. To find it take the "Par Vial" to bus Avenida de Las Americas, then ask directions. It's a short walk to Hidalgo.

LA PICCOLA TRATTORIA RISTORANTE, Av. Mexico 2219. Tel. 615-6643.
   Cuisine: ITALIAN.
$ **Prices:** Appetizers $2.50-$4; main courses $4.75-$15.50; pizza $6.90-$10.
   Open: Tues-Sat 1pm-midnight; live piano music 2-5pm and 9pm-midnight.

Dark, candelit, and casual, the decor here is in handsome black and maroon, with curtains half covering the big windows facing the avenida. Some people swear this restaurant makes the best pizzas in the city, but there are only four versions to choose from. Other main-course choices include seafood such as tequila shrimp brochette, or beef filet in wine or pepper sauce. The restaurant is near the corner of Avenida Mexico and Americas.

RESTAURANT LA RINCONADA, Morelos 86. Tel. 613-9914.
   Cuisine: MEXICAN/INTERNATIONAL.
$ **Prices:** Appetizers $5-$6.50; main courses $8-$14.
   Open: Mon-Sat 11:30am-9pm; Sun 1-6pm.

Housed in a beautiful old stone mansion on the Plaza Tapatía, La Rinconada draws diners in with live music, which is almost nonstop throughout the day. The dining room is set in the mansion's huge interior patio surrounded by arches and doors leading to smaller rooms with iron grill-covered windows. The setting is truly lovely, but the slow and inattentive service leaves something to be desired. Though some diners rave about the steaks, which are the house special, skip the daily special of cornish hen, pasta, and soup. It's especially popular at lunch but the crowd thins out by late afternoon. To find it from the Plaza de Armas, walk two blocks east of the plaza along Morelos. Look for the restaurant behind the theater.

RICCO, Libertad 1981. Tel. 625-0724.
   Cuisine: ITALIAN/CONTINENTAL.
$ **Prices:** Appetizers $3.25-$4; main courses $6.50-$13.50.
   Open: Daily 1-11:30pm.

Housed in an old mansion in one of Guadalajara's neighborhoods, this casually fashionable restaurant rates high with the locals. Dining rooms, all decked out in cloth-covered tables and cushioned chairs, are a bit too brightly lit to be intimate, but the service and food are good. Starters include small portions of pasta, seafood, and soup or perhaps pâté and prosciutto and canteloupe. Among the main courses you'll find pepper steak, seabass in brown beer, and veal with fettucine. To find it from the main plaza take a bus to Chapultepec and Vallarta. At Vallarta turn left for two blocks to Libertad and turn left again. You'll see it on the right less than half a block down.

SANBORN'S, Juárez at 16 de Septiembre. No phone.
   Cuisine: INTERNATIONAL.
$ **Prices:** Breakfast $3.85–$11.50; main courses $3.85–$12.
   Open: Sun–Wed 7:30am–midnight; Thurs–Sat 7:30am–1am.

Opened in 1992, Sanborn's is alive with patrons almost any time. Like other branches in Mexico, waitresses wear festive dresses and serve swiftly and politely. The menu is varied from tacos and hotcakes to steaks and sandwiches. When you're finished, the drugstore/gift/book section is *the* place to get back in touch with the world while browsing through the books, newspapers, and magazines in English; Sanborn's drug/gift stores are always well stocked. It's in the heart of downtown.

SANDY'S RESTAURANT, 16 de Septiembre and Independencia. Tel. 614-4236.
   Cuisine: INTERNATIONAL.
$ **Prices:** Breakfast special $4–$6.50; sandwiches $5–$7.75; main courses $5.75–$11.50.
   Open: Daily 7:30am–10:30pm.

This second-story restaurant has balconies overlooking the Rotonda de Los Hombres Ilustres and the cathedral. It's a nice place for breakfast, when the morning sun and mist play on the flowers and foliage in the park. For lunch, it's a slight escape from the bustle of city life below, and the menu includes soups, pasta, fajitas, hamburgers and sandwiches, filet mignon, and chicken parmesan. If you can't decide, gaze at one of the large colored photos of the house specialties on the wall. There's often music between 7 and 10pm, with complimentary botanas in the Bar Los Globos to the left as you enter. The restaurant is upstairs, two blocks north of the cathedral on Alcalde opposite the Rotonda de los Hombres Ilustres.

BUDGET

ACUARIUS, Prisciliano Sanchez 416. Tel. 612-6277.
   Cuisine: VEGETARIAN.
$ **Prices:** Breakfast $2.50–$3.50; comida corrida $7.
   Open: Mon–Sat 9:30am–9pm.

This tidy, airy little lunchroom has soft music playing, and shelves of soy sauce and vitamins. The restaurant serves breakfast and a comida corrida daily. For the comida there's a choice of two main dishes which you can sample first if you can't make up your mind. When I was there the choice was zucchini sautéed with mushrooms in a tangy tomato sauce or a mixed-vegetable stew. Whole-grain bread and whole-grain tortillas come with the meal, plus soup, fruit and yogurt or a salad, a tall, cool glass of fruit juice, and dessert. From the Plaza de Armas, walk 4 blocks south on 16 de Septiembre and turn right on P. Sanchez. Walk 3½ blocks and it's on the right. It's between Guerrero and O'Campo.

LA CHATA RESTAURANT, Corona 128. Tel. 613-0588.
   Cuisine: REGIONAL.
$ **Prices:** Breakfast $3–$5; main courses $5–$8.
   Open: Daily 8am–11pm.

La Chata doesn't look like much from the street, but the first sight of its gaily clad tables and bandana-topped women stirring and frying—not to mention the sounds and smells of the cookery—hooks just about everyone. Locals like La Chata for Tapatían fare from pozole and *torta ahogadas* (a spicy pork sandwich) to the steaming hot atole, which some people drink over ice. To find it from the Plaza de Armas, walk 1½ blocks south on Corona, and it's on the right between Juárez and López Cotilla.

PASTELERÍA LUVIER, Colón at Madero. Tel. 613-1343.
  Cuisine: PASTRIES/CROISSANTS.
$ Prices: 50¢–$1.
  Open: Mon–Fri 7am–9pm.

You'll see branches of this bakery all over the city and this one is particularly handy if you're downtown. Pick up a tray and tongs and browse the shelves for kaiser rolls, croissants with all kinds of fillings, giant cookies, and slices of cake. Cartons of milk are sold as well.

TAMALES SINALOENSES, 45B Galvez at Juárez.
  Cuisine: TAMALES/MEXICAN.
$ Prices: Tamales and tostadas 60¢–$1.50; pozole $2.50–$3.50; atole 75¢. No alcoholic beverages.
  Open: Dinner daily 5:30–10:30pm.

⑤ This evening-only restaurant serves pozole and tamales, plus atole, a thick, lightly sweet corn drink traditionally eaten before bedtime and at breakfast.
The tamales are huge, light, and tasty; one fills you up. They come with beef, pork, and chicken fillings, or in sweet varieties with raisins. The tamales are kept hot in large lidded cans, just the way they're sold in markets. Pozole comes in two sizes—large and small. The new restaurant is accented with tile, and the stainless-steel kitchen is open to view. This is a good place to grab a bite before one of the frequent films, art openings, or concerts at the Ex-Convento del Carmen just across Juárez. It's within easy walking distance of the Plaza de Armas. Walk one block to Juárez, turn right, and walk three or four blocks to the Templo del Carmen; the café is left of the templo facing the plaza.

CHAPTER 11

WHAT TO SEE & DO IN GUADALAJARA

- SUGGESTED ITINERARIES
1. THE MAJOR ATTRACTIONS
- WALKING TOUR—DOWNTOWN GUADALAJARA
2. MORE ATTRACTIONS
- FROMMER'S FAVORITE GUADALAJARA EXPERIENCES
3. ORGANIZED TOURS
4. SPECIAL EVENTS
5. SPECTATOR SPORTS
6. SHOPPING
7. EVENING ENTERTAINMENT

Visitors to Guadalajara and surrounding villages discover a variety of sightseeing opportunities to satisfy most interests.

One of the best ways to see Guadalajara's top attractions is by taking a walking tour. A walk through the downtown area will acquaint visitors with the major historical, cultural, and architectural highlights of the city.

SUGGESTED ITINERARIES

IF YOU HAVE 2 DAYS On your first day in Guadalajara, familiarize yourself with the historic downtown area by taking the walking tour below. Take your time browsing in the crafts section of the Libertad Market and walking the corridors of the Cabañas Cultural Institute, admiring Orozco's work there. Wind up the day with dinner near the Plaza Tapatía, then stroll over to Mariachi Square to hear the battle of the singers. If your second day happens to be a Thursday, make a shopping foray to Tlaquepaque and Tonalá and have dinner in Tlaquepaque or at the El Mesón del Chef at the Hotel El Tapatío overlooking the city. On other weekdays, you can spend a second day further exploring the city's museums and other attractions.

IF YOU HAVE 3 DAYS After you've spent a couple of days learning the lay of Guadalajara, begin early on your third day and make for Lake Chapala; you'll probably want to go to the lakeside villages of Chapala and Ajijic. Have breakfast in Chapala at one of the restaurants on the main street or on the malecón, then later take lunch at one of Ajijic's fine restaurants. After exploring the area and enjoying the lake, a sunset dinner at one of the lakeside restaurants is a nice way to wind up the day.

IF YOU HAVE 5 DAYS After a few days taking in the pleasures of the Guadalajara area as described above, you'll want to spend two nights at the mountain resort towns of Mazamitla and Tapalpa.

1. THE MAJOR ATTRACTIONS

There is no better way to explore the museums and architecture of historic downtown Guadalajara than by taking a walking tour.

WALKING TOUR — DOWNTOWN GUADALAJARA

Start: Plaza de Armas.
Finish: Libertad Market.
Time: Approximately three hours, not including museum and shopping stops.
Best Times: After 10am when museums are open.
Worst Times: Monday or holidays when museums are closed.

Begin the tour in the plaza beside the main cathedral on Alcalde between Hidalgo and Morelos in the charming:

1. **Plaza de Armas.** Beside the main cathedral, on Alcalde between Moreno and Morelos, is this pleasant plaza with wrought-iron benches and walkways leading like spokes in a wheel to the ornate iron, French-made, central bandstand, directly in front of:
2. **The Palacio del Gobierno.** This eye-catching arched structure that dominates the plaza was built in 1774 and combines the Spanish/Moorish influences prevalent at the time. Go inside to view the spectacular mural of Hidalgo by José Clemente Orozco over the beautiful wooden-railed staircase to the right. The theme in the center, quite obviously, is social struggle. The panel to the right is called *The Contemporary Circus,* and the one on the left, *The Ghost of Religion in Alliance with Militarism.* Orozco was a native of Guadalajara and is held in high esteem here and countrywide. Going back out the front entrance, turn right and walk to the:
3. **Cathedral.** Begun in 1561, the unusual, multispired facade combines several 17th-century Renaissance styles, including a touch of Gothic. An 1818 earthquake destroyed the original large towers. The present ones were designed by architect Manuel Gomez Ibarra. Inside, look over the sacristy to see the painting believed to be the work of renowned 17th-century artist Bartolomé Murillo (1617–82). Leave the cathedral and turn right out the front doors and walk along Alcalde to the:
4. **Rotonda de Los Hombres Ilustres.** Sixteen gleaming white columns without bases or capitals stand as monuments to Guadalajara's—and the state of Jalisco's—distinguished sons. To learn who they are, visitors need only to stroll around the green and flower-filled park and read the names on the 11 nearly life-size statues of the state's heroes. There are 98 burial vaults in the park, only four of which are occupied. East of the plaza, cross Liceo to the:
5. **Regional Museum of Guadalajara.** Built in 1701 in the Churrigueresque style, this museum contains archeological pieces, including a mammoth skeleton and an 18th-century meteorite, as well as art from the 17th and 18th centuries up to the present—both folk arts and crafts and works of art by modern masters Orozco, Rivera, Quiroga, Vizcarra, and Figueroa. Rooms 6 and 7 are devoted to the history of the state of Jalisco, and others display ethnography and European painting. Another section deals with paleontology, prehistory, and archeology, and features a gigantic reconstructed skeleton of a mammoth and the Meteorite

of Zacatecas found in 1792, weighing 1,715 pounds. The museum also includes the **National Institute of Anthropology and History,** which contains a large, colorful mural by J. G. Nuño showing scenes of the conquest. Frequent craft shows are held here as well. It's open Tuesday through Sunday from 10am to 3:45pm. Admission costs $5 for adults; children enter free. Outside the museum and to the right is the:

6. **Palacio de Justicia.** Built as the first convent in Guadalajara, Santa María de Gracia in 1588, it later became a Teachers College and girls school. In 1952, it was officially designated as the Palacio de Justicia. Inside above the stairway is a huge mural honoring the law profession in Guadalajara; it depicts historic events, including Benito Juárez with the 1857 constitution and laws of reform. Outside the palacio and directly to the right, continuing east on Hidalgo is the:

7. **Church of Santa María de Gracia,** one of Guadalajara's oldest churches, which was built along with the convent next door. Currently, it's being restored. Opposite the church is the:

8. **Teatro Degollado** (Deh-goh-*yah*-doh), a beautiful neoclassic-style, 19th-century opera house named for Santos Degollado. Degollado was a local patriot who fought with Juárez against the French and Maximilian. Notice the seven muses in the theater's triangular facade above the columns. The theater hosts various performances during the year, including the Ballet Folklórico Sunday at 10am. It's open to see Monday through Friday from 10am to 2pm. The **Plaza Liberación** links the cathedral and the Teatro Degollado. To the right of the theater on the opposite side of the plaza from the Santa María de Gracia church is the:

9. **University of Guadalajara School of Music and the San Agustín Church.** There are continuous services in the church, and sometimes the music school is open to the public. Continuing east on the plaza, be sure to notice the spectacular fountain behind the Teatro Degollado depicting Mexican history in low relief. You'll next pass the charming children's fountain, and then, the unusual sculpture of a tree with lions with nearby slabs of text by Charles V proclaiming Guadalajara's right to be recognized as a city. The plaza opens up into a huge pedestrian expanse called the **Plaza Tapatía,** framed by department stores and offices and dominated by the:

10. **Quetzalcoatl Fountain.** This towering, abstract sculpture/fountain represents the mythical plumed serpent, Quetzalcoatl, which figures so broadly in Mexican legend and ancient culture and religion. The smaller pieces represent the serpent/birds; the centerpiece is the serpents' fire. Looking down at the far end of the plaza, you'll spot the Hospicio Cabañas (see no. 11).

REFUELING STOP Take a short break at one of the small ice-cream shops or fast-food restaurants along the plaza, or wait and go to the small cafeteria inside the Hospicio, where they serve hot dogs, sandwiches, cake, soft drinks, coffee, and snacks.

11. **Hospicio Cabañas.** Formerly called the Cabañas Orphanage, and known today as the **Instituto Cultural Cabañas** (tel. 18-6003), this impressive structure was designed by the famous Mexican architect Manuel Tolsá. It housed homeless children from 1829 until 1980. Today it's a thriving cultural center offering art shows and classes for children and adults in all the fine arts. The main building has a fine dome and the walls and ceiling are covered by murals painted in 1929 by José Clemente Orozco (1883–1949). The powerful painting in the dome, *Man of Fire,* by Orozco, is a must to see; it's said to represent the spirit of

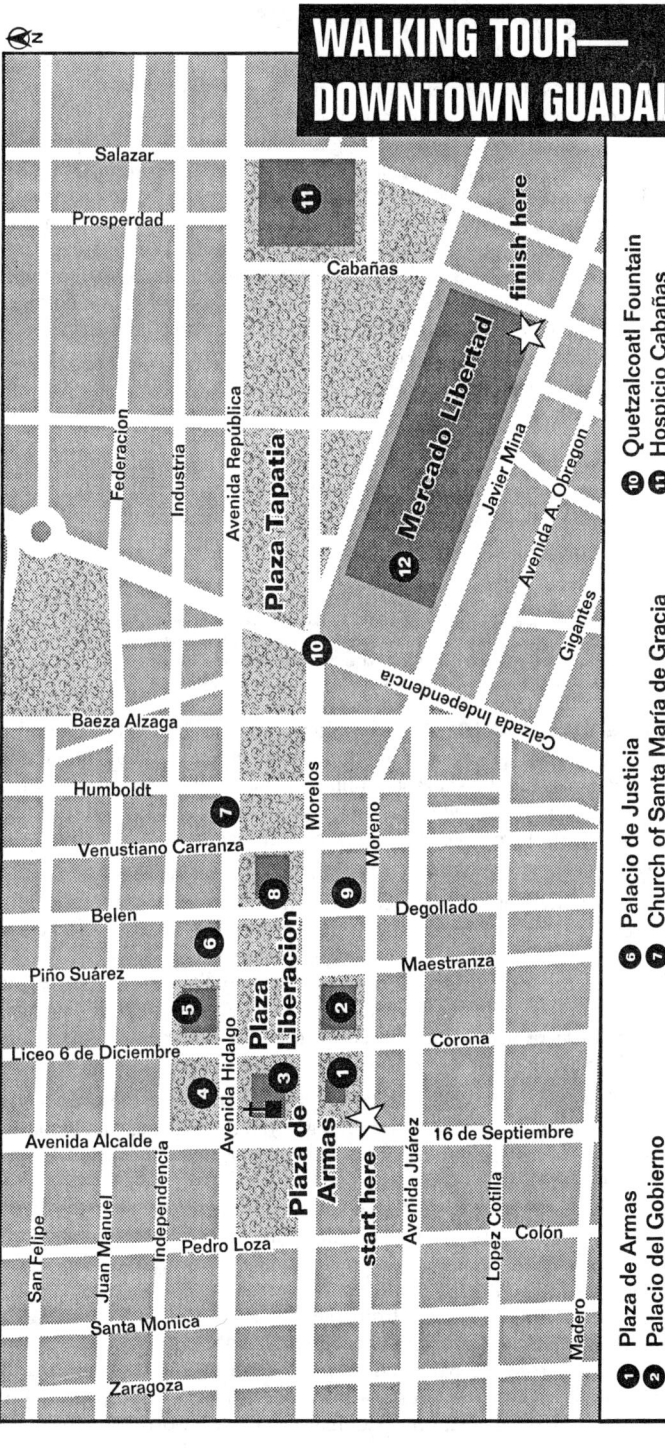

humanity projecting itself toward the infinite. Take a break and lie down on the viewing bench to see for yourself. Several other rooms hold more of Orozco's work, and there are also excellent temporary exhibits. For a free guided tour, ask for Ruben, at the front desk. He speaks English. Don't miss the contemporary art exhibit in the south wing, with the fascinating and unusual paintings by Javier Arevalo. The institute's own **Ballet Folklórico** performs here every Wednesday at 8:30pm and costs $5. The Instituto Cultural Cabañas is open Tuesday through Saturday from 10am to 6pm. Admission is $1.75 for adults, $1 for students, and 35¢ for children under 12. To the left of the entrance is a bookstore. In the far back, to the right, and down a hallway beyond the first patio after you enter, is a small café selling pizzas, sandwiches, sweets, and hot and cold drinks. The restaurant is open Monday through Friday from 10am to 8pm, Saturday from 10am to 6pm, and Sunday from 10am to 3pm.

For a real change of pace, turn left out the front entrance of the Cabañas and look for a stairway that leads down to the:

12. **Mercado Libertad.** Guadalajara's gigantic, covered central market, said to be the largest in Latin America. The site has been used for a market plaza since the 1500s and the present buildings were constructed in the early 1950s. This is a great place to buy leather goods, pottery, and just about anything else you can think of.

2. MORE ATTRACTIONS

PLAZA DE LOS MARIACHIS A half a block from the Mercado Libertad on Calzada Independencia and Javier Mina and beside the San Juan de Dios church is the Plaza de los Mariachis, actually a short street lined with restaurants and cafés. During the day, small bands of mariachis will be loafing around or sipping drinks, but at night the place is packed with them. (See also "Evening Entertainment," below.)

PLAZA & EX-CONVENTO DEL CARMEN At the Ex-Convento del Carmen, on Juárez four blocks west of the historic center, offers a full range of theater, films, and musical events almost nightly. It's open daily from 9am to 10pm. Tickets are usually sold here just a short while before the performance.

Across the street, the **Plaza del Carmen,** with a bubbling fountain, roses, and shade trees is a nice place to relax. Lovers' embraces may lead to a wedding at the small **Templo del Carmen,** an old church on the plaza. There's usually a mass, wedding, or christening in progress.

PARQUE AGUA AZUL Located near the former bus station at the south end of Calzada Independencia, this park is a perfect refuge from the bustling city. It contains plants, trees, shrubbery, statues, and fountains. The park is open daily from 10am to 6pm. Admission is 25¢.

For children there's a **Museo Infantil** (children's museum) with displays of traditional toys as well as shows. "El Chuku, Chuku," a rubber-tired minitrain, circulates through the grounds daily in the summer and the rest of the year on Saturday and Sunday from 11am to 6pm. A ride costs 45¢.

Across the Calzada Independencia from the Parque Agua Azul is the **Teatro Guadalajara del IMSS,** which offers experimental shows.

Across the calzada from the park entrance is the **Museo Antropología** in a small, one-story rock building. It houses a fine collection of pre-Hispanic pottery from the states of Jalisco, Nayarit, and Colima and is well worth your time. The museum is open daily from 10am to 12:45pm and 3:30 to 7:30pm. There's a small admission.

Also across the calzada (opposite Parque Agua Azul) is the **Casa de la Cultura** between 16 de Septiembre and Calzada Independencia (tel. 619-3611). It offers a variety of classes in local culture by day, as well as a packed evening schedule to which the public is invited. For details see "Evening Entertainment," below.

The state-run **Casa de las Artesanías** is just past the park entrance (heading toward town) at the crossroads of Calzada Independencia and Gallo (for details see "Shopping," below).

THE ZOO & PLANETARIUM Even those who don't like zoos will like the beautiful and spacious new Guadalajara Zoo (Jardín Zoológico; tel. 637-2478), which straddles the edge of the breathtaking Huentitlán ravine at the far northeast edge of town. It's next to the Technology Center of Guadalajara with its planetarium and Omnimax Theater. A few hours or half a day provides a nice respite from the hectic downtown pace and affords some great people as well as animal watching. Huge, happy families with toddlers, teens, and patriarchs roam the territory, ogling at the animals.

A striking monolithic fountain of bas-relief animals in the turquoise tones of oxidized metal greets visitors at the zoo entrance. Next, a flamboyant flock of flamingos lolls in a large pond. A sightseeing train straight ahead offers a 15-minute

FROMMER'S FAVORITE GUADALAJARA EXPERIENCES

The Battle of the Bands Sunday afternoon and evening listen to the battle of mariachis under the portals of El Parián in Tlaquepaque. Or go to any evening gathering round the spirited mariachi bands at Plaza de los Mariachis in downtown Guadalajara, where dining tables set out in the open fill with willing listeners. In the lobby bar of the Hotel Frances, between 8pm and 3am, enjoy pianist Goyo Flores, who learned his art by braille.

Visiting the Zoo Spend a half day at the new Guadalajara Zoo on the edge of the breathtaking Huentitlán ravine.

The Ballet Folklórico Attend an exhilarating performance of the Ballet Folklórico de la Universidad de Guadalajara, acclaimed as the best folkloric ballet company in all Mexico.

Walking Take a walk through the enormous Instituto Cultural Cabañas designed by Manuel Tolsá with fabulous murals by native son José Clemente Orozco. Walk through the pedestrian-only historic center, a magnificent example of urban renewal that preserves the city's history.

Museums Explore Tlaquepaque's Regional Ceramics Museum, and the National Ceramics Museum in Tonalá preserving examples of Mexico's master potters.

Glass Blowing Watch glass blowers in Tlaquepaque turn red-hot glass into fine utilitarian pieces.

The Markets Visit the Sunday and Thursday street markets in Tonalá.

tour of the area—a good way to get acquainted. The zoo is nicely integrated into the area's rolling topography, and all of the zoo's buildings have an attractive Aztec motif with stout round columns and zigzag painted designs. Modeled after other great zoos of the world such as those in San Diego and Berlin, this roomy zoo gives the larger animals plenty of space to roam and tries to approximate their natural habitat. Huge monkey islands with huge dead trees strung with vinelike ropes provide hours of entertainment. Most people stand mesmerized around the massive, moon-faced orangutans or the great, placid pumas and panthers. Multiple aviaries house screeching parrots and all types of colorful jungle birds. Informative signs throughout give habitat information and the status of threatened or endangered species. The zoo is open daily from 9am to 6pm (tel. 37-2478).

The **planetarium,** right next door, presents programs every evening, starting at 4, 5, and 6pm with earlier shows on Saturday (tel. 637-2119 or 637-2050). Movies at the **Omnimax Theater** are at 10am and noon, and at 1, 4, 5, and 8pm—but call to confirm these times.

By local bus no. 60-A north on Calzada Independencia, it's about a 30-minute ride. A taxi costs $5. Those going by bus, should look for the large, pale terra-cotta structure on the corner of Independencia Norte and Avenida Flores Magon, on the right-hand side of the street coming from downtown. From Independencia, it's another five- or six-block walk up Avenida Flores Magon to the zoo's entrance, past the huge parking lots.

Admission is $1.25, and the zoo and planetarium are open Tuesday through Sunday from 10am to 6pm.

MUSEO DE LA CIUDAD, Independencia 684 at M. Barcena. Tel. 658-2531.

Opened in 1992 in a wonderful old stone convent, this fine museum fills a giant gap in chronicling the city's interesting past. The eight salas, beginning with the first room to the right, start with the years before the city's founding when 63 Spanish families pioneered the area and fought to gain a toehold on the land. Each successive room progresses until the present. Among the artifacts displayed are many unusual and rare Spanish armaments and equestrian paraphernalia—enormous stirrups, charro costumes, spurs, and branding irons. You'll see a mock-up of the city in the 17th century that shows it to have been a city of convents. Other objects include jugs and medicinal containers, examples of iron filigree, an unusually well-preserved iron portfolio for keeping important papers, paintings on canvas and copper, alabaster sculptures, and bakers' stamps, which authenticated the origins and quality of a loaf of bread. Incorporated into each area are objects and text that give a sense of what life was like day-to-day. If you read Spanish, take time to read the explanations—they give many interesting details not otherwise noted in the displays.

Admission: $1.
Open: Tues–Sat 10am–5pm, Sun 10am–3pm.

3. ORGANIZED TOURS

Several times daily, **Panoramex** (tel. 610-5005, 610-5057, or 610-5109) offers bilingual tours of Guadalajara, Lake Chapala, Tequila, and Zapopan, ranging in price from $8 to $17.75. Those without a car might want to consider a tour or two, especially to the outlying regions. The office is open Monday through Friday from 9am to 7pm, or inquire at your hotel. **Viajes Copenhagen** (tel. 621-1890 or 621-1008) also organizes similar tours plus others such as golfing in Guadalajara, to the mountain resort towns, or more far-flung trips to the coast or to interior colonial villages. It's open Monday through Friday from 9am to 7pm.

THE TEQUILA PLANT You might want to take a tour of the Tequila Sauza bottling plant, at Avenida Vallarta 3273 (tel. 615-6990 or 630-0707), on the left on the way out of town. The tours begin at 10am Monday through Friday. After the tour there's a "happy hour" where you can enjoy a variety of tequila drinks, prepared by masters of the art. You can skip the tour and come just to drink from 10am to 1pm. Both the tours and drinks are free.

By the way, this is just a bottling plant. The distillery is in the town of Tequila, off Highway 15 about 25 miles of bad road east of Guadalajara. You'll see the spiny blue agave, from which tequila is made, growing everywhere around the little town.

4. SPECIAL EVENTS

In the **Plaza de Armas,** the Jalisco State Band puts on **free concerts** usually every Tuesday, Thursday, and Sunday evening starting about 7pm. Those who want a seat in the park should arrive early.

Special month-long festivals take place in Guadalajara in September, October, and February.

During September, Mexicans celebrate their **independence** from Spain, but Guadalajara really goes all out. Look for poster-size calendars listing attractions that include many performing arts in theaters all over the city. On the 15th, the Governor's Palace fills with well-dressed, invited guests as they, and the massive crowd in the plaza below, await his reenactment of the traditional *grito* (shout for independence) at 11pm. The grito commemorates Father Miguel Hidalgo de Costilla's pronouncement that began the War for Independence in Mexico in 1810. There's live music on a temporary street stage, spontaneous dancing, much shouting of "Viva Mexico," and fireworks. On September 16 there's a parade that lasts an hour or so. For the next couple of days the park in front of the Teatro Degollado resembles a county fair and Mexican market. There are games of chance with stuffed-animal prizes, and a variety of food, including cotton candy and candied apples. Among the many attention-getting gimmicks and games, look for a mechanized, growling, arm-flailing, stuffed gorilla wearing a sombrero. Live entertainment goes on in the park day and night.

October is another month-long celebration, called **Fiestas de Octubre,** that originally began with the procession of Our Lady of Zapopan, but has since added a celebration of all that is notable about Guadalajara and Jalisco. The month kicks off with an enormous parade, usually on the Sunday nearest the first of the month (but it could be Saturday). By the way, those Americans in the parade may be from San Antonio, Texas, Guadalajara's sister city. Festivities continue all month with performing arts, rodeos (charreadas), bullfights, art exhibits, regional dancing, a food fair, and a Day of Nations involving all the consulates of Guadalajara. Much of the ongoing displays and events take place in the Benito Juárez Auditorium.

On **October 12** around dawn, the small dark figure of **Our Lady of Zapopan** begins her five-hour ride from the Cathedral of Guadalajara to the Cathedral of

Zapopan, a suburb. The original figure dates from the mid-1500s and the procession tradition began 200 years later. Crowds spend the night all along the route and vie for position as the Virgin passes riding in a new car donated to her for the occasion. In the months before October 12, the figure is carried to churches all over the city. During that time, you may see neighborhoods decorated with paper streamers and banners honoring the passing of the figure to the next church.

The last two weeks in February are marked by a series of **cultural events** before the beginning of Lent.

5. SPECTATOR SPORTS

BULLFIGHTS Many say that Guadalajara and Mexico City have the best bullfights in the country, so if you want to see one, this is probably an excellent place to do it. Every Sunday at 4:30pm (4pm in summer) there's a bullfight at the Plaza de Toros Nuevo Progreso, across from the football stadium on Calzada Independencia Norte, north of town. Tickets range from $3 in the sun to $80 for the best seats in the shade. Buy tickets downtown in the reception area of the Hotel Frances on Thursdays from 10am to 2pm or from 4 to 7pm, or at the Plaza de Toros.

RODEOS & COCKFIGHTS To the east of Parque Agua Azul is **Aceves Galindo Lienzo,** or rodeo ring, where there's a Mexican rodeo (charreada) on Sunday at noon. Riding, roping and rope tricks, and a traditional grand promenade are all part of the action at the charreada. Sometimes there are evening shows, too. It's found at the corner of Dr. R. Michel and Calzada de las Palmas (tel. 619-3232).

Also nearby, cockfights are held in the **Palenque/Agua Azul,** at the corner of Washington and 16 de Septiembre (tel. 619-5993 or 619-5940), but only in the high seasons, from October to early November. For cockfights the rest of the year, visit the local "pit" at the **Plaza de Gallos, La Tapatía,** at Avenida Revolución 2120 (tel. 635-7506), on the way to Tlaquepaque (take a Tlaquepaque bus from along Calzada Independencia). Profits from the sport go to charity and matches are *usually* held daily. Arrive by 7pm.

6. SHOPPING

Besides the mammoth **Mercado Libertad,** described above, in which you can find almost anything, Guadalajara boasts the largest modern shopping center in Latin America. The **Plaza del Sol** megacomplex, spraws over 120,000 square yards in an area at the junction of Avenidas López Mateos and Mariano Otero, outside the center of town. Here you can buy anything from a taco to a Volkswagen; you can also cash a check, make a plane reservation, or buy a lottery ticket. There are even hotels and restaurants for weary shoppers! Take the no. 40 bus from Calzada Independencia near the Mercado Libertad.

There's a convenient pedestrian passageway that runs under Juárez where there are many stalls selling candied fruits, leather belts, and other goods. A better place to purchase **leather goods,** however, is down on Avenida Pedro Moreno, a street that runs parallel to Juárez, and for **shoes,** go to E. Alatorre northeast of the historic center, where 70 shoe stores are located.

One block past the entrance of Parque Agua Azul in the direction of the city center (on your right at the crossroads of the calzada and Gallo), is the **Casa de las Artesanías,** Gallo 20 (tel. 619-4664). It's an enormous two-story, state-run crafts store that sells pottery, silver jewelry, dance masks, and regional clothing from around the state. The best crafts aren't necessarily found here and prices seem somewhat steep, so if you are going to the villages, such as Tonalá, you may want to postpone buying. On the right as you enter are museum displays showing crafts and regional costumes from the state of Jalisco. The craft store is open Monday through Friday from 10am to 7pm, Saturday from 10am to 4pm, and Sunday from 10am to 2pm.

There's an **outdoor market** every Sunday at Santa Teresita, where you can buy clothes and anything else you have in mind, all at excellent prices; look on the map of Greater Guadalajara for an approximation of where to find it. It stretches out for blocks and blocks.

For the best shopping see Tlaquepaque and Tonalá in Chapter 12.

7. EVENING ENTERTAINMENT

MUSIC & DANCE

MAJOR PERFORMING ARTS COMPANIES

BALLET FOLKLÓRICO DE LA UNIVERSIDAD DE GUADALAJARA. Tel. 614-4773, ext. 144 or 143.

This wonderful dance company, acclaimed as the best folkloric ballet company in Mexico, provides the light, color, movement, and music that is pure Jalisco. Call for information. Performances are at the Teatro Degollado Sunday at 10am.
Prices: $4–$20.

BALLET FOLKLÓRICO NACIONAL OF THE INSTITUTO CULTURAL CABAÑAS. Tel. 618-6003.

Performances are every Wednesday at 8:30pm at the theater of the Instituto Cultural Cabañas.
Prices: Tickets $7.

THE STATE SYMPHONY ORCHESTRA. Tel. 613-1115 or 614-4773.

The orchestra performs regularly at the Teatro Degollado. Call for the schedule.
Prices: $4–$20.

CASA DE LA CULTURA, between 16 de Septiembre and Calzada Independencia. Tel. 619-3611.

A variety of performances is offered. The Association of Composers of Jalisco offer new works on Tuesday evenings at 8pm. The state chorus group, the Coral del Estado, also performs here. On Thursday there are literary readings at 8pm, as well as experimental dance performances and Aztec music. Call for information.

EX-CONVENTO DEL CARMEN, Juárez 638. Tel. 614-7184.

Many low-cost concerts, other performances, and movies are offered here.

Performances are usually on Monday and Tuesday evenings at 8 or 8:30pm. Open: Daily 9am–10pm.

THEATER

TEATRO EXPERIMENTAL, Calzada Independencia Sur near Parque Agua Azul. Tel. 619-3770.

Interesting experimental works are performed here and it's worth going even if you don't speak Spanish. Performances are Friday, Saturday, and Sunday. On Friday and Saturday performances begin around 8:30pm and at 5 and 7pm on Sunday. Call for information and prices.

TEATRO GUADALAJARA DEL IMSS, Av. 16 de Septiembre 868. Tel. 619-4121.

More conventional than the Teatro Experimental, the schedule of plays is usually modern. Call for current schedule and prices.

THE CLUB & MUSIC SCENE

For rousing music, and pure Mexico/Guadalajara ambience go to the **Plaza de los Mariachis,** down by San Juan de Dios Church and the Mercado Libertad, junction of Calzada Independencia and Juárez/Javier Mina. Every evening the colorfully dressed mariachis of the city, in various states of inebriation, play for money (if they can get it) or for free. Enjoy a meal here, or a snack or a soft drink, or just stand around spending nothing but time. It's fun and it's free; spend at least one evening here.

Few places in Guadalajara are more enjoyable to me than **El Parián** in **Tlaquepaque** where mariachis serenade diners under the portals. See Chapter 12 for more information.

NIGHTCLUB/CABARET

HOTEL FIESTA AMERICANA, Glorieta Minerva. Tel. 625-3434 or 625-4848.

Live jazz "English-pub style" is presented in the Caballo Negro Bar from 9pm until 4am. There is also continually changing low-key entertainment in the lobby bar daily from 7pm until 1am. In another salon, Estelaris, there are occasional performances by nationally known artists.

JAZZ/BLUES

RESTAURANT/BAR COPENHAGEN 77, Marcos Castellanos 140-Z. Tel. 625-2803.

This dark, cozy jazz club is by the little Parque Revolución, on your left as you

---

MAJOR PERFORMANCE HALLS

Teatro Degollado. Tel. 613-1115
Casa de la Cultura. Tel. 619-3611
Ex-Convento del Carmen. Tel. 614-7184

walk down López Cotilla/Federalismo. There are linen tablecloths and a red rose on every table. You can come just for a drink, or for the restaurant's specialty, the delicious paella Copenhagen al vino ($9.50). The pae'la takes a while to prepare, but it's an enjoyable wait, while you sip a drink and listen to the jazz. Open: Daily 8:30am-1:30am; live jazz trio plays Mon-Sat 3-4:30pm and 8:30pm-12:30am.
Admission: Free.

DANCE CLUBS/DISCOS

MAXIM'S DISCO CLUB, Hotel Francés, Maestranza 35. Tel. 613-1190.
Despite the name, Maxim's is not a disco, but a dance hall with singer or a live band. There are tables around the dance floor and in the lower bar section. While you're at the Hotel Francés, check out the lobby bar, open from 8am to 10:30pm, one of the most popular in the downtown area. There's a happy hour from noon to 8pm with two national (not imported) drinks for the price of one. There's often live piano music in the late afternoon and evening. Open: The disco is open daily 8pm-3 or 4am; 2-for-1 drinks Mon-Wed 8-11pm.
Admission: Free.

BAR EL CAMPAÑARIO, Hotel de Mendoza, Carranza 16. Tel. 613-4646.
There is a beautiful view from this penthouse perch in the Hotel de Mendoza. Only couples or mixed-sex groups are allowed in. There is music for dancing Monday through Saturday starting at 9pm. Open: Mon-Sat 11am-1am; happy hour 6-7pm. At this writing the bar is temporarily closed, but expected to reopen soon.

CHAPTER 12

EASY EXCURSIONS FROM GUADALAJARA

1. **TLAQUEPAQUE & TONALÁ**
2. **THE LAKE CHAPALA REGION**
3. **MAZAMITLA**
4. **TAPALPA**
5. **SAN JUAN DE LOS LAGOS & LAGOS DE MORENO**

By car the villages below take from 30 minutes to Tlaquepaque, the nearest, to around three hours to the farthest, Mazamitla and Tapalpa. By public transportation it will take longer.

Tlaquepaque and Tonalá, are 7 to 10 miles southeast of Guadalajara. Lake Chapala and the village of Chapala are 26 miles south. Ajijic is 4 miles west of Chapala; San Juan Cosalá, 9.5 miles of west of Chapala; Jocotepec, 12 miles west of Chapala. Mazamitla is 170 miles south of Guadalajara. Tapalpa is 133 miles south of Guadalajara.

1. TLAQUEPAQUE & TONALÁ

Tlaquepaque and **Tonalá** are Guadalajara suburbs that are a special treat for shoppers. **Market days** are Sunday and Thursday in Tonalá, but on Sunday many of Tlaquepaque's stores are open only from 10:30am to 2:30pm, if open at all. To combine a trip to both villages—about five miles apart—Thursday is the best day. Monday through Saturday, stores in Tlaquepaque usually close between 2:30 and 4pm. It makes a nice day to wear yourself out in Tonalá, then relax at one of Tlaquepaque's pleasant outdoor restaurants for a sunset meal and wait for the mariachis to warm up at El Parián.

To reach **Tlaquepaque** (a 25-minute ride) take the A or B no. 275 bus on 16th de Septiembre/Alcalde opposite the cathedral in front of the portals; wait by the blue bus signs. To get off at Tlaquepaque, get off one or two stops after you see the welcoming arch on the left, then ask for directions to El Parián, Tlaquepaque's central building. To **Tonalá,** stay on the bus (another 15 minutes) and Tonalá is the last stop the bus makes before turning around.

The **Tlaquepaque Tourism Office** is in the Presidencia Municipal (opposite El Parián), Calle Guillermo Prieto 80 (tel. 635-1503 or 635-0596); it's open Monday through Friday from 9am to 3pm, and Saturday from 9am to 1pm.

The **Tonalá Tourism Office** is in the Casa de Cultura, at Morelos 180 (tel.

IMPRESSIONS

Guadalajara is a bit too staid to go in for Acapulco-style night spots. The gaiety is left to Ajijic.
—JAMES NORMAN, *TERRY'S GUIDE TO MEXICO*, 1965

It is a pretty, somnolent town [Guadalajara] with a magnificent climate and is famous for its special style of pottery as well as for a certain type of hide chair which you will recognize instantly as the kind you have sat in wherever there was a terrace.
—LEONE AND ALICE LEONE-MOATS, *OFF TO MEXICO*, 1935

It is earthy and noisy and very pleasant in this potters' village [Tlaquepaque]. Mexico has a good time here and so will you.
—SYDNEY CLARK, *ALL THE BEST IN MEXICO*, 1952

683-0971), around the corner from the National Ceramics Museum, upstairs on the right. Hours are Monday through Friday from 9am to 3pm and Saturday from 9am to 1pm.

TLAQUEPAQUE

This suburban village is famous for its **fashionable stores** in handsome old stone mansions fronting pedestrian-only streets and its pottery and glass factories. The village is also known for **El Parián,** a circular building dating from the 1800s in its center, where innumerable mariachis belt out rousing songs to diners in sidewalk cafés. The mariachis are especially plentiful, loud, and entertaining on weekend evenings (Sunday is best). But just about any time of day you'll hear them serenading there. The stores, especially on Calle Independencia, offer all the pottery and glass for which the village is famous, plus the best of Mexico's crafts, such as equipales furniture, fine wood sculptures, and papier-mâché.

SPECIAL EVENTS The **Festival of the Immaculate Conception** is Tlaquepaque's biggest event with regional dances and parades December 8. During the **Christmas season** an almost life-size ceramic Nativity scene is set up in the central plaza. June 8 is the **Festival of St. Peter** with lively mariachis, folk dancing, and a parade.

WHAT TO SEE & DO

Tlaquepaque's **Regional Ceramics Museum,** Independencia 237 (tel. 635-5404), is a good place to see what traditional Jalisco pottery is all about. There are high-quality examples dating back several generations. Note the cross-hatch design known as petatillo on some of the pieces. It's one of the region's oldest traditional motifs. There's also a small display of pre-Hispanic pottery, Huichol costumes, and folk art. The museum is open Tuesday through Saturday from 10am to 4pm, and Sunday from 10am to 1pm. (See also the National Ceramics Museum in Tonalá.)

Across the street from the museum is **La Rosa Fábrica de Vidrio Soplado glass-blowing factory.** From 9:30am to 2:30pm the public is invited to watch. In a room at the rear of the patio, a dozen scurrying men and boys heat glass bottles and jars on the end of hollow steel poles. Then, blowing furiously, they'll chase across the room, narrowly missing spectators and fellow workers alike as they swing the red-hot glass within an inch of a man who sits placidly rolling an elaborate jug out of another chunk of the cooling glass. Nonchalantly, the old man will leave his own task long enough to clip off the end of the boy's vase at the exact moment at which it comes within reach of his hand. Then he drops the clippers and returns once more to his own task as the youth charges back across the room to reheat the vase in the furnace.

Shopping

Tlaquepaque has many fine shops. Below are a few special ones.

BAZAR HECHT, 158 Independencia. Tel. 657-0316. Fax 635-2241.
One of the village's longtime favorite stores, here you'll find wood objects, handmade furniture, and a few antiques. Open: Mon–Sat 10am–2:30pm and 3:30–6:30pm.

SERGIO BUSTAMANTE, 236 Independencia. Tel. 639-5519.
Sergio Bustamante's imaginative and original brass, copper, ceramic, and papier-mâché sculptures are among the most sought after in Mexico and the most copied. This is an exquisite gallery of his work. Open: Mon–Sat 10am–7pm.

CAOBA, 156 Independencia. Tel. 635-9770.
Unusual, rustic, but finely finished pottery and wood sculptures are the specialties here. Open: Mon–Sat 10am–7pm, Sun 11am–5pm.

CASA CANELA, 258 Independencia. Tel. 635-3717.
Step inside this grand mansion and discover one of the most elegant stores in Tlaquepaque. Browse through the rooms of decorative arts, among them imaginative use of Mexican and Guatemalan textiles on equipale furniture. Open: Mon–Fri 10am–2pm and 3–7pm, Sat 10am–3pm.

KEN EDWARDS, 70 Madero. Tel. 635-5456.
Ken Edwards was among the first artisans to produce high-fired, lead-free stoneware in Tonalá and his blue-on-blue pottery is sold all over Mexico. This showroom has a fine selection of his work not normally seen in such size or quantity elsewhere. There's a section of seconds as well. It's next door to the Restaurant With No Name. Open: Mon–Sat 10am–6:30pm. His factory is in Tonalá.

IRENE PULOS, 224-B Independencia. Tel. 657-8499.
The emphasis here is on designer clothing using hand-loomed textiles and designs from Guatemala and Mexico. There's an entire room devoted to the clothing of the Huichol of Jalisco and Nayarit. Open: Mon–Sat 10am–6pm, Sun 10am–3pm. The patio restaurant here is open daily from 10am to 3pm.

TETE ARTE Y DISENO, Juárez 173. Tel. 635-7347.
Here you'll find many large architectural decorative objects mixed in with the pottery, antiques, glassware, and paintings, all in a sort of organized jumble. Open: Mon–Sat 10am–7pm.

WHERE TO DINE

Read the fine print on menus. The 10% value-added tax, usually included in the written menu price elsewhere in Mexico, may not be included in Tlaquepaque. It may be added on when your bill is presented. Even if the fine print tells you it's included, ask—before ordering.

BIRRERÍA EL SOPE, D. Guerra 142. Tel. 35-6338.
  Cuisine: BIRRIA.
  $ Prices: Birria $5.75.
  Open: Daily 8am–10pm.
This is where locals go for that wonderful Jalisco specialty—birria. Cheery and clean, it's in a quiet neighborhood in a long, narrow room open at the front. The decor of cushioned French provincial chairs pulled up to plastic-over-cloth-covered tables topped with artificial carnations doesn't quite fit the country menu, but the food is tasty. Choose your birria by the meat—goat, lamb, or pork; and then by the cut—leg, ribs, etc. An order comes with fresh salsa, chips and tortillas, and beans. Side orders of quesadillas or queso fundido are extra. To find it from Tlaquepaque's main plaza, walk north on Madero two blocks and turn left on Guerra; it's half a block down on the right.

LOS CAZADORES, Chamizal 606. Tel. 635-1983.
  Cuisine: MEXICAN.
  $ Prices: Appetizers $7–$20; main courses $8–$25.
  Open: Daily 1–6pm.

This expansive and tranquil restaurant resembles a country hacienda and is noted for good service and food in a casual atmosphere. Patrons start drifting in about 1:30pm and the dining rooms and huge shady patio are full by 3pm. The large mariachi group is one of the best I've heard, and plays without charge. *Important Note:* Waiters will bring you extra appetizers (and charge you for them). They all speak English, so make sure they know what you do and don't want. Also, alcoholic drinks can be outrageously expensive, and cocktail prices are not on the menu. Ask the price before you order! As a special treat, folk dancing is presented Friday from 2 to 3pm, and Saturday and Sunday at 4pm. It's a bit tricky to find the restaurant if you're driving, so follow these directions. Leave from El Parián via Independencia (which is one-way). At the end of this street, turn left onto Revolución, and drive back toward Guadalajara nine-tenths of a mile. At the traffic circle, go down the street to the right of the Pemex station for two blocks. Cazadores is on the right with a huge parking lot. Taxis charge around $4 to $5.

MARISCOS PROGRESO, Progreso 80. Tel. 657-4995.
  Cuisine: SEAFOOD/MEXICAN.
  $ Prices: Appetizers $2.50–$8.50; main courses $8–$15.
  Open: Daily 10am–8pm.
Formerly the Restaurant Los Corrales, this renamed restaurant has an all-new, primarily seafood menu. Its cozy tree-shaded patio, filled with leather-covered tables and chairs, makes an inviting place to take a break from your shopping. Charcoal-grilled seafood is the specialty here. To find it, cross Juárez, one of the streets that borders El Parián, and look for this corner restaurant.

RESTAURANT EL ABAJENO, Av. Juárez 231. Tel. 635-9015.
  Cuisine: REGIONAL.
  $ Prices: Appetizers $3–$6; main courses $8–$15.
  Open: Daily 11am–9pm.
Once you walk through the dark passage into this huge garden restaurant, you'll be primed for relaxing over a good meal. Tables and fountains filled with flowers ring a huge old Fresnillo tree, and strolling mariachis give the place a festive air. Try the well-prepared favorites such as *borrego al pastor* (a countryside specialty that's hard

to find in the city), *birria de chivo* (goat), carnitas and pork ribs, or select from the seafood or steak section. Portions are huge, and the guacamole salad and margaritas are great.

To get here from El Parian, walk 2½ blocks west, immediately past FCO de Miranda.

RESTAURANT WITH NO NAME (Sin Nombre), Madero 80. Tel. 635-4520 or 635-9677.
   Cuisine: MEXICAN.
   $ Prices: Breakfast $4.75–$10; appetizers $4.50–$15; main courses $13–$22.
   Open: Mon–Sat 8:30am–8:30pm, Sun 8:30am–6:30pm.

This all-time favorite offers excellent cuisine in a spectacular garden shaded by banana, peach, palm, and other tropical trees and guarded by strutting peacocks. A trio plays music in mid-afternoon. The menu is spoken by the bilingual waiter, not written, so ask for prices as you order. The excellent "No Name Chicken" is cooked in onions, green peppers, and a buttery sauce, and spread around a mound of rice. The quesadillas are outstanding.

Why the unusual name here? When the restaurant first opened it didn't have a liquor license, so they operated as a speakeasy, and early clients gave the place its current appellation. It's 1½ blocks from the main plaza between Independencia and Constitución.

TONALÁ

Tonalá is a pleasant, unpretentious village about five miles from Tlaquepaque, that many will find more authentic and easier on the wallet. The streets were paved only recently, but there aren't any pedestrian-only avenues yet. The village has been a center for pottery making since pre-Hispanic times; half of the more than 400 artists who reside here produce high- and low-temperature pottery in different colors of clay with a dozen different finishes. Other local artists also work with forged iron, cantera stone, brass and copper, marble, miniatures, papier-mâché, textiles, blown glass, and gesso.

On Thursday and Sunday **market days** vendors and temporary street stalls under flapping shade cloths fill the streets; "herb-men" sell multicolored, dried medicinal herbs from wheelbarrows; magicians entertain crowds with sleight-of-hand tricks; and craftspeople spread their colorful wares on the plaza's sidewalks. Those who love the hand-blown Mexican glass and folksy ceramics will wish they had a truck to haul the gorgeous and inexpensive handmade items. There is certainly greater variety here than Tlaquepaque—tacky and chic are often side by side.

Tonalá is the home of the **National Museum of Ceramics,** Constitución 104, between Hidalgo and Morelos (tel. 683-0494). The museum occupies a huge two-story mansion with displays of Jalisco work as well as pottery from all over the country. There's a large shop in the front on the right as you enter. The museum is open Tuesday through Friday from 10am to 5pm, and Saturday and Sunday from 10am to 3pm, admission is free.

SHOPPING

KEN EDWARDS, Morelos 184. Tel. 683-0313.
   This is the factory where the famous Ken Edwards stoneware is made. You can see

the artisans at work and select pottery in the salesroom. Open: Mon-Fri 10am-2pm and 3-6:30pm.

JOSE BERNABE AND SONS, Hidalgo 83. Tel. 683-0040 or 683-0877.
Revered as among the best ceramic and stoneware artists in Tonalá, José Bernabe and his sons have a workshop and showroom ½ block from the Presidencia Municipal. Prices here are very expensive, but the quality is unsurpassable if a bit mass-produced looking; some pieces are museum quality and all are hand-painted by four generations of Bernabes trained in the art from boyhood. Open: Mon-Fri 10am-6:30pm, Sat-Sun 10am-2pm.

SANTIAGO DE TONALA, Madero 42. Tel. 683-0641 or 639-0543.
Blown glass is made at this factory ½ block off the plaza. Enter the factory by the back door to see how the work is done. There's a sales showroom as well where prices are higher than elsewhere because the glassware is commercial strength, made for heavy use in restaurants. Open: Mon-Fri 7am-3pm (factory to 7pm), Sat-Sun 7am-2pm.

ARTESANIAS MAYORGA, Madero 43. Tel. 683-0121.
This large shop has a little bit of everything, including all kinds of crafts, from masks to colorful hanging ceramic birds. Open: Mon-Sat 10am-6pm, Sun 10am-5pm.

WHERE TO DINE

LOS GERANIOS, Hidalgo 71. Tel. 683-0010.
  Cuisine: MEXICAN.
$ Prices: Appetizers $2.75-$3.25; main courses $4.50-$8.
  Open: Sun-Mon 11am-5pm.
This narrow, inviting restaurant next to El Bazar de Sermel offers a cool respite from the blazing sun. Diners can relax in the clean and comfortable white canvas chairs at white-clothed tables or in the small booths. The menu includes Mexican specialties. Try the fish with almonds and mushrooms or something quick like nachos. It's near the main plaza, so using that as a reference (facing the church), walk ½ block down Hidalgo. Look for a pretty stained-glass sign with red flowers on the left.

IMPRESSIONS

Chapala, which can more or less be called the Mexican Riviera, is situated on the lake of the same name and surrounded by picturesque Indian villages. It is gay with thousands and thousands of birds that migrate here from the north.
          —LEONE and ALICE LEONE-MOATS, OFF TO MEXICO, 1935

Winging their way across the lake are countless thousands of ducks and geese. And in the shallow waters near the shore wade longlegged cranes, blue herons, white pelicans, and awkward, timid egrets with their tufts of priceless white plumes on the lower part of their backs. Furthermore, the marshy lands about the lake and the woodland that dot its shores are the home of all sorts of colorful birds that have come here to avoid the chill winds of colder climates.
              —BURTON HOLMES, MEXICO, 1939

2. THE LAKE CHAPALA REGION

The Lake Chapala region, 26 miles south of Guadalajara, has long been popular with foreign vacationers because of its near-perfect year-round spring-like climate, its gorgeous scenery, and its several charming little lakeshore towns—Chapala, Ajijic, and Jocotepec among them. Because of the region's beauty and climatic appeal, a largely permanent expatriate community of around 4,000 people has settled along the shoreline and in the villages stretching all the way from Chapala to Jocotepec. In fact, the climate is so agreeable that few hotels offer air conditioning or fans; neither is necessary.

CHAPALA

Chapala, Jalisco (pop. 36,000), founded in 1538, is the district's business and administrative center as well as the oldest resort on Lake Chapala, Mexico's largest lake. Much of the town's prosperity comes from the retirees, primarily from the United States and Canada, who come from nearby lakeside villages into Chapala to change money, buy groceries, and check the stock ticker. Except on weekends, when throngs of visitors fill the area around the pier and lake's edge, it can be a pretty sleepy place.

Lake Chapala feeds the water needs of both Guadalajara nearby and Mexico City more than 300 miles away, and also provides irrigation for area farmers. From the mid-1970s until 1991 its depth and perimeter diminished dramatically due to population growth in the cities and poorly managed upstream use of the Lerma River, a major stream that feeds the lake. But heavy rains in 1991 and 1992 brought the lake's level up so that it almost laps its original shoreline; when you first see it as you come from Guadalajara it looks like an ocean. Nothing has changed about the government's management of the lake's water, so it could recede again, but for now it is a stunning sight, ringed by high forested mountains and fishing villages.

Buses to Chapala go from Guadalajara's *old* Central Camionera. The **Transportes Guadalajara-Chapala** company (tel. 657-8448) serves the route. Buses and minibuses run every half hour to Chapala, and every hour to Jocotepec. The last bus back to Guadalajara leaves around 9pm. In Chapala, the bus station (tel. 5-2212), is about seven blocks north of the lake pier. To get to Ajijic and San Juan Cosalá from Chapala, walk towards the lake (left out the front of the station) and look for the local buses lined up on the opposite side of the street. These travel between Chapala and San Juan Cosalá about every 30 minutes. From San Juan Cosalá change buses to Jocotepec. There are also buses direct to Jocotepec from the Chapala bus station leaving every half hour until 8pm.

Those driving will be able to enjoy the lake and its towns more fully. From Guadalajara, drive to Lake Chapala via the new four-lane Highway 15/80. Leave Guadalajara via Avenida Gonzalez Gallo, which intersects with Calzada Independencia just before Playa Azul Park. Going south on Independencia, turn left onto Gallo and follow it all the way out of town past the airport, where it becomes Highway 15/80 (but some signs may say Highway 44), the main road to Chapala. The first view of the lake isn't until just outside of the town of Chapala.

The highway from Guadalajara leads directly into Chapala and becomes Madero, which leads straight to Chapala's pier, Malecón (waterfront walkway and street), and

THE LAKE CHAPALA REGION • 189

small shopping and restaurant area. The one traffic light in town (a block before the pier) is the turning point (right) to Ajijic, San Antonio, San Juan Cosalá, and Jocotepec. Chapala's main plaza, is three blocks north of the pier and the central food market flanks the park's back side.

The **area code** for the whole northern lake shore (Chapala, Ajijic, San Juan Cosalá, and Jocotepec) is 376.

Libros y Revistas, at Madero 230 (tel. 5-2021), near the Chamber of Commerce and Lloyds and opposite the plaza, carries a wide assortment of English-language newspapers, magazines, and books—from the latest paperback novels to *Mirabella, Family Circle, Texas Monthly,* and *Scientific American.* It's open daily from 9am to 4pm.

Chapala's **Chamber of Commerce,** at Madero 232 (tel. 5-2149; fax 5-3598), has a small assortment of maps and local information. It's open Monday through Friday from 9am to 4pm. It's close to Banamex and upstairs over Lloyds. The **Jalisco State Information Office** is in Ajijic (see below).

To **exchange money,** there's a Banamex, on the right side of Madero just before the light. It's open Monday through Friday from 9am to 5pm. U.S. dollars can be changed all day and Canadian dollars between 9am and 1:30pm. There's a Banamex automatic-teller machine for VISA cards to the right of the bank's front door. Just down from Banamex (walking away from the lake), is Lloyds' money exchange (by Lloyds' front door), which is opposite the food market and main plaza. It's open Monday through Friday from 9am to 4pm.

There are several supermarkets on Madero. Probably the most convenient one is **Supergrisa** at the corner of Hidalgo and Madero opposite the Restaurant Superior. It's open Monday, Tuesday, Wednesday, Friday, and Saturday from 8am to 8pm, Thursday from 8am to 3pm, and Sunday from 8am to 6pm.

Several outlets offer fax, telephone, mail and message services. **Centro de Mensajes Mexicano-Americano,** is the local affiliate for UPS. They also have 24-hour telephone message and fax-receiving services, court-approved translation ability, and secretarial service. It's at Hidalgo 236 (Apdo. Postal 872), Chapala, Jal. 45900 (tel. and fax 376/5-2101). It's open Monday through Friday from 10am to 6pm and Saturday from 10am to 2pm. Almost next door **Aero Flash,** Hidalgo 236 (tel. 376/5-3696; fax 5-3063), has 24-hour fax service and specializes in package mailing. It's the local Federal Express office.

The **post office** is on Hidalgo two blocks from the intersection of Madero. Enter down the hill and in back. It's open Monday through Friday from 9am to 1pm and 3 to 6pm and on Saturday from 9am to 1pm. The **telegraph office** is upstairs in the same building and is open Monday through Friday from 9am to 3pm.

WHAT TO SEE & DO

GOLF The **Chula Vista Country Club** in Ajijic (2½ miles west of Chapala; tel. 5-2281) has a nine-hole golf course and accepts nonmembers daily from 9am to 6pm. However, beginners and children under 15 are allowed only Monday through Friday after 2pm. Monday through Friday a round costs $25; Saturday and Sunday, $27. Caddies cost $5 for nine holes and $7. The small restaurant serves drinks and on weekends offers light snacks.

LAKE TOURS Lake Chapala is dotted with several islands. Relatively nearby is the small **Isla de los Alacranes** (Scorpion Island), with a few outdoor restaurants where you can sip a drink or have a meal. Once nesting grounds for area birds, most of the trees were destroyed by rising water years ago. Fishermen net charales on the edge of the island early in the morning. Distant **Isla Mezcala** is larger and holds the ruins of a 17th-century prison fortress. Birds nest in the trees remaining on the highest part of the island, but much of the island is devoted to small plots for raising corn and chayotes (a vegetable called vegetable pear or mirliton in the United States). The **Cooperativo de Lanchas Guerreros Inmortales** has a small booth at the beginning of the pier in Chapala, staffed daily from around 7:30am until 5pm. Tour prices are per boat, most of which hold between 8 and 10 people. A short lakeshore tour costs $16; a 30-minute ride to Isla Alacranes costs $25—long enough to enjoy a soft drink at one of the little restaurants; an hour trip to Isla Alacranes is $35—time enough to eat or watch the fishermen; a tour to both islands costs around $115 and takes around four hours. Weekends are best to try for a boat excursion, since without others to share the price you'll have to pay for the whole boat, and it's not worth it. Ask for **Matias Estrada,** whose boat is the *Blanca Marcela.* He's usually around the pier mornings or call him at home (tel. 5-4326) a day in advance to arrange for an early-morning trip.

SHOPPING Chapala's main street, Madero, and Hidalgo, the intersecting street leading to Ajijic, have a few shops. To find the small collection of craft stalls at the **Mercado de Artesanías,** turn left at the pier in Chapala and follow it to the end. The market is on the left. Shopping is better in Ajijic.

HORSEBACK RIDING Horses for hire are gathered under the trees beside the Mercado de Artesanías (see above). Cost, including a guide, is $7.50 per hour for adults and $5 for children.

WHERE TO STAY

Expensive

QUINTA QUETZALCOATL, c/o Golden Ledger Bookkeeping, P.O. Box 1649, Tracy, CA 95378-1649. Tel. 209/832-8788. Fax 209/832-1204. 8 rms.

$ Rates (including daily breakfast, several meals, and four excursions): $100–$150 single or double daily. 8- or 10-night minimum; shorter stays on space-available basis. Discounts in summer.

★ The secluded, centrally located QQ, as it is dubbed, stands for *quinta* which means country inn and Quetzalcoatl, for the plumed serpent of Aztec/Toltec legend, and it's the place where D. H. Lawrence wrote part of *The Plumed Serpent.* It's owned by Californians Dick and Barbi Henderson, who personally attend guests. Rooms flank a large flower-, tree-, and plant-filled interior garden behind a 12-foot-high brick wall. Each room is tastefully furnished, entirely different, and intriguingly named. Lady Chatterley is one of the smaller rooms and has quaint Victorian touches with a stuffed Queen Anne chair, armoire, lace-covered table, and glass chandelier. The two-story *Castillo* (the castle) is the largest with two bedrooms, separate living and dining rooms, and an enormous tile kitchen. Henderson, an accomplished chef, prepares meals from a cozy kitchen brimming with interesting pots and jars. Summer visits, June through October, are arranged on request for eight guests minimum and require a 10-night minimum stay. During winter, December through May, there are fixed arrival and departure days and a stay of eight nights is

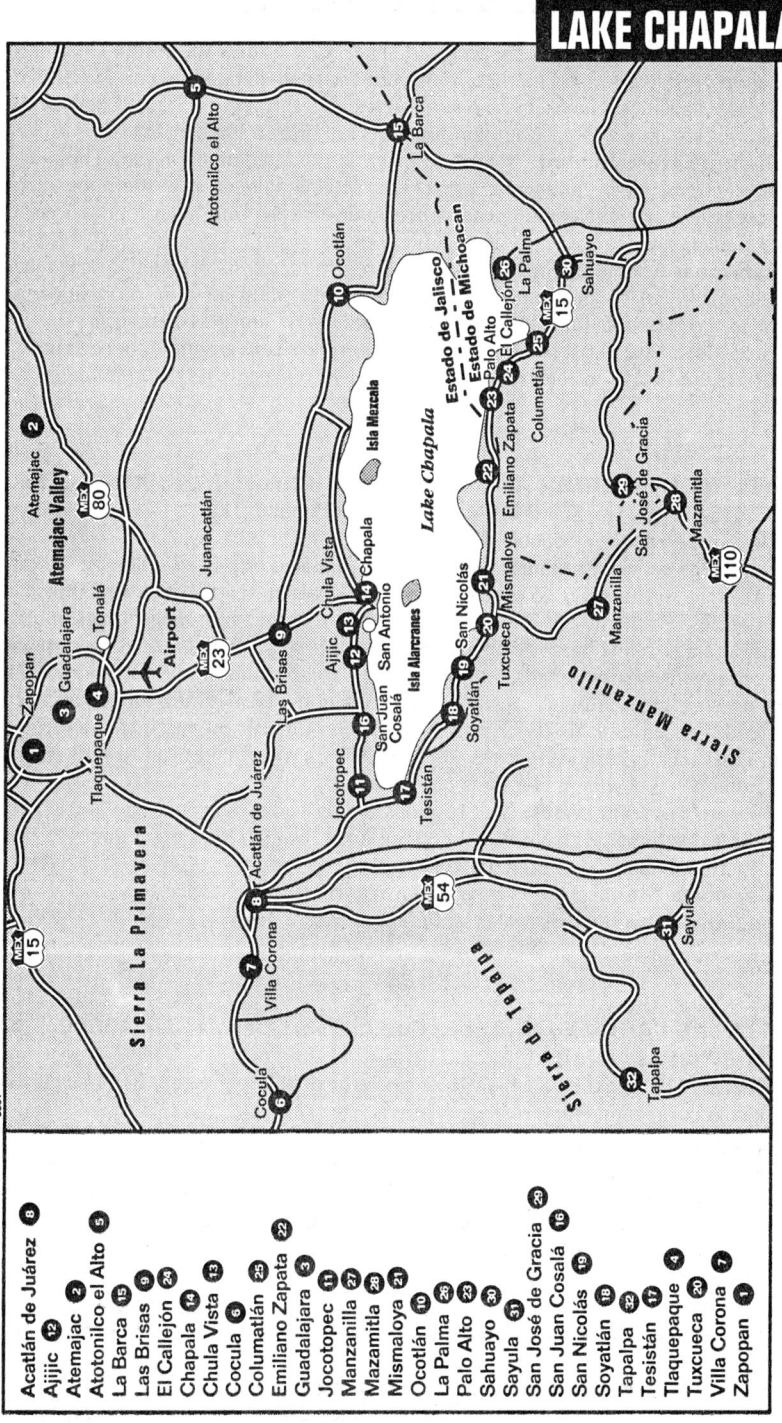

required. No children or pets are accepted. The QQ is a short walk from Chapala's pier, shops, restaurants, and market. Bring your own golf clubs and tennis rackets for use in area facilities. Guests must make reservations through the United States; no drop-in guests are accepted. Summer discounts are often a big bargain.

Dining/Entertainment: Meals are taken in the large dining room. The price includes several large continental breakfasts, several dinners, one afternoon taco fiesta, self-serve bar with complimentary beer and soft drinks and a day tour to Tonalá and Tlaquepaque.

Services: Afternoon airport pickup and return for guests on the QQ schedule; space-available guests may not fit this schedule, but transportation information is provided. Four optional fixed-schedule excursions in the inn's 14-passenger van.

Facilities: Several patios and sitting areas on the shady grounds; coffee makers, hairdryers, and robes in each room.

Moderate

HOTEL MONTECARLO, Av. Hidalgo 296, Chapala, Jal. 45900. Tel. 376/5-2120. Fax 376/5-2024. 46 rms (all with bath). TEL

$ Rates: $55 single or double. **Parking:** Free.

Behind a high wall, the setting is delightful here, situated on a rise overlooking lovely grounds that spread down to the edge of Lake Chapala. Red-tile walkways link the room areas, restaurant, and pools, and grounds are dotted with mango trees, pines, palms, and a strolling peacock or two. Rooms all have balconies facing the gardens and come with two twin beds, and tub/shower combination in the bathroom with separate sink area. Advance reservations are a good idea during winter and on weekends. It's a five- to six-block walk from here to Chapala proper. If you're driving from Guadalajara, turn right at the light in Chapala which takes you toward Ajijic. The hotel is less than a mile farther on the left.

Dining/Entertainment: The spacious dining room overlooks the lawns and lake. Breakfast is served from 8 to 11:30am; lunch from 1:30 to 5pm; dinner, from 7:30 to 10pm; Sunday buffet, from 2:30 to 5pm.

Services: Morning and evening room service; laundry service.

Facilities: Two thermal-water swimming pools.

Budget

HOTEL LAS CANDILEJAS, López Cotilla 663, Chapala, Jal. 45900. Tel. 376/5-2279. 9 rms.

$ Rates: $19 single or double; $100 single or double per week; $150 single or double per month. **Parking:** On Madero.

Opened in 1992, this two-story hotel is half a block up a steep hill from Madero. Rooms are sizable but plain, with brick ceilings, tile floors, small baths, armoires for belongings, and one or two comfortable double beds covered in frilly cotton bedspreads. Four have small balconies overlooking López Cotilla. There's no car access to the front door of the hotel, so the desk clerk will help with luggage from Madero.

HOTEL NIDO, Av. Madero 202, Chapala, Jal. 45900. Tel. 376/5-2116. 30 rms.

$ Rates: $19 single; $23–$27 double. **Parking:** On Madero.

A dowager among local hostelries, the red-brick Hotel Nido is in the center of

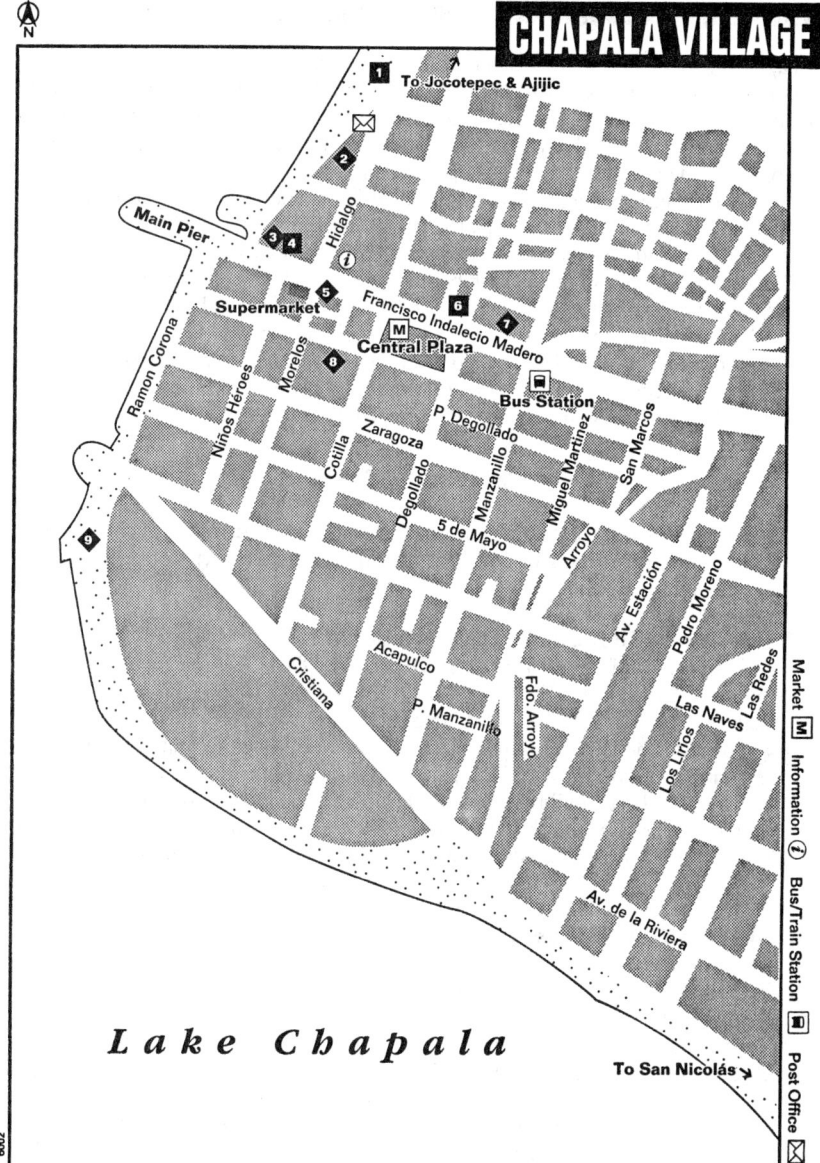

ACCOMMODATIONS:
Hotel las Candilejas 6
Hotel Montecarlo 1
Hotel Nido 4

DINING:
La India Bakery 8
Restaurant Bar Che Mary 7
Restaurant Beer Garden 3

Restaurant Don Juan 9
Restaurant Superior 5
San Francisco Grill 2

Chapala's action, only half a block from the water and pier on the right side of Madero. The two stories of rooms are built around two central lobbies. The main lobby, where you register, doubles as a restaurant with neat cloth-covered tables. To the left is the bar, which also serves drinks outside on the main street at umbrella-shaded tables. It's a well-kept, old-timey place with French doors covered with lace curtains opening to each room, tiled floors and bathrooms, armoires with lots of storage space, table and chairs, and comfortable beds with reading lamps. Avoid the rooms in both sections in the back—they are subject to loud noise until the wee morning hours from the nightclub around the corner (it's open weekends and for special events). On the first floor in back, there's a swimming pool and garden. Even if you don't stay here, come in to look at the old photographs of Chapala around the dining room and up the stairs. The hotel can have copies made but the process takes about three weeks. Especially look for the one showing the normally placid lake churning like an ocean and rolling over the pier.

WHERE TO DINE

Lake Chapala regional specialties include caviar de Chapala, caldo michi, charales, and tortas ahogados. Viuda de Sanchez Sangrita (a tequila chaser) is made locally as well as Cholula brand hot sauce.

LA INDIA BAKERY, Juárez 533. Tel. 5-3005.
  Cuisine: BOLILLOS/MUFFINS/COOKIES/PAN DULCE.
$ **Prices:** 25¢–$2.
  Open: Daily 6am–10am (or until sold out).

★ From this hole-in-the-wall bakery, with no visible sign to announce it, comes some of the best-tasting basic bakery products in the country. Certainly they make the best bolillos in town, but all of their cookies and pan dulce have a spark of flavor I've not tasted elsewhere. It's located directly behind the main plaza and market and next to the Casa Carocio. Get there early in the day; it sells out fast.

RESTAURANT BAR CHE MARY, Madero 429.
  Cuisine: ASIAN/MEXICAN.
$ **Prices:** Breakfast $3–$5; main courses $4–$9.
  Open: Daily 8am–10pm.

This small colorful restaurant, known for its margaritas, is the most inviting restaurant on Chapala's main street. Decked out in gay tablecloths, with open windows and a small balcony and deck facing the street, you'll notice it first thing when driving into town. The Asian specialties come with soup, salad, and main course. But there are numerous light meals, from sandwiches to Mexican specialties and fish and chips. The menu is in English and proprietress María Rivera caters to foreign needs with purified water and treated fresh vegetables.

RESTAURANT BEER GARDEN, Malecón at the pier. Tel. 5-2257.
  Cuisine: REGIONAL/MEXICAN.
$ **Prices:** Main courses $4–$8; comida corrida $10.
  Open: Mon–Sat 10am–6pm; Sun 10am–8:30pm.

Facing the lake and opposite Chapala's main pier where the Malecón begins, the Beer Garden is on the open patio of the long-defunct Hotel Arzapalo. Things really get going in the afternoon when strolling mariachis add a festive touch and locals begin to drift in for lunch and drinks. There's always a live band on weekends. The menu is in Spanish and English. The daily comida corrida starts with soup or consommé, rice with meat course, beans, dessert, and coffee or tea. Among the regional specialties served here are sweet or spicy tortas ahogados.

RESTAURANT DON JUAN, Paseo Ramón Corona 3. Tel. 5-3060.
Cuisine: REGIONAL/SEAFOOD.
$ Prices: Comida corrida $6.25–$7; tacos and quesadillas 75¢–$1.25 each; main courses $3–$8.
Open: Daily 9am–6pm; comida corrida 1–6pm.

This is one of the old established open-air eateries lined up facing the lake at the far right end of the malecón. It's opposite the market. Three different comida corridas are offered daily. Besides regional dishes like caldo michi, the restaurant specializes in batter-fried fish. Be sure to ask for their homemade salsa. As at other restaurants in central Chapala, mariachis usually play in the afternoon.

RESTAURANT SUPERIOR, Madero and Hidalgo. Tel. 5-2180.
Cuisine: MEXICAN.
$ Prices: Main courses $6–$8; breakfast $1.50–$4.
Open: Wed–Mon 8am–10pm, Tues 8am–5pm.

Right in the heart of Chapala this snappy clean little restaurant, owned by the Mungia family, has been operating at the same location for 30 years. The extensive menu of Mexican specialties includes chiles rellenos, enchiladas, and tacos. The Mexican plate comes with two tacos and enchiladas, a chile relleno, rice, beans, and salsa. There are several tables outdoors and a bar upstairs which has live music weekends and overlooks Madero.

SAN FRANCISCO GRILL, Hidalgo 236 A.
Cuisine: MEXICAN/AMERICAN.
$ Prices: Brunch $5–$11; main courses $5–$11.
Open: Daily 8am–9:30pm; brunch 8am–1pm.

Housed in a giant thatched palapa with windows all around, San Francisco Grill faces the lake and offers both indoor and outdoor dining. It's an agreeable place to begin or end the day. The house specialty is grilled meat and seafood and there's an assortment of hamburger platters with intriguing names—such as the Broadway Burger and the Nob Hill. The daily brunch includes a Bloody Mary, gin fizz, or margarita and the price varies with your main course selection; choices include eggs benedict, grilled steak and eggs, shrimp Louie, and a pâté, fruit, and cheese platter. There's an entrance on Hidalgo, 1½ blocks west of Madero, as well as an entrance from the Malecón where you see the restaurant's terrace decked out with umbrella-covered tables.

AJIJIC

Ajijic, another lakeside village, is a quiet place inhabited by fishermen, artists, and retirees. As you reach Ajijic, the highway becomes a wide, tree-lined boulevard through **La Floresta,** a wealthy residential district. The La Floresta sign signals you've entered Ajijic, but the central village is about a mile farther on the left. To reach Ajijic's main street, Colón (which changes to Morelos), turn left when you see the Danny's Restaurant sign. It leads straight past the main plaza and ends at the lake and the popular Restaurant La Posada Ajijic. The cobblestone streets and arts-and-crafts stores give the town a quaint atmosphere. (See "Chapala" above for bus information to Ajijic).

The area **tourist information office** is at km 6.5 on the road between Chapala and Ajijic (tel. 376/5-3135). When you see the modernistic cement sculpture on the left, turn left there, then immediately right on the interior street that parallels the highway. It's on the left, next to the Casa de Artesanías. They have maps of the lake and brochures about the area. Hours are Monday through Friday from 9am to 6pm and Saturday from 9am to 1pm. The telephone is an extension of the Casa de Artesanías.

The **Clinica Ajijic** (tel. 5-2023), on the main highway at the corner of Javier Mina, has a two-bed emergency section with oxygen and electrocardiogram, an ambulance, and five doctors with different specialties. Their 16-bed hospital was due to open in February 1993. The pharmacy there is available after hours for an emergency.

Should you decide to rent a car after arrival, two residents have a few cars to let. Call Michael Moore at 5-3415 or Herb Steever at 5-2692. But make reservations as soon as you can upon arrival—they're often all booked.

WHAT TO SEE & DO

THERMAL POOLS A mile and a half west of Ajijic is the lakeside settlement of San Juan Cosalá, known for its thermal water. The Balneario San Juan Cosalá allows day use of their pools. To enter adults pay $3.50, and children $1.75. There are two huge private pools and the cost to use them is $5 per person, but only you or your group, friends, et al, are allowed in.

RENTAL HORSES Horses for hire are tied up on the central median of 16 de Septiembre near the Hotel Real de Chapala. Sunset rides along the lakeshore are very popular. Adults pay $8 per hour and children $5.50.

ENTERTAINMENT There's almost always a group or a crowd at the **Posada Ajijic Cantina**, Calle 16 de Septiembre no. 2, where a band (of sorts) plays for dancing on Saturday and Sunday evenings. There's a happy hour daily from noon to 1:30pm and 5 to 6:30pm with complimentary snacks. The **Nuevo Posada Ajijic**, Donato Guerro 9, is a place to socialize almost anytime. Happy hour runs from noon to 1:30pm and 5 to 6pm both with complimentary snacks. For catching the latest in sports on a wide-screen TV or for just hanging out, **Los Veleros Video Bar**, on the Chapala Highway at Galeana Street in Ajijic, is another popular place. It's open Sunday through Friday from 10am to 10pm and Saturday from 10am to midnight.

SHOPPING

The **Casa de Artesanías** (tel. 5-3135) is on the left entering Ajijic just after the La Floresta sign. When you see the cement sculpture on the left, turn left and the casa is on the left. The shop has a good selection of pottery from all over Mexico as well as locally made weavings. It's open Monday through Wednesday from 10am to 6pm, Thursday from 10am to 2pm and 4 to 6pm, Friday and Saturday from 10am to 6pm, and Sunday from 10am to 1pm.

Most of Ajijic's shops line Colón/Morelos, but don't limit your shopping to that. Wander the side streets, especially Independencia which is the street just before the waterfront. Below are only a few of the shops you'll discover.

LOS ORIGINALAES TELLARES AJIJIC, corner of Morelos and Independencia. Tel. 5-2402 or 5-4320.

Founded in 1950, this was one of the first weavers' shops in the village. Visitors can still watch men working the large pedal looms and wander through the showrooms with bolts of material and ready-made decorative goods as well as clothing from other places. Open: Mon–Fri 8am–6pm.

OPUS 1, Colón 15.

 Here you'll find a fine line of designer clothing using Mexican colors and motifs made of handwoven cotton cloth. Open: Mon–Sat 10am–5pm.

WHERE TO STAY

Expensive

DANZA DEL SOL, Zaragoza 165, Ajijic, Jal. 45920. Tel. 376/5-2505; toll free 800/431-2822 in the U.S. and Canada, or 800/336-5454 in California. Fax 376/5-2836. 40 suites. TV TEL

$ Rates: $55 single; $70 double.

On secluded plant-filled grounds sequestered behind walls, this establishment gives you not simply a room, but a massive nicely furnished apartment complete with patio (in some cases a gigantic one), full-size living room with a fireplace, separate dining room, large complete kitchen, and from one to four spacious bedrooms (each with a separate bath). Used frequently as a small meeting hotel, Danza del Sol doesn't attract a lot of tourists, but it's one of the most comfortable places along the lake and a beautiful discovery. Danza del Sol is a little hard to find. Head out of Ajijic toward Jocotepec and look carefully on the left for the weathered sign. Turn there and go a short distance on a beat-up road.

Dining/Entertainment: The restaurant/bar by the pool is open daily from 7:30am to 10:30pm.

Facilities: Swimming pool.

HOTEL REAL DE CHAPALA, Paseo del Prado 20, Ajijic, Jal. 45900. Tel. 376/5-2416 or 5-2468; toll free 800/431-2822 in the U.S. and Canada, or 800/336-5454 in California. Fax 376/5-2836 or 5-2474. 85 suites (80 junior, 5 master). TV TEL

$ Rates: $78 single; $95 double; $110 master suite.

This hotel, with towering eucalyptus trees and tranquil interior gardens on its grounds, is a good choice right on the lake. The rooms could use some renovation, but all are large suites with two double beds or one king-size bed and large windows facing the interior garden or lake. Rooms on the lake side at the far end will be the least subject to spillover noise from the bar and special events room. A series of dining rooms with white wrought-iron furniture sprawls out on an enormous tree-shaded, flower-filled, lakeside patio with a pool. It's a most welcoming and popular place to come for a drink or meal even if you aren't a guest. Tucked in the La Floresta residential area, coming from Chapala, you'll see the sign for it at the large cement sculpture on the left. Turn left there and follow the signs to the hotel.

Dining/Entertainment: Restaurant Oscars is open from 6 to 11pm; Azulejos opens for breakfast only from 7 to 11am; and La Terraza/La Huerta on the terrace serves from 12:30 to 6pm or inside from 6 to 10:30pm. There's live piano music in the evenings at Oscars; and mariachis play frequently on weekends.

Services: Laundry, room service.

Facilities: Swimming pool off the terrace and facing the lake.

Moderate

LA FLORESTA, Paseo de la Cima 4, Ajijic, Jal. 45900. Tel. 376/5-3997. 102 bungalows.

$ Rates: $51 one-bedroom bungalow; $71 two-bedroom bungalow. **Parking:** Free.

In a residential neighborhood of Ajijic's suburb of La Floresta, this hotel is a tranquil alternative with a mountain backdrop. Individually separated, each of the one- or two-bedroom units has a fully equipped kitchen and small living/dining area. All bedrooms have two single beds and bathrooms have a separate sink area. If you're driving from Chapala the directional sign for the hotel will be on the right, after the Floresta subdivision sign. This is a better choice for those with cars, since the hotel is several blocks from the main boulevard, and taxis are on call, but not on-site.

Dining/Entertainment: Restaurant/bar.

Facilities: TV room, swimming pool, and Ping-Pong area.

LA NUEVA POSADA, Donato Guerra No. 9 (Apdo. Postal 30), Ajijic, Jal. 45900. Tel. 376/5-3395. Fax 376/5-4495. 12 rms.

$ Rates (including full breakfast): $53 single; $61–$73 double. **Parking:** Free.

This new posada (as the name indicates) was built by Michael and Elena Eager, the former owners of the popular Posada Ajijic (now a restaurant and bar under different ownership). Modeled after a gracious, traditional-style hacienda, La Nueva Posada looks a lot more expensive than it is. French doors, marble bathrooms, a wine cellar, and a small swimming pool are some of the amenities—which also include an elegant dining room with a glorious lake view. Original paintings hang in all of the color-coordinated rooms and public areas. Some rooms overlook the lake, others have intimate patios, but the former will have less disturbance from the after-hours kitchen crew. The Eagers' new venture is as popular as (but nothing like) their previous hostelry, and La Nueva Posada is often booked up way in advance for holidays. To find the hotel from the plaza walk toward the lake on Colón, then turn left on Independencia/Constitución; at Donato Guerro turn right and you'll see the hotel's blue facade on the right by the lake.

Dining/Entertainment: The hotel's restaurant La Rusa and casual bar (see "Where to Dine" below) are among the most popular meeting places in the village. There's live background music most evenings and some afternoons.

Facilities: Swimming pool.

Budget

LA LAGUNA BED AND BRUNCH, Zaragoza 29, Ajijic, Jal. 45900. Tel. 376/5-2264. Fax 376/5-2861. 4 rms.

$ Rates (including brunch): Nov 15–Apr 15 $25 single; $35 double. Apr 16–Nov 14 $20 single or double.

The rooms in this small inn, all with thick tile floors and fireplaces, are handsomely furnished with king-size beds covered with bright, loomed bedspreads. Brunch is served in a lovely glassed-in dining room facing the back patio; it includes fruit, apple bran muffins, and a choice of eggs as you like them. Free coffee is ready all day and "honor" pastries (pay as you eat) are on the table. Monday through Friday brunch is served from 9 to 11am; Sunday brunch, which starts with a bloody Mary, runs from 9:30am to 12:30pm. Nonguests can partake of brunch too at a cost of $3.85 on weekdays and $4.75 on Sunday. To reach La Laguna from the main highway, turn left on Colón and left again on the first street. It's 1½ blocks down on the left. It's also behind the Laguna Ajijic Real Estate office (which faces the main highway) and is operated by them.

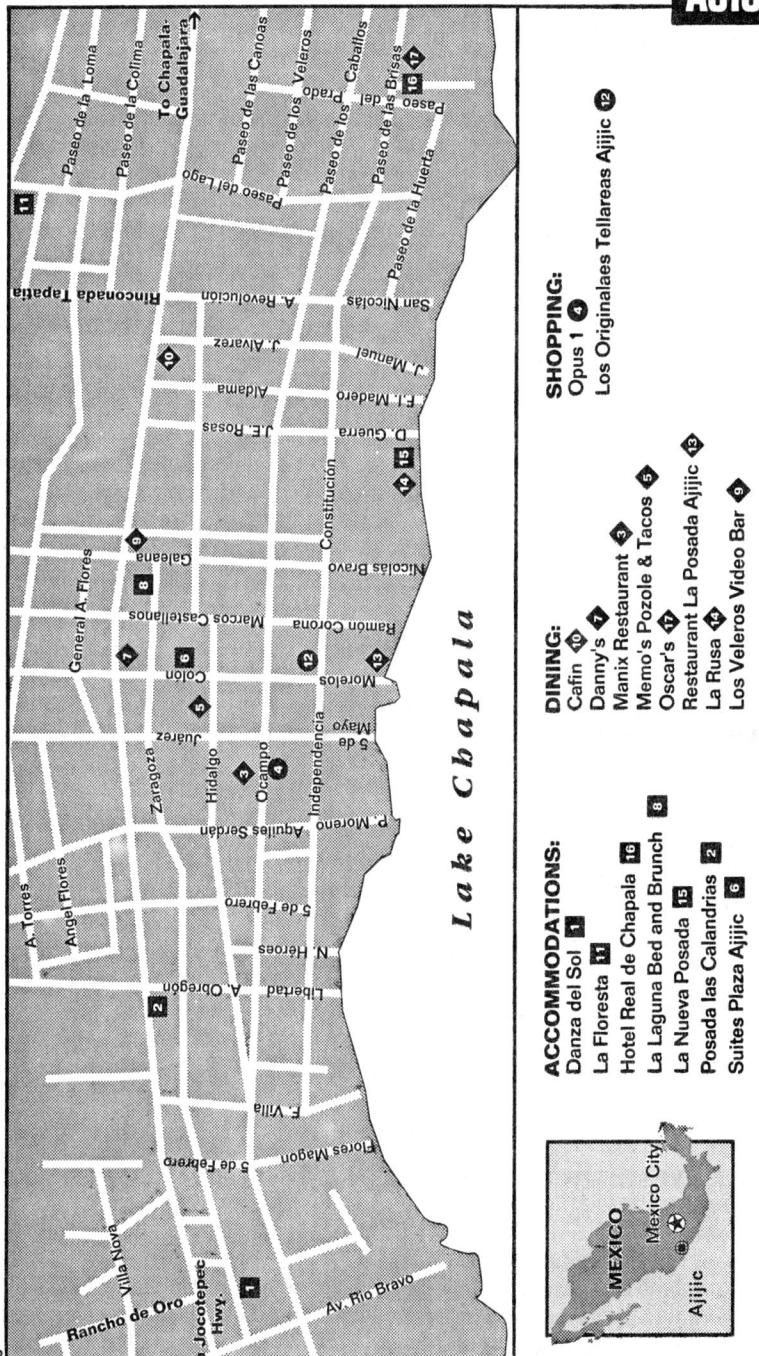

200 • EASY EXCURSIONS FROM GUADALAJARA

POSADA LAS CALANDRIAS, Carretera Chapala-Jocotepec poniente no. 8 (Apdo. Postal 76), Ajijic, Jal. 45920. Tel. 376/5-2819. 29 rms. TEL
$ Rates: $37 one bedroom; $56 two bedrooms.

Outside town on the main highway, this two-story brick hotel surrounds a swimming pool with bougainvillea everywhere. Guests come from all over, as the car license plates show: Rhode Island, Montana, and British Columbia. The rooms are large and comfortable and come with tile floors, fireplaces, and kitchens. There's an honor book exchange in the lobby. It's a good place to be for an extended stay, or while looking for long-term accommodations. Las Calandrias is on the main highway (left side if you're arriving from Chapala) at the west edge of Ajijic.

SUITES PLAZA AJIJIC, Colón 33, Ajijic, Jal. 45920. Tel. and fax 376/5-4802, or 3/622-4437 in Guadalajara. 10 rms.
$ Rates: $25 single or double; $175 per week; $517 per month; $345 for three months.

Located opposite Ajijic's central square, this simple but pleasant and clean hostelry reopened in 1992. The lobby, which faces the street, doubles as a real estate office. Rooms are behind the lobby and line up on two sides of a narrowish open patio. All are one-bedroom apartmentlike quarters with the bedroom separate from the kitchen area (where there's a dining table). A refrigerator and stove are available on request. A pleasant room in the far back of the patio serves as the common living room with game table, TV, stereo, and honor paperback library.

An RV Park

PAL RV PARK, Carretera Chapala-Jocotepec, San Antonio, Jal. 45900. Reservations: Madero 232, Chapala, Jal. 45900. Tel. 376/5-3764 or 5-3765. Fax 376/5-3567. 106 spaces.
$ Rates: $14 per day; $280 30 days; $211 permanent resident.

This immaculately kept park caters to visiting northerners who come for the winter. Each RV space has full hookups, a patio, and outdoor cooking grill. There's a nice recreation room for gatherings. The spotless bathrooms, separate for men and women, each have four showers and three toilets. To find the park, follow the highway from Chapala to San Antonio, which is between Chapala and Ajijic, just before the Floresta suburb, and it's easy to miss the town sign. There's a small sign to the park, but you'll also see a large Carta Blanca sign on the right. Turn right there. Make reservations by September for the winter months.

WHERE TO DINE

Moderate

MANIX RESTAURANT, Ocampo 57. Tel. 5-3449.
    Cuisine: INTERNATIONAL.
$ Prices: Comida corrida $11–$12.
    Open: Mon–Sat 1–9pm.

A favorite of American residents, this small, tranquil, and attractive restaurant, with rainbow-colored napkins to brighten up the dark, carved wood furniture, serves a different international comida daily. Seafood, beef, and sometimes chicken Cordon Bleu are served. To find Manix from the plaza walk away from the church on Morelos toward the lake and turn right on Ocampo. The restaurant is a block or so on the right, but the sign for it is hidden behind a tree.

OSCAR'S, Paseo del Prado 20. Tel. 5-2416.
　Cuisine: INTERNATIONAL.
$ Prices: Full meal $25–$35.
　Open: Daily 6–11pm.

★ This intimate little restaurant is part of the Hotel Real de Chapala. Named after the Academy Award figure, its candlelit tables are set inside in the cozy dining room or outside on the small terrace. Main courses of fish, chicken, steak, and pasta include a very tender and delicious beef filet médaillon named for Tom Selleck. John Huston would be honored by the outstanding Caesar salad prepared by José Luis Jimenez (ask for him to be your waiter). The crêpes Suzette named for Brooke Shields and prepared by Jimenez are something special to remember. A pianist plays softly in the background.

RESTAURANT LA POSADA AJIJIC, Morelos and Independencia. Tel. 5-4422.
　Cuisine: MEXICAN/INTERNATIONAL.
$ Prices: Sandwiches $3.25–$5.50; main courses $5.75–$11.
　Open: Mon–Fri noon–10:20pm.

Formerly managed by the owners of the Nuevo Posada Ajijic, this lakeside restaurant has reopened under new ownership and with gracious Mexican-inspired decor and good service. The menu covers the traditional with soups (ask about the daily specials), salads, sandwiches, and more filling Mexican specialties as well as beef, chicken, and seafood entrées. On Sunday lunch is served on the patio facing the gardens and the specialty is grilled meat—you pick the piece—which comes with soup or salad bar. The restaurant is at the end of Colón/Morelos and you enter through the back by the lake, where there's parking.

LA RUSA, Donato Guerra No. 9. Tel. 5-3395.
　Cuisine: INTERNATIONAL. **Reservations:** Suggested Dec–Apr.
$ Prices: Lunch $5.75–$8.50; dinner main courses $8–$15; Sun brunch $8.50–$10.50.
　Open: Mon–Sat 8am–9pm, Sun 9am–8pm; Sun brunch served 9am–1pm.

★ Step inside the dining/drinking area of the La Nueva Posada and you can't help but be pleased by La Rusa's looks, whether you're in the equipales-furnished bar, the elegant dining room with garden and lake view, or dining in the garden itself. La Rusa continues its reputation as a popular dining spot with the locals. The lunch menu is simple—crêpes, sandwiches, and salads. The dinner menu, printed on a large poster, has a dozen meat, seafood, and chicken entrées, plus soup, salad, and dessert. The Sunday brunch is entirely different; offerings include scrambled eggs in a potato nest with sausage, broccoli rarebit, and shrimp-asparagus crêpes newburg. The higher priced brunch includes wine. To reach the restaurant from the Ajijic plaza, walk toward the lake on Colón, turn left on Independence/Constitución and look for Donato Guerra. Turn right and the hotel/restaurant is on the right by the lake.

Budget

CAFIN, Carretera Chapala-Ajijic. Tel. 5-2572.
　Cuisine: PASTRIES/PIZZA/SANDWICHES.

$ Prices: Baked goods 35¢–$6; sandwiches and hamburgers $4.50–$6; pizza $5–$15.
Open: Mon–Sat 8am–7pm, Sun 8am–3pm.

You'll spot this cheery eatery by its green awning on the left just before Ajijic. The front part holds the bakery and booths lining one wall. There's a covered area in back beside a small lawn. Here you can purchase fresh croissants, cakes, and pies, plus sandwiches, hamburgers, and pizza. A lot of people come to enjoy the pastries with cappuccino and hot chocolate.

DANNY'S, on the highway at Colón Street.
Cuisine: AMERICAN/MEXICAN.
$ Prices: Breakfast $4.25; Mexican dishes $3–$7; sandwiches/burgers $2.50–$4.75.
Open: Mon–Sat 8am–6pm; Sun 8am–1pm.

Bright and cheerful with clean and colorful tablecloths, Danny's is one of the most popular restaurants in Ajijic due to the good food and service. The menu is fifty-fifty American and Mexican so you can enjoy a good sandwich or hamburger and fries, as well as something like the Mexican plate with chili relleno, enchiladas, beans, and rice. There are five breakfast specials that include coffee or tea, beans or hash browns, juice, and toast, bolillo, or tortillas. Danny's is the landmark I use on the highway to turn onto Colón, the main street into Ajijic proper.

MEMO'S POZOLE & TACOS, Hidalgo 27 at Juárez. No phone.
Cuisine: MEXICAN.
$ Prices: Pozole $2; tacos, tostadas, and enchiladas 35¢ each.
Open: Daily 6–11pm.

It's always a delight to discover a local favorite like Memo's. The simple specialties of pozole, tacos, enchiladas, sopes, and tostados are so good, housewives would rather buy them here than make them at home. The big bowl of pozole comes with lots of tender pork pieces. Operated by Memo Rameño and María Robledo, the place is simple but the prices and taste are hard to top.

LOS VELEROS VIDEO BAR, on the highway at Galeana Street. No phone.
Cuisine: ITALIAN/MEXICAN.
$ Prices: Breakfast $4.50; pizza $4.25–$35; main courses $4–$11.50.
Open: Sun–Fri 10am–10pm; Sat 10am–midnight.

Casual and comfortable, Los Veleros is a good place to meet some of the Americans and Canadians who live in the area. You can dine inside facing the large TV screen which is always bringing in the latest U.S. news or sporting event, or outside on the covered patio. The big brick oven is always turning out one of their 14 pizzas, but the menu also includes spaghetti, chicken, fish, and sandwiches. Spaghetti comes with salad and garlic bread; other entrées are served with salad, vegetable, and potatoes or rice.

SAN JUAN COSALÁ

Famed for its thermal waters, San Juan Cosalá is 8 miles west of Chapala and 1½ miles from Ajijic. Because of the string of establishments along the highway and dearth of signs, it's difficult to tell when you've arrived in Cosalá. The sign announcing Balneario San Juan Cosalá means you're there.

WHERE TO STAY & DINE

BALNEARIO SAN JUAN COSALÁ, Av. La Paz 420, San Juan Cosalá, Jal. 45900 (Apdo. Postal 181, Chapala, Jal. 45900). Tel. 376/3-0507 or 3/615-6728 in Guadalajara. 32 rms.

$ **Rates** (including breakfast): $44 single; $54 double; $64 triple. Fans $3 extra daily. **Parking:** Free.

Ⓢ The first established hotel using the area's thermal/mineral waters, it's still a popular place for day use of the huge swimming pool (with the mineral water) and for wintering northerners. Rooms are clean, freshly painted, and well-kept with decades-old veneer furniture, tile floors, and glass louvered windows. Each is furnished with two double beds and some have refrigerators. All have balconies or patios with a table and chairs facing the pool and lake. It can be a busy place on weekends with lots of good-natured noise from children enjoying the pools. The restaurant is open daily from 8am to 9pm.

VILLA BUENAVENTURA, Carretera Chapala-Jocotepec 13.5, San Juan Cosalá, Jal. 45900 (Apdo. Postal 181, Chapala, Jal. 45900). Tel. 376/3-0505. 6 condos, 9 villas (all with bath). TV

$ **Rates:** $80 one-bedroom villa for two; $85 two-bedroom villa for two. **Parking:** Free.

Next to the Balneario San Juan Cosalá is its modern rival, with rooms spread out around a small interior shady lawn with a nice-size thermal/mineral-water pool. All of the rooms have thermal/mineral water in the tap and bath. The condominium units are in a two-story building and all have two bedrooms each with a private bath and a large shared thermal-water tub. The one- or two-bedroom villas are farther back on the property. Each has a nice fully equipped kitchen, dining room, and sitting areas in the large bedrooms. Four of the villas are large, with a more stylish living room, kitchen with bar, and bubbling hot tubs in the bedrooms.

JOCOTEPEC

West of Ajijic, this small colonial-era village is becoming a weaving center. *Important note:* Formerly the main highway went straight through Jocotepec, but now it becomes one-way in the opposite direction as the highway approaches town center. Where the highway becomes one-way, a large sign over the highway points left to Guadalajara and Morelia and right to Guadalajara and Centro (Jocotepec town center). The sign with an arrow and line through it means it's illegal to continue straight ahead (all very confusing at first). So if you're headed to the town plaza turn right, then left at the next street and keep an eye to your left until you see the plaza. You can park and walk to the shopping street of Hidalgo from the plaza. Or instead of turning right off the highway, turn left and follow the Guadalajara/Morelia signs until you reach Avenida Hidalgo. Turn right on Hidalgo and park on the street; you'll be headed in the direction of Ajijic when it's time to leave.

The main street curving in front of the central plaza becomes Hidalgo, the main **shopping** street. Thursday is market day and the market is at the corner where the street curves and becomes Hidalgo. Beginning on Hidalgo at the plaza you'll find several weavers' shops with locally loomed rugs and wall hangings.

WHERE TO STAY

POSADA DEL PESCADOR, km. 73, Carretera Chapala-Jocotepec (Apdo. Postal 67), Jocotepec, Jal. Tel. 376/3-0028. 22 bungalows.

$ **Rates:** $35 bungalow for one or two people; $50 bungalow for four people.

Just east of Jocotopec, this pretty motor inn will do if everything in Ajijic is full or if you can't quite make it to your next destination. The single-story, red-brick bungalows are scattered around the swimming pool. Each has a kitchenette, dining area, fireplace, bedroom, and bath. There's a self-operated laundry room with washer and dryer, and iron and ironing board. Maintenance and housekeeping standards are always in flux here; once I arrived and no rooms could be let because they had no sheets! The office is frequently not staffed, so honk your horn. It's on the main highway, on the eastern edge of Jocotopec on the right if coming from Ajijic.

WHERE TO DINE

BAR JACAL, Miguel Arana Altos.
   Cuisine: SNACKS/DRINKS.
$ **Prices:** Nachos $3.50; sandwiches $1.50–$3.50; beer $1.25; margarita $3.
   Open: Tues–Sun 6–10pm.

To find this local watering hole, face the main plaza from the main street. On the right corner and upstairs (via a doorway without a sign) is the Bar Jacal overlooking Jocotepec's main street. It's a very casual place with equipales chairs and cloth-covered tables on an open, plant-filled balcony. The menu is mostly snack food that goes with a beer or margarita, such as queso fundido, hamburgers, burritos, fajitas, and pizzas.

NEVADO DE TOLUCA, Hidalgo 158. Tel. 3-0622.
   Cuisine: ICE CREAM.
$ **Prices:** Cone $1; one dip 60¢.
   Open: Daily 9am–8:30pm.

☆ Good for a light treat if you're just in town shopping, this is the best ice cream in the area. Scoops are generous and two will fill up one of the huge waffle cones. There's another branch of this chain on the right side of the highway as you head back to Ajijic.

3. MAZAMITLA

A three-hour drive from Guadalajara (70 miles south of Guadalajara and 45 miles south of Chapala) this mountain resort town (pop. 11,000; alt. 7,500 feet) is a popular weekend getaway in the state of Jalisco. By bus, **Auto Transportes Mazamitla**, at Guadalajara's central bus station, has more than a dozen daily departures from Guadalajara to Mazamitla. To return by bus from Mazamitla to Guadalajara, the bus station (tel. 8-0410), is opposite the market a block from the central square. In Mazamitla, six buses daily go to Guadalajara Monday through Friday and nine buses make the route on Saturday and Sunday. All are de paso and the last leaves Mazamitla for Guadalajara around 8:30pm—but double-check that time when you travel. **Flecha Amarilla** buses (tel. 8-0413) in Mazamitla, half a block from the market, can take you on to Colima, Manzanillo, or to San José de Gracia.

By car, the shortest way to get there from Guadalajara is by following Highway 44 west along the lake through Chapala, Ajijic, and Jocotepec, after which it becomes Highway 15 south as it goes along the lake's southern shoreline. Just after Tuxcueca you'll see the right turn and crossroads with a sign to La Manzanilla and Mazamitla only 25 miles farther. (Most maps don't show the turnoff—trust me, it's there and the road is paved). The long way from Guadalajara is along Lake Chapala's eastern shore through La Barca and Sahuayo. Soon after the turnoff at Tuxcueca, the road climbs and winds through the mountains, the landscape becomes covered in oak and pine trees, and the temperature drops considerably. A few miles before Mazamitla is La Manzanilla, a pretty village in which you may want to take a few minutes to walk around the plaza.

Founded soon after the conquest of Mexico, Mazamitla, only six miles from the state of Michoacán, is architecturally more Michoacán than Jalisco. Wide wood-beamed rooflines support dark red-tiled roofs, with pine balconies and window trim, all characteristic of Michoacán. Mazamitla retains its colonial-era charm; the village and it's cobblestone streets all branch out from the shady central plaza and church, which is devoted to the Virgin of Guadalupe.

For **tourist information,** follow directions below to Colina de los Ruiseñores restaurant where the owner, Guillermo Arias, acts as the village's unofficial tourist delegate.

Important Note: Bring a heavy sweater or jacket any time of year. Long johns and heavy socks might be called for at night in unheated hotels.

WHAT TO SEE & DO

Although this picturesque resort town is largely devoted to relaxing and strolling the streets, self-guided mountain hiking is one active option. Mazamitla is among several area villages where you can buy locally made cheese and rompope, and home-canned fruits temptingly displayed in glass jars. The town's patron, Saint Christopher, is honored with a large **festival** the last Sunday in July. Besides Saint Christopher, Mazamitla also honors the Virgin of Guadalupe December 4 to 12, and Fiestas Patrias (independence celebration) September 13 to 17. **Rental horses** are available for around $7 per hour, on the road to Monte Verde Centro Recreacional. Look left and you'll see them lined up under the trees. If you'd like to come just for the day, and look the town over, **Viajes Copenhagen** in Guadalajara (tel. 3/621-1008) offers a day-trip with picnic lunch.

WHERE TO STAY

Be aware that Mazamitla is a very popular getaway for Guadalajarans and hotels fill up on weekends, major Mexican holidays, and for village festival days (mentioned above). Should everything be full when you arrive, consider nearby San José de Gracia (see "A Side Trip to San José de Gracia" below).

HOTEL FIESTA MAZAMITLA, Reforma 6, Mazamitla, Jal. 49500. Tel. 353/8-0050. 24 rms (all with bath).

$ Rates: Weekday $10 single; $20 double. Weekend and holidays $14 single; $27 double.

A half block off the central plaza, this new hotel, with a natural pine balcony, has rooms facing the street and interior rooms facing a small upstairs restaurant. The rooms all have tile floors, one or two double beds, and small bathrooms. Those facing the street are brighter, but may also come with a lot of street noise. The restaurant wasn't operating when I was there.

HOTEL SIERRA DEL TIGRE, Reforma 3, Mazamitla, Jal. 49500. Tel. 353/8-0087. 11 rms. TV

$ Rates: $13.50 per person.

Opened in 1992, this cozy two-story hotel is a welcome addition to Mazamitla's sparse hotel scene. Without windows on the outside (all open to the interior) rooms are warmer than those in any other hotel in town. Each is nicely decorated with tile floors, pine furniture, and warm red-and-blue plaid bedspreads. Some come with bunk beds and a double bed, some with double beds, and some with two single beds. Most have a small refrigerator. There's a small sitting area on the second floor and the restaurant is open from 8am to 10pm daily. It's half a block off the main square.

MONTE VERDE CENTRO RECREACIONAL, Calle Constitucional, Mazamitla, Jal. 49500. Tel. 353/8-0150, Fax 353/8-0049. or 3/616-1826. Fax 3/615-6812 in Guadalajara. 51 cabins (all with bath).

$ Rates: $95 small; $115 large; $115 five-night honeymoon package Sun–Thurs.

On the far edge of town, Mazamitla's original resort is spread over a mountain side surrounded by forest and gardens. Steep, paved streets wind past the Swiss-style cabins. Small cabins are those with two bedrooms, two bathrooms, kitchen/dining room, and fireplace, and sleep six to eight persons. Large cabins have three bedrooms, two living areas, kitchen, dining room, two bathrooms, and two fireplaces, and sleep eight to ten people. Most people bring their food and do their own cooking. It's the town's best-known and most popular inn and is always crowded in summer as well as all Mexican holidays and weekends. Off-times, especially weekdays, ask for a discount. To find the Monte Verde, from the main plaza go straight past the plaza (the church front will be on your right) on Reforma through town, and bear right with the main street. It's ahead on the left.

Dining: The Restaurant Campestre La Carreta and Mazamitla Grillare across the street from the entrance to the resort and both are open for lunch and dinner.

Facilities: Three tennis courts, volleyball, basketball, jogging path.

POSADA ALPINA, Portal Reforma 8, Mazamitla, Jal. Tel. 353/8-0104 or 3/641-0681 in Guadalajara. 14 rms.

$ Rates: $14 single; $27 double; $35 triple. **Parking:** Free, in front.

Opposite the church and on the central plaza, this late 19th-century home has been converted into a rustically charming inn. Rooms in the front section with a large interior patio are part of the original home with polished plank floors and beamed ceilings. Those in the rear around a small patio have been added on and are smaller. Six of the rooms are large with three beds. Room no. 1 is one of these and opens onto the upper front porch which overlooks the plaza and church. Owner Guadalupe Toscano Hernandez will graciously help with directions or sightseeing suggestions.

POSADA LAS CHARRANDAS, Obregón 2, Mazamitla, Jal. 49500. Tel. 353/8-0254 3/614-9618 in Guadalajara. 10 rms.

$ Rates: $27 small room; $38 large room for two. **Parking:** Free, behind.

The Charrandas's natural pine exterior looks like it belongs in Switzerland and exudes the kind of quaint charm for which this village is known. The interior is brightly colored with orange walls, pine shutters and furniture, and fawn-colored tile floors. Rooms no. 5, 6, 7, and 8 have balconies with mountain views. Some rooms are a bit small, but cheery, and all come with one or two double beds. Owner Lourdes Azpeitia keeps the place spotless. There's a cozy restaurant off the lobby, open daily from 8am to 9pm.

SIERRA PARAISO, Loma Bonita s/n, Mazamitla, Jal. 49500. Tel. 353/8-0044. 7 villas.

$ Rates: $45 double.

This, one of Mazamitla's most beautiful inns, is on three beautifully groomed and grass-filled levels edged with flowers and trees. The villas are spread about the grounds. Each one comes with a sunken living room facing a fireplace, kitchen open to the living room, wood and tile floors, and one, two, or three bedrooms. The master bedroom has a king-size bed while other bedrooms have a bunk bed and a double bed. Each villa has a furnished patio and grill for cooking outdoors. The Sierra Paraiso is straight ahead, up the hill from the Monte Verde Centro Recreational mentioned above.

WHERE TO DINE

Among the regional specialities you may want to try are *bote*, which is meat cooked in pulque (the pre-Conquest alcoholic beverage made from the maguey plant); *parajito*, a mixture of fresh cow's milk, chocolate, and pure alcohol; and *atole de agua miel*, a kind of fruit wine. Everywhere you see shelves laden with quart jars of enticing home-preserved fruits, to buy and eat there or to go.

CIERVO ROJO, Pino Suarez at Reforma. Tel. 8-0129.
Cuisine: INTERNATIONAL.
$ Prices: Main courses $6.50–$9; daily special $6.75; Irish coffee $4.
Open: Wed–Thurs 11am–10pm; Fri–Sun 10am–11pm.

Another cozy eatery with red-brick and pine walls and a fireplace, this one is only a block from the central plaza. Although I wouldn't expect a memorable culinary treat, the international menu is a nice escape from totally Mexican fare. There's chicken curry and fish in white wine, as well as hamburgers. The daily special might be pork in a mushroom sauce with potato, vegetable, and salad. To find it from the plaza, with the Posada Alpina on your left, walk straight ahead one block and the restaurant is on the left corner.

COLINA DE LOS RUISENORES. Allende 50. Tel. 8-0484.
Cuisine: REGIONAL/INTERNATIONAL.
$ Prices: Breakfast $1–$4; main courses $3–$7.75.
Open: Daily 8am–8pm.

The food at this charming little pine-decorated restaurant, in a small garden setting, is some of the best in Mazamitla—and in the country for that matter. Owned by the Arias family, Señora Arias, whose family owns and operates the place, does all the cooking using recipes adapted from family favorites passed down through the generations. Her meat marinades are scrumptious. The pork adobada has a wonderful tangy taste, and the bistec de res Ruiseñores is yet another great marinated flavor, with a soy sauce and vinegar base. The pork ribs are meaty and flavorful. The special of the day is often trout in almond sauce. There's also chicken to stay or to go, Mexican antojitos, and *lonches* (sandwiches). Arias's children and relatives do most of the serving; Señor Arias, who also sells real estate and willingly helps tourists with area information, pitches in. A *ruiseñore*, by the way, is a bird. To find the restaurant from the main plaza, with the Posada Alpina on your right, walk straight ahead a block to the market which will be on your right, keep going to the bend in the road (about a block) and the restaurant is on the right.

EL PORTAL "VITO'S," Portal Reforma 12. Tel. 8-0016.
Cuisine: REGIONAL.

$ Prices: Main courses $3.50–$7.
Open: Mon–Wed and Fri–Sun 10am–11pm; Thurs 10am–6pm.
On the second floor overlooking the main square, Vito's, as it's called locally, has a long porch with tables and chairs overlooking the main plaza. Inside it's warm (important in this chilly town) with red tablecloths and a fireplace. Sunday the specialty is *borrego* (wood-roasted lamb). The long liquor list has plenty of options if you just want to take off the chill or relax while watching the plaza action.

RESTAURANT CAMPESTRE LA TROJE, Galeana 53. Tel. 8-0070.
Cuisine: REGIONAL/MEXICAN.
$ Prices: Appetizers $2.75–$8; main courses $5.75–$9.
Open: Wed–Mon 9am–7pm.
Campestre (country) restaurants are popular in this region and this one is certainly deserving of the crowds. Service is excellent and it's known for charcoal-grilled meat platters which come with rice and beans. Their specialties include chicken, beef, or shrimp fajitas (or a combination of the three), shrimp four different ways, and beef brochet. The restaurant is at the crossroads immediately outside Mazamitla opposite the Pemex station on the road leading to the highway and Chapala.

RESTAURANT POSADA MAZAMITLA, Hidalgo 2 at Reforma. Tel. 8-0161.
Cuisine: REGIONAL/MEXICAN.
$ Prices: Breakfast $2.50–$3.50; main courses $5–$6.
Open: Daily 8:30am–6pm.
On one corner of the square behind a small market, you'll find this popular restaurant fashioned out of an old home with a partly covered interior courtyard. Main courses are usually pork and beef, but there are lighter choices of beans, quesadillas, and soup, all very inexpensive.

A SIDE TRIP TO SAN JOSÉ DE GRACIA

Seven miles northeast of Mazamitla, just over the state line from Jalisco into the state of Michoacán, is San José de Gracia, an immaculately beautiful village once known for its potters, whose numbers are now dwindling. Besides being a delightful village in which to stroll around, San José's hotels come in handy when those in Mazamitla are full.

WHAT TO SEE & DO

The shady central square, which you'll find if you keep going through town on the main highway, is the village's quiet central hub. Take time to walk around and talk to the locals, who will be quite interested in you since few visitors come here. A few village potters still produce the green "pineapple" jugs with hooks and cups around the side that are popular for fiesta beverages in Mexican homes. These are still made by members of the family of Emilio Alejos Pérez and Aurelio Diego, so if you're interested ask someone to direct you to their homes.

WHERE TO STAY

HOTEL DE LARIOS, Reforma y Morelos, San José de Gracia, Mich. 59500. Tel. 353/7-0508. Fax 353/7-0236. 42 rms. TV TEL
$ Rates: $29 single; $33 double; $41 suite.

Some might count finding all of Mazamitla's hotels full a blessing—it's warmer overall in San José, and rooms in this three-story hotel have warmth even though they aren't heated. Modern and furnished in the latest style, most rooms have tile floors, while suites are carpeted. Just off the lobby there's a restaurant with irregular hours, but its posted hours are Tuesday through Sunday from 1:30 to 11pm.

WHERE TO DINE

RESTAURANT BAR EL DOÓN, Galeano 3. Tel. 7-0543.
  Cuisine: STEAK/MEXICAN.
  $ Prices: Main courses $4.75–$12.
  Open: Thurs–Tues 1–9pm.

Shiny and clean, with cloth-covered tables and good service, El Doón is *the* place to eat in San José de Gracia. Different beef cuts are the specialty here, grilled to your specification. You can have chicken and fish as well, or try a Mexican dish such as steak Tampiqueña, charro beans, and Tarascan soup. Ask directions from the main plaza; it's between Independencia and Melchor O'Campo.

4. TAPALPA

Another tidy, 16th-century mountain-resort town, Tapalpa (pop. 10,000; alt. 6,398 feet) is almost equidistant between Guadalajara, 133 miles to the south, and Manzanillo, 158 miles to the north. Driving in on the toll road (Highway 110) from either direction, you'll see a sign marking the turn-off to Tapalpa; from there it's approximately 20 miles farther to the town. The trip takes about three hours one-way from either Guadalajara or Manzanillo. Just before the Tapalpa turn-off coming either from Guadalajara or Manzanillo you'll pass the enormous, almost-dry lakebed of Sayula, which at certain times of year is a mecca for migrating birds. When you leave the toll road turn left at the next intersection (the old free highway) and follow it about four miles to another crossroad with a sign pointing right to Tapalpa. The road begins to wind up through the mountains, and you're at the pine level by the time you reach Tapalpa and the end of the highway.

The pavement gives over to cobblestones at the edge of Tapalpa; the streets in town are lined with whitewashed, red-tile-roofed buildings. Smaller and more of a quiet backwater than Mazamitla, it centers around a lovely plaza and is dominated by an enormous 18th-century red-brick church dedicated to the Purísma Concepción. Arcaded buildings more than 200 years old surround the central plaza. It isn't unusual to see horses, mules, and burros hitched outside local stores or men on horseback during their workday.

The locally maintained **tourism office** is on Portal Morelos on the main square. Printed information is scarce there as is staff, but you can try asking questions if anyone is around. The office doors are open Monday through Friday from 9:30am to 2pm and Saturday from 4:30pm to 8pm. **Bancomer** on the plaza is open from 9am to 1:30pm and will exchange dollars between 9:30 and 11:30am. The **bus station** is on Matamoros, a block down the hill from the main plaza. There are buses almost hourly to and from Guadalajara (a three-hour trip), beginning at 6am and the last at 6:30pm. There's one daily bus at 6am to Cuidad Guzman. If you're coming from Manzanillo, take a bus to Ciudad Guzman and change to a bus to Tapalpa. Buses to

Tapalpa leave from Guadalajara's old bus station near downtown. The **gas station** on the edge of town doesn't have unleaded gas.

Important note: Bring warm clothes—long johns, gloves, and a heavy sweater or jacket. The brick, stucco, and rock hotels here, with tile floors and no heat or fireplaces, retain the cold day and night. The temperature drops to freezing often at night and daytime temperatures can be nippy too.

WHAT TO SEE & DO

HIKING   Like Mazamitla, self-guided walks around town and in the mountains are what most people do when they aren't relaxing. The 300-foot **Nogales waterfall**, almost 20 miles from Tapalpa, is a pleasant place to hike. You'll have to leave your car a distance from the falls and walk the rest of the way. There are modest paths to follow and the bird life may prove interesting depending on the time of year. You could see deer and fox as well. Ask directions in town for how to get there. Another local diversion, **Las Piedrotas** (the rocks), is a strange outcropping of large rocks. Ask directions to them.

SHOPPING   Several shops around the central plaza sell wood carvings from Michoacán—napkin holders, Christmas ornaments, etc. The gift shop of the **Hacienda de las Fuentes** has a fine selection of Mexican and Guatemalan crafts. As in Mazamitla you'll see jars of home-canned fruit, stacks of cheese, and bottles of rompope for sale. Three blocks from the main square is the **Cooperativo Ojo Zarco de Tapalpa**, Ignacio López 266 (tel. 2-0165), open daily from 9am to 6pm. Here you can buy reasonably priced, nicely designed lambswool sweaters knitted locally. Back of the showroom, men machine-card the wool and dye the yarn. Besides sweaters knitted by women, a number of men in town loom rugs and serapes. **Jesús Delgado**, Independencia 140, may have a good selection to choose from. He sells from the patio of his family home and prices are by weight per kilo.

WHERE TO STAY

POSADA DE LA FUENTE, Matamoros 69, Tapalpa, Jal. 49340. Tel. and fax 343/20189. 8 rms.

$ Rates: $96 one bedroom; $135 two bedroom.

The front part of this hotel is a 200-year-old home built around a beautiful courtyard. High-ceilinged rooms with beamed ceilings and polished plank floors flank three sides and make up the reception area, restaurant, and gift shop. The eight cozy guest rooms, which are all new construction, are built around another courtyard in back. Designed with families in mind, the rooms with one bedroom can sleep four people. Those with two bedrooms have a master bedroom and bath downstairs and a large bedroom upstairs with four single beds and sleep six people. The drawback is only one small bathroom in each room no matter how many it sleeps. But the rooms are handsomely furnished with soft comforters, wood floors, rock and brick walls, and many Mexican decorative details.

POSADA EL CARRETERO, Augustine Yañez 12, Tapalpa, Jal. 49340. Tel. 343/2-0049. 18 rms.

$ Rates: $20 one bed; $40 two beds; $50 three beds.

One of the first hotels to open after the highway reached Tapalpa in the mid-1970s, was in times past a way station for mule drivers and other travelers called the Meson del Sur. The two stories of rooms are built around a nice plant-decorated courtyard. Rooms, all with tile floors, are large with large bathrooms, but are sparsely furnished with chenille or cotton bedspreads. Management is as spare and cold as the furnishings, so don't expect much in the way of hospitality. It's just half a block past the square.

POSADA LA HACIENDA, Matamoros 7, Tapalpa, Jal. 49340. Tel. 343/2-0193. 31 rms and bungalows.
$ Rates: $80 single or double; $95 one-bedroom bungalow. 40% discounts are common.

On the corner, opposite the central square, this overpriced hostelry is grouped around two large patios. Rooms are simply furnished with pine furniture and tile floors. All come with kitchen and dining area. Some have balconies and fireplaces. The bungalows are more spacious rooms around the back patio. Housekeeping standards are quite lax, so inspect your quarters and insist on cleanliness.

HOTEL TAPALPA, Matamoros 35, Tapalpa, Jal. 49340. Tel. 343/2-0607. 13 rms (all with bath).
$ Rates: $11 single; $20 double.

This is a good budget choice on the central plaza. Rooms in the two-story hotel are simple and clean and were being remodeled when I was there. Each has either one or two double beds, tile floors, and small all-tile bathrooms.

WHERE TO DINE

Roasted lamb (borrego) is the town specialty and, on weekends and holidays especially, restaurants all over town and lining the highway cook the meat over open fires.

POSADA DE LA FUENTE, Matamoros 69. Tel. 2-0189.
   Cuisine: REGIONAL.
$ Prices: Breakfast $4-$10; main courses $5-$10.
   Open: Mon-Thurs 9am-9pm; Fri-Sat 8:30am-10pm; Sun 8:30am-6pm.

The most pleasing dining setting in Tapalpa is this one at the Hotel Posada de la Fuente. Take a seat either on the sheltered patio or in interior rooms with shuttered windows facing the plaza. Colorfully and tastefully decorated, it's a pleasant setting for a drink or a meal. Among the breakfast offerings is yogurt with fruit. The lunch and dinner menu is a short one but includes borrego birria, beef or pork asada, and sandwiches.

RESTAURANT HACIENDA BUENAVISTA, Portal Morelos, upstairs. Tel. 2-0233.
   Cuisine: MEXICAN.
$ Prices: Breakfast $2.50-$4; main courses $2-$4.
   Open: Thurs-Tues 8:30am-9:30pm.

From the upper floor of an old mansion you can sit inside in the large, simply furnished dining room, or out on the narrow balcony and watch what's happening on the plaza. Choose from chicken and beef main courses or for something lighter, try quesadillas or birria.

RESTAURANT TAPALPA, Matamoros 35. Tel. 2-0607.
   Cuisine: MEXICAN.

$ Prices: Breakfast $2; main courses $2.50–$3.75.
Open: Wed–Mon 8:30am–9:30pm.

Next to the Hotel Tapalpa on the main square is this clean, large lunchroom with cloth-covered tables and pine furniture. The menu offers traditional Mexican specialties such as chicken in mole sauce, carne asada, chiles rellenos, and smoked pork.

RESTAURANT TAPALPA BORREGO, Hidalgo 275. Tel. 2-0156.
Cuisine: BORREGO/ROASTED LAMB.
$ Prices: Borrego dinner $7; borrego birria $4.
Open: Wed–Mon 11am–6pm.

You'll pass this humble but pleasant patio-centered restaurant as you drive in from the main highway—look on your right for its sign, which hangs askew. Most likely you'll see lamb roasting over an open fire just inside the doorway. Sheltered metal tables and chairs line one wall of the patio. The main dish, of course, is delicious and tender borrego, which comes with salsa, tortillas, and beans. The ribs have little meat, so ask for leg meat (*pierna*). On weekends they make borrego birria. It's about two blocks from the main square, walking towards the highway.

5. SAN JUAN DE LOS LAGOS & LAGOS DE MORENO

Two hours northeast of Guadalajara on Highway 80, San Juan de los Lagos (pop. 100,000; alt. 1,895 feet) receives more than five million visitors a year. The majority of people arrive during the months of February, May, and December and during Easter week. Most visitors are pilgrims paying homage to the Virgin of San Juan de los Lagos, whose tiny image is encased in gold leaf over the altar of the Basilica de San Juan de los Lagos. The village was founded soon after the conquest, but it wasn't until 1939 that the event that made it a famous religious site occurred. In that year, a small girl is said to have fallen on a knife and died in the garden in front of the home of Ana Lucia. The next day, before burying the child, Ana Lucia placed the figure of the Virgin de la Concepción (which had been in her care), on the child's chest. The mourning crowd was astounded when the child returned to life. Word of the miracle spread, and since then penitents from around the world come to ask favors of the Virgin and to give thanks for her intervention in their lives. For years they gathered at the chapel erected on the spot where the child came to life, which was the church of a small hospital with an adjacent guesthouse. Today that place is called the Capilla del Primer Milagro, or "Chapel of the First Miracle"; the figure has been moved to the larger Basilica de San Juan on the town's central square.

Located in an area of the state called Los Altos de Jalisco (the highlands of Jalisco), the region is rich in cattle and milk production. That abundance of milk is turned into candy, cheese, and rompope, which is sold widely, especially in San Juan de los Lagos. San Juan (as it's called locally) is a sunny city in a small deep valley (locals refer to it as a "well") with narrow streets which eventually climb in and out of the well.

Neighboring Lagos de Moreno (pop. 140,000; alt. 1,965 feet), a city with a beautiful colonial center, was also founded in the 16th century and is only 21 miles farther, but is colder and dryer than San Juan and has wide streets. Although San Juan is the focus of pilgrims, and has the most shops, Lagos (as it is referred to by locals) has the greater variety of hotels, restaurants, and beautifully preserved colonial buildings. *Lagos* means "lakes" in Spanish; once there were three lakes in the area, but only a small portion of one remains today. The latter part of the town's name honors Pedro Moreno, a valiant freedom fighter who was born here and gave his life in the Mexican War for Independence. Lagos has always been a way station for travelers— it's a natural stopping-point on a journey inland to or from either coast via Guadalajara. Both Lagos and San Juan are worth a detour in your journey through this part of Mexico.

Most of the year both cities are tranquil places, with orderly traffic and plenty of hotel space if you arrive early in the day. However, in February around 50,000 penitents arrive on foot for **Día de la Candelaria,** February 2, and they stay in and near San Juan until around the 8th of February. Large groups carrying banners can be seen streaming toward San Juan on all the major highways of Mexico around this time, and the national news charts the progress of these pilgrims daily. Around **Easter** at least 120,000 pilgrims come in a 15-day period. All of May is a festival month, called the **"Mez de María"** or (Mary's month), and **"Las Fiestas de la Primavera"** (spring festivals). It's a combination cultural, agricultural, and religious event. There are reunions of bricklayers and other commercial groups on different days, fireworks, music, parades, and charreadas. Between May 18 and 31 afternoon processions feature giant papier-mâché figures. A pilgrimage for the **Assumption of the Virgin,** which culminates on August 15th, attracts 80,000 pilgrims, most of them traveling by bicycle. The whole month of **December** is given over to religious devotion, with around 150,000 visitors arriving primarily between December 1 and 8.

San Juan de los Lagos is easily reached from Guadalajara's Central Camionera on the first class La Alteña, Transportes Frontera, Oriente, and Estrella Blanca lines. Servicios Coordinadores has luxury service twice daily. You'll arrive in San Juan's clean bus station, which is near downtown, but too far to walk with luggage. Taxis are always in front and cost around $2 to town center.

For returning to Guadalajara or going on to Lagos de Moreno there are several choices: La Alteña (tel. 5-1223), Oriente (tel. 5-0625), and Estrella Blanca (tel. 5-0051) go to Guadalajara every hour and to Lagos every 30 minutes. Transportes Frontera (tel. 5-0051) has buses every half hour to Guadalajara and to Lagos de Moreno every hour from 9am to 11pm. Servicios Coordinadores (tel. 5-1738) has luxury buses twice daily.

The **State Tourism Office,** Callejon Fortuna 5 (tel. 378/15-0979), is in San Juan de los Lagos, only a block from the central plaza at the corner of Rita Pérez de Moreno and Fray Antonio de Segovina. Ask for José Rangel, who can answer any questions in English. The office is on the second floor and is open Monday through Friday from 9am to 8pm and Saturday from 9am to 1pm.

SAN JUAN DE LOS LAGOS

The town spreads out below as you enter from Highway 80, and the towers of the Basilica de San Juan de los Lagos on the central plaza stand out prominently in the midst of it all. Parking is scarce on the narrow streets of the central city, so if you're driving, you might consider parking and taking a taxi to any sites beyond the downtown area.

WHAT TO SEE & DO

The heart of the city is the **Plaza Principal** with the Basilica de San Juan de los Lagos at one end and a parklike plaza with grand fountain at the other. Strolling musicians and sellers of religious memorabilia frequent the plaza, and streets fanning out from it are chock-a-block with stores selling milk and cream based candy, cajeta, and rompope. This is the place to get the heartbeat of San Juan—to watch religion and commerce meet.

BASILICA DE SAN JUAN DE LOS LAGOS, Plaza Principal. No phone.

The famed Virgin of San Juan de los Lagos is housed over the altar of the basilica, which is the focal point of the city and of the broad central square that is the city's hub. Made inside and out of rose cantera stone, the basilica is beautiful inside, especially the altar with the Virgin dressed in her blue and gold cape and crown. But it's plain compared to the Paroquia de la Asunción in Lagos de Moreno, owing to remodeling early this century that removed most of its colonial adornments. To the right of the altar is a room full of ex-votos (painted personal requests or tributes to the Virgin), made by people from all over the world. So many of these have been left over the years that the church is starting a small museum of them next to the Posito (church) de la Virgen at the end of Iturbide, which runs in front of the church and to the right of the basilica. In the basilica a private room below the altar holds religious paintings that—to set the record straight—are attributed to the school of Rubens, but don't bear the master's signature. Though not open to the public, the preserved bedroom made especially for Pope John Paul II's 1990 visit is in the priest's private living area. Other rooms in that section hold photographs of the pope made during his visit. On Sunday the first mass is at 5:30am and thereafter almost hourly until 7:30pm. Weekdays the first mass is at 8:30am with a daily schedule similar to Sunday and a final mass at 7:30pm. Visitors can enter any time, but are requested to respect a mass in progress.

CAPILLA DEL PRIMER MILAGRO, Lius Moreno at Primavera. No phone.

A short walk from the basilica, this small chapel and room next door commemorate the first miracle attributed to the Virgin of San Juan de los Lagos. More significant than beautiful, it is still a most revered spot where thousands of visitors spend a few moments during their visit to the city. To find it from the main plaza, with your back to the front of the basilica take the side street to the right of the basilica for four blocks. You'll see the white facade of the church on the right at the corner of Primavera.

MUSEO CRISTERO, Plaza Principal. No phone.

This small museum commemorates the Cristero Rebellion (1926–29), which was particularly brutal in this part of Mexico. When President Calles placed restrictions on the Catholic church, it set off a rebellion among the masses that is remembered to this day as one of the worst epochs in the country's history. This private museum has a small room full of photographs and newspaper clippings that chronicle the bloody event. It's open daily from 8am to 8pm. Admission is $1.

Shopping

In San Juan de los Lagos it's impossible to leave without seeing the many vendors of locally made coconut and milk candy, *cajeta* (caramelized cow's milk), *rompope* (similar to eggnog), and religious objects pertaining to the Virgin de San Juan. Shop after shop sells almost the same type of goods. Scattered among them are shops selling hand-knitted and embroidered objects—tablecloths, dresses, doilies, and sweaters—a cottage industry that's been thriving for decades. Often women set up a row of tables of these handmade items and continue knitting and embroidering while passersby browse. Besides these you can find a small selection of pottery from Tonalá and wooden toys from Michoacán. The streets fanning out from the basilica are the most prolific, but your San Juan shopping experience begins with a lineup of such stalls even at the bus station.

EL NEGOCIO, Plaza Principal 6. Tel. 5-0626.
If you're outfitting yourself or your horse, this is the place to visit. For more than 20 years at this location they've been dressing cowboys with straw and felt hats, boots, saddles, chaps, stirrups—well, the works. Just to satisfy tourists they have a few gawdy charro hats and sun hats for women. It's on the main plaza and it's open Monday through Saturday from 9am to 2pm and 4 to 8pm.

WHERE TO STAY

HOTEL POSADA ARCOS, Plaza Principal, San Juan de los Lagos, Jal. 47000. Tel. 378/5-1580. Fax 378/5-1590. 140 rms. TV TEL
$ Rates: $30 single; $42 double; $46 suite. **Parking:** Free.
This hotel's appealing and spacious pale gray marble lobby with black marble columns makes an inviting impression. Halls and rooms in this four-story hotel are carpeted. Rooms, all nicely furnished, have windows facing the halls and nice-size bathrooms. This is an excellent choice on the main plaza and there's a nice restaurant off the lobby.

HOTEL PRIMAVERA, Primavera 13, San Juan de los Lagos, Jal. 47000. Tel. 378/5-1506. Fax 378/5-2220. 62 rms. TV TEL
$ Rates: $37 single; $48 double.
A block from the famed Capilla del Primer Milagro, this neat little four-story hotel is another good choice (it also has an elevator). Tiled halls lead to rooms with windows opening to an airshaft and small all-tile bathrooms. Sinks are inside the shower stalls. Beds are firm and come in various sizes from king-size to twin. There's a restaurant serving all three meals. To find it, with your back to the front of the basilica, take the street on the right side and walk ahead about four blocks to the Capilla de la Primer Milagro (on the right) and turn left there onto Primavera; the Hotel is ahead on the left with a visible sign.

WHERE TO DINE

The two hotels mentioned above have nice restaurants and besides the restaurants mentioned below there are several other nice lunchroom-type eateries on the main plaza. The **market**, where there are always a dozen or so small cook shops, is catercorner from the basilica.

LONCHERIA ARCOS, Portal Hidalgo 5. Tel. 5-0219.
Cuisine: SANDWICHES.
$ Prices: Tortas $1.60–$2; tostadas $1.15.
Open: Daily 8am–10pm.
Just around the corner from the basilica, this *loncheria* (sandwich shop) is tucked in among the stores selling candy and clothing opposite the downtown market. A dozen stools are pulled up around a narrow counter facing the cook's stove so you can watch how clean it's kept during the miracle of producing quantities of fast food in such tight quarters. Sandwiches (tortas) come on delicious french bread and in several combinations. Plus they can serve up a hamburger with fries, tostadas, enchiladas, and

hot dogs. Coffee is serve-yourself—hot water and instant coffee. Service is quick and friendly. From the basilica it's on the right corner of the square, a few steps around the corner.

RESTAURANT SEÑORIAL, Plaza Principal. Tel. 5-1270.
Cuisine: MEXICAN.
$ Prices: Breakfast $2.75–$3.50; main courses $4.75 to $8.50; comida corrida $6.25.
Open: Daily 7am–10pm.

You can't miss this clean lunchroom with its polite waiters, located opposite the basilica on the main plaza. Take a seat in the front and watch the people on the plaza. Choose from a variety of preparations of chicken, beef, pork, and enchiladas. Service is quick, friendly, and efficient, but come before 1:30pm when the downtown lunch crowd begins to arrive.

LAGOS DE MORENO

Located 21 miles north of San Juan de los Lagos, Lagos de Moreno's beautiful central plaza is shaded by handsome Indian laurel trees and surrounded by colonial-era buildings made of the rose cantera stone so abundant in the area. On one side is the lovely 200-year-old Parroquía de la Asuncion, the downtown area's most prominent church. Lagos's preserved colonial city is worth a stop to stroll the streets and nose in and out of stores and churches. The city's main festival, **"Feria de Agosto,"** honors the Image of Calvario. The main day is August 6, but the fair goes on for a week before and after that date with dances, parades, charreadas, cock fights, painting expositions, and mechanical rides.

WHAT TO SEE & DO

If you're driving, you'll be glad to know parking is not as difficult in the downtown area of Lagos as it is in San Juan. Most places of interest are in and around the central plaza called the Jardín Juárez. The post office is the modern building (also made with rose cantera stone) that seems a bit out of place surrounded by colonial buildings to one side of the Jardín Juárez.

PARROQUIA DE LA ASUNCION, Jardín Juárez. No phone.

The most imposing building in the central city is the parroquía, finished in 1784 with a baroque facade of rose cantera stone and a beautiful wrought-iron fence defining its boundaries. It's in use today as the parish church. The interior mesquite floors with a geometric pattern lead to the altar, over which is a mural of the Virgin Mary ascending to heaven on a cloud of cherubs. Encased to the right is what is believed to be the visible body of Saint Hermon, which was sent to San Juan in 1791. Below the main floor are crypts of priests dating from the late 1800s to the early 1900s. In the Salon Cristo Rey (a side room off the sanctuary) are paintings of the bishops of Guadalajara and the first cardinal of Mexico, José Garibi y Rivera, who achieved that title in 1958.

MUSEO CASA DE CAPELLANES. Off the main plaza. No phone.

Built as a temple and convent in 1756, it also served as a jail during the Cristero Rebellion. Now it's a museum housing the murals of Gabriel Flores which were painted in 1964 and depict the often heated history of the country and the area. It's open Tuesday through Sunday from 9am to 2pm and 4 to 7pm.

TEMPLO EL CALVARIO, on a hill above town. No phone.
With sweeping views of the town from its grand front steps, this beautiful late-19th-century stone church hovers over the town. You notice first the grand mesquite wood doors and floors then the murals of saints in the cupola above the altar. In the sacristy is a painting of the last supper with 13 apostles. When asked why there were 13 apostles, the artist replied, "One ate and ran."

Shopping

There aren't as many candy shops here as in San Juan, and in fact shopping is a bit scant on the whole. You'll have to wander the streets to find deals you can't live without. Besides the antique shop mentioned below, there are several others in the downtown area. Shops are closed between 2 and 4pm Monday through Saturday and all day Sunday.

MONTECRISTO ANTIGUIDADES. Hidalgo 494. Tel. 2-0249.
A shop housed in a wonderful one-story 19th-century home, Montecristo has two patios surrounded with rooms full of antiques. Hallways brim over with old doors and other architectural embellishments scavenged from the country's once-grand estates. It's open Monday through Saturday from 10am to 2pm and 4 to 7pm and Sunday from 10am to 2pm.

WHERE TO STAY

Because Lagos is a commercial area, lodging here seems to cater more to the business traveler than the tourist, and is overpriced in comparison to similar towns elsewhere in the country.

CASA GRANDE, Carretera Lagos San Juan, Lagos de Moreno, Jal. Tel. 474/2-1392 or 2-1926. 119 rms. A/C TV TEL
$ Rates: $116 single or double. **Parking:** Free.
Certainly the nicest hotel in the area, it almost seems like a hotel better suited for Puerto Vallarta than an out-of-the-way inland town. Spacious and modern, it's built around a grand courtyard with a kiosk and large swimming pool. The all-tile hallways flow into handsomely decorated tile-floored rooms. Rooms come with a choice of a king-size bed or two double beds and some have a VCR. Two restaurants cover all three meals. Because it's next to the charro stadium just out of Lagos de Moreno on the road to San Juan de los Lagos, it's a bit inconvenient for those without cars. However, the hotel offers free transportation into Lagos.

HOTEL COLONIAL, Hidalgo 279. Lagos de Moreno, Jal. Tel. 474/2-0142. Fax 474/2-0142. 29 rms. TV TEL FAN
$ Rates: $71 single; $77 double. There's usually a 20% discount. **Parking:** Free.
Wonderful blue and yellow tile greets you upon arrival at the Hotel Colonial, the 17th-century house of the Conde Rul. Only the lobby area hints of grand days as a mansion; the two stories of rooms have long since taken on the look of a comfortable old hotel, complete with a sitting area on the landing. Most rooms are carpeted and have windows opening onto the tile hallway. A nice restaurant just off the lobby serves

all three meals. To find it, with your back to the parroquía, walk left ½ block and it's on the right.

HOTEL PARIS, Gonzalez León 339, Lagos de Moreno, Jal. Tel. 474/2-0200 or 2-0201. 36 rms.
$ **Rates:** $15.50 single; $19.25 double.

Just opposite the parroquía, this cavernous mansion-turned-hotel is a more reasonably priced alternative to the Hotel Colonial. It's 50 years old and undergoing a slow renovation. Rooms, all with high ceilings, have one double bed or two twin beds, nice plaid bedspreads, soft mattresses, and lights over each bed. Bathrooms are aging but clean and come with either showers or tub/shower combinations—but no shower curtain. It's on the main plaza next to the Banco Serfin.

WHERE TO DINE

ADOBES, Carretera Panamericana. Tel. 2-0625.
   Cuisine: MEXICAN/INTERNATIONAL.
$ **Prices:** Appetizers $5–$8; main courses $10–$20.
   Open: Mon–Sat 8am–11:30pm; Sun 8am–8pm.

The newest and also the most sophisticated restaurant in town, Adobes caught on big when it opened in 1992 and hasn't let up. As the name implies, the handsome adobe walls set a rustically beautiful background for the use of Mexican tile, cloth-covered tables, and elegant pewter serving plates. Beef and pork reign supreme, but there's seafood and chicken too. The *filete especial Adobes* is steak with bacon, mushrooms, and black-bean sauce. The pollo especial is a delightfully marinated chicken breast and comes with a fresh green salad. For dessert the café adobe, which is coffee flavored with ice cream and rum, may catch your eye. To find it ask directions; it's only slightly out of town across the railroad tracks on Highway 80 going towards San Luis Potosí.

LA HACIENDA, Hidalgo 460. Tel. 2-0665.
   Cuisine: MEXICAN.
$ **Prices:** Breakfast $2.50–$3; main courses $7–$12.
   Open: Daily 8am–11pm.

Another locally popular dining spot, La Hacienda is small but spiffy, with cloth-covered tables and waiters wearing black and white. Specialties include beef tampiqueña, *lomo de cerdo adobado* (pork loin baked in a spicy broth), and *sopa medula* (bone-marrow soup). Snacks include queso fundido, tacos, and guacamole with tostados. To find it from the main plaza, with your back to the church walk right two blocks and it's on the corner.

RESTAURANT RIVERA, Camarena 364. Tel. 2-0879.
   Cuisine: MEXICAN.
$ **Prices:** Breakfast $2.75; main courses $4.75–$9.75; comida corrida $5.75.
   Open: Daily 8:30am–9:30pm.

Dependable and plain with Formica tables and chairs, this is the place for a good meal at reasonable prices. The comida corrida includes soup, main course, beans, and dessert. Every Sunday a pot of menudo brings in the locals. It's on the street behind the parroquía church and a half a block to the left.

LA RINCONADA, Constituyentes 425. Tel. 2-3404.
   Cuisine: MEXICAN/REGIONAL.
$ **Prices:** Salad and soup $3.45–$5; main courses $7.75–$10.
   Open: Thurs–Tues 1–11pm.

A handsome, gleaming little place with tile floors and arched doorways, La Rinconada is very popular with locals who consider it a treat to eat here. There's usually a daily special of traditional Mexican food such as chiles rellenos or almond chicken. But the menu is a full one with fish, shrimp, and beef, and there's a lengthy bar list. To find the restaurant from the main plaza, with your back to the front of the church, turn right one block, then left and it's on the left.

APPENDIX

FOR YOUR INFORMATION

A. VOCABULARY
B. MENU SAVVY
C. CONVERSION TABLES

A. VOCABULARY

Traveling on or off the beaten track, you will encounter many people in service positions who do not speak English. Many Mexicans who can understand English are embarrassed to speak it. And finally most Mexicans are very patient with foreigners who try to speak their language; it helps a lot to know a few basic phrases.

Berlitz's *Latin American Spanish for Travellers*, available at most bookstores for $4, cannot be recommended highly enough. But for added convenience, I've included a list of certain simple phrases for expressing basic needs, followed by some menu items presented in the same order in which they'd be found on a Mexican menu.

BASIC VOCABULARY

Good day	Buenos días	bway-nohss *dee*-ahss
How are you?	¿Cómo esta usted?	*koh*-moh ess-*tah* oo-sted
Very well	Muy bien	mwee byen
Thank you	Gracias	*grah*-see-ahss
You're welcome	De nada	day *nah*-dah
Good-bye	Adios	ah-dyo*hss*
Please	Por favor	pohr *fah*-bohr
Yes	Sí	see
No	No	noh
Excuse me	Perdóneme	pehr-*doh*-ney-may
Give me	Déme	*day*-may
Where is . . . ?	¿Dónde esta . . . ?	*dohn*-day ess-*tah*
The station	la estación	la ess-tah-see-*own*
A hotel	un hotel	oon *oh*-tel
A gas station	una gasolinera	oon-nuh gah-so-lee-*nay*-rah
A restaurant	un restaurante	oon res-tow-*rahn*-tay
The toilet	el baño	el *bahn*-yoh
A good doctor	un buen médico	oon bwayn *may*-dee-co
The road to . . .	el camino a . . .	el cah-*mee*-noh *ah*
To the right	A la derecha	ah lah day-*ray*-chuh
To the left	A la izquierda	ah lah ees-ky-*ehr*-dah
Straight ahead	Derecho	day-*ray*-cho
I would like	Quisiera	keyh-see-*air*-ah
I want	Quiero	kyehr-oh
To eat	comer	*ko*-mayr

APPENDIX: VOCABULARY • 221

English	Spanish	Pronunciation
A room	una habitación	oon-nuh ha-bee-tah-see-*own*
Do you have?	¿Tiene usted?	tyah-nay *oos*-ted
How much is it?	¿Cuanto cuesta?	*kwahn*-to *kwess*-tah
When?	¿Cuando?	*kwahn*-doh
What?	¿Que?	kay
There is (Is there?)	¿Hay . . .	eye
Yesterday	Ayer	*ah*-yer
Today	Hoy	oy
Tomorrow	Mañana	mahn-*yawn*-ah
Good	Bueño	*bway*-no
Bad	Malo	*mah*-lo
Better (best)	(Lo) Mejor	(loh) meh-*hor*
More	Más	mahs
Less	Menos	*may*-noss
No Smoking	Se prohibe fumar	seh pro-*hee*-beh foo-*mahr*
Postcard	Tarjeta postal	tahr-*hay*-ta pohs-*tahl*
Insect repellent	Rapellante contra insectos	rah-pey-*yahn*-te *cohn*-trah een-*sehk*-tos

1 **uno** (ooh-noh)	15 **quince** (*keen*-say)	60 **sesenta** (say-*sen*-tah)
2 **dos** (dohs)	16 **dieciseis** (de-ess-ee-*sayss*)	70 **setenta** (say-*ten*-tah)
3 **tres** (trayss)	17 **diecisiete** (de-ess-ee-see-*ay*-tay)	80 **ochenta** (oh-*chen*-tah)
4 **cuatro** (kwah-troh)	18 **dieciocho** (dee-ess-ee-*oh*-choh)	90 **noventa** (noh-*ben*-tah)
5 **cinco** (seen-koh)	19 **diecinueve** (dee-ess-ee-*nway*-bay)	100 **cien** (see-*en*)
6 **seis** (sayss)	20 **veinte** (*bayn*-tay)	200 **doscientos** (dos-se-*en*-tos)
7 **siete** (syeh-tay)	30 **treinta** (*trayn*-tah)	500 **quinientos** (keen-ee-*ehn*-tos)
8 **ocho** (oh-choh)	40 **cuarenta** (kwah-*ren*-tah)	1,000 **mil** (meal)
9 **nueve** (nway-bay)	50 **cincuenta** (seen-*kwen*-tah)	
10 **diez** (dee-ess)		
11 **once** (ohn-say)		
12 **doce** (doh-say)		
13 **trece** (tray-say)		
14 **catorce** (kah-tor-say)		

USEFUL PHRASES

Do you speak English? **¿Habla usted inglés?**
Is there anyone here who speaks English? **¿Hay alguien aquí qué hable inglés?**
I don't understand Spanish very well. **No lo entiendo muy bien el español.**
What time is it? **¿Qué hora es?**
May I see your menu? **¿Puedo ver su menu?**
The check, please. **La cuenta por favor.**
What do I owe you? **¿Cuanto lo debo?**
What did you say? **¿Mande? (colloquial expression for American "Eh?")**
I want (to see) a room **Quiero (ver) un cuarto (una habitación)**
for two persons. **para dos personas**
with (without) bath. **con (sin) baño**

We are staying here only 1 night (1 week). **Nos quedaremos aqui solamente una noche (una semana).**

We are leaving tomorrow. **Partimos mañana.**
Do you accept traveler's checks? **¿Acepta usted cheques de viajero?**

BUS TERMS

Autobus Bus
Camión Bus or truck
Carril Lane
Directo Nonstop
Equipajes Baggage (claim area)
Foraneo Intercity
Guarda equipaje Luggage storage area
Llegadas Gates
Local Originates at this station

De Paso Originates elsewhere; stops if seats available
Primera First (class)
Recibo de Equipajes Baggage-claim area
Sala de Espera Waiting room
Sanitarios Toilets
Segunda Second (class)
Sin Escala Nonstop
Taquilla Ticket window

POSTAL TERMS

Aduana Customs
Apdo. Postal Post office box (abbreviation)
Buzón Mailbox
Correo Aéreo Airmail
Correos Postal service
Entrega Inmediata Special Delivery, Express

Estampilla or Timbre Stamp
Giro Postal Money order
Lista de Correos General Delivery
Oficina de Correos Post office
Paquete Parcel
Registrado Registered Mail
Seguros Insurance (insured mail)
Sello Rubber Stamp

B. MENU SAVVY

BREAKFAST [DESAYUNO]

Jugo de naranja orange juice
Café con crema coffee with cream
Pan tostada toast
Mermelada jam
Leche milk
Té tea
Huevos eggs
Huevos cocidos hard-boiled eggs

Huevos poches poached eggs
Huevos fritos fried eggs
Huevos pasados al agua soft-boiled eggs
Huevos revueltos scrambled eggs
Tocino bacon
Jamón ham

LUNCH, SUPPER & DINNER [ALMUERZO, COMIDA & CENA]

SOUP [SOPA]

Caldo broth
Caldo de pollo chicken broth

Menudo tripe soup
Sopa clara consommé

Sopa de lentejas lentil soup
Sopa de chicharos pea soup
Sopa de medula bone-marrow soup

SEAFOOD [MARISCOS]

Almejas clams
Anchoas anchovies
Arenques herring
Atun tuna
Bagre catfish
Cabrilla black sea bass
Calamares squid
Camarones shrimp
Caracoles snails
Corvina bass
Dorado dolphinfish
Gallo roosterfish
Huachinango red snapper
Jaiba crab
Jurel yellowtail
Langosta lobster
Lenguado sole
Lobina black bass
Macabi bonefish
Marlin azul blue marlin
Marlin blanco white marlin
Marlin rayado striped marlin
Mero grouper
Mojarra perch
Ostiones oysters
Pescado fish
Peto wahoo
Pez espada swordfish
Pez vela sailfish
Robalo sea bass/snook
Sabalo tarpon
Salmón salmon
Salmón ahumado smoked salmon
Sardinas sardines
Solo pike
Trucha arco iris rainbow trout

MEATS [CARNES]

Ahumado smoked
Alambre shish kebab
Albóndigas meatballs
Aves poultry
Bistec steak
Cabeza de ternera calf's head
Cabrito kid (goat)
Callos tripe
Carne meat
Carne fría cold cuts
Cerdo pork
Chiles rellenos stuffed peppers
Chicharrones pigskin cracklings
Chorizo spicy sausage
Chuleta chop
Chuleta de carnero mutton chop
Chuletas de cordero lamb chops
Chuletas de puerco pork chops
Conejo rabbit
Cordero lamb
Costillas de cerdo spareribs
Faisán pheasant
Filete de ternera filet of veal
Filete milanesa breaded veal chops
Ganso goose
Hígado liver
Jamón ham
Lengua tongue
Lomo loin
Paloma pigeon
Pato duck
Pavo turkey
Pechuga chicken breast
Perdiz partridge
Pierna leg
Pollo chicken
Res beef
Riñones kidneys
Salchichas sausages
Ternera veal
Tocino bacon
Venado venison

VEGETABLES [LEGUMBRES]

Aguacate avocado
Aceitunas olives
Arroz rice
Betabeles beets
Cebolla onions
Champinones mushrooms

Chicharos peas
Col cabbage
Coliflor cauliflower
Ejotes string beans
Elote corn (maize)
Entremeses hors d'oeuvres
Esparragos asparagus
Espinaca spinach
Frijoles beans
Hongos mushroom
Jícama potato/turnip-like vegetable
Lechuga lettuce
Lentejas lentils
Papas potatoes
Pepino cucumber
Rabanos radishes
Tomate tomato
Verduras greens, vegetables
Zanahoras carrots

SALADS [ENSALADAS]

Ensalada de apio celery salad
Ensalada de frutas fruit salad
Ensalada mixta mixed salad
Ensalada de pepinos cucumber salad
Guacamole avocado salad
Lechuga lettuce salad

FRUITS [FRUTAS]

Chavacano apricot
Ciruela prune
Coco coconut
Durazno peach
Frambuesa raspberry
Fresas con crema strawberries with cream
Fruta cocida stewed fruit
Granada pomegranate
Guanabana green pearlike fruit
Guayaba guava
Higos figs
Lima lime
Limón lemon
Mamey sweet orange fruit
Mango mango
Manzana apple
Naranja orange
Pera pear
Piña pineapple
Platano banana
Tuna prickly pear fruit
Uva grape
Zapote sweet brown fruit

DESSERTS [POSTRES]

Arroz con leche rice pudding
Brunelos de fruta fruit tart
Coctel de aguacate avocado cocktail
Coctel de frutas fruit cocktail
Compota stewed fruit
Fruta fruit
Flan custard
Galletas crackers or cookies
Helado ice cream
Nieve sherbet
Pastel cake or pastry
Queso cheese
Torta cake
Yogurt yogurt

BEVERAGES [BEBIDAS]

Agua water
Brandy brandy
Café coffee
Café con crema coffee with cream
Café de olla coffee with cinnamon and sugar
Café negro black coffee
Cerveza beer
Ginebra gin
Hielo ice
Jerez sherry
Jugo de naranja orange juice
Jugo de tomate tomato juice
Jugo de toronja grapefruit juice

Leche milk
Licores liqueurs
Manzanita apple juice
Refrescos soft drinks
Ron rum
Sidra cider
Sifón soda
Té tea
Vaso de leche glass of milk
Vino blanco white wine
Vino tinto red wine

CONDIMENTS & CUTLERY

Aceite oil
Ajo garlic
Azúcar sugar
Bolillo roll
Copa goblet
Cilantro coriander
Cuchara spoon
Cuchillo knife
Manteca lard
Mantequilla butter
Mostaza mustard
Pan bread
Pimienta pepper
Sal salt
Sopa de arroz plain rice
Taza cup
Tenedor fork
Tostada toast
Vinagre vinegar
Vaso glass

PREPARATIONS

A la parrilla grilled
Al horno baked
Asado roasted
Bien cocido well done
Cocido cooked
Cocina casera home cooking
Empanado breaded
Frito fried
Milanesa Italian breaded
Poco cocido rare
Tampiqueño long strip of thinly sliced meat
Veracruzana tomato, garlic, and onion-topped

MENU ITEMS

Achiote Small red seed of the annatto tree
Achiote preparada A prepared paste found in Yucatán markets made of ground achiote, wheat and corn flour, cumin, cinnamon, salt, onion, garlic, oregano; use mixed with juice of a sour orange or vinegar and put on broiled or charcoaled fish (tikin chick) and chicken
Agua fresca Fruit-flavored water, usually watermelon, cantaloupe, chia seed with lemon, hibiscus flour, or ground melon-seed mixture
Antojito A Mexican snack, usually masa based with a variety of toppings such as sausage, cheese, beans, onions; also refers to tostadas, sopes, and garnachas
Atole A thick, lightly sweet, warm drink made with finely ground rice or corn and flavored usually with vanilla; often found mornings and evenings at markets
Birote Similar to a bolillo, but rounder and used often as a dinner roll or for sandwiches around Lake Chapala
Birria Lamb or goat meat cooked in a tomato broth spiced with garlic, chiles, cumin, ginger, oregano, cloves, cinnamon, thyme, and garnished with onions and cilantro and fresh lime juice to taste; a specialty of Jalisco state
Borrego al pastor A specialty around Tapalpa, Jalisco, is roast lamb basted and cooked over an open wood fire
Botana A light Mexican snack—an antojito
Buñelos Round, thin, deep-fried crispy fritters dipped in sugar or dribbled with honey

Burrito A large flour tortilla stuffed with beans or sometimes potatoes and onions

Cabrito Roast kid; a northern Mexico delicacy

Cajeta Caramelized cow or goat milk often used in dessert crêpes

Caldo Michi A Lake Chapala specialty of catfish soup in a base of onions and tomatoes

Carnitas Pork that's been deep-cooked (not fried) in lard, then steamed and served with corn tortillas for tacos

Caviar de Chapala Carp eggs, usually seasoned and fried and made into tacos or soup

Ceviche Fresh raw seafood marinated in fresh lime juice and garnished with chopped tomatoes, onions, chiles, and sometimes cilantro and served with crispy, fried whole corn tortillas; in Colima sailfish is preferred and they use less lime in the preparation

Charales Dried minnows, a specialty around Lake Chapala and Lake Pátzcuaro, served with lime and sprinkle of chile pepper

Chayote Vegetable pear or mirliton, a type of spiny squash boiled and served as an accompaniment to meat dishes

Chiles rellenos Poblano peppers usually stuffed with cheese, rolled in a batter and baked; but other stuffings may include ground beef spiced with raisins

Chorizo A spicy red pork sausage, flavored with different chiles and sometimes with achiote, or cumin and other spices

Churro Tube-shaped bread fritter, dipped in sugar and sometimes filled with cajeta or chocolate

Cilantro An herb grown from the coriander seed, chopped and used in salsas and soups

Cochinita pibil Pig wrapped in banana leaves, flavored with pibil sauce and pit-baked; common in Yucatán

Corunda A triangular-shaped tamal wrapped in a corn leaf, a Michoacán specialty

Enchilada Tortilla dipped in a sauce and usually filled with chicken or white cheese and sometimes topped with tomato sauce and sour cream (enchiladas suizas—Swiss enchiladas) or covered in a green sauce (enchiladas verdes) or topped with onions, sour cream and guacamole (enchiladas potosiños)

Epazote Leaf of the wormseed plant, used in black beans, and with cheese in quesadillas

Escabeche A lightly pickled sauce used in Yucatán chicken stew

Frijoles boda A specialty of Colima, "married beans" are refried beans (*frijoles refritos*) mixed with bacon, guajillo chile, and black papper and sprinkled with dry cheese

Frijoles charros Beans flavored with beer, a northern Mexico specialty

Frijoles refritos Pinto beans mashed and cooked with lard

Garnachas A thickish small circle of fried masa with pinched sides, topped with pork or chicken, onions, and avocado, or sometimes chopped potatoes and tomatoes, typical as a botana in Veracruz and Yucatán

Gorditas Thickish fried corn tortillas, slit and stuffed with choice of cheese, beans, beef, chicken, with or without lettuce, tomato, and onion garnish

Guacamole Mashed avocado, plain or mixed with onions and other spices

Gusanos de maguey Maguey worms, considered a delicacy and delicious when charbroiled to a crisp and served with corn tortillas for tacos

Horchata Refreshing drink made of ground rice or melon seeds, ground almonds, and lightly sweetened

Huevos mexicanos Scrambled eggs with onions, hot peppers, and tomatoes

Huevos motuleños Eggs atop a tortilla, garnished with beans, peas, ham, sausage, and grated cheese, a Yucatecan specialty

Huevos rancheros Fried egg on top of a fried corn tortilla covered in a tomato sauce

Huitlacoche Sometimes spelled "cuitlacoche," mushroom-flavored black fungus that appears on corn in the rainy season; considered a delicacy

Machaca Shredded dried beef scrambled with eggs or as salad topping; a specialty of northern Mexico

Manchamantel Translated means "tablecloth stainer," a stew of chicken or pork with chiles, tomatoes, pineapple, bananas, and jícama

Masa Ground corn soaked in lime used as basis for tamales, corn tortillas, and soups

Menudo A stew made with cow entrails; Jalisco style is without ground masa (corn) but with a tomato base, spiced with oregano and chile arbol and often with a few leaves of yerba buena

Mixiote Lamb or chicken baked with carrots, potatoes, and sauce in parchment paper from a maguey leaf

Mole Pronounced "*moh*-lay," a sauce made with 20 ingredients including chocolate, peppers, ground tortillas, sesame seeds, cinnamon, tomatoes, onion, garlic, peanuts, pumpkin seeds, cloves, and tomatillos; developed by colonial nuns in Puebla, usually served over chicken or turkey; especially served in Puebla, state of Mexico, and Oaxaca with sauces varying from red to black and brown

Molletes A bolillo cut in half and topped with refried beans and cheese, then broiled; popular at breakfast

Pan de muerto Sweet or plain bread made around the Days of the Dead (November 1–2), in the form of mummies, dolls, or round with bone designs

Pan dulce Lightly sweetened bread in many configurations, usually served at breakfast or bought at any bakery

Papadzules Tortillas are stuffed with hard-boiled eggs and seeds (cucumber or sunflower) in a tomato sauce

Pavo relleno negro Stuffed turkey, Yucatán style, filled with chopped pork and beef, cooked in a rich, dark sauce

Pibil Pit-baked pork or chicken in a sauce of tomato, onion, mild red pepper, cilantro, and vinegar

Pipian Sauce made with ground pumpkin seeds, nuts, and mild peppers

Poc-chuc Slices of pork with onion marinated in a tangy sour orange sauce and charcoal-broiled; a Yucatecan specialty

Pozole A soup made with hominy and pork or chicken, in either a tomato based broth Jalisco-style, or a white broth Nayarit-style, or green chile sauce Guerrero-style, and topped with choice of chopped white onion, lettuce or cabbage, radishes, oregano, red pepper, and cilantro

Pulque Drink made of fermented sap of the maguey plant; best in state of Hidalgo and around Mexico City

Quesadilla Flour tortilla stuffed with melted white cheese and lightly fried or warmed

Queso relleno "Stuffed cheese" is a mild yellow cheese stuffed with minced meat and spices, a Yucatecan specialty

Rompope Delicious Mexican eggnog, invented in Puebla, made with eggs, vanilla, sugar, and rum

Salsa mexicana Sauce of fresh chopped tomatoes, white onions, and cilantro with a bit of oil; on tables all over Mexico

Salsa verde A cooked sauce using the green tomatillo and puréed with mildly hot peppers, onions, garlic, and cilantro; on tables countrywide

Sopa de calabaza Soup made of chopped squash or pumpkin blossoms

Sopa de lima A tangy soup made with chicken broth and accented with fresh lime; popular in Yucatán

Sopa seca Not a soup at all, but a seasoned rice which translated means "dry soup"

Sopa Tarascan A rib sticking pinto bean-based soup, flavored with onions, garlic, tomatoes, chiles, and chicken broth and garnished with sour cream, white cheese, avocado chunks, and fried tortilla strips; a specialty of Michoacán state

Sopa Tlalpeña A hearty soup made with chunks of chicken, chopped carrots, zucchini, corn, onions, garlic, and cilantro

Sopa tortilla A traditional chicken broth-based soup, seasoned with chiles, tomatoes, onion, and garlic, bobbing with crisp fried strips of corn tortillas

Sope Pronounced "*soh*-pay," a botana similar to a garnacha, except spread with refried beans and topped with crumbled cheese and onions

Tacos al pastor Thin slices of flavored pork roasted on a revolving cylinder dripping with onion slices and juice of fresh pineapple slice

Tamal Incorrectly called tamale (*tamal* singular, *tamales* plural), meat or sweet filling rolled with fresh masa then wrapped in a corn husk, a corn or banana leaf and steamed; many varieties and sizes throughout the country

Tepache Drink made of fermented pineapple peelings and brown sugar

Tikin xic Also seen on menus as "tikin chick," charbroiled fish brushed with achiote sauce

Tinga A stew made with pork tenderloin, sausage, onions, garlic, tomatoes, chiles, and potatoes; popular on menus in Puebla and Hidalgo states

Torta Sandwich, usually on bolillo bread, usually with sliced avocado, onions, tomatoes, with a choice of meat and often cheese

Torta ahogados A specialty of Lake Chapala is made with scooped out roll, filled with beans and beef strips, and seasoned with either a tomato or chile sauce

Tostadas Crispy fried corn tortillas topped with meat, onions, lettuce, tomatoes, cheese, avocados, and sometimes sour cream

Venado Venison (deer) served perhaps as pipian de venado, steamed in banana leaves and served with a sauce of ground squash seeds

Ztabentun Pronounced "*shtah*-ben-toon," a Yucatán liquor made of fermented honey, and flavored with anise; it comes seco (dry) or crema (sweet)

Zacahuil Pork leg tamal, packed in thick masa, wrapped in banana leaves and pit baked; sometimes pot-made with tomato and masa; specialty of mid- to upper Veracruz

C. CONVERSION TABLES

METRIC MEASURES

Length

1 millimeter = 0.04 inches (or less than 1/16 in)
1 centimeter = 0.39 inches (or just under 1/2 in)
1 meter = 1.09 yards (or about 39 inches)
1 kilometer = 0.62 miles (or about 2/3 of a mile)

To convert kilometers to miles, multiply the number of kilometers by .62 (for example, 25 km × .62 = 15.5 mi).

To convert miles to kilometers, multiply the number of miles by 1.61 (for example, 50 mi × 1.61 = 80.5 km).

Capacity

1 liter = 33.92 fluid ounces or 1.06 quarts or 0.26 gallons.

To convert liters to gallons, multiply the number of liters by 0.26 (for example, 50 liters × .26 = 13 gallons).

To convert gallons to liters, multiply the number of gallons by 3.79 (for example, 10 gal × 3.79 = 37.9 liters).

Weight

1 gram = 0.04 ounces (or about a paperclip's weight)
1 kilogram = 2.2 pounds

To convert kilograms to pounds, multiply the number of kilograms by 2.2 (for example, 75kg × 2.2 = 165 pounds).

To convert pounds to kilograms, multiply the number of pounds by 0.45 (for example, 90 lb × .45 = 40.5 kg).

Temperature

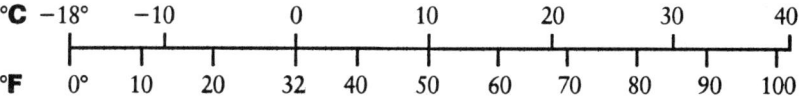

To convert degrees C to degrees F, multiply degrees °C by 9, divide by 5, and add 32 (for example 9/5 × 20°C + 32 = 68°F).

To convert degrees F to degrees C, subtract 32 from degrees F, then multiply by 5, and divide by 9 (for example, 85°F − 32 × 5/9 = 29°C).

CLOTHING SIZE EQUIVALENTS

You'll want to try on clothing you intend to buy, but here are some equivalents in case you're buying gifts for friends. Note that women's blouse sizes are the same in the United States and Mexico.

Women's				Men's					
Dress		Shoes		Collar		Jacket		Shoes	
U.S.	Mex.	U.S.	Mex.	U.S.	Mex.	U.S.	Mex.	U.S.	Mex.
6	36	5	35	14	36	38	48	8	41
8	38	5.5	35.5	14.5	37	40	50	8.5	41.5
10	40	6	36	15	38	42	52	9	42
12	42	6.5	36.5	15.5	39	44	54	9.5	42.5
14	44	7	37	16	40	46	56	10	43
16	46	7.5	37.5	16.5	41	48	58	10.5	43.5
18	48	8	38	17	42	50	60	11	44
20	50	8.5	38.5	17.5	43	52	62	11.5	44.5
22	52	9	39	18	44	54	64	12	45

INDEX

GENERAL INFORMATION

Accommodations:
  Ajijic, 197-8, 200
  Barra de Navidad, 131-2
  Bucerías, 104
  Chapala, 190, 192-4
  Colima, 144
  Costa Careyes, 140-2
  El Tamarindo, 139
  Guadalajara, 157-65
  Jocotepec, 203-4
  Lagos de Moreno, 217-18
  Las Alamandas, 142-3
  Manzanillo, 116-20
  Mazamitla, 205-7
  Melaque, 135-6
  money-saving tips, 79, 158
  Puerto Vallarta, 77-88
  rental options, 69
  San Blas, 107-8
  San José de Gracia, 208-9
  San Juan Cosalá, 203
  San Juan de los Lagos, 215
  Tapalpa, 210-11
  Tecuan, 138-9
  Tenacatita, 138
Adventure/wilderness travel, 46
Airports:
  Guadalajara, 148
  Manzanillo, 110
  Puerto Vallarta, 70
Air travel, to and within Mexico, 48-9, 53-4
Ajijic, 195-202
  map, 199
Alternative and adventure travel, 46
Altitude sickness, 40
American Express:
  Guadalajara, 154
  Manzanillo, 115
  Puerto Vallarta, 73
Architecture, 16-18
Arriving:
  in Guadalajara, 147-8
  in Manzanillo, 110-11
  in Puerto Vallarta, 70-1
Art, 16-18
  Guadalajara, 179
  Puerto Vallarta, 100-1

Barra de Navidad, 129, 131-5
Beaches:
  Manzanillo, 129-30
  Puerto Vallarta, 97
  San Blas, 106-7
Beverages, 24
Birdwatching:
  Manzanillo, 130
  San Blas, 107
Boat tours:
  Barra de Navidad, 135
  Puerto Vallarta, 97
  San Blas, 107

Boat travel and cruises, 52-3
Books, recommended, 24-6
Bribes, 34
Bucerías, 103-5
Bullfights:
  Guadalajara, 178
  Puerto Vallarta, 97
Business hours, 62
Bus travel:
  Guadalajara, 148-50
  Manzanillo, 111, 114, 115
  Mexico, 49, 55-6
  Puerto Vallarta, 70-1, 72-3
  vocabulary terms, 222

Calendar of events, 36-9
Camera/film, 62
Camping, 61-2
  San Blas, 108
Car rentals, 57-9
  confirmation, 58
  costs, 57-8
  damage, 58-9
  Guadalajara, 154-5
  insurance, 58
Cars and driving:
  to and within Guadalajara, 148, 154
  to Manzanillo, 111
  to Mexico, 49-52
    crossing the border, 52
    documents required, 50-1
    insurance, 51-2
    preparation, 52
  within Mexico, 56-62
    breakdowns, 61
    driving rules, 60-1
    gasoline, 59-60
    parking, 61
  to Puerto Vallarta, 71
Cash, 30
Chapala, 188-95
  map, 193
Charter flights, 49
Children, travel tips, 45
Cigarettes, 62
Climate, 35
Clothing sizes, converting, 230
Colima, 143-5
Colimilla, 135
Comala, 145-6
Consulates, 63-4
  Guadalajara, 155
  Puerto Vallarta, 73
Conversion tables, 229
Costa Careyes, 139-42
Cost of everyday items, 32-4
Crafts and folk art:
  Guadalajara, 179
  Puerto Vallarta, 100
Credit cards, 32
Crime, 34-5, 66-7

232 • INDEX

Cruises to Mexico, 52-3
Cuisine, 23-4
Cultural life, 20-1
Currency, 30
  exchange, 32, 155, 189
Customs, 30, 63
  dining, 23
Cuyutlán, 143

Dance, 21-2
Dentists, 63
Departing:
  Guadalajara, 148-50
  Manzanillo, 111, 114
  Puerto Vallarta, 71
Disabled travelers, tips for, 43
Diseases, 40-2
Diving and snorkeling, Puerto Vallarta, 97-8
Doctors, 63
Documents for entry, 29-30
  for cars, 50-1
Drinks, 24
Driving rules, 60-1
Drug laws, 63
Drugstores, 63

Ecology, 3, 6
Educational/study travel, 46
Electricity, 63
El Tamarindo, 139
Embassies and consulates, 63-4
Emergencies, 64
  evacuation procedures, 42
Entertainment and nightlife:
  Ajijic, 196
  Barra de Navidad and Melaque, 137-8
  Guadalajara, 179-81
  Manzanillo, 130
  Puerto Vallarta, 101-3
Entry requirements, 29-30
Etiquette, 64-5

Families, tips for, 45
Famous and historical figures, 11-16
Fast facts, 62-9
  Chapala, 189
  Guadalajara, 154-6
  Manzanillo, 115
  Puerto Vallarta, 73, 76
Ferry service, 62
  to Playa Yelapa, 103
Festivals, 36-9
  Guadalajara, 177-8
  Lagos de Moreno, 216
  Mazamitla, 205
  Puerto Vallarta, 99
  San Juan de los Lagos, 213
  Tlaquepaque, 183
Films, 26-7
Fishing:
  Manzanillo, 130
  Puerto Vallarta, 98
Folklore, 19-20
Food, 22-4

Gasoline, 59-60
Geography, 3, 6
Golf:
  Chapala, 189
  Manzanillo, 130
  Puerto Vallarta, 98
Guadalajara, 147-219
  accommodations, 157-65
  cost of everyday items, 33-4

entertainment and nightlife, 179-81
excursion areas, 182-219
  Lagos de Moreno, 216-19
  Lake Chapala region, 188-204
  Mazamitla, 204-9
  San Juan de Los Lagos, 212-16
  Tapalpa, 209-12
  Tlaquepaque, 183-6
  Tonalá, 186-7
fast facts, 154-6
Frommer's favorite experiences, 175
itineraries, suggested, 170-1
maps, 153
  downtown, 163, 173
  environs, 151
orientation, 147-52
restaurants, 165-9
shopping, 178-9
special events, 177-8
transportation, 152, 154
walking tour, 171-4
Guides, tour, 64-5

Health concerns and precautions, 39-42
History, 6-11
Hitchhiking, 62, 65
Holidays, 36
Homestays, 46
Horseback riding:
  Ajijic, 196
  Chapala, 190
  Mazamitla, 205

Information sources, 28-9
  Ajijic, 194, 196
  Barra de Navidad, 131
  Chapala, 189
  Colima, 144
  Guadalajara, 155
  Manzanillo, 115
  Mazamitla, 205
  Puerto Vallarta, 73, 76
  San Blas, 106
  Tapalpa, 209
  Tlaquepaque, 182
  Tonalá, 182-3
Insurance:
  for car rentals, 58
  for cars, 51-2
  health, 42
Isla de los Alacranes, 189-90
Isla Mezcala, 190

Jocotepec, 203-4
Jungle cruises, San Blas, 107

Lagos de Moreno, 216-19
Lake Chapala region, 188-204
  map, 191
Languages, 20, 65
Las Alamandas, 142-3
Legal aid, 65
Liquor, 24
Literature, 18-19

Mail, 65
Manzanillo, 110-46
  accommodations, 116-20
  cost of everyday items, 33
  entertainment and nightlife, 130
  excursion areas, 132-46
    Barra de Navidad, 129, 131-5
    Colima, 143-5
    Comala, 145-6

GENERAL INFORMATION INDEX • 233

Manzanillo (cont'd)
  Costa Careyes, 139-42
  Cuyutlán, 143
  El Tamarindo, 139
  Las Alamandas, 142-3
  Melaque, 135-8
  Tecuan, 138-9
  Tenacatita, 138
  fast facts, 115
  Frommer's favorite experiences, 129
  itineraries, suggested, 128
  maps, 112-13
    Bay area, 131
    downtown, 123
  orientation, 110-11, 114
  restaurants, 121-7
  sports and recreational activities, 129-30
  transportation, 115
Maps:
  Ajijic, 199
  to buy, 65
  Barra de Navidad Bay area, 133
  Chapala, 193
  Guadalajara, 153
    downtown, 163
    environs, 151
    walking tour, 173
  Lake Chapala region, 191
  Manzanillo, 112-13
    downtown, 123
  Mexico, 4-5
  Mid-Pacific Coast, 31
  Puerto Vallarta, 74-5
    downtown, 91
Matanchen, 106
Mazamitla, 204-9
Measurements, converting, 229-30
Melaque, 135-8
Money, 30, 32-3
Music, 21-2
  Guadalajara, 179-81
  Manzanillo, 130
  Puerto Vallarta, 102
Mythology, 19-20

Neighborhoods:
  Guadalajara, 150, 152
  Manzanillo, 114
  Puerto Vallarta, 72
Newsletters, 29, 44
Newspapers, 65-6

Package tours, 53
Packing for your trip, 42-3
Parking your car, 61
Peoples, 20-1
Performing arts, 21-2
Pets, 66
Photographic needs, 62
Phrases, useful, 221-2
Planning and preparing for your trip, 28-69
  alternative and adventure travel, 46
  calendar of events, 36-9
  climate, 35
  entry requirements, 29-30
  fast facts, 62-9
  getting around: see Transportation, within Mexico
  getting there: see Transportation, to Mexico
  health concerns and precautions, 39-42
  holidays, 36
  information sources, 28-9
  insurance, 42
  money, 30, 32-3
  packing, 42-3

  shopping, 46-8
Playa Yelapa, 103
Police, 66
Post office, 65
  Guadalajara, 156
  vocabulary terms, 222
Puerto Vallarta, 70-109
  accommodations, 77-88
  cost of everyday items, 32-3
  entertainment and nightlife, 101-3
  evening entertainment, 101-3
  excursion areas, 103-9
    Bucerías, 103-5
    Playa Yelapa, 103
    San Blas, 105-9
  fast facts, 73, 76
  Frommer's favorite experiences, 99
  itineraries, suggested, 96
  maps, 74-5
  orientation, 70-2
  restaurants, 88-95
  shopping, 99-101
  sports and recreational activities, 97-9
  transportation, 72-3

Recordings, 27
Recreational activities: see Sports and recreational activities
Religion, 19-20
Rental options, 69
Restaurants:
  Ajijic, 200-2
  Barra de Navidad, 126-7, 132-5
  Bucerías, 104-5
  Chapala, 194-5
  Colima, 144
  Guadalajara, 165-9
  Jocotepec, 204
  Lagos de Moreno, 218-19
  Manzanillo, 121-7
  Mazamitla, 207-8
  Melaque, 136-7
  money-saving tips, 89, 166
  Puerto Vallarta, 88-95
  San Blas, 108-9
  San José de Gracia, 209
  San Juan Cosalá, 203
  San Juan de los Lagos, 215-16
  Tapalpa, 211-12
  Tlaquepaque, 184-6
  Tonalá, 187
  vocabulary terms, 222-8
Restrooms, 66
Rodeos and cockfights, Guadalajara, 178

Safety, 66-7
San Blas, 105-9
San José de Gracia, 208-9
San Juan Cosalá, 202-3
San Juan de los Lagos, 212-16
San Patricio: see Melaque
Scams, 34-5
Senior citizen travelers, tips for, 44
Shopping, 46-8
  Ajijic, 196-7
  Chapala, 190
  Guadalajara, 178-9
  Lagos de Moreno, 217
  Manzanillo, 130
  Puerto Vallarta, 99-101
  San Juan de los Lagos, 214-15
  Tapalpa, 210
  Tlaquepaque, 184
  Tonalá, 186-7

Sights and activities:
  Ajijic, 196
  Barra de Navidad, 135
  Bucerías, 103-4
  Chapala, 189-90
  Colima, 145
  Guadalajara, 170-8
  Lagos de Moreno, 216-17
  Manzanillo, 128-30
  Mazamitla, 205
  Puerto Vallarta, 96-109
  San Blas, 106-7
  San José de Gracia, 208
  San Juan de los Lagos, 213-14
  Tapalpa, 210
  Tlaquepaque, 183-4
  Tonalá, 186
Single travelers, tips for, 44-5
Snorkeling & diving, San Blas, 106-7
Spanish lessons, 46
  Guadalajara, 156
Special events, 36-9
  Guadalajara, 177-8
  Lagos de Moreno, 216
  Mazamitla, 205
  Puerto Vallarta, 99
  San Juan de los Lagos, 213
  Tlaquepaque, 183
Sports and recreational activities, 22
  Chapala, 189-90
  Guadalajara, 178
  Manzanillo, 129-30
  Puerto Vallarta, 97-9

Tapalpa, 209-12
Taxes, 67
  airport, 53
Tecuan, 138-9
Telegrams/telex/fax, 68-9
Telephone, 67-8
Telephone numbers, useful, 64
Temporary Car Importation Permit, 50-1
Tenacatita, 138
Tennis:
  Manzanillo, 130
  Puerto Vallarta, 98
Time, 69
Tipping, 69
Tlaquepaque, 182-6
Toilets, 66
Tonalá, 182, 186-7
Tourist information, 28-9
  Ajijic, 194, 196

Barra de Navidad, 131
Colima, 144
Guadalajara, 155
Manzanillo, 115
Mazamitla, 205
Puerto Vallarta, 73, 76
San Blas, 106
Tapalpa, 209
Tlaquepaque, 182
Tonalá, 182-3
Tourist permit, 29
Tours, organized, 46, 53
  Guadalajara, 176-7
  Manzanillo, 129
  Puerto Vallarta, 96-7
  for single travelers, 44-5
Train travel, to and within Mexico, 49, 54-5
Transportation:
  to Barra de Navidad and Melaque, 132
  to Chapala, 188-9
  to Colima, 143
  to Comala, 145
  within Guadalajara, 152, 154
  within Manzanillo, 115
  to Mexico, 48-53
    by bus, 49
    by car, 49-52
    by plane, 48-9
    by ship, 52-3
    by train, 49
  within Mexico, 53-62
    by bus, 55-6
    by car, 56-62
    by plane, 53-4
    by train, 54-5
  within Puerto Vallarta, 72-3
  to San Blas, 105-6
  to San Juan de los Lagos, 213
  to Tapalpa, 209
  to Tlaquepaque and Tonalá, 182
Traveler's checks, 32
Turista, 39-40

Villas/condos, 69
Vocabulary terms, 220-8

Walking tours:
  Guadalajara, 171-4
  Puerto Vallarta, 98-9
Water, 69
Weather, 35
Whale watching, Puerto Vallarta, 98, 106

SIGHTS & ATTRACTIONS

PUERTO VALLARTA & ENVIRONS

Borrego Beach, San Blas, 106
Cathedral, 98
El Rey Beach, San Blas, 106
Gringo Gulch, 99
La Contadura, San Blas, 106
Las Islitas Beach, San Blas, 106-7
Libertad, 99

Matanchen Bay, San Blas, 106
municipal building, 98
Museo del Cuale, 99
Playa de Oro, 97
Playa Los Cocos, San Blas, 107
Playa Mismaloya, 97
Playa Olas Altas, 97

ACCOMMODATIONS INDEX • **235**

Playa Yelapa, 103
Port of San Blas, 106
Punta Negra, 97

Tovara Springs, 107
Zaragoza, 99

MANZANILLO & ENVIRONS

La Audiencia beach, 129
Laguna de Cuyutlán, 130
Laguna de las Garzas, 130
Laguna de San Pedrito, 130
Museo de Occidente de Gobierno de Estado (Museum of Western Cultures), Colima, 145
Museu de Historia de Colima, Colima, 145

Museum of Popular Culture María Teresa Pomar, Colima, 145
Playa Azul, 130
Playa Las Brisas, 129
Playa Miramar, 129
Sala de Exposiciones, Colima, 145

GUADALAJARA & ENVIRONS

Ballet Folklórico, 174
Capilla del Primer Milagro, San Juan de los Lagos, 214
Casa de la Cultura, 175
Cathedral, 171
Guadalajara School of Music, University of, 172
Hospicio Cabañas, 172
Instituto Cultural Cabañas, 172
Las Piedrotas, Tapalpa, 210
La Rosa Fábrica de Vidrio Soplado glass-blowing factory, Tlaquepaque, 183-4
Mercado Libertad, 174
Museo Antropología, 174-5
Museo Casa de Capellanes, Lagos de Moreno, 216-17
Museo Cristero, San Juan de los Lagos, 214
Museo de la Ciudad, 176
Museo Infantil, 174
National Institute of Anthropology and History, 172
National Museum of Ceramics, Tonalá, 186
Nogales waterfall, Tapalpa, 210
Palacio de Justicia, 172
Palacio del Gobierno, 171
Parroquía de la Asunción, Lagos de Moreno, 216

Parque Agua Azul, 174
Planetarium, 175-6
Plaza de Armas, 171
Plaza de los Mariachis, 174
Plaza & Ex-Convento del Carmen, 174
Plaza Liberación, 172
Plaza Tapatía, 172
Plaza Principal, San Juan de los Lagos, 213-14
Quetzalcoatl Fountain, 172
Regional Ceramics Museum, Tlaquepaque, 183
Regional Museum of Guadalajara, 171-2
Rotonda de Los Hombres Ilustres, 171
San Agustín Church, 172
San Juan de los Lagos, Basilica de, San Juan de los Lagos, 214
Santa María de Gracia, Church of, 172
Teatro Degollado, 172
Teatro Guadalajara del IMSS, 174
Templo el Calvario, Lagos de Moreno, 217
Tequila plant, 177
thermal pools, Ajijic, 196
Zoo, 175-6

ACCOMMODATIONS

PUERTO VALLARTA & ENVIRONS

Belaire Resort Puerto Vallarta, Marina Vallarta (VE), 78
Buenaventura, Hotel, north of the Río Cuale (M),* 83
Camino Real, south of Mismaloya (E), 86
Casa Corazón, south of the Río Cuale (M), 84
Continental Plaza Vallarta Tennis & Beach Resort, hotel zone (VE), 81
Costa Flamingos Hotel, Bucerías (M), 104
Encino, Hotel, north of the Río Cuale (B)($), 84
Fiesta Americana Puerto Vallarta, hotel zone (VE), 81-2
Fontana del Mar, Hotel, south of the Río Cuale (M), 84
Hacienda Buenaventura, north of the Río Cuale (M), 83
Hyatt Coral Grand, south of Mismaloya (E), 86-7
Krystal Vallarta, hotel zone (VE), 82
La Jolla de Mismaloya, south of Mismaloya (E), 87-8
Las Brisas Resort, Hotel, San Blas (M),* 107-8
Los Bucaneros, Hotel, San Blas (B), 108

Los Cocos Trailer Park, San Blas (CG), 108
Los Cuatro Vientos, north of the Río Cuale (B), 83-4
Marriott Casamagna, Marina Vallarta (VE), 78-9
Marsol, Hotel, south of the Río Cuale (B), 85
Melia Puerto Vallarta, Marina Vallarta (VE), 79-80
Molino de Agua, Hotel, south of the Río Cuale (M), 84-5
Playa Los Arcos, south of the Río Cuale (M),* 85
Plaza Las Glorias Puerto Vallarta, hotel zone (E), 82-3
Posada Del Rey, Motel, San Blas (B), 108
Posada de Roger, Hotel, south of the Río Cuale (B)($), 85
Posada Olas Altas, Bucerías (B), 104
Posada Río Cuale, south of the Río Cuale (B), 85-6
Radisson Paraiso Nuevo Vallarta, 77-8
Velas Vallarta Grand Suite Resort, Marina Vallarta (VE), 80-1

Key to abbreviations * = Author's favorite; $ = Super-value choice; B = Budget; M = Moderately priced; E = Expensive; VE = Very expensive.

MANZANILLO & ENVIRONS

America, Hotel, Colima (M), 144
Bel-Air Costa Careyes, Hotel, Careyes (VE), 140-1
Bel-Air El Tamarindo, Hotel, El Tamarindo (VE), 139
Bungalows Villamar, Melaque (B), 135-6
Cabo Blanco, Hotel, Barra de Navidad (E), 131-2
Ceballos, Hotel, Colima (B), 144
Club Med Playa Blanca, Costa Careyes (E), 141-2
Club Náutico Melaque (M),* 136
Club Vacacional Las Brisas (M), 117
Coco Club Melaque (M), 136
Colonial, Hotel, downtown (B), 116
Condominios Arco Iris, Salahua, 117-18
Delphín, Hotel, Barra de Navidad (B)($),* 132
El Tecuan, Tecuan (M)($),* 138-9
Emperador, Hotel, downtown (B), 116

Fiesta Americana Los Angeles Locos Tenacatita, Tenacatita (E), 138
La Posada, Hotel, Las Brisas (M), 117
Las Alamandas (VE),* 142-3
Las Hadas, Santiago Peninsula (VE), 118-19
Legazpi, Hotel de, Melaque (B)($), 136
Marlyn, Hotel, Santiago Peninsula (M), 120
Playa de Santiago, Hotel, Santiago Peninsula (M), 120
Plaza Las Glorias, Hotel, Santiago Peninsula (E), 119
Posada Pablo de Tarso, Melaque (M), 136
Ruiseñores, Hotel, downtown (B), 116-17
Sands, Hotel, Barra de Navidad (M), 132
Sierra Manzanillo, Hotel, Santiago Peninsula (E), 120
Tropical, Hotel, Barra de Navidad (M), 132

GUADALAJARA & ENVIRONS

Aranzazu, Hotel, downtown (M), 161
Balneario San Juan Cosalá, San Juan Cosalá (M)($), 203
Calinda Roma, downtown (M), 160-1
Canada, Hotel, near old bus station (B), 164-5
Carlton Hotel, Agua Azul Park (E), 157
Casa Grande, Lagos de Moreno (E), 217
Colonial, Hotel, Lagos de Moreno (E), 217-18
Danza del Sol, Ajijic (E), 197
Don Quijote Plaza, Hotel, downtown (B), 162
El Parador, Hotel, near the new bus station (B), 165
El Tapatío Gran Spa & Resort, near airport (E), 160
Fiesta Americana, Glorieta Minerva (E), 157-8
Fiesta Mazamitla, Hotel, Mazamitla (B), 205
Holiday Inn Crowne Plaza, downtown (E), 158-9
Hyatt Regency, Plaza del Sol (E), 159
La Floresta, Ajijic (M), 198
La Laguna Bed and Brunch, Ajijic (B), 198
La Nueva Posada, Ajijic (M), 198
Larios, Hotel de, San José de Gracia (B), 208-9
Las Candilejas, Hotel, Chapala (B)($), 192
Mendoza, Hotel de, downtown (M), 161
Montecarlo, Hotel, Chapala (M), 192
Monte Verde Centro Recreacional, Mazamitla (E), 206
Nido, Hotel, Chapala (B), 192-4

Pal RV Park, Ajijic (CG), 200
Paris, Hotel, Lagos de Moreno (B), 218
Posada Alpina, Mazamitla (B), 206
Posada Arcos, Hotel, San Juan de los Lagos (M), 215
Posada de la Fuente, Tapalpa (E), 210
Posada del Pescador, Jocotepec (B), 203-4
Posada el Carretero, Tapalpa (B), 210-11
Posada la Hacienda, Tapalpa (M), 211
Posada Las Calandrias, Ajijic (B)($), 200
Posada Las Charrandas, Mazamitla (B), 206
Posada Regis, downtown (B)($), 162, 164
Primavera, Hotel, San Juan de los Lagos (M), 215
Quinta Quetzalcoatl, Chapala (E),* 190, 192
Quinta Real, Minerva Circle (E),* 159-60
Real de Chapala, Hotel, Ajijic (E), 197
Río Caliente Spa, Primavera forest (M),* 161-2
San Francisco Plaza, Hotel, Pricilano Sanchez square (B),* 162
Sierra del Tigre, Hotel, Mazamitla (B), 205-6
Sierra Paraiso, Mazamitla (M), 206-7
Suites Bernini, downtown (B)($),* 164
Suites Plaza Ajijic, Ajijic (B), 200
Tapalpa, Hotel, Tapalpa (B), 211
Villa Buenaventura, San Juan Cosalá (M), 203

RESTAURANTS

PUERTO VALLARTA & ENVIRONS

AMERICAN
The Pancake House (Casa de Pancakes), south of the Río Cuale (B),* 94
Tuti Frutti, north of the Río Cuale (B), 92

CHICKEN
El Edén, south of town (E), 95

CHINESE
Archie's Wok, south of the Río Cuale (M), 92

CONTINENTAL
Bogart's, hotel zone (VE), 88
Chez Elena, north of the Río Cuale (E), 89-90

ECLECTIC
Archie's Wok, south of the Río Cuale (M), 92
Bogart's, hotel zone (VE), 88

ICE CREAM
Helados Bing, north of the Río Cuale (B), 90

Key to abbreviations * = Author's favorite; $ = Super-value choice; B = Budget; M = Moderately priced; E = Expensive; VE = Very expensive.

RESTAURANTS INDEX

INTERNATIONAL
Café Adobe, south of the Río Cuale (M)($),* 92
Café des Artistes, north of the Río Cuale (E), 88-9
El Palomar de los Gonzalez, south of the Río Cuale (M), 93
El Set, south of town (M), 95
La Casa del Almendro, north of the Río Cuale (M), 90
Restaurant el Delfín, San Blas (M),* 108-9

ITALIAN
Pietro Pastas & Pizzas, north of the Río Cuale (B), 90
Pizza Joe, south of the Río Cuale (M), 93

JAPANESE
Mikado Restaurant, Marina Vallarta (VE), 88

MEXICAN
Chef Roger, north of the Río Cuale (E), 89
Chico's Paradise, south of town (M), 94
El Dorado, south of the Río Cuale (M),* 92
Fonda la China Poblana, south of the Río Cuale (M)($),* 92-3
La Casa del Almendro, north of the Río Cuale (M), 90
McDonald's, San Blas (B), 109
The Pancake House (Casa de Pancakes), south of the Río Cuale (B),* 94
Puerto Nuevo, south of the Río Cuale (M), 93
Restaurant/Bar Aquarena, south of the Río Cuale (M), 93-4
Restaurant Juanita, north of the Río Cuale (B), 90, 92

PASTRIES
Pie in the Sky Bakery, Bucerías (B), 105

PIZZA
Mark's, Bucerías (B), 105

SANDWICHES
Mark's, Bucerías (B), 105

SEAFOOD
Adriano's, Bucerías (M), 104
Chico's Paradise, south of town (M), 94
Chino's Paraiso, south of town (E), 94-5
El Edén, south of town (E), 95
El Set, south of town (M), 95
La Isla, San Blas (B),* 108
Puerto Nuevo, south of the Río Cuale (M), 93
Restaurant/Bar Aquarena, south of the Río Cuale (M), 93-4

STEAK
Chino's Paraiso, south of town (E), 94-5
El Edén, south of town (E), 95
El Set, south of town (M), 95
La Isla, San Blas (B),* 108

VEGETARIAN
Tuti Frutti, north of the Río Cuale (B), 92

MANZANILLO & ENVIRONS

AMERICAN
Juanito's, Costera Madrid (M), 127

BOTANEROS
Bar Social, downtown, 122
El Ultimo Tren, downtown, 122

CHINESE
Ly Chee, downtown (M), 121

GRILLED SPECIALTIES
Carlos 'n' Charlies, Santiago Road (E), 124
El Vaquero Campestre, Santiago Road (E), 124-5

ICE CREAM
Helados Bing, downtown (B), 121-2

INTERNATIONAL
El Dorado, Melaque (E), 137
Hotel Delphín, Barra de Navidad (B), 132-4
La Plazuela Restaurant, Santiago Peninsula (E), 125-6
Legazpi, Santiago Peninsula (VE), 125
Los Pelicanos, Melaque (B), 137
Ly Chee, downtown (M), 121
Manolo's Bistro, Santiago Road (E), 124
Osteria Bugatti, Santiago Road (E), 124
Restaurant La Audiencia, Santiago Peninsula (B), 126
Viva Maria, Melaque (M), 137
Willy's LAs Brisas (M), 125

MEXICAN
Cafetería/Neveria Chantilly, downtown (M), 121
El Buen Gusto, Melaque (B)($), 136-7
Juanito's, Costera Madrid (M), 127
La Perlita Restaurant, downtown (M), 122
Las Palmas, Colima (B), 137
Los Naranjos (The Orange Trees), Colima (B), 137
Restaurant y Café, Barra de Navidad (B), 134
Restaurant y Ceñaduría Patty, Barra de Navidad (B), 134

PIZZA
Benedetti's Pizza, downtown (M), 121

SEAFOOD
Oasis, Barra de Navidad (E), 126-7
Panchos, Barra de Navidad (M),* 134
Restaurant Bar Pacifico, Barra de Navidad (B), 134
Viva Maria, Melaque (M), 137
Willy's, LAs Brisas (M), 125

SEAFOOD/STEAK
L'Récife Restaurant & Bar, Barra de Navidad (E), 126
Manolo's Bistro, Santiago Road (E), 124
Velleros, Barra de Navidad (M)($),* 134-5

VEGETARIAN
Restaurant y Café, Barra de Navidad (B), 134

GUADALAJARA & ENVIRONS

AMERICAN
Danny's Ajijic (B)($),* 202
San Francisco Grill, Chapala (M), 195

ASIAN
Restaurant Bar Che Mary, Chapala (B), 194

BAKERY
Cafin, Ajijic (B), 201-2
La India Bakery, Chapala (B),* 194
Pastelería Luvier (B), 169

BIRRIA
Birrería el Sope, Tlaquepaque (B), 185

BORREGO
Restaurant Tapalpa Borrego, Tapalpa (B), 212

CONTINENTAL
Ricco (M), 167-8

ICE CREAM
Nevado de Toluca, Jocotepec (B),* 204

INTERNATIONAL
Adobes, Lagos de Moreno (M), 218
Ciervo Rojo, Mazamitla (M), 207
Colina de los Ruisenores, Mazamitla (B), 207
El Mesón del Chef (E), 165-6
La Copa de Leche (E), 165
La Rusa, Ajijic (M),* 201
Manix Restaurant, Ajijic (M),* 200-1
Oscar's, Ajijic (M),* 201
Restaurant La Posada Ajijic (M), 201
Restaurant La Rinconada (M), 167
Rose Cafe (E), 166
Sanborn's (M), 168
Sandy's Restaurant (M), 168

ITALIAN
La Piccola Trattoria Ristorante (M), 167
Los Veleros Video Bar, Ajijic (B),* 202
Ricco (M), 167-8

MEXICAN
Adobes, Lagos de Moreno (M), 218
Cafe Madrid (M),* 166-7
Danny's, Ajijic (B)($),* 202
La Hacienda, Lagos de Moreno (M), 218
La Rinconada, Lagos de Moreno (B), 218-19
Los Cazadores, Tlaquepaque (M),* 185
Los Geranios, Tonalá (B), 187
Los Otates (M), 167

Los Veleros Video Bar, Ajijic (B),* 202
Mariscos Progreso, Tlaquepaque (M), 185
Memo's Pozole & Tacos, Juárez (B)($), 202
Restaurant Bar Che Mary, Chapala (B), 194
Restaurant Bar El Doón, San José de Gracia (B), 209
Restaurant Beer Garden, Chapala (M), 194-5
Restaurant Campestre La Troje, Mazamitla (B), 208
Restaurant Hacienda Buenavista, Tapalpa (B), 211
Restaurant La Posada Ajijic (M), 201
Restaurant La Rinconada (M), 167
Restaurant Posada Mazamitla (B), 208
Restaurant Rivera, Lagos de Moreno (B), 218
Restaurant Señorial, San Juan de los Lagos (B), 216
Restaurant Superior, Chapala (B)($), 194
Restaurant Tapalpa (B), 211-12
Restaurant With No Name, Tlaquepaque (M),* 186
San Francisco Grill, Chapala (M), 195
Tamales Sinaloenses (B)($), 169

REGIONAL
Colina de los Ruisenores, Mazamitla (B), 207
El Portal "Vito's," Mazamitla (B), 207-8
La Chata Restaurant (B), 168-9
La Rinconada, Lagos de Moreno (B), 218-19
Posada de la Fuente, Tapalpa (B), 211
Restaurant Beer Garden, Chapala (M), 194-5
Restaurant Campestre La Troje, Mazamitla (B), 208
Restaurant Don Juan, Chapala (B), 195
Restaurant El Abajeno, Tlaquepaque (M), 185-6
Restaurant Posada Mazamitla (B), 208

SANDWICHES
Bar Jacal, Jocotepec (B), 204
Cafin, Ajijic (B), 201-2
Loncheria Arcos, San Juan de los Lagos (B), 215-16

SEAFOOD
Mariscos Progreso, Tlaquepaque (M), 185
Restaurant Don Juan, Chapala (B), 195

STEAK
Restaurant Bar El Doón, San José de Gracia (B), 209

VEGETARIAN
Acuarius (B),* 168

Now Save Money on All Your Travels by Joining FROMMER'S ™ TRAVEL BOOK CLUB
The World's Best Travel Guides at Membership Prices

FROMMER'S TRAVEL BOOK CLUB is your ticket to successful travel! Open up a world of travel information and simplify your travel planning when you join ranks with thousands of value-conscious travelers who are members of the FROMMER'S TRAVEL BOOK CLUB. Join today and you'll be entitled to all the privileges that come from belonging to the club that offers you travel guides for less to more than 100 destinations worldwide. Annual membership is only $25 (U.S.) or $35 (Canada and foreign).

The Advantages of Membership

1. Your choice of three FREE travel guides. You can select any **two** FROMMER'S COMPREHENSIVE GUIDES, FROMMER'S $-A-DAY GUIDES, *or* FROMMER'S FAMILY GUIDES—plus **one** FROMMER'S CITY GUIDE *or* FROMMER'S CITY $-A-DAY GUIDE.
2. Your own subscription to **TRIPS AND TRAVEL** quarterly newsletter.
3. You're entitled to a **30% discount** on your order of any additional books offered by FROMMER'S TRAVEL BOOK CLUB.
4. You're offered (at a small additional fee of $6.50) our **Domestic Trip-Routing Kits.**

Our quarterly newsletter **TRIPS AND TRAVEL** offers practical information on the best buys in travel, the "hottest" vacation spots, the latest travel trends, world-class events and much, much more.

Our **Domestic Trip-Routing Kits** are available for any North American destination. We'll send you a detailed map highlighting the best route to take to your destination—you can request direct or scenic routes.

Here's all you have to do to join:

Send in your membership fee of $25 ($35 Canada and foreign) with your name and address on the form below along with your selections as part of your membership package to **FROMMER'S TRAVEL BOOK CLUB, P.O. Box 473, Mt. Morris, IL 61054-0473**. Remember to select any **two** FROMMER'S COMPREHENSIVE GUIDES, FROMMER'S $-A-DAY GUIDES, *or* FROMMER'S FAMILY GUIDES—plus **one** FROMMER'S CITY GUIDE *or* FROMMER'S CITY $-A-DAY GUIDE.

If you would like to order additional books, please select the books you would like and send a check for the total amount (please add sales tax in the states noted below), plus $2 per book for shipping and handling ($3 per book for all foreign orders) to:

FROMMER'S TRAVEL BOOK CLUB
P.O. Box 473
Mt. Morris, IL 61054-0473
(815) 734-1104

[ ] **YES.** I want to take advantage of this opportunity to join FROMMER'S TRAVEL BOOK CLUB.
[ ] **My check is enclosed.** Dollar amount enclosed_____*

Name_____
Address_____
City_____ State_____ Zip_____

To ensure that all orders are processed efficiently, please apply sales tax in the following areas: CA, CT, FL, IL, NJ, NY, TN, WA and CANADA.

*With membership, shipping and handling will be paid by FROMMER'S TRAVEL BOOK CLUB for the three free books you select as part of your membership. Please add $2 per book for shipping and handling for any additional books purchased ($3 per book for foreign orders).

Allow 4–6 weeks for delivery. Prices of books, membership fee, and publication dates are subject to change without notice.

AC1

Please Send Me the Books Checked Below:

FROMMER'S COMPREHENSIVE GUIDES
(Guides listing facilities from budget to deluxe, with emphasis on the medium-priced)

	Retail Price	Code		Retail Price	Code
☐ Acapulco/Ixtapa/Taxco 1993–94	$15.00	C120	☐ Jamaica/Barbados 1993–94	$15.00	C105
☐ Alaska 1994–95	$17.00	C130	☐ Japan 1992–93	$19.00	C020
☐ Arizona 1993–94	$18.00	C101	☐ Morocco 1992–93	$18.00	C021
☐ Australia 1992–93	$18.00	C002	☐ Nepal 1994–95	$18.00	C126
☐ Austria 1993–94	$19.00	C119	☐ New England 1993	$17.00	C114
☐ Belgium/Holland/Luxembourg 1993–94	$18.00	C106	☐ New Mexico 1993–94	$15.00	C117
☐ Bahamas 1994–95	$17.00	C121	☐ New York State 1994–95	$19.00	C132
☐ Bermuda 1994–95	$15.00	C122	☐ Northwest 1991–92	$17.00	C026
☐ Brazil 1993–94	$20.00	C111	☐ Portugal 1992–93	$16.00	C027
☐ California 1993	$18.00	C112	☐ Puerto Rico 1993–94	$15.00	C103
☐ Canada 1992–93	$18.00	C009	☐ Puerto Vallarta/Manzanillo/Guadalajara 1992–93	$14.00	C028
☐ Caribbean 1994	$18.00	C123	☐ Scandinavia 1993–94	$19.00	C118
☐ Carolinas/Georgia 1994–95	$17.00	C128	☐ Scotland 1992–93	$16.00	C040
☐ Colorado 1993–94	$16.00	C100	☐ Skiing Europe 1989–90	$15.00	C030
☐ Cruises 1993–94	$19.00	C107	☐ South Pacific 1992–93	$20.00	C031
☐ DE/MD/PA & NJ Shore 1992–93	$19.00	C012	☐ Spain 1993–94	$19.00	C115
☐ Egypt 1990–91	$17.00	C013	☐ Switzerland/Liechtenstein 1992–93	$19.00	C032
☐ England 1994	$18.00	C129	☐ Thailand 1992–93	$20.00	C033
☐ Florida 1994	$18.00	C124	☐ U.S.A. 1993–94	$19.00	C116
☐ France 1994–95	$20.00	C131	☐ Virgin Islands 1994–95	$13.00	C127
☐ Germany 1994	$19.00	C125	☐ Virginia 1992–93	$14.00	C037
☐ Italy 1994	$19.00	C130	☐ Yucatán 1993–94	$18.00	C110

FROMMER'S $-A-DAY GUIDES
(Guides to low-cost tourist accommodations and facilities)

	Retail Price	Code		Retail Price	Code
☐ Australia on $45 1993–94	$18.00	D102	☐ Mexico on $45 1994	$19.00	D116
☐ Costa Rica/Guatemala/Belize on $35 1993–94	$17.00	D108	☐ New York on $70 1992–93	$16.00	D016
☐ Eastern Europe on $30 1993–94	$18.00	D110	☐ New Zealand on $45 1993–94	$18.00	D103
☐ England on $60 1994	$18.00	D112	☐ Scotland/Wales on $50 1992–93	$18.00	D019
☐ Europe on $50 1994	$19.00	D115			
☐ Greece on $45 1993–94	$19.00	D100	☐ South America on $40 1993–94	$19.00	D109
☐ Hawaii on $75 1994	$19.00	D113	☐ Turkey on $40 1992–93	$22.00	D023
☐ India on $40 1992–93	$20.00	D010	☐ Washington, D.C. on $40 1992–93	$17.00	D024
☐ Ireland on $40 1992–93	$17.00	D011			
☐ Israel on $45 1993–94	$18.00	D101			

FROMMER'S CITY $-A-DAY GUIDES
(Pocket-size guides with an emphasis on low-cost tourist accommodations and facilities)

	Retail Price	Code		Retail Price	Code
☐ Berlin on $40 1994–95	$12.00	D111	☐ Madrid on $50 1992–93	$13.00	D014
☐ Copenhagen on $50 1992–93	$12.00	D003	☐ Paris on $45 1994–95	$12.00	D117
☐ London on $45 1994–95	$12.00	D114	☐ Stockholm on $50 1992–93	$13.00	D022

FROMMER'S WALKING TOURS
(With routes and detailed maps, these companion guides point out the places and pleasures that make a city unique)

	Retail Price	Code		Retail Price	Code
☐ Berlin	$12.00	W100	☐ Paris	$12.00	W103
☐ London	$12.00	W101	☐ San Francisco	$12.00	W104
☐ New York	$12.00	W102	☐ Washington, D.C.	$12.00	W105

FROMMER'S TOURING GUIDES
(Color-illustrated guides that include walking tours, cultural and historic sites, and practical information)

	Retail Price	Code		Retail Price	Code
☐ Amsterdam	$11.00	T001	☐ New York	$11.00	T008
☐ Barcelona	$14.00	T015	☐ Rome	$11.00	T010
☐ Brazil	$11.00	T003	☐ Scotland	$10.00	T011
☐ Florence	$9.00	T005	☐ Sicily	$15.00	T017
☐ Hong Kong/Singapore/			☐ Tokyo	$15.00	T016
Macau	$11.00	T006	☐ Turkey	$11.00	T013
☐ Kenya	$14.00	T018	☐ Venice	$9.00	T014
☐ London	$13.00	T007			

FROMMER'S FAMILY GUIDES

	Retail Price	Code		Retail Price	Code
☐ California with Kids	$18.00	F100	☐ San Francisco with Kids	$17.00	F004
☐ Los Angeles with Kids	$17.00	F002	☐ Washington, D.C. with Kids	$17.00	F005
☐ New York City with Kids	$18.00	F003			

FROMMER'S CITY GUIDES
(Pocket-size guides to sightseeing and tourist accommodations and facilities in all price ranges)

	Retail Price	Code		Retail Price	Code
☐ Amsterdam 1993–94	$13.00	S110	☐ Montreál/Québec		
☐ Athens 1993–94	$13.00	S114	City 1993–94	$13.00	S125
☐ Atlanta 1993–94	$13.00	S112	☐ New Orleans 1993–94	$13.00	S103
☐ Atlantic City/Cape			☐ New York 1993	$13.00	S120
May 1993–94	$13.00	S130	☐ Orlando 1994	$13.00	S135
☐ Bangkok 1992–93	$13.00	S005	☐ Paris 1993–94	$13.00	S109
☐ Barcelona/Majorca/			☐ Philadelphia 1993–94	$13.00	S113
Minorca/Ibiza 1993–94	$13.00	S115	☐ Rio 1991–92	$9.00	S029
☐ Berlin 1993–94	$13.00	S116	☐ Rome 1993–94	$13.00	S111
☐ Boston 1993–94	$13.00	S117	☐ Salt Lake City 1991–92	$9.00	S031
☐ Cancún/Cozumel 1991–			☐ San Diego 1993–94	$13.00	S107
92	$9.00	S010	☐ San Francisco 1994	$13.00	S133
☐ Chicago 1993–94	$13.00	S122	☐ Santa Fe/Taos/		
☐ Denver/Boulder/Colorado			Albuquerque 1993–94	$13.00	S108
Springs 1993–94	$13.00	S131	☐ Seattle/Portland 1992–93	$12.00	S035
☐ Dublin 1993–94	$13.00	S128	☐ St. Louis/Kansas		
☐ Hawaii 1992	$12.00	S014	City 1993–94	$13.00	S127
☐ Hong Kong 1992–93	$12.00	S015	☐ Sydney 1993–94	$13.00	S129
☐ Honolulu/Oahu 1994	$13.00	S134	☐ Tampa/St.		
☐ Las Vegas 1993–94	$13.00	S121	Petersburg 1993–94	$13.00	S105
☐ London 1994	$13.00	S132	☐ Tokyo 1992–93	$13.00	S039
☐ Los Angeles 1993–94	$13.00	S123	☐ Toronto 1993–94	$13.00	S126
☐ Madrid/Costa del			☐ Vancouver/Victoria 1990–		
Sol 1993–94	$13.00	S124	91	$8.00	S041
☐ Miami 1993–94	$13.00	S118	☐ Washington, D.C. 1993	$13.00	S102
☐ Minneapolis/St.					
Paul 1993–94	$13.00	S119			

Other Titles Available at Membership Prices

SPECIAL EDITIONS

	Retail Price	Code		Retail Price	Code
☐ Bed & Breakfast North America	$15.00	P002	☐ Marilyn Wood's Wonderful Weekends (within a 250-mile radius of NYC)	$12.00	P017
☐ Bed & Breakfast Southwest	$16.00	P100	☐ National Park Guide 1993	$15.00	P101
☐ Caribbean Hideaways	$16.00	P103	☐ Where to Stay U.S.A.	$15.00	P102

GAULT MILLAU'S "BEST OF" GUIDES
(The only guides that distinguish the truly superlative from the merely overrated)

	Retail Price	Code		Retail Price	Code
☐ Chicago	$16.00	G002	☐ New England	$16.00	G010
☐ Florida	$17.00	G003	☐ New Orleans	$17.00	G011
☐ France	$17.00	G004	☐ New York	$17.00	G012
☐ Germany	$18.00	G018	☐ Paris	$17.00	G013
☐ Hawaii	$17.00	G006	☐ San Francisco	$17.00	G014
☐ Hong Kong	$17.00	G007	☐ Thailand	$18.00	G019
☐ London	$17.00	G009	☐ Toronto	$17.00	G020
☐ Los Angeles	$17.00	G005	☐ Washington, D.C.	$17.00	G017

THE REAL GUIDES
(Opinionated, politically aware guides for youthful budget-minded travelers)

	Retail Price	Code		Retail Price	Code
☐ Able to Travel	$20.00	R112	☐ Kenya	$12.95	R015
☐ Amsterdam	$13.00	R100	☐ Mexico	$11.95	R128
☐ Barcelona	$13.00	R101	☐ Morocco	$14.00	R129
☐ Belgium/Holland/Luxembourg	$16.00	R031	☐ Nepal	$14.00	R018
			☐ New York	$13.00	R019
☐ Berlin	$13.00	R123	☐ Paris	$13.00	R130
☐ Brazil	$13.95	R003	☐ Peru	$12.95	R021
☐ California & the West Coast	$17.00	R121	☐ Poland	$13.95	R131
			☐ Portugal	$16.00	R126
☐ Canada	$15.00	R103	☐ Prague	$15.00	R113
☐ Czechoslovakia	$15.00	R124	☐ San Francisco & the Bay Area	$11.95	R024
☐ Egypt	$19.00	R105			
☐ Europe	$18.00	R122	☐ Scandinavia	$14.95	R025
☐ Florida	$14.00	R006	☐ Spain	$16.00	R026
☐ France	$18.00	R106	☐ Thailand	$17.00	R119
☐ Germany	$18.00	R107	☐ Tunisia	$17.00	R115
☐ Greece	$18.00	R108	☐ Turkey	$13.95	R027
☐ Guatemala/Belize	$14.00	R127	☐ U.S.A.	$18.00	R117
☐ Hong Kong/Macau	$11.95	R011	☐ Venice	$11.95	R028
☐ Hungary	$14.95	R118	☐ Women Travel	$12.95	R029
☐ Ireland	$17.00	R120	☐ Yugoslavia	$12.95	R030
☐ Italy	$18.00	R125			